AF600308

TRADITIONAL SUBJECTIVITIES:
THE OLD ENGLISH POETICS OF MENTALITY

BRITT MIZE

Traditional Subjectivities

The Old English Poetics of Mentality

UNIVERSITY OF TORONTO PRESS
Toronto Buffalo London

Toronto Buffalo London
www.utppublishing.com

ISBN 978-1-4426-4468-7

Library and Archives Canada Cataloguing in Publication

Mize, Britt
Traditional subjectivities : the Old English poetics of mentality / Britt Mize.

(Toronto Anglo-Saxon series)
Includes bibliographical references and index.
ISBN 978-1-4426-4468-7

1. English poetry – Old English, ca. 450–1100 – History and criticism. 2. Folk poetry, English (Old) – History and criticism. 3. Oral tradition – England – History – To 1500. 4. Subjectivity in literature. 5. Emotions in literature. 6. Characters in literature. I. Title. II. Series: Toronto Anglo-Saxon series

PR203.M59 2013 829'.1009 C2012-907033-5

University of Toronto Press gratefully acknowledges the financial assistance of the Centre for Medieval Studies, University of Toronto, in the publication of this book.

University of Toronto Press acknowledges the financial assistance to its publishing program of the Canada Council for the Arts and the Ontario Arts Council.

Canada Council for the Arts Conseil des Arts du Canada

University of Toronto Press acknowledges the financial support of the Government of Canada through the Canada Book Fund for its publishing activities.

Contents

Acknowledgments

I owe a great general debt to the scholarly example of the English faculty of the University of North Carolina and to the mentorship in particular of Joseph S. Wittig and Edward Donald Kennedy. Hardly less influential on my ability eventually to carry out a project of this kind were many stimulating academic friendships with peers at UNC, where I benefited from an extraordinarily active and supportive community of medievalists.

More interlocutors than I will remember to name have improved this work as it has taken shape. My analysis has been sharpened by the questions or conversation, during and around conference sessions, of Daniel Donoghue, Michael Drout, Carolin Esser, Johanna Kramer, Leslie Lockett, Andrew Rabin, and Miranda Wilcox, among others. Thomas A. Bredehoft, George Clark, and Paul Roberge responded graciously to requests for help on particular points. My current colleagues Robert Boenig and J. Lawrence Mitchell offered valuable perspectives on parts of the book in draft form, and Bryan Carella and William Smith gave liberally of a scarce resource, their time, to comment with attentiveness and care on the whole of the first full draft, as the University of Toronto Press's anonymous evaluators also did on the near-final version. Tom Bredehoft, Bryan Carella, and Leslie Lockett shared some of their own forthcoming work with me, kindly guiding me through, or enabling me to steer out of, hazardous waters they had already expertly navigated. Jackeline Bevering checked quotations and played devil's advocate on translations, and Jonathan Quick helped me compile the index.

Generous financial support for the writing and final preparation of this book was provided at Texas A&M University by the Department of English, the College of Liberal Arts Rothrock Fellowship, and the Office of the Vice President for Research. The Centre for Medieval Studies at the

University of Toronto subsidized its publication. Less tangible but no less important has been the encouragement of departmental friends, both at Texas A&M and in my previous appointment at California State University, Long Beach, as well as the interest of participants in the Medieval Studies Working Group sponsored by Texas A&M's Glasscock Center for Humanities Research. The least tangible and most important debt of all I owe to the companionship of Nandra Perry, my roller coaster co-pilot, and Ruby Wynn, our treasure and our joy.

TRADITIONAL SUBJECTIVITIES: THE OLD ENGLISH POETICS OF MENTALITY

Introduction

One of the better-understood things about the Franks Casket is the inscription on its front panel indicating the material, whalebone, from which it is made. A small eighth-century box of unknown intended use,[1] the casket bears on its four upright sides and top an intricate program of textual and pictorial carving that has made the object as famous for its cyclonic complexity as for its beauty: its conjunctions of word and image inspire elaborate interpretations that may succeed less in persuading than in further highlighting perplexities.[2] Even the front-panel text to which I refer is not without its difficulties, but these are superficial. The runic inscription, running all the way around a diptych juxtaposing scenes from the pagan legend of Weland with the visit of the Magi to Mary and Jesus, is partly retrograde with the individual characters reversed as well, but it is easily enough transcribed apart from one minor uncertainty;[3] it contains some lexical isolates, but none whose referent cannot be determined; and it trips us up with a morphological puzzlement that may be irresolvable as such

1 This date accommodates almost all scholarly opinion. The divergent view of Vandersall ('Date and Provenance') has not won approval; see in response Webster, 'Stylistic Aspects.' On the environment of its production, see esp. Wood, 'Ripon, Francia, and the Franks Casket.'

2 Peeters, 'Judaeo-Christian Interpretation'; Webster, 'Iconographic Programme'; Lang, 'Imagery'; Neuman de Vegvar, 'Reading'; and Osborn, 'Lid as Conclusion' (culminating a series of her articles published over several years).

3 The uncertainty is the meaning, if any, of the double dot that appears in the middle of the sequence ᚷᚪ:ᛋᚱᛁᚳ (=ga:sric). Osborn ('Picture-Poem') takes it as a vowel-sign and transcribes *gaesric*. Alternatively, the dots may only be pellets to fill an awkwardly large space between the lower half of two adjacent letters, and I follow most commentators in reading *gasric*.

but need not finally disrupt comprehension.[4] By the standards of the Franks Casket, this amounts to forthrightness.

The main part of the inscription, running along the top, right, and bottom of the panel, forms a metrically regular distich of English verse that can be transliterated thus, with word-division and modern punctuation supplied:

> Fisc flodu ahof   on fergenberig;
> warþ gasric grorn   þær he on greut giswom.[5]

> [The sea cast the fish onto a mountain; the *gasric* grew miserable where he swam onto the sand.]

Nobody really knows what the mysterious compound *gasric* means,[6] but whatever its component morphemes may be, it is clearly a nominal reference to the beached whale identified explicitly by the short remainder of the inscription, carved upward along the fourth (left) edge of the panel.[7] This concluding phrase, a paratextual label external to the metrical and syntactic boundaries that define the main discourse unit,[8] reads 'hronæs

---

4 It is unclear on morphological grounds which of the words *fisc* and *flodu* is the subject of the first verb (text quoted below); serious problems exist with both construals. However, semantics determines *flodu* almost certainly to be the subject and *fisc* the object (Mize, 'Meaning of "Fisc Flodu Ahof"').

5 Unless otherwise noted, Old English poems are cited from Krapp and Dobbie, *Anglo-Saxon Poetic Records* (hereafter *ASPR*). I silently change editorial punctuation where I think doing so clarifies sense or syntax. Unattributed translations are my own.

6 Interpretations can be grouped as those that require emendation (the transposition of the runes ᛋ and ᚱ from their carved order to give *garsic*) and those that do not. The argument for emendation is based on the similarity of the emended form to *garsecg* 'ocean,' of which some have taken **garsic* to be a plausible spelling. But *hapax legomena* are often encountered among Old English compound words, and contextually meaningful construal of the unemended form is possible. 'Terror-king' (Page, *Introduction*, 175) is the most-repeated gloss.

7 *Fisc*, *gasric*, and *hron* reference the same creature in this poem. We know a whale to be dead at the end of the text; we know the *fisc* to have been thrown onto the land, where it will die; and we know that the *gasric* is unhappy with the situation. The most recent to attempt a distinction is Schürr ('*Hron* und *Fisc*').

8 Paratexts accompany and in some way control or shape access to a 'main' text but are understood by readers to be marginal or auxilliary to it (see Genette, *Paratexts*); examples include titles, incipits, prefaces, and footnotes. The extrametrical and extrasyntactic phrase 'hronæs ban' is joined to but not intrinsic to the poem proper.

ban' [whale's bone], thus relating the text that it titles or glosses to the substance from which the casket was fashioned and revealing the poem to be a riddle, to which it provides the answer.[9]

What it answers is not just the preceding part of the inscription, however; the words 'hronæs ban' declare the connection of the front panel text to the whole box, whose physical presence is necessary to complete the sense of what is in effect a multimedia enigma. The poem is less a puzzle to be solved – the solution, after all, is there, once the practical challenges of reading it are overcome – than an evocative recollection that this small, disciplined masterwork of human artifice has ties to a natural world of mighty elemental forces. The front panel inscription, unlike the other panels' texts, lacks a direct thematic link to the images it surrounds. But if its primary functional identity as a part of the whole artefact consists in its referentiality to the substance of which the casket is made, its primary discursive identity is as a classical Old English poem, identifying that material by saying the kinds of things that Old English poems say in the kinds of ways Old English poems say them.

The inscription says two things, to be exact, and one of them is about the mood of a stranded whale. Why does it matter, in this little poem, that the creature is sad? Most of us are likely to be less satisfied with a presumption of verisimilar naturalism (or a foray into veterinary psychology) than E.V.K. Dobbie was when he dryly (?) observed, in his notes to *The Anglo-Saxon Poetic Records*, that despondency upon being beached is 'a normal reaction for a whale.'[10] Our more usual modes of reading take the emotional content as a signifying element of the poem's construction, whether we interpret the whale as pitiable or consider the detail a sign less of sympathy than of Schadenfreude.[11] But the question I ask as a point of entry to this study is more fundamental than any particular interpretation, and I will suggest that it leads deep into both the techniques and the aesthetics of Old English poetry in the classical style. Why did it matter at all in the sensibilities of the riddle's creator to imagine the whale's state of

9 See Sorrell, 'Like a Duck to Water,' for brief but insightful discussion of this inscription as a riddle. Webster ('Iconographic Programme' and 'Encrypted Visions') treats the whole casket as a riddle using this concept more broadly.

10 *ASPR*, 6:205.

11 That the detail is meant to evoke pity seems to be the predominant assumption, but Wadstein (*Clermont Runic Casket*, 18) considered the inscription a jeer at the animal, and patristically informed interpretations may also see the whale as an antagonistic figure (e.g., Osborn, 'Picture-Poem' and 'Lid as Conclusion').

mind, such that a remark of this kind seemed more apt than any number of other possibilities? Put reductively, my answer will be that it mattered because the composer of these lines was writing Old English verse. Subjectivizing moments like this one are so rooted in Old English compositional priorities and methods as to be part and parcel of making poems in the traditional register.

The Variety and Extent of Emphasis on Mentality in Old English Poetry

As a rule, Old English verse gives generous attention to mental and emotional qualities and states, placing strong emphasis on what we are accustomed to conceptualizing (using a model that was also favoured by Anglo-Saxon poets) as interiority.[12] The prominent elegiac mode, with its continually recurrent motifs of grief, exile, and worldly ephemerality, consists largely of the representation of such a state of mind as we see in *The Wanderer*:

      ic modsefan   minne sceolde
oft earmcearig,   eðle bidæled,
freomægum feor   feterum sælan,
siþþan geara iu   goldwine minne
hrusan heolstre biwrah,   ond ic hean þonan
wod wintercearig   ofer waþema gebind,
sohte seledreorig[13]   sinces bryttan,
hwær ic feor oþþe neah   findan meahte
þone þe in meoduhealle   min mine wisse,
oþþe mec freondleasne   frefran wolde.   (ll. 19–28)

[Often I, miserable, parted from my homeland, far from lordly kin, have had to fasten my mind with fetters: ever since a long time ago I covered my gold-friend in the darkness of the earth and went downcast from there, winter-sorrowful, over the binding of waves; sought – longing for a hall – a treasure-giver wherever, far or near, I might be able to find someone who took consideration of me in a meadhall or would be willing to help me, friendless.]

12 The mental and the emotional are not systematically distinguished in Old English poetry: see Godden, ‘Anglo-Saxons on the Mind,’ esp. 295.

13 *ASPR* presents *seledreorig* as two separate words.

Similar are the poignant descriptions of life on the ocean and its correlative interior hardships in *The Seafarer*:

Mæg ic be me sylfum   soðgied wrecan,
siþas secgan,   hu ic geswincdagum
earfoðhwile   oft þrowade,
bitre breostceare   gebiden hæbbe,
gecunnad in ceole   cearselda fela,
atol yþa gewealc ...
. . . .
Calde geþrungen
wæron mine fet,   forste gebunden,
caldum clommum,   þær þa ceare seofedun
hat ymb heortan.   Hungor innan slat
merewerges mod.   Þæt se mon ne wat
þe him on foldan   fægrost limpeð,
hu ic earmcearig   iscealdnę sæ
winter wunade   wræccan lastum,
winemægum bidroren.   (ll. 1–6a, 8b–16)

[I can deliver a truth-song about myself, tell of trials, how in days of trouble I have often suffered times of hardship, endured bitter heartache, known in my ship many places of care, terrible tossing of waves ... My feet were hemmed in by cold, bound with frost – cold chains! – even as cares sighed hot around my heart. Hunger within tore at the spirit of one sea-weary. No man to whom it befalls most pleasantly on land knows how I, wretchedly sorrowful, have passed winter on an ice-cold sea in the paths of exile, deprived of caring kin.]

Whatever ends such poems are designed to achieve, writers working in this mode devote their craft to creating an atmosphere dominated by the portrayal of private emotion.

They often do so in conjunction with descriptions of nature's harshness, like the wintry weather the travellers in the passages above must endure, and the compound *wintercearig* in *The Wanderer* confirms the conscious nature of that association. The exterior reality in this poetry is intimately bound up with the interior one and indeed can function as a poetic resource for expressing human mood: physical discomfort and exposure to the elements materialize the psychological state accompanying separation from hall and community.[14] So strong is the emotive resonance of such sequences as these, pitting a lonely, displaced human against the indifferent natural world, that it could provoke the *Andreas* poet to call down upon southerly Mermedonia a winter with northern teeth, prompted only by a brief statement of the protagonist's distress as is found in the Greek *Praxeis Andreou* from which *Andreas* ultimately derives.[15] The Anglo-Saxon writer's environmental expression of this idea trades on the traditional association of stormy weather with the interior experience of people in predicaments like that of the imprisoned apostle: the motif sufficiently connotes the hardship of one parted from kin and country to supplant the source's plain denotation of his subjective state, and the impulse to deploy this poetic set-piece overcomes geographic illogic.[16]

The swift climate change the *Andreas* poet unleashes on the Mermedonians is still less bold, though, than the turnabout that becomes apparent in its fuller context. In the English text, the hero actually is not distressed, but courageous and blithe-hearted (*Andreas*, ll. 1262b–9a), an incongruity of psyche with season noted by both Peter Clemoes and Roberta Frank.[17] In creating this contrast the poet has gone directly against both vernacular convention and a specification of Andreas's state of mind found in the source text. In effect, the adapter has handled the source's statement of the apostle's misery twice: first by transmuting it into the onset of winter, and again by returning to Andreas's interiority and reversing the state of mind he was given in the *Praxeis*. The double move of exteriorizing the source's direct indication of the prisoner's subjective state while inverting the interior experience itself distinguishes Andreas's saintly mind by showing that

14 Cf. Stanley, 'Old English Poetic Diction,' 427 and 434–41, and Neville, *Representations*, 21.

15 *Andreas*, ll. 1255b–65a. For the relationship of *Andreas* to the *Praxeis*, seeing the Greek text as ancestral to the Old English one with the probable but not necessary mediation of a Latin version, see Boenig, *Saint and Hero*, 23–9, and *Acts of Andrew*, ii–ix.

16 Cf. Stanley, 'Old English Poetic Diction,' 440, and Foley, *Traditional Oral Epic*, 351–4. Foley sees this lyrical addition in *Andreas* as not directly motivated by the source because he believes its purpose is to represent Andreas as an exile; however, the Greek text's statement of the apostle's distress cues it, through the association for Anglo-Saxon poets of harsh weather with misery. Other, similar mismatches between traditional poetic 'themes' and contextual logic have occasionally been noted: e.g., G. Clark, 'Traveler Recognizes His Goal,' 648; Battles, '*Genesis A* and the Anglo-Saxon "Migration Myth,"' 46–7 and 59.

17 Clemoes, *Interactions of Thought and Language*, 267; Frank, 'Unbearable Lightness,' 494–5.

it defeats the expected conjunction of mentality with meteorology in Old English poetry.[18] Like *The Seafarer*, which in an equally sudden turn reveals its speaker's paradoxical attraction to the trials of the elements and separation from earthly community, *Andreas* illustrates at once both the traditionality of the weather-to-psychology correlation and its viability as a manipulable element in the making of new meaning.

That Anglo-Saxon poets frequently worked in an elegiac mode, which naturally has much to do with someone's state of mind, will not come as news to anyone acquainted with even the widely anthologized Old English poems. But the obvious needs to be newly contextualized by the further observation that it is but one aspect of a much broader aesthetic system. There was a perception on the part of the poets, presumably shared by their audiences, that the matter of interior experience was interesting in ways that made it suitable not just for mention, or even for frequent mention, but for prominent, continual presence via the highly stylized expression of traditional alliterative verse. Their manner of treating virtually any topic gravitates to virtually any available locus of subjectivity. Much Old English poetry is straightforwardly about mental states, but even that which is not in the ordinary sense 'about' mentality still, somehow, is, returning insistently to qualities, conditions, and actions of the mind. *Deor*, for example, is a rather different kind of poem from *The Wanderer* and *The Seafarer*. Nevertheless it is often numbered among the elegies, in part because its topic ultimately is the speaker's own troubles and the prospect of their resolution; but this is revealed only at the end, and the common perception of the monologue as elegiac also owes something to the way it has handled its serial allusions to legendary stories throughout, line by line. *Deor* could have made its point about the speaker's problems through reference merely to the situations of the historical and legendary characters it cites, but instead it focuses heavily, in its succession of micronarrative vignettes, on evocation of those figures' emotional states in response to their misfortunes.[19] Doing so feels natural within the conventions of Old English poetic practice; to do otherwise would seem unusual, aloof, insulated.

18 Higley (*Between Languages*, 157) suggests that the poet opposes the 'hardness' of the weather with the 'hardness' of Andreas's mind. Cf. Neville, *Representations*, 47.

19 Critical readings that recognize this feature of *Deor* include Eliason, '*Deor* – A Begging Poem?'; Olsen, 'Old English Women'; Biggs, 'Deor's Threatened "Blame" Poem'; Molinari, 'Overcoming Pagan Suffering'; Bueno Alonso, '"Less Epic Than It Seems"'; and Trilling, *Aesthetics of Nostalgia*, 42–9.

Deor arguably lies within the bounds of what we have come to call the elegy, but the same tendency to emphasize qualities and states of mind is easily found far from that territory. Probably the earliest extant Old English poem, *Cædmon's Hymn*, highlights 'metudæs ... modgidanc' [the Creator's ... mind-thought] (l. 2), here his providential forethought, as one of the two qualities of God (the other is his 'maecti' [power] in the same line) that an audience is called upon to praise.[20] Right at the start of the poetic tradition as it is known to us, *Cædmon's Hymn*, formed around the widespread 'mind and might' collocation,[21] strikes the note with the clarity of a tuning fork. Nearer the other end of the chronological range and in a very different genre, the protagonist of a late heroic poem, *Judith*, is continually affirmed through epithets of mental quality to be *gleaw on geðonce* 'wise in understanding' (l. 13b), *ferhðgleaw* 'wise-minded' (l. 41a), *snottor* 'wise' (ll. 55a, 125a), *ellenrof* 'bold' (ll. 109a, 146a), and so on, and her mental states and processes are frequently made part of the story as well.[22] Her antagonist Holofernes's interiority is equally laid open,[23] and the mentality of other, less personalized figures in the poem is similarly revealed when they enter the field of view.[24] This narrative far outstrips its biblical source in its density of reference to what every available mind is like and what it is busy doing.

Interior qualities and experiences to which readers may be granted imaginative access are not even reserved to humans in Old English poetry.

---

20 I cite the Northumbrian version as given in *ASPR*. Even if the extant English poem were reverse-engineered from Bede's Latin paraphrase (so Kiernan, 'Reading Cædmon's "Hymn"'; but see O'Donnell, 'Bede's Strategy'), the marginal inscriptions of the poem in the Moore and Leningrad MSS of Bede would still be old enough to make it perhaps the earliest surviving poem in English.

21 First discussed by Greenfield (*Interpretation of Old English Poems*, 51–2).

22 Ll. 73b–7a, 86b–8a, 93b–4a, 97b–8a, etc. Cf. Kaske, '*Sapientia et Fortitudo* in the Old English *Judith*.'

23 He is *swiðmod* 'arrogant' (l. 30a), *se modiga* 'the prideful one' (l. 52b), and *þearlmod* 'cruel-minded' (l. 66a); he becomes 'on gytesælum' [joyous at (wine-)pouring] (l. 22b), 'on mode / bliðe' [happy at heart] (ll. 57b–8a), and 'swa druncen / ... swa he nyste ræda nanne / on gewitlocan' [so drunk that he did not know any counsel in (his) thought-chamber] (ll. 67b–9a).

24 Holofernes's retainers in the opening scene are *wlance* 'proud' (l. 16a), *bealde* 'bold' (l. 17a), and *stercedferhðe* 'stout-minded' (l. 55b); Judith and her handmaid are together *ellenþriste* 'courageous' (l. 133b) and *glædmode* 'glad-minded' (l. 140a); the citizens of Bethulia, previously *geomormode* 'sad-minded' (l. 144a), become *bliðe* 'happy' (l. 159a) and *on lustum* 'joyful' (l. 161b).

The writer of *The Rune Poem* considers the mental disposition of the aurochs as important as its physical traits:

ᚢ [=ur] byþ anmod and oferhyrned,
felafrecne deor, feohteþ mid hornum,
mære morstapa; þæt is modig wuht. (ll. 4–6)

[The aurochs is single-minded and horn-crested: a very bold (or dangerous) beast, it fights with horns, the famous moor-walker. That is a brave creature.]

Is the point that the aurochs is in its own right brave, resolute, and daring, or that it is, more objectively, dangerous (to people, since it is people who make and read poems)? The former interpretation seems adequate at the beginning of this passage, as its first line alliteratively pairs a dispositional trait with a physical one in a kind of definition – it is *anmod* 'resolute, single-minded' and *oferhyrned* 'horned above' (or possibly 'having great horns'[25]) – and the last line quoted makes a similar complementary pairing of outward behaviour and inward disposition in the alliterating *morstapa* 'moor-walker' and *modig* 'brave, spirited.'[26] However, in the middle line *felafrecne* is difficult, meaning either 'bold' or 'dangerous' and apparently forcing a translator to choose between an interior, dispositional, imaginative understanding of the creature's nature and an exterior, interactional, implicitly anthropocentric one.

Of course, in the poem's own language no such quandary arises; *felafrecne* is a single word having both connotational valences, and as such it may simultaneously capture something about both the animal's subjective being and the way it objectively interacts with its environment. 'Aggressive' is a Modern English word that can do the same, being frequently applied to animals in just this way, and would decently render *felafrecne*. The animal is also *mære* 'famous, widely known,' its habits and disposition the topic of traditional lore (like that expressed in the *Rune Poem* itself) that circulates in human communities. These lines on the aurochs, in taking for

25 This is the gloss suggested by Hall, 'Perspective and Wordplay,' 453; Halsall, *Old English Rune Poem*, 106; and Acker, *Revising Oral Theory*, 50 and 59 n. 22.

26 Hall ('Perspective and Wordplay,' 454) suggests that 'antithesis between different aspects of the same concept or object is fundamental to the [this] poet's mode of thought' and finds the antithesis here to arise from the juxtaposition of this stanza and the one that follows. One might see the inner/outer distinction within the ᚢ=*ur* stanza as a more compact fulfillment of the same principle.

granted human investment in what they describe, begin to illustrate what I will suggest is an intrinsically relational way of thinking that saturates Old English poetic practice. This is a minimal example, but the craft of Anglo-Saxon poets often involves placing multiple subjectivities before readers to form networks of interaction in which each party's interior nature or mental state exists in essential relation to others.

This passage from *The Rune Poem* is far from an isolated instance of poetic attentiveness to zoological interiority. In the parade of prosopopoeic speakers found in the Exeter Book riddles, as also in some of the Latin riddle collections that were known in Anglo-Saxon England, several are animals.[27] In principle, a prosopopoeic text need not do more than transpose objective physical and behavioural description to first-person discourse. But the poets of the Old English riddles tend to go beyond the structural implementation of this device and make creative choices that imply active exploration of an imagined consciousness complete with perception, cogitation, will, and emotion, as when we become privy to a mother beast's strategizing to protect her young (riddle 15: a fox? a porcupine?) or a toiling ox's recollection of its carefree days as a calf from the perspective of its miserable adult life of labour (riddle 72).[28] The looking-glass world of the riddles allows even broader extension of this tendency to include inanimate objects and insensate creatures as well: mail-shirts can ponder their origins in the thoughts of their hearts, nicked shields can be weary of battle and long for healing, and trees can flourish joyfully.[29] Elsewhere in the Exeter Book, *The Phoenix* includes many indications of its legendary central figure's states and qualities of mind, but the poet also lets readers in on the emotions of the other birds that flock to it: hu-

27 On the range of riddles in Anglo-Saxon England, see Orchard, 'Enigma Variations.' Bitterli (*Say What I Am Called*, chaps 1–3) treats many of the Exeter Book animal riddles together.

28 If Exeter Book riddle 15 describes a fox, it may take its inspiration from Symphosius's *Aenigmata*, no. 34, but if so it is made incomparably more elaborate and subjective. Bitterli ('Exeter Book Riddle 15') revives a nineteenth-century suggestion that it refers to the more exotic porcupine. On the ox's elegiac attitude in riddle 72, cf. Bitterli, *Say What I Am Called*, 34.

29 Exeter Book riddles 35, ll. 3–4 (detail unparalleled in Aldhelm, *Aenigmata*, no. 33, which it translates; cf. Steen, *Verse and Virtuosity*, 96); 5 (details unparalleled in Aldhelm's enigma 87, also Shield); and 53, ll. 2b–3a (detail unparalleled in any of Aldhelm's several tree enigmata – 69, 76, 77, 91 – or those about things made of wood in either Aldhelm's or Symphosius's *Aenigmata*). Niles (*Old English Enigmatic Poems*, 52–4) suggests that the riddles' tendency to subjectivize expresses certain aspects of Anglo-Saxon worldview by dramatizing relational features of human society.

mankind looks on (in wonder, their own subjective position also being acknowledged) as mundane birds escort the phoenix 'mid wynnum' [joyously] (l. 345b), a 'drymendra gedryht' [joyful company] (l. 348a), and when it flies away from them they are left 'geomormode' [sad-minded] (l. 353b). We gain sustained access to the mentality of Noah's dove and raven, too, in the Junius Manuscript poem *Genesis A*, in a passage I will treat in chapter 1. In the much-discussed Beasts of Battle motif,[30] the core narrative proposition regarding the wolf, the raven, and the eagle is not that they congregate near battlefields, or that they follow armies, or that they devour the fallen, but that they rejoice in anticipation of an impending battle, giddily mindful of the carrion on which they expect to feast. And we have already seen the poem on the front of the Franks Casket, after setting the scene with an objectively narrated situation in the first of its two lines, shift focus in its second to a beached whale's state of mind.

In another poetic account of a whale we are granted access to its disposition, much as in the case of the aurochs in *The Rune Poem*. In the Old English version of parts of the Latin *Physiologus*, and without specific parallel in the Latin, the whale is *frecne* (the same word used in compound for the aurochs) and 'ferðgrim ... / niþþa gehwylcum' [fierce-hearted in every confrontation] (*The Whale*, ll. 5–6a). But in this case some of the attraction to subjective experience centres on humans' interests within the poem, not just those arising in the hermeneutic space between text and reader. The nearest Latin version says that sailors mistakenly draw their boats alongside this gigantic creature, supposing it to be an island, and then 'ut coquant sibi cibos post laborem, faciunt ibi focos super arenam quasi super terram' [in order to cook themselves a meal after their work they make fires on the sand, just as they would on the ground].[31] The English poet transforms this statement, writing that

gewiciað werigferðe,
faroðlacende, frecnes ne wenað,
on þam ealonde æled weccað,
heahfyr ælað; hæleþ beoþ on wynnum,
reonigmode, ræste geliste. (*The Whale*, ll. 19–23)

30 Identified by Magoun ('Theme of the Beasts of Battle') and recently surveyed by J. Harris ('Beasts of Battle'). Among many others, see esp. Bonjour, '*Beowulf* and the Beasts of Battle'; Foley, *Immanent Art*, 224–31; and Griffith, 'Convention and Originality.'

31 Quoted from Carmody, *Physiologus Latinus*, 44; translation from Allen and Calder, *Sources and Analogues*, 160.

> [the weary-hearted ones, the sailors, make camp, do not suspect danger, kindle a fire on the island, build a bonfire; the men are joyful, weary-minded, glad of rest.]

The matter-of-fact Latin gives no hint of interest in the sailors' interiority apart from the necessary condition of their having assumed the whale to be an island, but clearly it is important to the Anglo-Saxon poet to make them weary of heart and mind, insensible of danger, and joyful at a chance to rest. This cannot be a case of metrical 'filling,' because the phrases involved do not always provide alliterative complements to opposing half-lines with differing content.[32] Rather, what was entirely implicit has now been made explicit and indeed has become the focal point of the passage. External actions have been reframed entirely in terms of interiority, and a comment which in Latin had been about what the men do is now about what they feel, think, and know (or do not know). This is a profound act of translation: not just from Latin into English or from prose into verse, but from one discursive universe into another, intersecting but distinct one. As the account of the whale has made its way into the vernacular poetic idiom and the frames of reference through which that idiom customarily reckons with the world, the principal target of representation has moved inward. The introduction of emphasis on mentality into works lacking such emphasis in known earlier versions or close analogues illustrates the strength of the tendency I am describing.

Thus far I have concentrated on references to animals' mentality in Old English poems because this manifestation of the phenomenon I wish to analyse is perhaps unexpected and therefore highly visible once attention is called to it. But Old English poets' inclination to speak of mentality was general. Its significance becomes clearest in narrative poetry, which (unlike shorter lyric poems) normally takes its structure and paraphrasable subject matter from sequences of outward action. For this reason the chapters below will focus on narrative verse, with its greater demonstrational value for my argument. Narration as a discursive mode is built to recount events and to explore agency within the forward movement of time, not primarily to crystallize past and present moments reflectively as the lyric poem often does. Thus it is under no compulsion to give pronounced attention to

32 In l. 22b, the poet, under no constraint as to initial sound, could have said many other things about the 'hæleþ' than that they were 'in wynnum'; and l. 23 is dedicated in full to explaining their interiority, a fact for which there can be no formal explanation.

interiority, although of course writers may always choose to do so through various means, such as descriptive psychological portraiture or the technical device known as narrative focalization.

As I will use the term, focalization is the practice of creating access to and knowledge of a particular subjective position within a narrative, through the godlike liberty afforded by heterodiegetic narration (the so-called third-person point of view), such that a reader's understanding of the account is selectively informed by that subjective perspective on it or private experience with respect to it.[33] The passage from *The Whale* considered above is focalized through the sailors. The narrative point of view is third-person and uninvolved – there is no homodiegetic 'I' here telling a fish tale of firsthand experience – and yet readers are made momentarily privy to the thoughts, feelings, and perspective on events of the men disembarking atop the whale. Because we have not been limited to their perspective throughout, we happen already to know that the sailors' *ealond* 'island' is in fact (as the poet has called it a few lines earlier) an *unlond* 'not-land.' The wordplay underscores for readers the information deficit that endangers the mariners: *ealond* is their concept of where they are, and *unlond* is ours. When the poet refers to the whale as an *ealond*, he or she is focalizing a perception through the sailors. Focalization, like any other narrative technique, can of course contribute to all manner of larger, context-driven effects, as here its role in highlighting a failure of knowledge or awareness creates the 'uh-oh' factor of dramatic irony. The point to recognize for now is that at this moment in the text, the poet has deemed it at least as important as anything else that we see the situation through the sailors' eyes and understand the state of mind through which they experience it.

Focalization has particular informative potential in the study of Old English narrative verse because its use there deviates from the norms of other traditions, ancient, medieval, and modern, and thus signals something

33 My articulation of the concept here meets the needs of the analysis I will present as determined by the practice of Anglo-Saxon poets. My usage is in some ways more restricted and in others more permissive than technical definitions of focalization by structural narrative theorists whose goal is to taxonomize the full range of possible authorial techniques – yet whose schemas remain, for the most part, tethered to the genre of the novel and thus sometimes unsuited to medieval narratives. For influential, more strictly narratological discussions of the concept (disagreeing on some points), see Genette, *Narrative Discourse*, 189–94, and *Narrative Discourse Revisited*, 72–8; and Bal, *Narratology*, 100–15.

distinctive about the practice of Anglo-Saxon poets.[34] Storytelling that focalizes actively typically uses that technique to bias the game, making protagonistic characters' minds more open to readers than those of other parties. Indeed, in most imaginative narration, enhanced access to the thoughts, perceptions, intentions, and desires of certain characters is one of the chief identifiers of positions of agency inviting sympathy, while antagonists may be objectified, more often viewed from the outside, and thereby made 'other.'[35] What is striking about focalization in Old English narrative verse is its continual, seemingly compulsory use combined with its shifting and apparently indiscriminate application: this tradition is characterized by free perspectival movement from one subjectivizing opportunity to another.[36] There is little or no technical privileging of perspectives otherwise identified as protagonistic; the usual practice of Anglo-Saxon poets is to let the third-person narration circulate its focalization through multiple loci of subjectivity, granting readers access to a variety of perceptual and cognitive orientations toward events.

The Priority of Subjectivity over Subject in Old English Poetic Tradition

When we left our unfortunate sailors they had, incautious from exhaustion, made *unlond*fall on a surfaced whale. The encyclopedic bestiary tradition, within which *The Whale* and the other two *Physiologus* poems in the Exeter Book form an early vernacular cul-de-sac, instructs readers on the nature of various animals, starting in each case with summaries of their supposed behaviours and then turning to an exposition of each creature's allegorical Christian meaning. *The Whale* is not primarily a narrative text,

---

34 As far as I know, the only applications of the concept of focalization, technically defined, to any Old English poem have been by Ericksen ('Lands of Unlikeness') and Richardson ('Point of View and Identification') although the term has occasionally been used in passing and apparently in different senses. Earlier writers sometimes discussed features of particular texts that I would say have to do with focalization (e.g., Renoir, '*Judith* and the Limits of Poetry'; Renoir, 'Point of View and Design for Terror'; Greenfield and Calder, *New Critical History*, 213) but without clearly distinguishing it from narrative point of view.

35 This effect seems so automatic that it has sometimes been taken by narrative theorists as an axiom of response: e.g., Bal, *Narratology*, 104.

36 This observation is also made, from a different theoretical perspective leading to a different understanding of the phenomenon, by Huisman ('Subjectivity/Orality,' esp. 316 and 320).

then, but the systematic recounting of consuetudinal action gives it an intermittently narrative aspect. In the midst of one of the two behavioural sequences of *The Whale*, we have a single narrative moment involving humans: a scenario in which people make themselves vulnerable to the (allegorically diabolical) creature. It is here that the Anglo-Saxon poet elaborates generously to grant us knowledge of the sailors' minds, as if no enticement other than the mere opportunity were needed. Notice, too, that our access to their interiority has a strong descriptive element, not just presenting exterior reality as coloured by the sailors' perceptions but also affixing adjectival labels to their state of mind. We learn that they 'frecnes ne wenað' [do not suspect danger] (l. 20b), information on the same narrative order as the earlier statement that upon seeing the whale they 'wenaþ ... / þæt hy on ealond sum eagum wliten' [deem that with their eyes they are looking upon an island] (ll. 11–12), but we also find out that they are 'werigferðe' [weary-hearted] (l. 19b), 'on wynnum' [joyful] (l. 22b), 'reonigmode' [weary-minded] (l. 23a), and 'ræste geliste' [glad of rest] (l. 23b).[37]

These remarks in no way 'characterize' this unindividuated group of sailors. The mariners function, in the Old English version, to embody a state of mind: what the poet wanted here, I think, is weary-mindedness of a kind that will accept at face value something resembling an island and begin to cook dinner atop it without the necessary factual assurances. Psychological portraiture relies on the logically prior importance of a person or persona, with some sort of topical presence in the text, awaiting predication and definition. This is not psychological portraiture because a moment earlier there was no one sitting for a portrait. A moment later there will be nobody once again, for the sailors' only importance in this poem is as performers of an imprudent action, allegorized as spiritual unwariness, who are about to be carried swiftly to the bottom of the ocean

37 In theory, information presented through description rather than narration is distinct from focalization (the latter being a technique of perspective-bound event-narration). However, the two methods of supplying information about interiority are often entangled. Take the narrative proposition, combined with a state-of-mind epithet, that the sailors 'in þæt eglond up gewitað / collenferþe' [go up into that island, bold-hearted] (ll. 16–17a): the use of the term *eglond* definitely marks focalization through the sailors, because it names the whale according to their faulty perception of it; but the adjective *collenferþe* is only marginally a part of the narration proper and might be considered merely descriptive. What matters for my purposes is readers' knowledge of the interior qualities and states attached to subjective positions within a text. Both techniques accomplish this, and for the needs of this project surgically dividing them would be arbitrary.

in a passage that begins with a brief switch back to the whale's mental qualities and perception of events:

Þonne gefeleð facnes cræftig
þæt him þa ferend on fæste wuniaþ,
wic weardiað, wedres on luste,
ðonne semninga on sealtne wæg
mid þa noþe niþer gewiteþ
garsecges gæst, grund geseceð,
ond þonne in deaðsele drence bifæsteð
scipu mid scealcum. Swa bið scinna þeaw,
deofla wise, þæt hi drohtende
þurh dyrne meaht duguðe beswicað,
ond on teosu tyhtaþ tilra dæda,
wemað on willan, þæt hy wraþe secen
frofre to feondum. (ll. 24–36a)

[When the one crafty in trickery feels that the travellers are resting securely on him, keeping the camp, taking pleasure in the weather, then suddenly the sea-enemy plunges down into the salt wave with those presumptuous ones and reaches the bottom, and then secures (them) in a death-hall by drowning, ships together with men. Such is the custom of demons, the practice of devils, that through secret power they deceive people interacting (with them) and entice them to the injury of their (own) good deeds, persuade them in their wills so that they may horribly seek comfort in enemies.]

We would have the relationship of dependency backward if we saw the subjective qualities and states of the seafarers as the definition or specification of conceptually prior characters. Rather, the sailors are a narrative vehicle for a desired subjectivity, a peg on which the poet may hang something that matters more than they do. Likewise the whale is primarily a textual repository of subjective animosity to humans' best interests. In the Latin analogue, the whale's subjectivity is limited to its feeling the fire upon its back, a detail needed to provoke its dive. The English version gives a much more pointed sense of antagonism, as the whale seems spitefully aware of the encamped sailors' comforts and pleasures (which we ourselves know about due to another quick recurrence to their experiential perspective).

It may go without saying that these techniques of subjectivization are not used with the aim of psychologically nuanced depiction of the sailors (or the whale). But while a number of factors make such a reading unlikely in this case, intimations of mentality like the ones we see here have often been mistaken, when found in other contexts that may give an impression of greater cultural familiarity, as 'characterization' in some modern sense that implies an individuating psychological fictionalization. Against this interpretive tendency it is critical to recognize that what is happening in *The Whale* is normal, and it is everywhere, and it is intrinsically poetic within classical Old English tradition. The kinds of language and subjectivizing methods used here are common to Old English verse texts at large, including but not limited to those which (like some of the elegiac poems) might appear to lend themselves to a less tradition-conscious kind of reading that regards each reference to mentality as sufficiently determined by the text putatively circumscribing and containing it. Too often, studies of individual poems have begun by isolating them from the discourse in which inheres the means of their signification. I will argue that the continual reference to qualities and states of mind in classical Old English poetry works less to create distinctive fictional persons than to evoke a system of ethical positions and relationships, even when such a system is not fully articulated within a given text. The defamiliarization brought about by the zoological content of examples like *The Whale* or the front panel inscription on the Franks Casket may enable us to develop interpretive approaches that respond productively to such intimations as a normal part of Old English tradition.

The Latin *Physiologus* already included sailors, albeit mentally undefined ones, and we have seen the poet of *The Whale* remake them through focalization and epithets of subjectivity. He or she took them up as blanks, like unstruck coins, provided by the Latin source and collectively occupying an unrealized perspectival position, and impressed them with the mental attributes and actions that endow them with poetic as well as didactic worth within vernacular tradition. Sometimes Anglo-Saxon poets go one better still: at times the poetic attraction to subjectivity generates a perspectival position ex nihilo if none is already implicit in the story matter or scenario, eligible for actualization. In other words, so little does the fact of emphasis on emotion and mentality seem to depend on any prior notion of 'character' that the textual presence of a potential subject of experience to use as a starting point is no prerequisite: the felt need for a locus of mentality and perception to set into relation with the topical matter could conjure one up.

Even so unpopulous a poem as *The Ruin*, for example, summons the minds of the absent, managing before all is done to accommodate several lines' worth of sharply situated subjectivity. After beginning with objective description of the deteriorated city, the poet admires the intelligence of the unknown architects using quality-of-mind terms to describe their ingenuity (ll. 16–20) and then considers how the collapsed buildings must once have resounded '·ᛗ· [=mon]-dreama full' [full of human joys] (l. 23b), a phrase suggesting that the imagined joy of the citizens is at least as important as their imagined clamour. So far the city's residents have remained abstract and ghostly, subordinated to the physical presence of the ruins themselves. But the poet next creates and foregrounds an ancient human consciousness that gives a sense of immediacy to the greatness that has now decayed:

iu beorn monig
glædmod ond goldbeorht gleoma gefrætwed,
wlonc ond wingal wighyrstum scan,
seah on sinc, on sylfor, on searogimmas,
on ead, on æht, on eorcanstan –
on þas beorhtan burg bradan rices. (ll. 32b–7)

[long ago many a warrior – glad-minded and bright with gold, adorned splendidly, proud and wine-giddy – gleamed in war-garments, gazed on treasure, on silver, on cunningly wrought gems, on wealth, on property, on a jewel: on this bright city of the broad kingdom.]

The device of organizing some of the poem's meaning around a burst of particularized perception – dramatizing the scene now not just through speculation about the city's builders and occupants, but through the mediation of a fictional consciousness – moves *The Ruin* beyond impersonal description. Entire generations of what had until this point been indistinct figures of the remote past, the gulf between their ancient time (*iu*) and the present of the poetic voice unbridged, find representation now in an individuated perspective that is at the same time, paradoxically, collective in its import: the perspective of *beorn monig* 'many *a* warrior' – one warrior, whom we envision and through whose eyes we also see, but one who is feeling emotions and doing things which, the same phrase asserts, countless others like him also felt and did. The poem's content in this passage comes to us through the many-times-iterated workings of some hypothetical mind, proud of human accomplishment, and pair of eyes, surveying with pleasure the tokens of power and seemingly secure prosperity. In the variational sequence that forms a list of these tokens in lines 35–7, the *beorn*'s satisfied gaze lingers on first one item and then another; but a reader's vision is double as the poet catalogues what the audience knows to be lost, concluding with a totalizing equation of all that has gone before with the last item in apposition, the splendid city itself.

The juxtaposition of this vignette of sanguine pleasure with what is (for poet and reader) its conspicuous failure to endure helps give *The Ruin* the feel of a meditative poem despite its lacking *The Seafarer*'s construction of self-revealing intimacy or *The Wanderer*'s reflecting consciousness made wise by hard experience. The sudden introduction of a nameless representative of his long-departed people, essentially as a textual site for subjective activity, contributes forcefully to *The Ruin*'s elegiac impact, providing a locus of emotional access to past glories and also to the past unsuspicion of their fragility, which has already been revealed to readers in a present of shards and rubble. The interjection is brief, but it has made its point: like the Last Survivor in *Beowulf*, this *beorn* is gone from the text as quickly as he came, having done the work the poet needed him to do.[38]

Until recent decades academic study of *The Ruin* had largely aimed to determine which ruin the poet had in mind.[39] That would be a worthwhile thing to know, just as it is nice to have lately gained an informed judgment as to the species of whale that furnished the bone of the Franks Casket.[40] Peering from our distant vantage point we will take any hard facts we can get. But within the sphere of poetic signification that these texts occupied for early audiences, where to pinpoint *The Ruin*'s setting on a map probably did not matter any more than whether the Franks Casket's account of a stranding was journalistically accurate or what kind of whale it describes. It is not that the Anglo-Saxons lacked a factual sense of geography or history or detailed knowledge of their physical world. After all, they wrote land charters, recorded Othhere's and Wulfstan's voyages, produced important works of historiography, engineered and built large structures, grew crops, and achieved feats of artisanship requiring expert manipulation of metal, stone, and other substances. The point, rather, is that Old English poetic discourse takes a reader very far from forms of intellection centred on information, whether geographic, historical, or physical. When these areas of knowledge intersect with classical-style Old

38 Other examples of apparently ad hoc focalization include *Judgment Day I*, ll. 68b–77a; *Christ III*, ll. 1376b–8; and Cain in *Genesis A* (on the last, see Magennis, 'Treatments of Treachery').

39 See Orchard's summary in 'Reconstructing *The Ruin*,' 46 nn. 4–5.

40 Szabo, *Monstrous Fishes*, 55 n. 79.

English verse they become something else: the symbolic topography of *Beowulf* and *Guthlac A*,[41] or the ideological traditionalizing of *The Battle of Maldon* and the formally conservative poems among those in the *Anglo-Saxon Chronicle*,[42] or heirloom weapons, gifts of twisted gold, and the material remains of something once great, now gone. I will argue that the poets' choice, again and again, to provide their readers with perceptual, cognitive, and emotional access to practically any available subjective position participates in this same partly afactual process of constructing meaningful Old English verse in the traditional way.

Preliminaries to Further Analysis

I am not the first to stress the ubiquity of reference to mental states and processes as a bedrock-level truth about Old English poetry deserving of our attention. Antonina Harbus's monograph *The Life of the Mind in Old English Poetry* precedes me in arguing that emphasis on mentality is a consistent and notable feature of Anglo-Saxon literary art, and our work is mutually confirming in assigning importance to this basic but crucial observation. From that common starting point, our projects pursue different objectives and accordingly differ greatly in approach to the material. Whereas Harbus's methodological commitments lie principally within the field of cognitive literary studies,[43] it is not my goal here to discover the characteristics or operation of 'the mind' as the Anglo-Saxons understood that constituent part of the whole person. Previous general surveys of Old English terminology pertaining to mental faculties and functions have laid semantic foundations that need not be rebuilt here,[44] and Anglo-Saxon concepts of the mind's nature and activity have also received study from a range of perspectives.[45] This book takes as its topic not the nature of minds

41 See Stanley, 'Old English Poetic Diction,' 441; Howe, *Migration and Mythmaking*, chap. 5; Clemoes, 'King and Creation'; Magennis, *Images of Community*, 121–43 and 178–88; and Gelling, 'Landscape of *Beowulf*.'

42 See, e.g., J.M. Hill, *Anglo-Saxon Warrior Ethic*, chaps 4–5, and O'Brien O'Keeffe, 'Deaths and Transformations,' 164–78.

43 Harbus ('Anglo-Saxon Mentalities' and 'Cognitive Studies') explains cognitive literary studies and provides literature reviews.

44 Godden, 'Anglo-Saxons on the Mind'; North, *Pagan Words*, chap. 4; Low, 'Approaches'; and Harbus, *Life of the Mind*, chap. 2. More specialized or limited studies include Šileikytė, 'In Search of the Inner Mind'; Kiricsi, 'From *Mod* to *Minde*'; Low, 'Pride, Courage, and Anger'; and Mize, 'Representation,' 62–72.

45 E.g., Jager, 'Word in the "Breost"'; Harbus, *Life of the Mind*; Harbus, 'Medieval Concept'; Matto, 'War of Containment,' 67–70, and 'True Confessions'; Šileikytė, 'In

according to the testimony of Anglo-Saxon poets, but the nature of fictive access to them in Old English verse, and especially to the experiential positions they occupy with respect to narrated events. That is, instead of 'the mind' as an object of analysis or representation, I am chiefly interested in the powerful attraction to loci of subjectivity that we encounter at every turn in Old English poetry: more specifically, the traditionality of that attraction itself and of its manifestations in versecraft. It is this special feature of poetic expression in the classical style, embedded within and (I will argue) inextricable from the larger discursive traditionality of Old English verse composition, that I call the 'poetics of mentality.' Between us and real, historical Anglo-Saxon concepts of the mind – at least, as approached through their classical poetry – stands a massively stylized verbal art whose traditional representations mediate non-transparently, and the image that we receive is in part formed by the window through which we look. I am interested in that art, that artifice, the composition and optics of the window.

The word 'subjectivity' has several related but distinct meanings in contemporary literary study, some more technical than others. Sometimes it denotes linguistically constituted sites of agency that a text constructs and projects through the features of its own textuality, such as the interested positions that may be implied for originators and audiences of the text yet remain distinguished theoretically from real writers and readers (even if partly mirroring or mapped onto them).[46] Another major branch of contemporary thought focuses on the subject as a hypothetical extratextual entity, more presumed than projected by a text anchored in the material world of human affairs, and whose situatedness defines a socially, economically, and historically contingent 'subject position' from which the statements that constitute the text are conceivable and utterable.[47] Either of these postmodern approaches to the concept of subjectivity, or a blend of them,[48] can be useful in the study of medieval texts, not least in enabling critics to sidestep some inappropriate tendencies inherited from methods

Search of the Inner Mind'; Tyler, *Old English Poetics*, 29–31 and 52–73; Mize, 'Representation'; McIlwain, 'Brain and Mind'; Lockett, *Anglo-Saxon Psychologies*.

46 The usage of, for example, Pasternack (*Textuality of Old English Poetry*), Huisman ('Subjectivity/Orality'), and Dailey ('Questions of Dwelling') falls into this general class.

47 E.g., in Foucault, *Archaeology of Knowledge*, a work that does have some influence on my thinking in chap. 3 below (although for consistency I will not shift my usage of terminology there).

48 As in Matto, 'True Confessions.'

of analysis originally formed on the Romantic lyric, the dramatic monologue, and the Victorian and modernist novel. Paradoxically, at times it is the more innovative theoretical movements of the past few decades that most effectively expose and break some of the shackles of anachronism.

Nevertheless, as may already have become evident, I am reverting to something closer to an everyday-language, dictionary sense of the term 'subjectivity,' because it will suffice for describing and addressing the phenomenon studied in the following chapters. In my usage, subjectivity is non-objectivity, that is, experience- or perception-bound consciousness of events; and *a* subjectivity, in the context of Old English poetry, is an imagined locus of such consciousness, which for the purposes of my discussion will always lie within the fictive world of poetic representation (hence the qualifier, 'imagined'). Here, a 'subjectivity' will be the site of experiencing that is implicit in a portrayal of experience, the site of perceiving that is implicit in a statement of perception; it is a function and a product of narrative and descriptive technique. A 'subject,' then, is a discrete fictive agent occupying such a site, the entity to which belongs the consciousness that experiences and perceives what is said to be experienced and perceived. I define the terms 'subjectivity' and 'subject' in this order because, as suggested above, I believe that doing so reflects the logical relationship between the things they name that prevails in Old English poetic discourse: the priority of a subjectivity over a subject, with the subject sometimes starting out as a mere potentiality actualized by the poetic production of a subjectivity.[49]

I limit my analysis to and make claims concerning only Old English poetry in the 'classical' mode: that is, poems which generally conform to the conservative poetic metre first described by Eduard Sievers and more recently theorized according to a different model by Geoffrey Russom and Thomas A. Bredehoft.[50] Poems judged by various dating methods to

49 Otherwise – if subjects had strict priority to the production of subjectivities – my 'subjects' could simply be called 'characters.' Sometimes, when a subject is in fact firmly established by the text such that the distinction does not matter, I will use the words 'subject' and 'character' interchangeably.

50 Russom, *Old English Meter*, and Bredehoft, *Early English Metre*. Throughout this book I will follow Bredehoft's metrical system, a further development of Russom's elegant alternative to the received Sieversian model. The approach to metre that Russom and Bredehoft share (which identifies interfaces of grammar and metre as a link between linguistic competency and developed skill in versification) better accounts for the observable facts of the corpus than does the older system and connects more plausibly to hypothesizable compositional methods.

be among the earlier ones exhibit the classical form; some poems known to be late adhere to it as well, and I grant them membership in the tradition which by means of their metre and diction they assert themselves to share. It may be difficult to define non-arbitrary boundaries between classical poetic construction and the more open and varied forms found in late Old English verse, or between verse with characteristic late features and showy prose, but in any case it has been clear for a long time now that the simple categories of 'verse' and 'prose' cannot describe either the synchronic or the diachronic gradations in Old English literary form, nor are the problems put to rest by the insertion of 'rhythmic prose' into the spectrum (which arguably distorts analysis in one way as it facilitates it in another).[51] Rather than join the continuing confrontation of these important definitional challenges, I will avoid resting any part of my argument on cases that might be considered dubious on formal grounds without explicit justification. As it happens, delimiting the material in this way proves apt, because the poetics of mentality seems to belong to the classical style: its manifestations strongly coincide with the use of the traditional metre and other features long recognized as marking the classical poetic register, such as its special lexical resources and constraints.

Those special resources and constraints involve dictional and other structures that are commonly understood to diagnose the tradition as an 'oral-derived' one, but my arguments and analysis will have no dependence on any theory of actual oral composition.[52] I think it probable that many features of the traditional register of Old English verse took shape prehistorically in oral composition, and a real oral/written interface must historically have occurred, probably complexly and over a protracted period.[53] However, for two reasons I have no interest in attempting to

51 Seminal to the ongoing discussion are McIntosh, 'Wulfstan's Prose'; Blake, 'Rhythmical Alliteration'; Kuhn, 'Was Ælfric a Poet?'; and Stanley, 'Alliterative Ornament' and '*Judgement of the Damned*.' More recently, see Cable, *English Alliterative Tradition*, chaps 1–2; Richards, 'Prosaic Poetry'; Wright, 'More Old English Poetry'; Mitchell, 'Relation'; and Trahern, 'Working the Boundary.' Of particular importance are Momma, *Composition*, and several writings by Bredehoft: *Textual Histories*, esp. 73–99; 'Ælfric and Late Old English Verse'; 'Boundaries between Verse and Prose'; *Early English Metre*; and *Authors, Audiences, and Old English Verse*, esp. chaps 4–5.

52 This is not to deny that the poems we have may often have been declaimed aloud and heard rather than read. The involvement of the ear and voice with writing and reading in Anglo-Saxon England has been treated fruitfully by O'Brien O'Keeffe (*Visible Song* and 'Listening to the Scenes of Reading').

53 Niles (*Homo Narrans*, chap. 4) considers the processes that may have been involved.

identify genuine (pre)historically oral features as such. First, I do not think it is possible to do so, precisely because the tradition succeeded in reinventing itself in textual form.[54] The classical poems that we have took their extant shape within a culture of writing, a fact which alone (in my view) both proves the existence of a register of traditional-style written poetry and also prevents the evidentially sound discernment of anything else. I will work with the written poetic tradition as such and will resist speculative excavation beneath it. My assumption throughout, in accordance with the imperative of relying on as few untested and untestable premises as possible, is that all observable relations of poetic language among different surviving texts are or may be textual relations, in some cases perhaps direct (i.e., comprising a closed system of texts both or all of which happen still to exist) though most of the time indirect (involving one or more texts now unknown). Operating on the working assumption of textual relations among the attested instances of repeated patterns will ground analysis in what we have material evidence of – a written poetic tradition – rather than in conjecture about what we do not have.

Second, I do not think the oral origin of the classical poetic register bears on the interpretation of the written poems as they are known to us and as literate Anglo-Saxons produced and received them. Reading a text successfully does not require explanation of the origins of its style, provided that one is fluent in that style's operation within synchronic linguistic and cultural systems, any more than reading this sentence requires a speaker of English who is already acquainted with its words to etymologize them. Nor does approaching Old English poetry as the product of a textual poetic culture automatically imply anything about how a given text did or did not make meaning for its writer and early readers.[55] Questions of the relevant modes and systems of signification in any single instance belong to the pragmatics of culturally circumscribed language use and thus are logically discrete from any consideration of how texts, or any of their constituent elements (down to the individual phrase or motif), may be related to one another diachronically in a stemmatic or 'genealogical' configuration. In other words, I firmly separate the question of active, robust poetic traditionality from that of orality: although they have often been treated as concomitants, neither descriptor requires or implies the other.

---

54 Niles's reasoning ('Toward an Anglo-Saxon Oral Poetics') makes no claim that the criteria he offers could yield certainty, but I doubt they can even justify judgments of likelihood: it does not seem to me that any feature in his descriptions would be unsustainable in written composition given a strong enough sense of tradition.

55 Cf. Amodio, *Writing the Oral Tradition*, 57–9.

I will illustrate my position with an example. Let us suppose we can know with complete certainty something many scholars consider probable, that the writer of *Andreas* had specific knowledge of *Beowulf* and drew directly upon it.[56] Why did he or she do so, and to what purpose? The *Andreas* poet was not citing *Beowulf*, I would maintain, or quoting from or alluding to it, but borrowing from it: more precisely, borrowing aspects of its language, or more precisely yet, attempting to redirect and use that language's tried-and-true rhetorical ability to operate in desirable ways within a highly marked poetic register. The later poet's hope surely was not that audiences of *Andreas* would say to themselves, 'Ah, yes, there's another bit from *Beowulf*,' but that they would greet a new iteration of patterned diction with a kind of response the *Andreas* poet, as a reader, could identify with, and as a writer, sought to recreate to the advantage of a new poem about the apostles Matthew and Andrew.

'Imitate' is probably a better word than 'borrow' for such activity, even when the correspondence is verbatim, because conceiving of the relation as imitative avoids reifying either text in a way more typical of our culture than that of the Anglo-Saxons. While this may seem counterintuitive in our age of intellectual and verbal property supported by technologies of typography and manufacture, and especially in the more recently developed environment of digital textuality with its power of rapid fragmentation, manipulation, and reconstitution of text, premodern poetic practice in a well-defined traditional style was primarily a performance of a familiar kind of language: a process, not an assemblage of data. Its traditionality in relation to previous productions consisted not of a later writer's acquisition of textual objects (whether verbal or notional), implicitly conceptualized as having been formerly possessed by another – as is the case with citation, quotation, or allusion – but rather in its quality of attempting to do again, recognizably and to desired effect, as had been done before. What the *Andreas* poet did was make a poem in the way the *Beowulf* poet had done – here and there, in almost exactly the same way.

The role of direct imitation in the production of traditional verse should hardly come as a surprise, since poetry is a subset of language and the marked idiom of traditional Old English poetry a special register of ordinary Old English. Imitation of the adept is a key means by which language is learned, including specialized language, and it is also part of how practitioners of any craft continually hone their own skills. A medieval poet working in a conservative style, practising both a craft and a discourse, can

56 Best argued by Riedinger ('Formulaic Relationship').

be expected to have picked up formulaic and other diction and techniques from other poets just as any language user may pick up new vocabulary and expressive forms from effective speakers and writers; and prior to the Romantic theorizing and celebration of individual genius, he or she might have had little desire to conceal or minimize the relationship. What is exceptional is not the existence of such imitative acts as may be visible in the case of *Andreas* and *Beowulf*, but our occasional ability to track them, and far from arguing for the impoverishment of tradition, these acts may just as well bespeak a lively and informed traditional sensibility. The question of whether visible textual connections imply superficial mimicry or participation in an ongoing tradition of poetic discourse must be decided on the merits, through evaluation of interpretive cogency and the explanatory power of a given hypothesis. Such judgments must take multiple axes of traditional art into account, including not only repeated dictional units but also more complex features of the specialized register like the gravitation to traditional subjectivities through the distinctive use of focalization.

This book is not a study of focalization per se, although the manipulations of narrative matter through access to perspectivally limited positions that I have begun to describe are one major element of the system of compositional priorities whose importance to classical Old English versecraft I seek to demonstrate. The poetics of mentality manifests across all scales of poetic structure, from whole episodes and conceptual motifs centrally concerned with thought and emotion down to the smallest, most basic components of the traditional poetic register, including the lexicon itself,[57] as well as the formulaic diction that is used to construct metrical lines and the distinctive variational syntax of Old English poetry. I have laid such stress on focalization in this introductory chapter not only because in its own right it is a technical feature to which we will need to be sensitive, and a concept that may require some explanation, but also because of its special role in the system I describe, providing a means of connecting the elements of the poetics of mentality across scales. Focalization intersects with the details provided at the level of word, phrase, and half-line, as well as with episode- and poem-level concerns with subjective experience and interiority, making it an essential vehicle of represented subjectivities in third-person narration.

57 For example, of the fifteen almost-exclusively poetic words Frank selects for analysis ('Poetic Words in Late Old English Prose'), three (*hyge*, *ferhð*, and *sefa*) are frequent lexical items involved in constructions of emotion or mentality. See also the studies cited in nn. 44 and 45 above.

The way forward must begin with close analysis describing the Old English poetics of mentality and its continual generation of traditional subjectivities, but it is no less important to take the further step of considering how this feature of classical versecraft can affect interpretation. Each of the chapters below will contribute to the first, descriptive side of the argument using a comparative method. Different groupings of comparanda – drawn from Old English, Latin, and Old Saxon texts, prose and verse, original compositions and translations – are selected to bring different configurations of evidence to bear. At the same time, increasing attention will be given to the second, interpretive side of the argument with each successive chapter: chapter 1 will undertake little interpretation and concentrate on making the basic case for the poetics of mentality as a closely integrated set of priorities and practices in classical-style Old English poetry; chapter 3 will give the fullest attention to its impact on holistic reading of an entire poem.

Chapter 1 focuses on formal and technical aspects of *Genesis A*, an early, long text (near-consensus assigns it to the eighth century, and probably the earlier rather than later part),[58] to show manifestations of the poetics of mentality that pervade that poem and, I allege, typify classical Old English narrative verse on the whole. This first chapter will anatomize the phenomenon, starting with its smallest-scale expressions in the lexical, formulaic, and metrisyntactic elements of traditional composition; then expanding the scope of analysis to narrative techniques such as focalization and the use of characters' direct speech; and concluding with the role of the poetics of mentality in the formation of larger-scale narrative episodes and evocations of recurrent conceptual themes and motifs. This study of *Genesis A*, showing the integral place of the poetics of mentality in the craft of a single, thoroughly traditional poet, will provide a baseline of normal poetic practice that chapters 2 and 3 will help to solidify by documenting the same tendencies in poems that stand in different compositional relations to their own comparanda.

Chapter 2 examines a small number of changes made by the poet of *Genesis B*, a ninth-century text, to its source, the Old Saxon *Genesis*, and concentrates on the ways those alterations function within an English

58 For recent summary of the major factors in the poem's dating, see Orchard, 'Intoxication, Fornication, and Multiplication,' 334. The fullest chronological account of Old English poetry that is informed by Ashley Crandell Amos's critical evaluation of earlier dating methods (Amos, *Linguistic Means*) is Fulk, *History of Old English Meter* (for *Genesis A* see esp. pp. 368–81). See also Russom, 'Dating Criteria.'

literary environment.[59] Analysis of the formulaic language that the changed lines share with other surviving Old English poems finds the *Genesis B* poet working actively and comfortably within the norms of English poetic diction, making full use of traditional networks of association; and strikingly, the greater number of the changes made can be shown to participate in the poetics of mentality. Chapter 2 is also the theoretical heart of the book: here it becomes necessary to consider categorically the semantic and other communicative properties of formulaic poetic language. I will take a new approach to this problem, attempting to break the impasse of assertion and counterassertion that has often characterized commentary on the meaning of conventional elements in Old English poetic language by setting such diction in the context of current thinking on linguistic pragmatics and discourse analysis, and bringing into the account as well a recent contribution to the cultural theory of tradition. Informed by these investigations taking place in allied fields of inquiry, my analysis of *Genesis B* will result in a more complete picture of the poetics of mentality as a normal part of the special linguistic register for traditional poetry.

Chapter 3 takes up another narrative poem, Metre 1 of the Old English *Boethius* (a work usually associated with the West Saxon court of King Alfred and the flurry of translational activity near the turn of the tenth century), and tracks the changes wrought by the *Boethius* poet on Metre 1's prose source, the historiographical introduction to the first, all-prose version of the *Boethius*. As a complement to chapter 2's focus on dictional manifestations of the poetics of mentality, the demonstration of its emergence from the priorities and procedures of verse composition in the first half of chapter 3 will concentrate more on larger-scale matters of narrative treatment to show how the *Boethius* poet's traditional techniques shape not just the verbal but also the rhetorical and intellectual construction of a whole poem. The second half of the chapter will explore several features of Metre 1 generated by the poetics of mentality that also seem to root that

59 Neither the manuscript of *Genesis A* (Junius 11) nor the edition of it in *ASPR* marks it as separate from *Genesis B*, a text of different origin which *Genesis A* envelopes. From a reception standpoint a strong argument can be made for regarding the two as a single work: for such analyses, see, e.g., Lucas, 'Loyalty and Obedience'; Karkov, *Text and Picture*; and Buchelt, 'All about Eve.' However, any kind of design-oriented interpretation must consider that *Genesis B* appears to have been brought in scribally to fill a lacuna in a defective exemplar (see below, chap. 2, n. 1). Because my argument focuses on the making of Old English verse, the fact that *Genesis A* and *B* originated in different ways at different times mandates their treatment as separate entities.

text in a particular ideological milieu. Chapter 3 will thus complete the broadening of this book's case studies from description of phenomena that I argue are typical into analysis of the role those phenomena played in the making of meaning for writers and readers who, through their attraction to poetry in the classical style, functioned as agents of a persistent but adaptable tradition.

With Metre 1 of the *Boethius*, a text written at least one and a half centuries after *Genesis A* and tentatively assignable to a relatively well-known political and literary context, it becomes possible to consider the management of subjectivity as an aspect of not just *traditionality* but also *traditionalism*: that is to say, not just practice that is recognized as traditional, but the use of traditionality to do something, to bring about some effect on historically situated audiences. To inquire into traditionalism is to recognize that the invocation of tradition is a discursive operation with its own rhetorical properties and purposes. Classical Old English verse of the kind represented by *Genesis A* was a model for the later *Genesis B* and *Boethius* poets' work. But whatever earlier poetry remained in circulation (and we know it did: *Genesis A* survives along with *Genesis B* in a manuscript that actually postdates that of the later, prosimetrical *Boethius*)[60] was also, more dynamically, a kind of elder interlocutor with which subsequent poets interacted in making their compositional choices. Any literary tradition, however conservative, is constituted from an indefinite number of singular, situated engagements – with discursive fields, with cultural and textual environments, and with sociohistorical conditions – by persons creating texts for reasons that make sense to them. Metre 1 and *Genesis B* are new instalments in a classical tradition that cannot ever truly have been static or monolithic, however it might appear from a great chronological remove and without the benefit of much extratextual information. These poets continued to produce tradition at the same time as they tapped into its cultural power through what Elizabeth Tyler felicitously terms an 'aesthetics of the familiar.'[61] Alertness to the poetics of mentality gives us one way of seeing how they did it.

60 Bodleian Library MS Junius 11, holding the *Genesis* compilation, is best assigned to the period 960×990 (Lockett, 'Integrated Re-Examination'); British Library MS Cotton Otho A.vi, the sole surviving copy of the version of the *Boethius* that includes the Metres, dates from near the middle of the tenth century (Godden and Irvine, *Old English Boethius*, 1:22).

61 The subtitle of Tyler, *Old English Poetics*.

1 The Poetics of Mentality

The claim that a systemic, continual attraction to subjectivity partly governed the production of traditional Old English verse is far-reaching and, if correct, will imply a need to reevaluate some of the ways we interpret Old English poems when our goal is to understand how they made meaning in Anglo-Saxon England. My introductory chapter illustrated Old English poetry's attentiveness to interiority and experiential perspective, preliminarily suggesting only that it is a prominent feature of the surviving corpus and is largely unconstrained by conditions of subject matter or genre. This and the following chapters will argue more rigorously that it is almost a sine qua non of Old English poetic thought and expression: in other words, a given poem will tend to emphasize mentality because that is one of the things that make it sound and work 'right' as an Old English poem in the classical style. The poetics of mentality inhabits the versecraft itself, having an ever-emergent presence in the traditional idiom and its compositional techniques as well as finding expression in topical interests that are in their own right traditional to the culture of Anglo-Saxon vernacular poetry as we know it.

Some evidence for this phenomenon's intrinsic involvement in the making of traditional Old English verse is found in its total integration in the lexical, phrasal, and metrisyntactic building blocks from which that poetry is formally constructed. By itself, however, the ubiquity of mentality language in the nuts and bolts of the poetic register need not imply that poets inclined toward opportunities to explore states and qualities of mind beyond accepting the words and formulaic units most readily available to them in the practical task of producing acceptable verses. Just as important as its permeation of the irreducible components of classical-style diction is the way the poetics of mentality cuts across all structural scales of poetic expression, also driving the creation of larger narrative and thematic units and shaping their presentation. This chapter will survey both the smaller- and larger-scale subjectivizing methods of traditional Old English poetry and show the continuity between them that is maintained in part through focalization. This overview will enable subsequent chapters to focus on how specific components of the poetics of mentality make meaning without losing sight of the fuller range of constantly interacting techniques.

I will proceed by means of a case study that allows comparison of an Old English poem with an Old English prose work corresponding closely in content. The extant corpus provides several such opportunities, and a number of these pairings afford the additional possibility of comparison with a known Latin source which they share, whether through independent parallel descent or in a line of descent in which one vernacular version depends on the other. *Genesis A* and the Ælfrician/Hexateuch prose *Genesis* both translate scripture. *Judith* and its Ælfrician prose counterpart both likewise come from the biblical book of Judith, and the Old English verse and prose renderings of various psalms from Latin versions of the book of Psalms.[1] *Guthlac B* and the two Old English prose lives of Guthlac all derive from Felix of Crowland's Latin *Life of St. Guthlac*; the verse portions of the Old English *Boethius* rewrite chapters of the all-prose version that for the most part translate *metra* from Boethius's *Consolation of Philosophy*; and both *Judgment Day II* and the prose homily (Napier 29) with which it has material in common are based on the Latin poem *On the Day of Judgment* attributed to Bede.[2]

1 Verse: Psalms 51–150 from the *Paris Psalter*, the verse translation of Psalm 50 in Cotton MS Vespasian D.vi, and *Fragments of Psalms* from MS Junius 121. Prose: the parts of Psalms 1–50 in the *Paris Psalter* that correspond to individual verse versions, and the continuous interlinear glosses of psalms in several surviving glossed psalters. K.J. Quinn and K.P. Quinn (*Manual*, items H008–H020) and Frank and Cameron (*Plan*, 224–6) list psalters glossed in Old English; Stanton (*Culture of Translation*, chap. 1, esp. 34–46) discusses the relationship of continuous glosses to translation practices for free-standing prose. I exclude *Exodus* from my list of eligible biblical poems because it is not a direct enough sequential rendering from the scriptural book of Exodus to function as a close analogue to the English prose *Exodus* of the Hexateuch (see Remley, *Old English Biblical Verse*, chap. 3).

2 The *Judgment Day II*/Napier 29 pairing is part of a complex series of correspondences and overlaps between verse and prose material in Cambridge, Corpus Christi College MS 201, Oxford, Bodleian Library MSS Hatton 113 and 114, and the Vercelli Book. See Whitbread, '"Wulfstan" Homilies,' 'Two Notes,' and 'Notes on the Old English *Exhortation*'; Stanley, '*Judgement of the Damned*,' esp. 364–5; Richards, 'Prosaic Poetry'; Wright, 'More Old English Poetry'; and Bredehoft, *Authors, Audiences, and Old English Verse*, 179–85.

While any of these sets of texts might have evidential value, some will have far more to tell us than others. For the purpose of isolating qualities of expression that are inherent to classical Old English poetic discourse, our most information-rich starting point will be a pair comprising a lengthy verse and lengthy prose text that share a known Latin source and whose relationships to that source are as direct and as precisely definable as possible. Most of the works listed above are less than optimal for various reasons. *Judith*'s prose cognate is a compressed paraphrase of the biblical text, and the abbreviating tendency of the prose would interfere. *Guthlac B*'s prose analogues bring an unhelpful complication of textual history by deriving from Felix's *Life* through a now-unknown prose intermediary.[3] The relationship between *Judgment Day II* and its prose counterpart is direct, but which version is the source of the other remains uncertain.[4] That poem, like the various poetic versions of psalms and most of the Metres of the Old English *Boethius*, is predominantly non-narrative, thus ruling out the technique of focalization whose distribution among different perspectival positions is so informative; and the *Paris Psalter* verse is very untraditional.[5]

The best candidate for case study at this stage is *Genesis A*. At over 2300 lines, this poem offers much material for comparison with its Latin source and with the Ælfrician prose *Genesis* that became incorporated into the Old English Hexateuch. But understanding what *Genesis A* does, and therefore what it can tell us about Old English versecraft, requires first understanding as fully as possible what it is. The next section below will define its intellectual orientation to the biblical source, establishing the English poem's fundamentally translational character. We will then turn in the remainder of the chapter to the case study proper with detailed

3 J. Roberts, 'Old English Prose Translation.'

4 It used to be thought that the homilist of Napier 29 used a variant version of the vernacular poem as a source (see, e.g., Dobbie's comments in *ASPR*, 6:lxxii, and Whitbread, 'Two Notes,' 197–8); but Stanley ('Studies in the Prosaic Vocabulary,' 389–90) suggests that some prose version different from Napier 29 itself underlies the poem, and Frank ('Poetic Words in Late Old English Prose') thinks priority remains undetermined.

5 The untraditional style of the *Paris Psalter*'s verse renderings of psalms 51–150 is widely remarked, but see esp. K. Sisam and C. Sisam, 'Psalm Texts,' 17, and Griffith, 'Poetic Language.' They appear to depend heavily on glosses: Keefer, *Old English Metrical Psalter*; Toswell, '"Awended on Engliscum Gereorde,"' 171; and Toswell, 'Translation Techniques,' passim but esp. 404–5. Toswell's caveat about Keefer's methodology (ibid., 405 n. 40) is well-taken, but however one sorts the evidence it is hard not to conclude that the verse translation is greatly indebted to the gloss tradition.

analysis of a representative episode of *Genesis A*, proceeding from smaller- to larger-scale realizations of the poetics of mentality.

Genesis A's Relationship to Latin Learning and to Scripture

Genesis A can meaningfully be contextualized by the Latin hexameter biblical poems of several late antique writers: on New Testament subject matter, Juvencus, Sedulius, and Arator; and on Old, Cyprianus Gallus, Victorius, and Avitus. These works, especially those by the three New Testament poets and Avitus, enjoyed wide currency in the early Middle Ages. All six were known in Anglo-Saxon England, and at least some of them influenced the writings of Aldhelm, Bede, and Alcuin,[6] whose careers spanning the late seventh and the eighth centuries cover the period of *Genesis A*'s composition. There can be little doubt that the Latin tradition of versified biblical narrative known to and used by those pillars of Anglo-Saxon intellectual culture was a literary foundation on which the *Genesis A* poet built as well: even though no definite signs of direct borrowing have been identified in the Old English biblical poems, the widely studied Latin biblical epics were important precedents for the radical stylistic conversion of scripture to heroic poetry.[7]

To differing degrees those Latin authors – and most clearly the first of them to treat New and Old Testament subject matter respectively, Juvencus and Cyprianus, who were also the most straightforward in their handling of their biblical material – worked with scripture in ways that can be described using the classical concept of paraphrase.[8] Paraphrases might stay close to the wording and meaning of the source text at a relatively fine level of detail, but they also could depart from it considerably, treating only the narrative thread as the inviolable essence of the work that must be carried over without substantive change. All other aspects of the source, everything that might be considered to fall within the province of art and

6 Lapidge, *Anglo-Saxon Library*, 281, 292, 298, 299, 319, and 331–2.

7 Lapidge, 'Study of Latin Texts,' 470–94, and 'Versifying the Bible.' See also Kartschoke, *Bibeldichtung*, 218; Godman, *Bishops, Kings, and Saints*, lxix–lxxiv; Springer, *Gospel as Epic*, 129–35; Orchard, *Poetic Art of Aldhelm*, 161–70, 216–17, and 225–38; and Green, *Latin Epics*, esp. 356–9.

8 In this paragraph I summarize the views of M. Roberts, *Biblical Epic*, while taking into account critiques by Springer (*Gospel as Epic*, 9–21) and Green (*Latin Epics*), both of whom see Roberts's argument as too totalizing but allow that the rhetorical paraphrase tradition has relevance to at least the earliest Latin biblical epics.

style as distinguished from essential matter, could be acted upon freely and creatively while transplanting its narrative core into a new outward form. In the early centuries of Christianity this aspect of the paraphrase tradition made it a suitable instrument for dignifying the presentation of scriptural narrative's all-important content for the delectation of educated, culturally elite audiences averse to the Bible's plain style, and this consideration appears to have played a part in motivating at least Juvencus, the first of the biblical epic poets (writing during the reign of Constantine) and a model for the later ones.[9]

The *Genesis A* poet replicates in the vernacular the melding of scripture with poetic tradition that the Latin biblical epics effected, creating in his or her own composition something conceptually proximate to the earliest of them, Juvencus's *Evangeliorum libri* and Cyprianus's *Heptateuchos*. Studies of the Christian hexameter poems have documented their increasing complexity, both in style and in rhetorical positioning vis-à-vis scripture, as successive treatments of biblical matter grew more ornate, allusive, and exegetical.[10] In its disinclination to interrupt the narrative with overt exegetical explanations, *Genesis A* groups with the paraphrase-like poems of Juvencus and Cyprianus, suggesting a comparatively restricted notion of the new work's desirable relationship to the letter of the scriptural account: the primary goal is not to explain the biblical narrative but to transmit it through the full resources of heroic poetry. The avoidance of shifts into a commentary mode does not, of course, rule out the influence of learned interpretation, but the analytical distinction advocated by Roger P.H. Green in discussion of the Latin biblical epics is equally salient in the case of *Genesis A*: the difference between a poet's performing exegesis and merely leaving signs that his or her own understanding of the recounted matter has been shaped by it.[11] This distinction can provide a very useful

---

9 Green, *Latin Epics*, 128–34 and 373–4, and 'Birth and Transfiguration,' 161; M. Roberts, 'Vergil and the Gospels' and *Biblical Epic*, esp. 67–74 and 107–10; Lapidge, 'Versifying the Bible,' 12–15.

10 For comparison of the six Latin biblical epic poets' techniques, see M. Roberts, *Biblical Epic*, esp. chaps 5–6; for the New Testament poets only, Green, *Latin Epics* and 'Birth and Transfiguration'; and for these plus Avitus, Lapidge, 'Versifying the Bible.' Sedulius is discussed individually by Springer (*Gospel as Epic*) and Juvencus by Green ('Approaching Christian Epic' and '*Evangeliorum Libri*').

11 Green, '*Evangeliorum Libri*,' 71–5, with approving reference to this differentiation as made previously by Wilfrid Röttger. Lapidge, 'Versifying the Bible,' sees Sedulius as adding a typological dimension to the stylistic dignity that had been found by Juvencus and shows its further development by Avitus and Arator.

index to what the *Genesis A* poet believed he or she was doing – that is, his or her intellectual project – that must inform analysis of that project's execution with respect to the poetics of mentality.

Useful for defining this aspect of the *Genesis A* poet's work will be an episode in the English poem that indisputably engages with exegetical tradition and has attracted scholarly comment on those grounds: the sequence from the story of the Flood in which Noah sends out first a raven and then, repeatedly, a dove to search for dry land (*Genesis A*, ll. 1436–82; Gen. 8:6–12).[12] The raven, which according to the book of Genesis did not return, and the dove, which twice came back to the ark but the third time found enough dry land to stay away, were read according to the 'spiritual' or 'mystical' senses of scripture as well as the 'literal' or 'historical' sense by early authorities, who often constructed their interpretations of the birds around the figural identification of the ark as an antetype of the church. Christian exegetes adopted from Talmudic scholars a speculation explaining why the raven did not return – because it found a floating corpse on which it could feed[13] – and began partly on that basis to allegorize the bird negatively, as signifying (for example) sin being expelled from the body of Christ or people devoted to the corrupt world rather than to the church that might provide safety for their souls. The first two journeys of the dove were said by commentators to teach fortifying lessons: for instance, that rest is not promised to the faithful, who must persevere (prompted by the scriptural statement that the dove could find no place to set its foot), or that through Christian love those outside the church might be brought into its peace (suggested by the dove's olive twig). The dove's third flight, from which it did not return, was taken to signify the soul's eventual arrival at its eternal home.[14] Interpretation was by no means fixed, but the putative meanings listed here represent patterns sustained through lines of conservative influence from one commentator to another.

In *Genesis A*, this episode becomes, as it happens, a veritable study in the narrative technique of focalization. In this section of Genesis 8, including the verses leading up to the grounding of the ark and releases of the birds, the biblical account contains two narrative references to some kind

12 Bible references are to *Biblia sacra iuxta Vulgatam versionem*, ed. Weber et al., 5th corr. ed., rev. Gryson; where I quote, translations will be supplied from the Douay-Rheims Bible.

13 Doane, *Genesis A*, 271; Mirsky, 'On the Sources,' 391.

14 See Doane, *Genesis A*, 271–2; Huppé, *Doctrine and Poetry*, 174–5; Anlezark, *Water and Fire*, 39, 61–5; and Gatch, 'Noah's Raven,' 4–6.

of mental state or process. The first comes in 8:1, where God is said to remember Noah and the ark's other occupants, and the second is Noah's surmise in 8:11c that the waters are subsiding when the dove brings back the green twig from its second exploration. The poet elaborates the first of these, extending it to four lines of verse (*Genesis A*, ll. 1407–10), and transforms Noah's recognition of an objective fact about the floodwaters into a much more emotionally invested anticipation of 'relief' and 'comfort.'[15] But more important than amplifications or adjustments of the subjective elements that do already appear in the original are the examples of focalization in *Genesis A*'s presentation of the episode that lack any direct scriptural prompting. These begin with the proposition that the ark's passengers yearn for the time they can leave the vessel:

Hæleð langode,
wægliðende, swilce wif heora,
hwonne hie of nearwe ofer nægledbord
ofer streamstaðe stæppan mosten
and of enge ut æhta lædan. (ll. 1431b–5)

[The man longed, the wayfarers and likewise their wives, for when they would be able to step out of straitness, over the nailed board upon the shore, and bring their property out from confinement.]

A few lines later, Noah mistakenly believes that the raven he releases will come back, also without precedent in the Genesis account:

Noe tealde þæt he on neod hine,
gif he on þære lade land ne funde,
ofer sid wæter secan wolde
on wægþele eft – him seo wen geleah.[16] (ll. 1443–6)

[Noah reckoned that if it did not find land in the journey, it would necessarily seek him again, in the ship, over the wide water: that expectation misled him.]

15 'Þa ongeat hraðe / flotmonna frea þæt wæs frofor cumen, / earfoðsiða bot' [Then the lord of seamen immediately understood that comfort had come, relief from troublesome journeys] (ll. 1474b–6a).

16 I depart from *ASPR* in my distribution of words into half-lines in l. 1446, moving *eft* from the b- to the a-verse. This metrically acceptable grouping suggests a syntactic parsing that yields better sense. Cf. analogous statements nearby, in ll. 1471b and 1478b–9a.

Neither of these added statements requires a great inferential leap: it is reasonable enough to assume that the men and women aboard the ark were eager to leave it and that Noah's plan with the raven, though unstated in Genesis, was exactly as the poet spells it out. The point is that these things are stated in *Genesis A* whereas in the biblical text they were not.

The added focalization through and reference to characters' mentality conforms to patterns of expressive and technical choice made throughout this long poem; adaptations of this particular kind are encountered again and again throughout *Genesis A*. More is happening here than a steady, continual elaboration of the scriptural matter such as would inflate it in all directions, so to speak. Rather, these translational habits and apparent priorities suggest that helping readers keep track of what the ark's occupants are thinking and feeling, what they intend and desire, is somehow important to the English poet's work. A part of the biblical story of Noah and his family has become the story of their yearning and its eventual fulfilment when they disembark, their emotional as well as corporeal journey to safety. Within that larger narrative capsule, a part of the scriptural story of Noah and the birds has become the story of the patriarch's intelligence and its interaction with the animals' instinctive behaviour. These two mental stories, one of longing and one of foresight, converge a few lines later when the 'rædfæst' and 'gleaw' [prudent and wise] Noah (ll. 1498a, 1501a), having learned what he needed to know from the dove's actions, leads his family, 'wraðra lafe' [survivors of the hostilities], 'ofer streamweall ... / lustum miclum' [onto shore with great joy] (ll. 1493–6, where 'ofer streamweall' echoes the synonymous 'ofer streamstaðe' in the passage about their desire to leave the ark, cited above).

Most striking in the raven and dove passage, however, is the intense focalization through the birds themselves. When the raven does not come back to the ark, it is because 'se feonde gespearn fleotende hreaw; / salwigfeðera secan nolde' [that rejoicing one set foot on a floating corpse; the dark-feathered one did not want to return] (ll. 1447–8), adapting the unadorned scriptural statement that the bird '[non] revertebatur' [did not return] (Gen. 8:7).[17] Next comes a sustained passage that

17 *Feonde* 'rejoicing' is an editorial emendation of MS *feond*. Gatch ('Noah's Raven,' 5) states that nowhere in the exegetical tradition is the raven of this biblical verse taken to signify the devil. Doane (*Genesis A*, 271) contradicts Gatch on this point but offers no references. *Feonde* 'rejoicing' joins the epithet *salwigfeðera* in associating the raven here with the conventional nature of that animal as so often encountered in the Beasts of Battle motif (which Doane, ibid., rightly points out the latter word does, aligning it with the traditional exuberance of Old English poetic carrion-feasters), conforms to the

emphasizes the other bird's perspective to a remarkable degree. After Noah releases the dove,

Heo wide hire willan sohte
and rume fleah. Nohweðere reste fand,
þæt heo for flode fotum ne meahte
land gespornan ne on leaf treowes
steppan for streamum, ac wæron steap hleoðo
bewrigen mid wætrum. Gewat se wilda fugel
on æfenne earce secan
ofer wonne wæg, werig sigan,
hungri to handa halgum rince.
    Ða wæs culufre eft of cofan sended
ymb wucan wilde. Seo wide fleah
oðþæt heo rumgal restestowe
fægere funde and þa fotum stop
on beam hyre; gefeah bliðemod
þæs þe heo gesittan swiðe werig
on treowes telgum torhtum moste.
Heo feðera onsceoc, gewat fleogan eft
mid lacum hire: liðend brohte
elebeames twig an to handa,
grene blædæ.
. . . .
                Þa gyt se eadega wer
ymb wucan þriddan wilde culufran
ane sende. Seo eft ne com
to lide fleogan, ac heo land begeat,
grene bearwas; nolde gladu æfre
under salwed bord syððan ætywan
on þellfæstenne, þa hire þearf ne wæs. (ll. 1455–74a, 1476b–82)

[She searched widely for what she desired and flew broadly. However, she did not find a resting place, so that she could not set foot on land due to the sea-flow nor step onto the leaf of a tree on account of the currents; rather, the steep slopes were hidden by the waters. In the evening the wild bird went to

parallel representation of the dove's emotion to be discussed below, and better fits the poet's general habit of not advancing allegorical interpretation.

seek the ark over the dark sea, sank weary and hungry into the hands of the holy man. Then the wild dove was sent again, after a week, out of the enclosure. She flew widely, happy with freedom, until she found a pleasant resting place and stepped onto a tree with her feet; blithe-minded, she rejoiced because she could sit, very weary, on the beautiful branches of a tree. She flapped her wings, went flying back with her gift: the traveller brought a twig of an olive branch to hand, a green sprig ... Yet again, after the third week, the blessed man sent the wild dove one last time. She did not come flying back to the vessel, but she found land, green groves; the glad one did not wish to show herself ever afterward under pitch-covered boards in a plank-fastness, now that it was not necessary for her.]

The biblical basis for these lines, Genesis 8:9–12, says only that after the raven Noah sent forth a dove,

(9) quae cum non invenisset ubi requiesceret pes eius reversa est ad eum in arcam
aquae enim erant super universam terram
extenditque manum et adprehensam intulit in arcam
(10) expectatis autem ultra septem diebus aliis rursum dimisit columbam ex arca
(11) at illa venit ad eum ad vesperam
portans ramum olivae virentibus foliis in ore suo
....
(12) expectavitque nihilominus septem alios dies et emisit columbam
quae non est reversa ultra ad eum

[(9) But she, not finding where her foot might rest, returned to him into the ark: for the waters were upon the whole earth: and he put forth his hand, and caught her, and brought her into the ark. (10) And having waited yet seven other days, he again sent forth the dove out of the ark. (11) And she came to him in the evening, carrying a bough of an olive tree, with green leaves, in her mouth ... (12) And he stayed yet other seven days, and he sent forth the dove, which returned not any more unto him.]

The dove's weariness and hunger, her joy at being able to fly unconfined, her pleasure with the tree she finds and her gladness at the opportunity to rest there, her desire never to return to the ark now that her duty has been fulfilled – these intimations of the bird's mentality and emotion in *Genesis*

A are unanticipated by the biblical model, which offers, as the only thing resembling a precedent, the single, matter-of-fact perceptual statement that the dove did not find 'where her foot might rest.' The whole sequence makes for a pronounced example of focalization through what might seem an unlikely perspective, had we not already come to recognize movement into non-human as well as human subjectivities to be part of the Old English poetic repertoire.

This is no mere enlargement upon what is given in scripture: the very opportunities for expressing the dove's emotions are created by the *Genesis A* poet. We might say, to use a cinematic analogy, that the camera travels with the dove in *Genesis A* and presents events from her perspective, whereas in the biblical version it stays behind with Noah. But even that analogy does not capture the kind of mental access to the dove that the audience receives in this passage, for we do not just see what her eyes see. Through the poet's narrative choices and constitutive voice, which determines the facts within the fiction, we know the bird's wishes, thoughts, and emotions. The entire Noah's ark episode exhibits very plainly the *Genesis A* poet's tendency to frame story events in terms of the perceptions and feelings of those involved. He or she makes not just the degree of such access, or its line-by-line frequency, but even its wide distribution among various agents – in this episode including God, the raven, the dove, the occupants of the ark collectively, and Noah individually – a feature of the narrative's perspectival scheme.

Yet amid all of this elaboration there is no exegesis or commentary. Readers would be free, as they always are, to draw allegorical meaning from this paraphrase of scripture, but they would have to do so in much the same way they drew it from most parts of scripture itself: by applying a preconceived, highly theorized hermeneutic program to textual details that do not self-sufficiently point in that direction. A.N. Doane stresses that 'the specific approach of *Genesis A* [to the Bible] is predominantly literal'; Roberta Frank has noted the poet's ability to 'hint' at exegesis-driven relationships 'without ever leaving the literal level of narrative' or 'forging an overt theological equation'; and other scholars too have rightly emphasized the poem's construction first and foremost as a work of biblical history.[18] Recently, Daniel Anlezark has argued plausibly that in the

18 Doane, *Genesis A*, 53; Frank, 'Some Uses of Paronomasia,' 76. Cf. Gatch, 'Noah's Raven,' 6–7; Boyd, 'Doctrine and Criticism'; Garde and Muir, 'Patristic Influence'; T. Hill, '"Variegated Obit"'; and Trilling, *Aesthetics of Nostalgia*, 72–7. Perhaps the most marked case in *Genesis A* of the influence of 'spiritual' exegesis on the poet's chiefly literal or historical retelling of scripture is the much-expanded heroic episode of Lot's

Genesis A Flood episode 'the account is embellished so as to emphasize the theme of weariness,' such that its psychologizing features participate in the development of a theme around the etymology of Noah's name as 'rest' or 'comfort';[19] but this analysis still does not leave the literal level of interpretation: Noah's name is said straightforwardly in Genesis 5:29 to have that meaning, so narration that shows Noah providing such comfort or rest requires no movement into the 'spiritual' levels of tropology, typology, or anagogy.[20] Even if we were to grant that while not reproducing commentary, the text somehow cues a reader to the figural and tropological dimensions of this Genesis episode, this still would do nothing to explain the prominent role of the birds' mentality in the poetic treatment, because patristic tradition does not particularly psychologize the birds, only moralize or allegorize them: in other words, even the full light of commentary poorly illuminates that feature of the English text.

Michael Lapidge has maintained that Anglo-Saxon poets were likely less directly influenced by commentaries than by the Christian hexameter poets, whose works were standard school reading.[21] The case of Noah's raven and dove illustrates his point. Bringing the biblical epics to bear, I will suggest, elucidates some aspects of *Genesis A*'s treatment of the scene that would otherwise remain mysterious while also confirming the absence from the English poem of any significant exegetical agenda.[22] The birds' release from the ark was emphasized by versifiers of Old and New Testament subject matter alike. For the New Testament poets, any reference to this event from Genesis would arise through exegetical connections. Sedulius's mention of Elias's feeding by ravens in the wilderness (1 Kings 17:2–6) leads him by contrastive association to the raven of the Flood; the two scenes pair to form a moral narrative of expiation with the raven's scriptural appearances plotting a penitential trajectory as its service

---

capture and recovery by Abraham. Orchard ('Conspicuous Heroism') has shown the probable influence of Prudentius's *Psychomachia*, including its heroic allegorization of Abraham, on this long passage. Even here, however, while awareness of Prudentius may have prompted the poet's radical expansion of the text, it did so by fleshing out the story for him or her; what is actually told in *Genesis A* remains literal narrative, however elaborated. As with the Flood episode, a reader would have to bring knowledge of allegorical exegesis to find it there: the text does not supply it.

19 *Water and Fire*, 192–4; quotation from 193.

20 The development of a 'rest' or 'comfort' motif could even be construed as the poet's representation of the literal statement about Noah's name in Gen. 5:29, which as Anlezark notes (*Water and Fire*, 192) is not reproduced directly in the poem.

21 'Versifying the Bible.'

22 A useful background to the following paragraphs is Nodes, *Doctrine and Exegesis*.

to the holy man 'abluit in terris quidquid deliquit in undis' [washes away on land all that it did wrong in the waves] (*Carmen paschale*, 1.175). Arator treats both raven and dove, bringing them up through an allegory of the ark as the church's sacrament of baptism that delivers Christians through the waters into life.[23] His treatment shows a narrative impulse: for Arator, the allegorical correspondences centre on the actions of Noah's two birds within a single continuous time frame, unlike Sedulius's quasi-typological comparison of Noah's raven with Elias's. From references like these – and through poetry, not just explicative commentary – educated Anglo-Saxons could inherit a heightened awareness of the birds' actions as loaded with supernarrative meaning.

One Anglo-Saxon, Aldhelm, picks up Sedulius's remark about the raven and develops it in a pair of Latin enigmata about raven and dove. Aldhelm's conceptual starting point is unquestionably the two birds' contrasting behaviour when released from the ark: for him as for the *Genesis A* poet, their role in the episode has a certain prominence in his mind, due no doubt to the creatures' literary afterlives among the Latin poets. The juxtaposition of the birds in adjacent riddles implies the narrative association provided by the Flood account, and the poems' openings make that association explicit. First comes the raven:

Dum genus humanum truculenta fluenta necarent
Et noua mortales multarent aequora cunctos
Exceptis raris, gignunt qui semina saecli,
Primus uiuentum perdebam foedera iuris
Imperio patris contemnens subdere colla. (63.1–5)

[When savage floods were destroying the human race and new-made oceans were punishing all mortals – with very few exceptions, (namely those) who carried the seeds of the world – I first of all living things flaunted the bonds of the law by refusing to bow my neck to the commandment of the patriarch.][24]

The Dove enigma likewise begins by alluding to the Flood, and in doing so it emphasizes the dove's reversal of the raven's disobedience to which the previous enigma has called attention:

---

23 *Historia apostolica*, 1.643–63.

24 I cite Aldhelm's *Aenigmata* from the edition of Glorie and give translations from *Aldhelm: The Poetic Works*, trans. Lapidge and Rosier.

Cum Deus infandas iam plecteret aequore noxas
Ablueretque simul scelerum contagia limphis,
Prima praecepti compleui iussa parentis. (64.1–3)

[When God had punished (man's) unspeakable sins with the Flood and at the same time had washed away the contagion of evil with those waters, I carried out the first words of the command (issued by) the patriarch.]

In the remainder of these two brief poems, each moves from the Noachic narrative backdrop to another scriptural episode alongside which the respective birds' roles in the Flood account are placed like the panels of a diptych. On the raven, Aldhelm goes on to cite verbatim Sedulius's statement that the raven's feeding of Elias at God's command rectified its wrongdoing in the Flood (63.7); and the dove's actions, according to Aldhelm, indicated 'fructu terris uenisse salutem' [with the (olive-)leaf that well-being had returned to earth] (64.4), a phrase with which Aldhelm evokes both the second flight of Noah's dove and its figural fulfilment in the descent of the Holy Spirit in the form of a dove at Christ's baptism.[25] In third position in each enigma comes a pseudonaturalistic statement making a loose etiological connection between the scriptural incidents and the birds' supposed natures: the raven does not feed its young until they grow black feathers (63.8–9), and the blessed dove has a mild heart free of black bile (64.5–6).[26]

An important dissimilarity is evident between the two roughly contemporaneous Anglo-Saxon treatments, that in *Genesis A* and Aldhelm's in his Latin riddles. Aldhelm explains each bird's meaning beyond its immediate literal function in the Flood account and indeed only alludes to the event itself, shifting emphasis entirely onto its significance. Both the raven and the dove are given two kinds of meaning by Aldhelm according to the familiar templates of scriptural hermeneutics. Each bird has a tropological interpretation, brought out explicitly in the contrasting comments about

25 A double reading of the ablative 'fructu' arises through the concept of Christ as the fruit of Mary's womb and the word's syntactic association with either 'portendens' (preceding the quotation given here), to stand for that through which salvation is signified to Noah (i.e., the leaf), or 'uenisse,' to stand for that through which salvation has come to the earth (i.e., Christ). Both meanings cannot be accommodated simultaneously in translation because the rendering of 'fructu' must be put either inside or outside of the 'that' clause.

26 The Raven enigma concludes (63.10) with a word-play clue unparalleled in the Dove enigma.

their obedience; and each reference to the Flood then gives way to a second, paired event from scripture in the manner of a figural association. This is what poetry with an exegetical bent looks like. Even allowing for the difference in genre, its intellectual priorities bear little resemblance to those of the *Genesis A* poet.

Nevertheless, the influence on *Genesis A* of exegetical traditions like those partially reproduced by Aldhelm is not in doubt: the English poet's extreme interest in the raven and the dove is surely a trace of that influence, as comparison with the treatments of Sedulius, Arator, and Aldhelm helps to clarify. Reference to the Latin hexameter poets who narrate Old Testament subject matter, and thus tell the tale of the Flood rather than just alluding to it, implies the same. Cyprianus's account is attracted to the actions of the birds and follows the dove as it gobbles as many olives as possible in the fruitful grove it finds on its second journey before returning to Noah's fire at nightfall, outwardly trembling, but not subjectively feeling cold or exhausted, as far as we are told; the detail remains external and objective.[27] There is no real focalization in his telling, and even though Cyprianus maintains a predominantly literal orientation to scripture, he sets a moral frame of reference for the birds' behaviour by remarking, as Aldhelm would later do in his enigma, on the raven's failure to return as an act of disobedience to Noah's command. Victorius includes a touch of focalization through the dove – when it locates enough land not to return to the ark and finds the prospect of returning abhorrent – but explicitly allegorizes its actions as representing the soul's hope of reception into heaven only at the proper time, not before being called by God.[28] Avitus focalizes more significantly through the birds, but the role of the stylistic device in a larger project of explication becomes clear when Avitus breaks into the narrative with a polemical apostrophe to the Jews, allegorically represented by the raven in its disobedience, in which he accuses them of violating their covenant with God; and finally the dove that returns with the olive branch is, by direct contrast to the Jews, mindful of the commands it has been given.[29]

All of these verse retellings of scripture reflect a perception of the raven and dove as central to the story and follow their actions in ways not strictly motivated by the biblical narration. The difference lies in the kind of

27 *Heptateuchos*, ll. 302–10.

28 *Alethia*, 2.512–23.

29 *De spiritalis historiae gestis*, 4.548–50, 563–73, and 579–84.

attention the poets give them. Cyprianus has nothing approaching *Genesis A*'s emphasis on subjectivity and perspective. Victorius and Avitus take the exegetical assignment of special meaning to the birds as a cue to heighten the emphasis on their motivations through manipulations of narrative perspective, but solely to set up the exegetical dimension. These analogues put into sharp relief the difference between the didactic transmission of exegesis, on the one hand, and on the other, a restatement of the literal, narrative sense in the poetic mode. No comments of an explanatory nature are offered in *Genesis A* apart from the fact of the raven's attraction to carrion; and even then, in this clearest specific outcrop of an exegetical substrate, the poet's treatment notably remains on the literal level of scriptural interpretation and focuses at least as much on the bird's subjective reaction to the grisly find as on the factual cause of its failure to return. In episodes like this one, then, the Anglo-Saxon poet's reading of the scriptural source is influenced by access to exegetical learning, but the purpose of his or her own writing is not the conveyance of exegesis. If it were, the literary product would fail utterly in that purpose, the information it actually provides being hopelessly oblique to that body of knowledge: nowhere does the poet assign, in the manner of a scriptural commentator, any significance to the birds and their actions.

What the writer of *Genesis A* infuses scriptural matter with is not exegesis, but poetic style. What sets *Genesis A* apart from its Latin semi-analogues in the handling of this scene is the intensity of the focalization through the birds combined with the absence of any apparent exegetical purpose in the narration. If the *Genesis A* poet was influenced by the approach taken by one or more of the Christian Latin poets, as I imagine was the case, he or she stripped away exegesis from his or her sense of the project at hand. The commentary tradition prompted the Latin poets to elaborate on the birds' dispositions by drawing attention to their motivations through the interpretation of their actions, but as received by the English writer the birds' dispositions became a thing to dramatize and emphasize, apparently for their own intrinsic interest, even as the exegetical framework, within which the heightened rhetoric developed in the Latin texts, proved dispensable.

The Anglo-Saxon poet's commitment to representations of subjectivity is not a local feature of this episode, but consistent with his or her normal poetic method, as I will show. I have used *Genesis A*'s treatment of Noah's raven and dove strictly to establish this text's relationship to exegetical discourse, and thus also one aspect of its relationship to scripture. It shows both the background influence of exegesis – implying that its reproduction would have been a live option if that had been the *Genesis A* poet's wish – and the absence of any inclination to follow that path in favour of retelling the scriptural narrative in a stylized way. However, because the English poem is known to have a freer relationship to the biblical account in this section than elsewhere, the Flood story is not an appropriate case study on which to found a more general argument that will rely on immediate treatment of a known source.[30] A positive claim about poetic method must depend on *Genesis A*'s last two-thirds, where it has a more direct textual connection to scripture, like that of the Ælfrician prose *Genesis*.

The prose *Genesis* of the Old English Hexateuch is based on Jerome's Vulgate with few deviations[31] and is not much given to abbreviation through omission, as its companion texts in the Hexateuch often are.[32] The portions that can be confidently attributed to Ælfric, and which have not undergone revision for the Hexateuch compilation,[33] translate the biblical source plainly and with close correspondence at the level of phrase and clause; yet the translation is also real Old English prose, not a running gloss.[34] Both Ælfric and the anonymous other translator or translators whose work joined with his in the vernacular Hexateuch do intervene regularly in ways designed to guide interpretation, such as by supplying occasional explanatory phrases and by omitting or shifting the emphasis of passages that might seem to cast a negative light on important biblical figures.[35] But mediations of the former kind are not such as will disrupt the relationships among texts that we need to observe, and episodes that

---

30 On *Genesis A*'s correspondence to scripture, least direct in the Creation and Flood accounts but closely parallel in the material representing Gen. 3–5 and 8–22, see Remley, *Old English Biblical Verse*, esp. 105–15 and 120–43.

31 Bible texts in Anglo-Saxon England were overwhelmingly Vulgate rather than Old Latin in character (Marsden, *Text of the Old Testament*, esp. 49–55), and the prose *Genesis* can be shown to rest primarily upon Vulgate texts (ibid., 406–17; Marsden, 'Old Latin Intervention').

32 Marsden, 'Old Latin Intervention,' 232, and *Text of the Old Testament*, 406.

33 The prose *Genesis* up through 24:10 was originally authored by Ælfric and is represented in its unrevised Ælfrician version in one late non-Hexateuch manuscript. Much of it was brought essentially unaltered into the Old English Hexateuch, although some parts, avoided in my selection of text for analysis below, were revised by someone else. See Dodwell and Clemoes, *Old English Illustrated Hexateuch*, 42–53; Marsden, 'Translation by Committee?' and Marsden, '*Old English Heptateuch,*' 1:lxix–xcvi.

34 Marsden, 'Ælfric as Translator.'

35 Barnhouse, 'Shaping the Hexateuch Text'; Biggs, 'Biblical Glosses.'

provoke the latter type of intervention are easily avoided. Ælfric moved in and out of a more stylized alliterative diction in the later chapters of his translation,[36] but the text to be considered here does not come from that portion of his work. The material selected for comparative analysis below, rendering Genesis 16:1–8, represents Ælfric's translation practices in their state least conditioned by competing formal or aesthetic priorities and least obscured by vicissitudes of textual history.

My primary object of analysis, *Genesis A*, is based a little less straightforwardly on the Vulgate version of Genesis than is the Ælfrician prose translation, relying instead on a Vulgate exemplar with some Old Latin mixing.[37] However, the mixed character of the Latin original will have minimal impact for our purposes: behind the section of the poem with which we will be chiefly concerned, lines 2216–79 (corresponding to Gen. 16:1–8), Paul G. Remley finds only one 'probable' sign of an underlying Old Latin reading, which I will note in due course, and no 'unambiguous' or less likely but 'possible' ones.[38] All other features of the Latin original reflected by this portion of *Genesis A* are either diagnostically Vulgate or equally associable with both Vulgate and Old Latin versions, so use of the Vulgate as a backdrop for comparison between the two English texts creates no methodological problems.

The critical literature on *Genesis A*, like that on the vernacular prose *Genesis*, has established a widely accepted view of the poem's textual relationship to its source: it is a systematic, sequential translation-into-verse rather than a free adaptation. The poet's evident desire to follow the biblical source text very directly, for the most part thought by thought and statement by statement despite thorough aesthetic remodelling, has been emphasized by the major studies of *Genesis A*, which have observed that for much of its length its writer deliberately stays close to not just the narrative of the scriptural Genesis, but its arrangement and frequently its wording as well, while refashioning it as Old English verse. In the most recent full textual examination of the poem, Remley has shown that the final two-thirds of *Genesis A* follow a single, continuous Latin exemplar of Genesis 8–22 very closely, with no dislocation of more than one

36 See Biggs, 'Biblical Glosses,' 287.

37 Remley, 'Latin Textual Basis'; cf. Remley, *Old English Biblical Verse*, 148–9, affirming but slightly refocusing the evidence for this view.

38 'Latin Textual Basis,' 188–9. Cf. Marsden, *Text of the Old Testament*, 443, acknowledging the influence of Old Latin readings on *Genesis A*, as shown by Remley, but also reasserting the fundamentally Vulgate nature of the underlying Latin exemplar.

scriptural verse at any point, and that the Old English poem's verbal debt to this source is often pronounced enough to enable differentiation between underlying Vulgate and Old Latin readings.[39] Similarly, in the introduction to his edition, Doane characterizes the translator as distinguished by the 'ability to see Genesis *as a text*, as a fixed form of words which must be reproduced as entirely as possible' in the process of converting it into 'the only formal discourse available in the vernacular, dealing with the text as such' so that 'any transformation of the original that takes place as a result of his art is at the level of stylistic detail.'[40] Remley agrees that in the last two-thirds of *Genesis A*, the 'few conspicuous poetical enhancements of the matter of the biblical Genesis ... are better regarded as natural features of an Anglo-Saxon versification' than as undisciplined or casual substantive alterations of the scriptural text.[41]

Let us now examine the *Genesis A* poet's 'transformation' of a source 'at the level of stylistic detail' (in Doane's words), the English text's 'natural features of an Anglo-Saxon versification' (in Remley's) which we will want to isolate if we hope to understand the significance of different modes of presenting similar material in Old English verse and prose. Any systematic distinctions we observe between the two versions of Genesis in Old English (setting aside the *Genesis A* Creation and Flood accounts) may be, for all practical purposes, symptomatic of classical-style poetic techniques, because both versions are first and foremost – as we have reason to believe their translators understood them – faithful renderings of the scriptural source in the forms encouraged or allowed by, seemingly 'natural' to, their respective vernacular media. Provisionally, assuming that observations made here can be confirmed by reference to other texts as well, we may take consistent patterns of difference between *Genesis A* and the Ælfrician *Genesis* as indicative of specifically poetic tendencies of expression.

Traditionalizing Scripture: *Genesis A*'s Poetics of Mentality

The episode on which the following analysis centres, lines 2216–79 (corresponding to Gen. 16:1–8), recounts the childless Sarai's suggestion that Abraham produce an heir with her slave Agar, the ensuing discord

39 *Old English Biblical Verse*, 98–124 and 143–9. Cf. Remley, 'Latin Textual Basis," 166; Doane, *Genesis A*, 59–60.

40 *Genesis A*, 49–60 and 68–96; quotations from 54 and 55.

41 *Old English Biblical Verse*, 113–14.

between Sarai and the pregnant Agar, and Agar's flight from Sarai and encounter with an angel.[42] At sixty-four lines, it is a long enough run of text to exhibit most of the poet's habits with respect to the treatment of mentality, emotion, and perspective, yet short enough to consider closely within a reasonable space. I will work upward from smaller- to larger-scale manifestations of the poetics of mentality, and discussion will frequently range more widely within the poem to affirm that the features highlighted within this single episode also fit patterns and normalities in the *Genesis A* writer's practice. In order to mark clearly my resumptions of sequential reading of the Abraham–Sarai–Agar episode, I divide it into five parts to be taken up in a series of headed subsections below: lines 2216–19a (which I designate as segment A), 2219b–33 (segment B), 2234–43 (segment C), 2244–60 (segment D), and 2261–79 (segment E).

Segment A: Formulaic Subjectivity

Genesis 16:1 begins,

> igitur Sarai uxor Abram non genuerat liberos.
>
> [Now Sarai the wife of Abram, had brought forth no children.]

This statement is reproduced in the Ælfrician *Genesis* as

> Abrames wif wæs þa git wuniende butan cildum.[43]
>
> [At that time Abram's wife still remained without children.]

Genesis A renders the same sentence thus:

A   Þa wæs Sarran   sar on mode
þæt him Abrahame   ænig ne wearð
þurh gebedscipe   bearn gemæne,
freolic to frofre.   (ll. 2216–19a)

---

42 In general I will give biblical names as they appear in the Douay-Rheims translation. When referring to the character in *Genesis A*, I will follow the Anglo-Saxon poet's practice in using the post-covenant name form Abraham (rather than Abram).

43 I cite the prose *Genesis* from Marsden, *'Old English Heptateuch.'*

[Then it was painful in Sarai's mind that there had come no child in common to her and Abraham through intercourse, a noble one as a comfort.]

Where the biblical Genesis presents Sarai's childlessness in a perspectivally neutral statement, and the Old English prose *Genesis* retains this impersonal perspective in a very close paraphrase, the poet immediately emphasizes Sarai's emotional experience by focalizing this moment in the narrative through her subjective position. The primary narrative proposition in the poetic translation is no longer that Sarai is childless, but that she is sad: the objective fact that she and Abram have no heirs becomes in *Genesis A* a logically subordinate proposition serving an explanatory purpose.

This shift is brought about through traditional language. The verse 'freolic to frofre' is a realization of the widespread formula *q to frofre*, where *q* is a polysyllabic noun or substantive adjective bearing primary stress and normally alliterating with *frofre* to make an a-verse.[44] It takes exactly the same form elsewhere in *Genesis A*, where in line 1108a the phrase 'freolic to frofre' describes Seth, the 'noble one' given to Adam and Eve 'as a comfort' after Cain's murder of Abel. This is not a direct mental-content formula, but it is an implicitly focalizing one, because the

44 I designate variable lexical elements of formulas with the letter *q*. A substitutional system like *q to frofre* has most often been described as a 'formula system' rather than as a simple 'formula,' which term is then usually reserved for lexical sequences that recur verbatim and thus may appear to be fixed units. But that is not how formulaic diction operates in Old English, as has been recognized ever since Fry's insight ('Old English Formulas and Systems') that the 'system,' and not any particular instantiation of it, is the primary entity of formulaic structure in that language (he defined the individual 'formula' simply as a verse generated by a system). Many alternative approaches to defining the Old English poetic formula have been tried (see Foley, *Theory of Oral Composition*, 69–72), but Fry's, as refined by Niles ('Formula and Formulaic System') and Riedinger ('Old English Formula in Context'), remains the most satisfactory. Riedinger's reasoning leads toward elimination of any need for the concept of the 'formula system' as distinct from the 'formula,' although she stops short of that conclusion (see ibid., 305). It is most logical to think of the basic, paradigmatic Old English formula as having built into it a variable element, and this will be my practice. The much more unusual 'fixed formula' (an unvarying repetition) is the special case that merits adjectival marking in the nomenclature. See further chapter 2, n. 21, below. My identification of formulas and other units of traditional diction throughout this book has been greatly aided by Bessinger, Smith, and Twomey's *Concordance*, and claims about distributions and frequencies within the poetic corpus have used consultation of the same resource as their starting point.

semantics of *frofre* strongly implies an interested party, and in both of these instances it plays a part in bringing out a particular subjective position.[45] The direct statement of Sarai's sadness in line 2216 is likewise presented through a very familiar formula, *q on mode*, where *q* is a mono- or disyllabic adjective or noun bearing strong stress and participating in the line's alliterative scheme. Several other instances of this formula of mentality occur in *Genesis A*:

1. Hæfde styrne mod,
gegremed grymme, grap on wraðe
faum folmum, and him on fæðm gebræc
yrre on mode. (ll. 60b–3a)

[Fiercely provoked, (God) had a stern mind, in wrath gripped (them) with hostile hands, and angry in mind, broke them in his embrace.]

2. cwæð þæt him wære weorce on mode,
sorga sarost, þæt his suhtriga
þeownyd þolode. (ll. 2028–30a)

[(Abraham) said there to be unrest in his mind, sorest of sorrows, because his nephew suffered compulsion of slavery.]

3. Ða wearð unbliðe Abrahames cwen,
hire worcþeowe wrað on mode,
heard and hreðe. (ll. 2261–3a)

[Then Abraham's wife grew displeased, angry in mind toward her work-slave, harsh and fierce.]

4. heht þæt segn wegan
heah gehwilcne, þe his hina wæs
wæpnedcynnes, wære gemyndig,
gleaw on mode, ða him god sealde
soðe treowa. (ll. 2372b–6a)

45 In the lines following the mention of Seth as a 'comfort,' Adam describes his own earlier sorrow, defining both the subjective position and the situational context that make the *q to frofre* formula apt.

[When God had given him true promises, mindful of the covenant, wise in mind, (Abraham) commanded each one of the male kind who was of his household to bear that holy sign.]

5. Ælmihtig wearð
milde on mode, moncynnes weard,
Abimeleche, swa hine Abraham bæd. (ll. 2757b–9)

[The Almighty, mankind's guardian, grew mild in mind toward Abimelech, as Abraham asked.]

6. Þa wæs Abrahame
weorce on mode þæt he on wræc drife
his selfes sunu. (ll. 2791b–3a)

[Then there was unrest in Abraham's mind because he had driven his own son into exile.]

Q on mode is one of the most common of all Old English poetic formulas, and it is a prime example of the embeddedness of reference to mentality in traditional phraseology.

It is sometimes assumed that formulas are 'filler,' contributing nothing to the meaning of the lines in which they appear, even though careful work on formulaic composition over the past several decades has discredited this view. Chapter 2 will consider the pragmatics of formulaic language in some detail, but for the moment it is enough to demonstrate that these *q on mode* verses cannot serve a strictly formal function of supporting the alliteration of their companion verses to build full lines. The *q* term in examples 5 and 6 above participates essentially (not additively or in parallel with other sentence elements) in syntactic constructions extending beyond the half-line, so that the clause in which the formula occurs would not make sense without it: *q* is a grammatical subject in number 6 and a required predicate adjective in number 5, as it is also in segment A, on Sarai's sadness. In examples 1–4 the *q on mode* verse has a real conceptual role that is affirmed in each case by syntactic apposition, poetic variation, or some other near-synonymy in the statement, indicating that it participates in a structure of thought extending, again, beyond the metrical unit in question. Examples 2, 3, 5, and 6 are in fact entire statements topicalizing mentality. In several of the listed examples, then, dropping the *q on mode* formula would leave other elements that also semantically emphasize mentality, and in some, dropping those remaining mentality elements as well would leave effectively no narrative proposition at all, because mentality is what the poet has chosen to talk about.[46] Yet only in one case, number 6, is this subjectivity cued by the language of the biblical source.[47]

Other mentality formulas operate like *q on mode*, providing a metrisyntactic framework with a variable element that can be manipulated to suit the context, both meeting formal needs and contributing to meaning. This kind of formula is constructed, for instance, around every single occurrence of the adjective *gemyndig* in *Genesis A*, always in a verse *q gemyndig* in which *q* is a genitive disyllable participating in the line's alliteration:

7. Him þa feran gewat   fæder ælmihtiges
lare gemyndig   land sceawian. (ll. 1779–80)

[He set out to travel then, mindful of the almighty Father's teaching, to see the land.]

8.   Þa se halga ongan
ara gemyndig   Abraham sprecan. (ll. 1898b–9)

[Then the holy one, Abraham, began to speak, mindful of honour.]

9. emne þon gelicost,   lara gemyndig,
þe he ne cuðe   hwæt þa cynn dydon. (ll. 1943–4)

[… just exactly as if, mindful of teachings, he did not know what those people were doing.]

10. Gewat him þa se healdend   ham siðian
. . . .
Ebrea leod   arna gemyndig. (ll. 2162–4)

46 It would be defensible in instances of the *q on mode* formula in which *q* is adjectival, if taken in isolation from any special properties of traditional diction, to claim that *on mode* is filler: without the prepositional phrase Sarai could still be *wrað* (example 3), Abraham *gleaw* (example 4), and God *yrre* or *milde* (examples 1 and 5). But the status of the prepositional phrase alone is irrelevant to the question; the alliterating adjectives create the references to mentality in those cases. The metrisyntactic formula is not *on mode* but *q on mode*, and the assumption I dispute is that formula equals filler.

47 Gen. 21:11. The first example in this list has no biblical source; for the others see Gen. 14:13–14, 16:6, 17:23, and 20:17.

[The defender, the prince of the Hebrews, mindful of honours, then set out to journey home.]

11. heht þæt segn wegan
heah gehwilcne, þe his hina wæs
wæpnedcynnes, wære gemyndig. (ll. 2372b–4)

[mindful of the covenant, (Abraham) commanded each one of the male sex who was of his household to bear that holy sign.]

12. Spræc þa ofer ealle æðelinga gedriht
sunu Arones, snytra gemyndig. (ll. 2464–5)

[The son of Aaron, mindful of wisdom, spoke then to the whole company of nobles.]

In five of the six underlying biblical verses (Gen. 12:6, 13:8, 13:13, 15:1, and 19:6, corresponding to examples 7–10 and 12 as listed above), no concept occurs that is represented by the *gemyndig* phrase used by the *Genesis A* poet. In example 11, the clause 'sicut praeceperat ei Deus' [as God had commanded him] in Genesis 17:23 prompts the phrase 'wære gemyndig' [mindful of the covenant], but is not subjective.

Of course, formulaic language did present Anglo-Saxon poets with convenient metrical and alliterative units. Formulas like *q on mode* and *q gemyndig* create niches for stressed words that sustain the alliterative framework: that is what makes them useful from a compositional standpoint. But they cannot be dismissed from interpretive relevance on that account, because in a formulaic poetics, the use of patterned language endorsed by tradition is a way of building poetic meaning from the ground up – not just cranking out metrically acceptable lines regardless of content, or filling holes left after the 'real' content has been decided. Formulas contain words, those words have semantic value, and that value does not vanish when a reader or hearer recognizes familiar language, as if the poet had been caught trying to pass a counterfeit bill. The honour of which Abraham is mindful in examples 8 and 10, for instance, does not disappear from the text on account of being part of a traditional metrisyntactic construction that generates a half-line; and according to the construction that put it there, we cannot have the honour without also having Abraham's mindfulness of it. The participation of phrases like *q on mode* in a traditional discourse announces something about the way the poem makes meaning, and their semantic content impacts the meaning that is made; so if language about mental states, qualities, and processes is one fundamental component of the formulaic toolkit, then it matters fundamentally.

Segment B: Foregrounding of Interior States and Qualities through Poetic Style

The episode continues with Sarai's proposal to Abram in Genesis 16:1b–2:

> habens ancillam aegyptiam nomine Agar (2) dixit marito suo
> ecce conclusit me Dominus ne pararem
> ingredere ad ancillam meam si forte saltem ex illa suscipiam filios.
>
> [Having a handmaid, an Egyptian, named Agar, (2) She said to her husband: Behold, the Lord hath restrained me from bearing: go in unto my handmaid, it may be I may have children of her at least.]

This text is given as follows in the Ælfrician *Genesis*:

> heo hæfde ane þinene, þa Egiptiscan Agar, (2) and heo cwæð to hire were: 'Ðu wast þæt ic eom untymende. Nim nu mine þinene to þinum bedde þæt ic huru underfo sum fostercild of hyre.'
>
> [She had one slave, the Egyptian Agar, (2) and she said to her husband, 'You know that I am infertile. Now take my slave to your bed, so that I can at least receive a foster child from her.']

Genesis A elaborates:

> B Ongann þa ferhðcearig
> to were sinum wordum mæðlan:
> 'Me þæs forwyrnde waldend heofona,
> þæt ic mægburge moste þinre
> rim miclian roderum under
> eaforum þinum. Nu ic eom orwena
> þæt unc se eðylstæf æfre weorðe
> gifeðe ætgædere. Ic eom geomorfrod!
> Drihten min, do swa ic þe bidde:
> Her is fæmne, freolecu mæg,

ides Egyptisc, an on gewealde.
Hat þe þa recene reste gestigan,
and afanda hwæðer frea wille
ænigne þe yrfewearda
on woruld lætan þurh þæt wif cuman.' (ll. 2219b–33)

[The care-minded one then began to address her husband with words: 'The ruler of the heavens has denied me this, that I should be allowed to increase with your descendents the count of your lineage under the heavens. Now I am without hope that an heir (lit. family-support) ever may be granted to the two of us together. I am sad and old! My lord, do as I ask: here there is a woman, a beautiful maiden, a certain Egyptian lady in (my) power. Quickly command her to go up to you in bed and find out whether the Lord wishes to let any heirs come into the world to you through that woman.']

As these lines begin, the substantive adjective *ferhðcearig* 'care-minded one,' an epithet of emotional state, stands in reference to Sarai as the subject of a sentence. Denominative epithets are a type of traditional language that overlaps with but can be distinguished from metrisyntactic formulas like those previously considered, in that they may or may not be formulaic in their construction. Epithets like this one present themselves as definitions of a subject's essence as it is conceived at that poetic moment rather than as descriptions of a mental state or process, as the *q on mode* formula discussed above often is. The difference is that while description will predicate certain qualities or actions of an agent whose topicality is presupposed, a free-standing epithet topicalizes the quality itself, giving it an embodied presence in the narrated scenario. It helps to establish a traditional subjectivity. The term *ferhðcearig* in a sense constitutes Sarai, simultaneously communicating and delimiting the nature of her relevance at this point in the story.

The two functions that I have called definition and description are not mutually exclusive; in an environment of continuous narration they are more like points on a spectrum than rigid alternatives. For instance, we know intellectually that the reference to Sarai as *ferhðcearig* in this passage has to do with her circumstances, specifically her lack of a son with Abraham. She need not always remain *ferhðcearig*, and indeed she will not. But regardless of actual constancy or absoluteness, this denominative epithet uses the emotional quality as a sufficient marker standing in for her semantically at this point in the text. Calling Sarai, as an agent initiating action, 'the care-minded one' (topicalizing care-mindedness) is not precisely the same as stating declaratively that 'Sarai was preoccupied with cares' (topicalizing Sarai). It is more like calling the *Physiologus* whale *facnes cræftig* 'the one crafty in trickery' (*The Whale*, l. 24b). Whether whales are always crafty in trickery or only become so when exhausted sailors are in the neighbourhood is not at issue: in the only instant that matters to the sailors or to the poet – the fatal instant which (in that case) will be crystallized in the ensuing allegorical interpretation – baleful deception is the whale's defining principle, from which its actions will be understood to proceed. We have at this moment in *Genesis A* a sadness that is Sarai as much as a Sarai who is sad.

Ferhðcearig is used substantively here to denominate and define Sarai, but lexically it is simply an adjective, and the kind of usage we see here is a subset of adjectival behaviour more generally. The *Genesis A* poet is strongly drawn to terminology of mental state or quality in all adjectival functions, whether used as personal descriptors, denominative epithets, or some hybrid of the two such as often develops through the marked poetic syntax of apposition and variation. Abraham is *frod frumgara* 'the wise chieftain' (l. 2579a), *tilmodig eorl* 'the good-minded nobleman' (l. 1887a), and *beorn bliðemod* 'the glad-minded man' (l. 1800a); his enemies in battle are *wraðe wælherigas* 'angry slaughter-hosts' (l. 1983a). As the descendents of Noah populate the earth, the tribe of Shem are collectively *anmod* 'resolute, single-minded' (l. 1650b); a few lines later (ll. 1660–7) they enact the same quality in hatching the plan to build the Tower of Babel, narrated using the device of ad hoc focalization through grammatically individuated yet representative subjectivities that we saw in *The Ruin*. Once they carry out this ambition, God will be named as *stiðferhð cining* 'the stern-hearted king' (l. 1683a), as he repeatedly is in contexts of his anger or displeasure (cf. ll. 107a and 1406b). Only God is *stiðferhð*, but he shares the more violent epithet *reðemod* 'fierce-minded' with his enemies (ll. 47b, 1684a, and 2494a). Every time the word *wishydig* 'wise-minded' occurs in *Genesis A* (ll. 1816b, 1823a, 2053a, and 2257a), it refers to Abraham, alliterates, and lacks any parallel in the Vulgate source passages,[48] and in the last three of its four instances it participates in a full-line formula *wishydig wer wordum q*, where *q* is (as metre requires) a non-alliterating, stress-bearing polysyllable. Examples of adjectival usage akin to these I list, having to do with mentality and functioning as an integral component of

48 Gen. 12:10, 12:11, 14:14–15 (loosely), and 16:6.

the traditional phraseology in which the *Genesis A* poet fashions verse could be multiplied indefinitely.

In Sarai's speech following her designation as *ferhðcearig*, the *Genesis A* account differs from the Vulgate and Old English prose versions chiefly in its continuing emphasis on her sorrow. Previously the poet has made direct statements about her mentality, giving a reader or auditor narrative access to her interiority. Now the heightened emotional content of the passage is sustained by Sarai's outward articulation of her feelings, first in a new declaration of her hopelessness that is not in the source at all, and then when she calls herself *geomorfrod* 'sad-old' (or, arguably, 'sad-wise,' 'wise in sorrow'). Throughout, the variational syntax typical of Old English poetic style enhances the subjective dimension of this segment by discouraging rapid movement from one thought to the next: this recursive form of conceptual development has the effect of causing us to linger on Sarai's sorrow over her childlessness, giving it greater emphasis than would a more concise statement, however explicit.

The compound *geomorfrod* is a *hapax legomenon*, probably formed off of the rhyming and fairly common *geomormod* 'sad-minded' (which will itself occur a little later in this episode),[49] and the likeness helps to draw the unique construction into the matrix of traditional diction. The important role of compounding, including the frequent creation of new poetic compounds, is well-known as a characterizing feature of Old English versecraft. Its role in the practice of one virtuoso poet is nicely illustrated by Andy Orchard's breakdown of an enormous interlocking complex of compound words (some elsewhere attested and others *hapax*) in *Beowulf*,[50] and systems of this kind can be found throughout classical Old English verse. Given that word-formation by composition is a prominent feature of English morphology, like that of other Germanic languages, the continual generation of poetic compounds from free morphemes which are themselves constituents of poetically marked systems simultaneously partakes of normal linguistic processes yet produces some of the poetic register's dictional distinctiveness. Moreover, whereas compounds in Old English prose are normally used for conceptual specification, those in verse often have a metaphorical or aesthetically evocative nature as well, while of

49 I surmise the association to be direct both because of the rhyme, recalling to the ear the familiar *geomormod*, and because *geomor–* is not a highly productive first element in compounds (the sole other case being *geomorgydd*, with two occurrences).

50 *Critical Companion*, 69–72.

course presenting semantically viable options in the stress-bearing determinative elements (the leftward component, since endocentric compounds in English are right-headed) for the satisfaction of alliterative requirements.[51] Thus the tendency of poets to the dense use of compound words optimally combines stylistic marking, lexical flexibility in the service of concept and aesthetics, and an efficient means of fulfilling metrical demands.

Our understanding of this pervasive feature of Old English poetic diction continues to improve: Janie Steen has recently called attention to the use of compounds by some vernacular poets to help naturalize highly rhetorical Latin material to Old English diction;[52] and Don Chapman, approaching the topic from a very fresh direction, gives evidence that Anglo-Saxons conceptualized word composition as a creative act focused on the process of making rather than on the resulting product.[53] In showing that compounds were not necessarily assumed to be stable or permanent lexemes like simplices, Chapman's findings clarify the mode of poetic traditionality in which even unique specimens like *geomorfrod* can participate: what is traditional is not the word itself, but the act of forming a compound, especially using elements that may themselves have poetic resonance from their familiarity in other contexts and combinations.[54] At the

51 On the balance struck by poetic compounds between the potentially competing necessities of form and meaning, see Strauss, 'Compounding.'

52 *Verse and Virtuosity*, 62–4 and 136–7. Steen's observations tell against Lapidge's suggestion ('Old English Poetic Compounds') that this dictional feature is an imitation of a Latin device which is, after all, far less frequent in Latin than in Old English: simple operations using Lapidge's own tabulations show that among the poets he includes, the Latin writer with the highest incidence of tetrasyllabic compounds only approaches the English one with the lowest incidence. This is the case judging by line counts, Lapidge's method; but since hexameter lines are longer than Old English ones, frequency per 1000 words or per 1000 poetic feet would be a more valid basis for comparison, and using either of these ratios the measured differences are even more pronounced. Similarly, Lapidge's limitation of the data to tetrasyllabic compounds makes a drastic difference on the Old English side of the comparison, where most compounds are not tetrasyllabic, whereas in Latin, including compounds of different lengths alters the figures (as Lapidge points out) only very slightly.

53 'Composing and Joining.' Remarks on poetic compounding are limited to the very end of Chapman's essay, but the context created by the foregoing material is enlightening.

54 The process is analogous to that by which the unique phrases *bliðe on mode* (found only in *Andreas*, l. 1583b), *hold on mode* (only in *The Phoenix*, l. 446b), and *sorge on mode* (only in *Guthlac B*, l. 1068b) can recognizably actualize the *q on mode* formula discussed above. For discussion of how several *hapax legomena* in a passage of *Beowulf* participate in formulaic and other traditional structures, see Foley, *Traditional Oral Epic*, 211–12, 222–3, and 226–7.

most foundational level, current thinking on Old English metre goes beyond observing the dictional practice of compounding as an omnipresent stylistic device and reveals its connection to structural components of the poetic line itself via the role of compounds in the natural language: they are a key element of Geoffrey Russom's and Thomas A. Bredehoft's word-foot theory.[55]

Ælfric, by contrast with the *Genesis A* poet, has done nothing to stress Sarai's mental state in his prose version of this passage. Both Anglo-Saxon translators stay close to the Vulgate text, but to the poet, the transformation into traditional verse seems inherently to mean foregrounding the emotional elements of the biblical story that are strictly between the lines in the Vulgate and would remain so in its Old English prose translation. Similar heightening of reference to thought and emotion, with the increased use of reported speech as one of its instruments, occurs throughout *Genesis A*, even including at times the outright creation of opportunities for it. Outside of the Flood account, the clearest example of this practice in *Genesis A* may be lines 2024–38, where the poet narrates Abraham's learning of Lot's capture in the war of the four kings against the five kings and his intention to rescue him. The scriptural source (Gen. 14:13) simply states that a messenger brought the news of Lot's capture to Abram where he lived near his allies, the brothers Mambre, Escol, and Aner; no psychological information is given in the biblical version.[56] From this germ the English poet produces a much more elaborate scene. In *Genesis A*, once Abraham hears the report,

Þa þæt inwitspell   Abraham sægde
freondum sinum;   bæd him fultumes
wærfæst hæleð   willgeðoftan,
Aner and Manre,   Escol þriddan,
cwæð þæt him wære   weorce on mode,
sorga sarost,   þæt his suhtriga
þeownyd þolode;   bæd him þræcrofe

55 Russom, *Old English Meter*; Bredehoft, 'Ælfric and Late Old English Verse,' 85–6, and *Early English Metre*. Griffith ('Whole-Verse Compound Placement') and Terasawa (*Nominal Compounds*) identify particular restrictions or conditions according to which compound words' morphology as such interacts with metre.

56 Unless one counts the perceptual clause in the next verse ('quod cum audisset Abram …' [Which when Abram had heard …], 14:14a), serving as an indicator of sequence and motivation for the next action (gathering a force of 318 men).

þa rincas þæs ræd ahicgan,
þæt his hyldemæg ahreded wurde,
beorn mid bryde. Him þa broðor þry
æt spræce þære spedum miclum
hældon hygesorge heardum wordum,
ellenrofe, and Abrahame
treowa sealdon, þæt hie his torn mid him
gewræcon on wraðum, oððe on wæl feollan. (ll. 2024–38)

[Then Abraham told his friends that evil news; the pledge-secure man asked them, (his) companions Aner, Mambre, and Escol, for help: said there to be unrest in his mind, sorest of sorrows, because his nephew suffered compulsion of slavery, (and) asked them, those mighty men, to devise a plan accordingly so that his dear kinsman might get rescued, man and wife together. In their speech the three brothers very quickly remedied his mind-sorrow with sure words, the brave ones, and gave promises to Abraham that with him they would avenge his grief on the cruel or else fall amid the slaughter.]

After he gathers his troops, we are told that he 'wolde his mæg huru / Loth alynnan of laðscipe' [badly wanted to free his kinsman Lot from (that) hateful condition] (ll. 2047–8).

The central topic of this passage is Abraham's emotional reaction to Lot's capture, presented by several means: focalization (the designation of the news as 'evil' privileges his perception of it, for instance), indirect narration of his speech, direct narrative access to his state of mind, and dramatization of his friends' solicitous response to it. This passage is itself part of a longer stretch of much more freewheeling elaboration on scripture than is the translator's normal practice, in which he or she expands laconic biblical references to two battles into a pair of fully formed accounts of them.[57] But throughout that longer episode, mentality is treated indistinguishably from the way it is handled elsewhere in the poem, and it is clear that the writer's attraction to this opportunity for expansion reflects zeal for a traditional kind of poetry and the desire to develop traditional subject matter. The fact that Abraham's subjectivity is featured in this passage placed between the two similarly elaborated battle narratives – all apparently for the purpose of development in expected poetic directions, and with virtually no scriptural warrant for the existence of such a scene –

57 See Orchard, 'Conspicuous Heroism,' for analysis showing the influence of Prudentius.

speaks volumes on the traditional importance of the subjectivized material, right alongside the outwardly heroic.

Segment C: Shifts in Focalization and Other Mental Access

Genesis A does not directly represent Genesis 16:3, and neither does the Ælfrician prose *Genesis*.[58] We pick up, then, with Genesis 16:4:

qui ingressus est ad eam
at illa concepisse se videns despexit dominam suam.

[And he went in to her. But she, perceiving that she was with child, disdained her mistress.]

The Old English prose *Genesis* in this case is even simpler and less subjectivizing than the original, omitting Agar's act of perception:

Abram þa dyde swa swa him dihte Sarai, and Agar þa geeacnode, and eac forseah hire hlæfdian.

[Then Abram did just as Sarai had said to him, and then Agar became pregnant and also disdained her lady.]

The analogue in *Genesis A* opens by having Abraham agree to Sarai's advice, whereas the source had simply had him follow it:

C Þa se eadega wer idese larum
geðafode, heht him þeowmennen
on bedd gan bryde larum.
Hire mod astah þa heo wæs magotimbre
be Abrahame eacen worden.
Ongan æfþancum agendfrean
halsfæst herian, higeþryðe wæg,
wæs laðwendo, lustum ne wolde

58 But see next note. The avoidance of this verse by Ælfric and at least partially by the *Genesis A* poet is probably an evasion of its statement that Abraham married Agar, as Anlezark suggests ('Ideal Marriage,' 198). Barnhouse ('Shaping the Hexateuch Text,' esp. 97) documents patterns of omission in the Hexateuch *Genesis*, including some with similar subject matter.

þeowdom þolian, ac heo þriste ongan
wið Sarran swiðe winnan. (ll. 2234–43)

[Then the blessed man agreed to the lady's advice, commanded the slave to come into the bed to him according to the ways of a bride.[59] Her spirit rose up when she had become pregnant with a child by Abraham. The haughty one began to disdain her owner spitefully, bore arrogance, was hateful, would not endure slavery willingly; rather, she boldly began to struggle greatly against Sarai.]

While the narration at the start of the poetic version is not necessarily focalized through Abraham – *geþafian* does not in itself determine whether the consent is interior or outwardly expressed – the statement indicates the poet's interest in Abraham's decision-making prior to his taking a course of action. It foregrounds the fact that he has heard Sarai, considered her plan, and become convinced.

A pronounced shift into knowledge of Agar's subjectivity follows. Here the biblical source text uncharacteristically provides an explicit, if bare, statement of a character's attitude for the translator to work with. In *Genesis A*, this plain narrative proposition bursts into seven lines of Old English verse (ll. 2237–43). When the Anglo-Saxon poet says that Agar's 'mod astah' [spirit rose up] (l. 2237a), he or she responds directly to the verb in the source (Agar 'despexit' Sarai: literally, 'looked down upon' her). But then the poet returns a second time to that small subjective detail in the biblical text and amplifies it out of all proportion to its prominence in the source, where it was just a narrative datum needed to prepare causally for the next one. Now Agar – even before she has been named by the poet – is defined by a denominative epithet, *halsfæst* 'the haughty (lit. stiff-necked) one,' and we are given a comprehensive picture of her attitude

59 My translation of 'bryde larum' in l. 2236b is one of two possibilities; the other is 'according to the wife's advice.' My preference for 'according to the ways of a bride' is based on (1) its appropriateness to signify not just that Agar and Abraham are having sexual relations but that Agar's status in the household is undergoing, or may undergo, a change due to the liaison – precisely what Sarai (the real *bryd*) worries about, and a dimension of the episode emphasized by the poet; and (2) the fact that Gen. 16:3b, in which Sarai 'dedit eam viro suo uxorem' [gave her to her husband to wife], is not otherwise represented. Either way, the phrase reinforces one or another of the points I am making about the passage: the fact of Sarai's counsel, or the change in Agar's status (see further discussion below) as she physically takes the place of Sarai.

toward Sarai: spite, contempt, arrogance, hostility, and bold rebelliousness are each individually cited.

Besides vastly elaborating on the Latin original, the English verse translation has changed the environment of these statements such that they now contrast with the subjective perspective that dominated segments A and B. Because of the way the previous material has been handled, most of segment C, after the statement calling attention to Abraham's decision based on Sarai's advice, now constitutes a strong technical shift to focalization through Agar. The Flood episode discussed above showed the *Genesis A* poet augmenting focalization in general, adding it where there is none in the original and expanding its development and intensity where some gesture in that direction had been made by the biblical writer. The present episode confirms that tendency. The many other comparable examples of the poet's introduction or intensification of information about characters' interiority include the treatment of Abraham's journey to Bethel (ll. 1793–804; cf. Gen. 12:8a–b); his disbelief in God's promise that he and Sarai will have a son (ll. 2338–46; cf. Gen. 17:17); Sarai's similar disbelief and God's perception of it (ll. 2382–9; cf. Gen. 18:10c, 12); and God's response to Abimelech's abduction of Sarai (ll. 2742–6 and 2757–9; cf. Gen. 20:17–18). In lines 1847–68, another outstanding example of the poet's practice of shifting audience access to minds from one agent to another, focalization moves swiftly from Pharaoh's men, who consider Sarai beautiful, to God, whose anger the poetic voice narrates, and then to Pharaoh himself, who understands the source of the punishment that has befallen him and is driven by fear to return Sarai to Abram. The scriptural source for those lines (Gen. 12:14–19) suggests the first instance of focalization, that of Pharaoh's men; but the shift from there to God's state of mind and then to Pharaoh's own perception and cogitation is the *Genesis A* poet's own stylistic embellishment, without precedent in the biblical version or parallel in the Old English prose translation.

Focalization in *Genesis A* is widely distributed, not discriminating discernibly among characters and apparently being driven by textually local attraction to subjective positions that are found poetically desirable and conformable to traditional scenarios or situations. Such desirable positions, to judge by the practice of this and other poets, include those of agents interacting with one another in a hierarchical scheme of relationships, or in agonistic tension or conflict, or (as in Sarai and Agar's case) both. Thus there is nothing unusual about the development here of Agar's perspective, despite the fact that the narrative context within this episode has until this point presented Sarai as the central character and has treated

Agar strictly in relation to her. As conflict between the two women emerges, some stress on Agar's perspective as well as Sarai's is in fact predictable; it complements the establishment of Sarai's that has already occurred. The poet's choice at this moment to emphasize Agar's subjectivity is a major step in developing and particularizing the scheme of relationships inherited from scripture as the situation grows more complicated. Additional features of that relational scheme, including some further aspects of its representation here in segment C, will be best treated together with the following segment of text.

Segments C–D: Relational Subjectivities

Abraham's wisdom is stressed continually in *Genesis A*; by the time a reader reaches this episode the patriarch's thought processes and decisions are already marked as important. His agreement with Sarai at the beginning of segment C draws attention to her previous words to him as a very specific type of language, namely counsel, and to Abraham's acceptance of it. The translator's choice to narrate Abraham's acceptance of Sarai's advice – rather than following the Vulgate by merely recounting his subsequent actions without indicating deliberative process or mental movement on his part – implies something about the notional relationship of Sarai to Abraham at this moment and accords with the public, dynastic importance of the production of an heir and a nation which the poet has already emphasized in segment B's treatment of her desire for a child. This conception of Sarai's interaction with Abraham lays groundwork for the development of a scheme of ethical interests and relationships. That the poet imagines Sarai to be acting here as an advisor to the wise Abraham dignifies her and tends to legitimize her experiential perspective on events while affirming her husband's position of hierarchical superiority: the prudent Abraham listens to her advice (*lar*, l. 2234b) from his position of authority as her lord (*drihten*, l. 2227a).[60] In the portrayal of a biblical married couple different paradigms of social status are in play from those we find in poetic evocations of gift-hall and warband, but not without some points of intersection, and the representation of Sarai's plan as counsel puts her in the

60 Anlezark also recognizes in this episode the presence of a household hierarchy and its conceptual importance to the poet. I disagree with his view that Sarai is portrayed as dominant over Abraham and that primary responsibility for Abraham's liaison with Agar is placed upon Sarai more in this text than in others ('Ideal Marriage,' esp. 198, 200).

position of a beloved and highly esteemed subordinate who has a privileged place and the lord's ear.[61]

Status within the household is exactly what is at issue in this scene, and the emphasis on Agar's mentality in segment C solidifies her involvement in this relational scheme and gives her equal perspectival footing. Sarai had intended to bring about a temporary liaison for a specific purpose, not a reorganization of the domestic hierarchy. Yet the latter is what has happened, as the still-nameless Agar, defined epithetically as 'the haughty one,' assumes a position independent of her mistress, shrugging off her rule and realigning herself so that her own status, like Sarai's, now depends directly and only on her link to Abraham. The poet's additions to the biblical statements heavily stress Agar's violation of her social and legal place, thus following up the accentuation and naturalization of Sarai's place by Abraham's mental engagement with her counsel: it is Agar's 'owner' that she disdains, and it is 'slavery' that she refuses to endure. The scriptural cue can be understood as having to do with either Agar's attitude (contempt) or her behaviour (insubordination) toward Sarai, but either way it is a very simple statement. The poet's expansion of it actualizes both the psychological and the behavioural possibilities, and his or her energetic development of that cue, in language both strong in itself and strongly emphasized by the spiralling variational syntax, conveys a thorough preemption by Agar of rightful hierarchy. Segment C establishes with clarity and detail that in both self-esteem and action Agar sets herself above Sarai. She does so not in isolation – the story is not truly about a personality conflict between two women – but within a frame of reference formed by other relationships and an abstract model by which those relationships are supposed to be patterned. A relational structure that sets the environment in which the interactions begin and will continue to occur is implicit in the scriptural source, but it is given more definite shape by the poet, largely through the production of a powerful subjective position in opposition to Sarai's.

The source passage in Genesis 16:5–6 continues,

(5) dixitque Sarai ad Abram
inique agis contra me
ego dedi ancillam meam in sinum tuum
quae videns quod conceperit despectui me habet

61 Considering also the gendered nature of the relationship, one might compare the roles of the wise or prudent queens Wealhtheow and Hygd in *Beowulf*.

iudicet Dominus inter me et te
(6) cui respondens Abram
ecce ait ancilla tua in manu tua est utere ea ut libet.

[(5) And Sarai said to Abram: Thou dost unjustly with me: I gave my handmaid into thy bosom, and she perceiving herself to be with child, despiseth me. The Lord judge between me and thee. (6) And Abram made answer, and said to her: Behold thy handmaid is in thy own hand, use her as it pleaseth thee.]

The Vulgate source text is rendered very literally in the Ælfrician *Genesis*:

(5) Ða cwæð Sarai to Abrame: 'Þu dest unrihtlice wiþ me. Ic let mine wylne to þe; nu wat heo þæt heo ys eacniende and forsihð me for þig. Deme God betwux me and þe.' (6) Abram hire andwirde: 'Efne heo ys þin wyln under þinre handa: þrea hig locahu þu wylle.'

[(5) Then Sarai said to Abram, 'You act wrongly toward me. I gave my slave to you; now she knows she is pregnant and disdains me before you. May God judge between you and me.' (6) Abram answered her: 'Indeed, she is your slave, under your hands; punish her however you wish.']

Genesis A develops the material thus:

D Þa ic þæt wif gefrægn wordum cyðan
hire mandrihtne modes sorge,
sarferhð sægde and swiðe cwæð:
'Ne fremest þu gerysnu and riht wið me.
Þafodest þu gena þæt me þeowmennen,
siððan Agar ðe, idese laste,
beddreste gestah, swa ic bena wæs,
drehte dogora gehwam dædum and wordum
unarlice. Þæt Agar sceal ongieldan,
gif ic mot for þe mine wealdan,
Abraham leofa. Þæs sie ælmihtig,
drihtna drihten, dema mid unc twih.'
Hire þa ædre andswarode
wishidig wer wordum sinum:
'Ne forlæte ic þe, þenden wit lifiað bu,
arna lease, ac þu þin agen most
mennen ateon, swa þin mod freoð.' (ll. 2244–60)

> [Then I heard that the woman revealed (her) mind's sorrow to her husband with words: the one pained at heart spoke and strongly said, 'You do not do what is proper and right toward me. You have continued to allow – ever since she went up to you in bed, on the path of a lady, as I asked – that the slave Agar should disgracefully torment me each day with deeds and words. Agar must pay for that if I can rule my own in your eyes, dear Abraham. May the Almighty, Lord of Lords, be judge of that between us two.' The wise-minded man quickly answered her then with his words: 'While the two of us both live, I will not let you be deprived of dignities; rather, you can treat your own slave as your mind likes.']

Where the Bible gives only exteriorized narration here, recounting Sarai's words to Abram, the poet begins by returning to direct statement of Sarai's sorrow through a definitional epithet that simultaneously subjectivizes and traditionalizes her: she is now *sarferhð* 'the one pained at heart.' The expanded lead-up to her speech in lines 2244–6 resumes our earlier narrative access to Sarai's mind, as she reacts to Agar's behaviour before beginning her complaint proper. Notably, although she will become furious with Agar, she is said in *Genesis A* to approach Abraham in sorrow rather than anger. This doubtless has something to do with the poet's attraction to wordplay with her name, noticed by Roberta Frank;[62] but it also has to do with another, more traditional attraction to the way an Old English poetic agent conventionally reacts to the loss of a relationship of privilege with a beloved social superior. Paronomasia and situation converge to produce Sarai's misery.

Within her complaint, *Genesis A* makes explicit the nature of her grievance against her husband, which is elided in the biblical source and likewise in the literal translation of the Old English prose *Genesis.* In the biblical account, despite Sarai's invocation of God to act as judge between her and Abram, readers are left on their own to notice, and can easily pass by, his complicity in Agar's scorn of Sarai based on her newfound status as expectant mother of his child. But that is what captures the English poet's attention and here becomes topical. Instead of turning immediately from Sarai's accusation of Abraham's injustice to the description of Agar's behaviour, *Genesis A* devotes four and a half lines (2248–52a) to stressing that Abraham is implicated: he has permitted Agar to disrespect Sarai. Moreover, he has allowed this to go on continually since (as Sarai says)

62 'Some Uses of Paronomasia,' 76.

Agar 'ascended to you in bed' (ll. 2249–50a). This is the second time we have seen this curious phrase: the first was also spoken by Sarai, twenty lines earlier in segment B, and it has acquired new and ironic meaning since she first used it in proposing to Abraham that he should bring Agar into his bed. Its representation of Agar's approach to Abraham as following a vertical axis of movement ('on the path of a lady,' as Sarai now says) when she becomes his procreative partner turns out to double as a metaphor for the real elevation of her household status that has occurred, making Sarai's own position ambiguous.

Yet her position should be anything but ambiguous, according to the prior configuration of status understood by all parties: she is Abraham's wife and Agar's owner, placing her securely between the two in a well-defined hierarchy, and closer to Abraham than to Agar. One effect of *Genesis A*'s foregrounding of Abraham's role in this network of relationships is the continued affirmation of the importance of Sarai's perspective, because her fuller articulation of how the hierarchy has broken down in her husband's plain sight lends validity to her complaint. Sarai's objection questions the justice of Abraham's practice of lordship. Much more clearly here than in the biblical account, the *wishidig wer* 'wise-minded man' (l. 2257a) again hears Sarai out, considers her words, and changes his course of action, now to restore an order that he had allowed to deteriorate. He does not simply take sides or tell Sarai the case is in her hands, although either would be a tenable interpretation of the Vulgate's language, which does not require him to accept the responsibility Sarai claims he bears. In *Genesis A*, when he affirms his support of Sarai's continuing authority over her slave he does so in terms of her dignity and his duty to guard it, and in so responding he accepts her construction of him as a fully involved party, her reassertion of her own status, and her resumption of a position nearer to him than Agar can rightfully occupy. As the poet fleshes out what the Vulgate offers, he or she determines the telegraphic original text's meaning in a particular direction and in particular ways that bring it fully into conformity with some of the priorities of Old English verse.

The translator's interest in situating ethical agents within interactional, relational structures, and the inseparability of subjective representations from this mode of development, is evident elsewhere in *Genesis A* too, in keeping with the importance of lordship and counsel throughout the text. A notable and convenient example is a passage already quoted in the discussion of segment B above, in which Abraham finds out Lot has been captured by enemy kings. There, where the biblical account says only that a messenger brought the news, in *Genesis A* Abraham summons a council, calling together Mambre, Escol, and Aner – said in the Bible to be his neighbours and allies and made his friends as well by the English poet – explaining his anguish to them and charging them to formulate a plan by which Lot may be rescued. The relationship here, as with Sarai in segments B and C but more freely elaborated, is one of trusted counsel, with consolation and heroic loyalty also part of the picture in this all-male interaction. The men reassure Abraham and pledge their military support to him, swearing like the hearth-companions of heroic verse that alongside Abraham they will either achieve their objective of recovering Lot or die. Their loyalty, their counsel, and their courage are of a piece; and all of these things are likewise of a piece with Abraham's need, not just military but emotional and intellectual, and with the three brothers' role in this passage, completely invented by the poet, as his comforters, advisors, and warriors.

In segments C–D we twice see Abraham hearing and being influenced by Sarai's words, the first time to address a dynastic concern and the second to correct an injustice. Both times Sarai's emotional perspective on the situation drives the narration and helps to define the relational network which, for the *Genesis A* poet, endows these events with traditional poetic meaning.

Segment E: Traditional Poetic Themes and Their Engagement with Mentality

Another significant element added by the *Genesis A* poet in segment D is Sarai's threat of punishment against Agar, by which she will both demonstrate her renewed superiority in the household and take revenge. She acts on this intention in the last segment to be examined. The Vulgate source continues, from the middle of verse 6:

> adfligente igitur eam Sarai fugam iniit
> (7) cumque invenisset illam angelus Domini iuxta fontem aquae in solitudine qui est in via Sur (8) dixit ad eam
> Agar ancilla Sarai unde venis et quo vadis
> quae respondit a facie Sarai dominae meae ego fugio.

> [And when Sarai afflicted her, she ran away. (7) And the angel of the Lord having found her, by a fountain of water in the wilderness, which is in the way to Sur in the desert, (8) He said to her: Agar, handmaid of Sarai, whence comest thou? and whither goest thou? And she answered: I flee from the face of Sarai, my mistress.]

The prose *Genesis* version is as follows:

> Sarai hig þa geswencte and heo sona fleah ut to þam westene. (7) þær ðær wæs an wyllspring. Đa ofseah hig Godes engel (8) and hi sona clipode: 'Agar, Saraies þinen, hu færst þu oððe hwider wylt ðu?' Heo andwirde þam engle: 'Ic forfleo mine hlæfdian.'

> [Then Sarai tormented her, and she soon fled out to the desert. (7) There was a wellspring there. Then God's angel saw her (8) and immediately spoke to her: 'Agar, Sarai's slave, how is it you are travelling, or where do you wish to go?' She answered the angel: 'I am fleeing my mistress.']

The source material is represented by these lines of *Genesis A*:

E Đa wearð unbliðe Abrahames cwen,
hire worcþeowe wrað on mode,
heard and hreðe, higeteonan spræc
fræcne on fæmnan. Heo þa fleon gewat
þrea and þeowdom; þolian ne wolde
yfel and ondlean, þæs ðe ær dyde
to Sarran, ac heo on sið gewat
westen[63] secan. Þær hie wuldres þegn,
engel drihtnes an gemitte
geomormode. Se hie georne frægn:
'Hwider fundast þu, feasceaft ides,
siðas dreogan? Þec Sarre ah.'
Heo him ædre andswarode:
'Ic fleah wean, wana wilna gehwilces,
hlæfdigan hete, hean of wicum,
tregan and teonan. Nu sceal tearighleor
on westenne witodes bidan,
hwonne of heortan hunger oððe wulf
sawle and sorge somed abregde.' (ll. 2261–79)

[Then Abraham's wife grew displeased, angry in mind toward her work-slave, harsh and fierce, viciously spoke deliberate injuries to the woman. She

63 According to Remley, 'Latin Textual Basis,' 189, 'westen' in l. 2268a is the sole 'probable' reflection of an Old Latin reading in this episode of *Genesis A*.

left then to flee abuse and slavery, did not wish to endure harm and retaliation for that which she had done before to Sarai, but rather she went on a journey to find a deserted place. There a thane of glory, an angel of the lord, met her alone, the sad-minded one. He asked her intently, 'Where are you trying to take (your) travels, miserable woman? Sarai owns you.' She quickly answered him: 'I fled woes, lacking in each desired thing: (fled) my mistress's hate, pains and injuries, miserable out from the town. Now in a deserted place, teary-faced, I must await what is fated, when either hunger or the wolf may take from the heart both soul and sorrow together.']

A return to Sarai's emotional state dominates the opening of the poetic exposition as the writer indicates that she becomes 'unbliðe,' 'wrað on mode,' and 'heard and hreðe,' the onset of anger stressed by vigorous syntactic variation. This statement shifts away from Abraham's judicious affirmation of her continued authority over Agar and overwhelms with interior information her sole outward action in the first sentence in these lines, namely saying something hurtful to Agar. The term *hygeteona*, a compound whose first element indicates its involvement with mentality, might mean 'deliberate injury' (*hyge* signalling Sarai's calculation to hurt) or 'mental injury' (*hyge* signalling Agar's emotional pain at what Sarai says). It occurs only in this poem: there are two other instances, and the three taken together favour the sense 'deliberate injury.'[64]

As Sarai's narrated emotion shifts from sorrow to anger, she also begins to act unjustly herself, or at least excessively harshly. The negative description of her action toward Agar as 'yfel and ondlean' [harm and retaliation], in the context of the sentence in which it occurs, is inseparable from the renewed access to Agar's attitude and intentions and thus focalizes events through Agar's way of viewing them; but Sarai has also indicated earlier to Abraham that she intends to take revenge for Agar's disrespect, and when Sarai speaks 'deliberate injuries' to Agar, who is now firmly reestablished as her subordinate, she does so *frecne* 'viciously, aggressively' – in a line that precedes the shift back to Agar's subjectivity and would appear therefore to be a straightforward declaration of her intention and manner uninflected by Agar's perspective, although obviously beginning to bring her

64 In l. 2732, the word appears in Abimelech's reconciliation speech to Abraham and Sarai, in reference to the offence done to Abraham when Abimelech took Sarai, and could have either of the two senses. However, the occurrence in l. 1380, where it describes the wilful sins of humankind which God punishes with the Flood, indicates that the 'thought' referred to is that of the one causing offence, not the one suffering it.

interests into the picture. Sarai's actions in this segment are presented less as a reassertion of her rightful authority than as a vindictive assault launched from her newly fortified position against one unable to protect herself. It is not a fair fight. The angel whom Agar meets in the wilderness will go on in the lines following this segment to validate Sarai's authority and instruct Agar to return to her, but at this moment the slave's flight is made understandable.

Yet it remains a flight from one whose rule Agar herself acknowledges (in all versions she will still refer to Sarai as her 'lady' or 'mistress'). *Genesis A* develops the Sarai–Agar conflict by constructing partially parallel dilemmas that play each woman's self-interested expectation of just treatment against the unjust exercise of power by an authority figure who nevertheless has a recognized claim upon her loyalty or obedience.[65] We have seen Sarai's anguish at being caught between her husband's apparent wishes, in the form of his permissiveness toward Agar, and her sense of her own right to a position close to him. For Agar the dilemma consists of a tension between her acceptance in principle of her subservience, which she has overstepped, and her experience as a victim of retaliatory abuse in her resumed position under Sarai's rule. As was the case earlier with Abraham, the poet's particular choices of presentation now bring Sarai's actions into communication with concepts of virtuous lordship and right rule. Unlike Sarai earlier with respect to Abraham, Agar does not have a close alliance of another kind with her own superior, Sarai, that can provide a counterbalancing opportunity to persuade and prompt reconsideration; nor, because Abraham has already supported Sarai's autonomy in her dealings with Agar, can Agar appeal to the judgment of an authority higher than her abuser, as Sarai had done in invoking the judgment of God upon her grievance against Abraham.

While in the poet's development of the biblical material Sarai and Agar face structurally similar dilemmas, then, and while the binds in which they find themselves enhance the poetic attractiveness of both their subjectivities, the difference is that Agar has no recourse within the hierarchy, and this makes her especially eligible for the experience of anguish and abjectness to which Anglo-Saxon poets so often gravitate. Here Agar's perspective becomes appealing to the poet as that of a person suffering what seems

65 Although he does not put it in terms of access to characters' mentality, Lucas's study of the relationships in *Genesis A* ('Loyalty and Obedience,' esp. 123–8) shows incidentally that much of the ethical positioning can be tracked in terms of who is mindful of what.

to her to be irreparable loss: of the goodwill of her mistress, her temporarily elevated place in the household and Abraham's special favour, and now even her ability to remain peaceably in Sarai's service. The solution she attempts in the inherited biblical storyline, her flight, now becomes not just avoidance but self-destructive voluntary isolation and converges perfectly with a familiar Anglo-Saxon poetic motif, as this shift in focalization combines with the narrative situation to create a traditional elegiac subjectivity: Agar becomes an exile, sliding smoothly into a narrative groove associating her with a whole complex of Old English poetic concomitants of displacement and dispossession.[66]

After her flight Agar is again defined paraphrastically, now with the substantive adjective *geomormod* 'sad-minded one' – a telling change from her earlier designation as *halsfæst* 'haughty one,' particularly given that her actions will still be interpreted by the angel (as in the biblical original) as a kind of rebellion against her owner, to whom she must return. The haughtiness previously emphasized is not gone; Agar leaves because she refuses to endure slavery, when she is in fact a slave, and the angel will instruct her to go back and resume that role. But at this moment her narratively essential pride takes a back seat to her poetically attractive misery. When she encounters the angel, his direct speech, too, emphasizes Agar's emotional state: he addresses her as 'feasceaft ides' [miserable woman] even as he affirms Sarai's rightful ownership of her. The only particularizations of Agar in these lines, and indeed in the entire episode, centre on her feelings, and now her feelings highlight her status as an exile, not a headstrong resister of authority, even as events confirm that she has not ceased to be the latter.

Agar's answer to the angel sustains the emphasis on her emotions. In this sequence the poet has Agar's self-description take on the conventional qualities of Old English lamentation, with its recurrent motifs of dislocation and isolation, and in doing so, the writer subscribes to a traditional source of emotive content in the poetic idiom. Agar's sentiment as

66 The seminal discussion of the traditional theme of Exile is Greenfield, 'Formulaic Expression'; see also Frey, 'Exile and Elegy,' esp. 296–7. Traditional clusters of concept, detail, and association have been variously and contradictorily differentiated into technically defined 'themes,' 'motifs,' 'type-scenes,' and so on by theorists of Old English traditional poetics (for discussion of the early proliferation of definitions, see Fry, 'Old English Formulaic Themes,' 49–51). Such taxonomies of these conceptual conventions seem over-exact and unnecessary to me. In discussion I will avoid reliance on specialized senses of words like 'theme' and 'motif' and will attempt simply to be clear about what I mean in a given case.

expressed in this speech differs in circumstantial detail, but not in overall mode, from the elegiac pronouncements of *The Wanderer*, *The Wife's Lament*, and other poems. The affinity is especially marked in the last sentence of the quoted passage, where the concept of awaiting one's fate alone – along with the stylized reference to hunger and the wolf as the two forces one of which will eventually rid Agar of both her sorrow and her soul – strikes a chord not only with elegiac discourse in general, but also with the pithy ironies so characteristic of poetic desperation in Old English.

Here in her lament Agar verges on the kind of language that is also a knowledge-form, the apothegm or maxim encapsulating communal truth. The grimly witty turn of phrase the poet allows her about hunger and the wolf (one unhappy end brought about by lacking food, the other by becoming it) epitomizes a type of fatalistic summing-up rhetoric found elsewhere and usually bound up with self-conscious reference to mental states, couched in traditional structures of thought and language, as in Byrhtwold's exhortation in *The Battle of Maldon* – 'hige sceal þe heardra, heorte þe cenre, / mod sceal þe mare þe ure mægen lytlað' [thought must be the firmer, heart the keener, mind must be the greater as our strength declines] (ll. 312–13) – focused squarely on mentality in an adversative retooling of the 'mind and might' topos; or the Last Survivor's wry consignment of his tribe's treasure for safekeeping to the earth, from which (he implies) the jewels and metals might just as well never have been taken in the first place (*Beowulf*, ll. 2247–9a), before he goes on to describe his own miserable solitude;[67] or the Seafarer's neat triad of a man's possible fates, with its evocation of the fear or doubt that becomes inevitable just at the threshold of death:

Simle þreora sum   þinga gehwylce,
ær his tid aga,   to tweon weorþeð;
adl oþþe yldo   oþþe ecghete
fægum fromweardum   feorh oðþringeð.   (*The Seafarer*, ll. 68–71)

[Always one of three things, in every single case, becomes (cause for) uncertainty before one's time comes: infirmity or old age or sword-hate will drive life out of the doomed one about to die.]

Such statements sound proverbial, whether they really are or not, and from that resonance with the register of shared wisdom they derive their force.

67 References to *Beowulf* are to Fulk, Bjork, and Niles, *Klaeber's 'Beowulf.'*

The prospect of the wolf's preying on the helpless Agar participates as well in the motif of the ravenous, desperate lone wolf, itself an outcast. This reviled creature is one of the three gleefully scavenging Beasts of Battle, a widespread poetic theme the *Genesis A* poet repeatedly exploits,[68] and appears solo, as it does here, in *Maxims I* (ll. 146–51), *Maxims II* (ll. 18b–19a), and *The Fortunes of Men* (ll. 10–14). *Genesis A* is rich in such traditional parcels of detail or image, which help naturalize the biblical material to Old English poetic discourse. Others include the sighting of the towering city in lines 1820–2a (cf. Gen. 12:11) and 2399–406a, a well-distributed theme (sometimes called The Traveller Recognizes His Goal) that has counterparts outside of *Genesis A* in both Beowulf's and Grendel's approaches to Heorot (*Beowulf*, ll. 306b–11 and 710–16a), Judith's triumphant return to Bethulia with Holofernes's head (*Judith*, ll. 132b–41a), *Maxims II* (ll. 1b–3a), and elsewhere;[69] the motif of Women in the Captivity of Strangers to which the *Genesis A* poet recurs several times (ll. 1969b–73, 2009b–13a, 2085b–92a, and 2630–3a), with parallels in *Beowulf* (ll. 3015a–21b; cf. 3150–5a) and *Wulf and Eadwacer* (ll. 9–12); and the Migration theme that Paul Battles has convincingly identified.[70] That every single one of these poetic motifs often or always entails an imagined subjectivity – a fact that has been noticed only piecemeal, in reference to individual ones[71] – underscores the pervasiveness of the poetics of mentality. There is more to a poetic theme than the words and situations that conventionally constitute or signal it; in all of these cases, the handling of perspective through the technique of focalization appears to be equally traditional.

---

68 *Genesis A*, ll. 1983–5, 2086–9, 2159–61, and perhaps a partial reflex in ll. 1443–8 as discussed above. For fuller listings and analysis, see studies referenced above, introduction, n. 30.

69 See G. Clark, 'Traveler Recognizes His Goal,' for additional examples.

70 '*Genesis A* and the Anglo-Saxon "Migration Myth"' (a reinterpretation of a pattern previously noticed by Doane, *Genesis A*, 81–2).

71 E.g., Riedinger, discussing a theme that she calls The Victor Returns Home with His Reward, points out in two articles that pride and exultation generally accompany the other elements of the pattern ('Old English Formula in Context,' 309–11, and '"Home,"' 55–7); Greenfield ('Formulaic Expression') treats the emotions associated with the situation of the exile as an integral part of that theme; and Griffith's itemization of the elements of the Beasts of Battle theme ('Convention and Originality,' 185) includes two ('eager' and 'joy') that centre on emotion.

* * *

The analysis of this typical episode in *Genesis A*, taken from a portion of that text commonly agreed to represent disciplined poetic translation of the Latin scripture underlying it, lays a cornerstone for my argument that the practice of Old English versecraft as a rule entails strong emphasis on characters' mental states and positions of subjectivity. We have seen that in a project best described as a faithful translation into the vernacular poetic style, the *Genesis A* poet consistently heightens the emphasis on mental and emotional states by several means. In making these adjustments to the content of his or her source text, the poet can be seen interacting with features of that source, but never being fully guided by them. His or her expression was shaped in part too by the formal constraints of Old English verse, but they likewise do not create the phenomena we have observed. Most of the time the translator evidently adds and develops reference to mentality because doing so was perceived as appropriate or desirable in the act of refashioning scripture as English poetry. Attention is likely to be given to the emotional states or mental qualities of any character who occupies an experiential position for which there exists a traditional repertoire of expressive devices, or who will be involved in a scenario of hierarchical relations or agonistic conflict; and entire opportunities to provide access to different minds may even be created for no other apparent reason than to have subjectivities available with which to work in such situations.

Thus the emphasis on mentality and emotion frequently shifts from one character to another and does not especially prefer those we would identify as protagonists. If *Genesis A* has a protagonist, it is Abraham, yet his perspective does not play a large part in the episode we have looked at in detail (although his wisdom, as the poet has previously established it, is important). Neither Sarai nor Agar behaves in a way that would suggest a desire by the writer to create stable, character-based sympathy; both experience victimhood, and both also violate their assigned ethical roles, each abusing the other in the process. But in part because of their entanglement, both of the women's perspectives lend themselves to vignettes of traditional subjectivity that the poet finds attractive and develops in accordance with the priorities and values of classical Old English verse. Tellingly, we hear about Abraham's subjectivity much more intensively when Lot is captured and the patriarch himself occupies a position suspended between the elegiac and the heroic.

This flexibility of perspective in interaction with local situational factors, the pervasiveness of the complex of related techniques as I have outlined them, and their presence across scales, in the smallest building-blocks as well as the larger structures of Old English verse texts, all point to the poetics of mentality as a fundamental component of design and expression according to traditional methods. This chapter has taken *Genesis A* as a representative of classical Old English versecraft to use as a starting point. The next two will turn to the work of other poets to confirm that the features and techniques found in *Genesis A* do indeed typify Old English poetry of the traditional kind.

2 Traditional Diction, Emergent Subjectivities

The Old English *Genesis B*, comprising lines 235–851 of the composite *Genesis* text that MS Junius 11 presents continuously, is part of an English translation from a longer poem in continental Old Saxon.[1] Although the manuscript as it stands gives no indication of a textual splice with the *Genesis A* material that precedes and follows it,[2] since the early nineteenth century this 617-line poetic segment has been recognized as an interpolation due to differences of style and handling of story matter. In 1875 Eduard Sievers hypothesized its dependence on an unknown Saxon *Genesis*, reasoning primarily from unusual linguistic features of the English text, and his surmise suddenly proved correct in 1894 upon the discovery that three fragments of this underlying work had survived in the margins

1 The surviving portion of *Genesis B* is best explained as a narrative patch used to fill a lacuna in a defective exemplar of *Genesis A* (Raw, 'Probable Derivation'; Doane, *Genesis A*, 8–10, 20–3, and *Saxon Genesis*, 41–2). It is unknown whether *Genesis B* was always a partial translation only, made for the purpose of supplying a defective *Genesis A* manuscript with material representing Gen. 3:1–7, or whether a full English rendering of the Old Saxon *Genesis* once existed (cf. Schwab, *Bruchstücke der altsächsischen Genesis*, 29). The interpolation predates the production of Junius 11 (Lucas, 'MS Junius 11,' 22; Raw, 'Construction of Oxford, Bodleian Library, Junius 11,' 193–6); the immediate exemplar of Junius 11 probably already contained not just the already-united *Genesis A* and *Genesis B* but the full sequence *Genesis A/B–Exodus–Daniel* (Doane, *Genesis A*, 12, and *Saxon Genesis*, 34; Remley, *Old English Biblical Verse*, 24–9).

2 The first transition point between *Genesis A* and *Genesis B* (between ll. 234 and 235 in *ASPR*), and thus at least a small part of *Genesis B*, has been lost through physical damage to Junius 11, but the end of the extant *Genesis B* runs straight into the resumption of *Genesis A*.

of a manuscript dated to the third quarter of the ninth century.[3] As it happens, the shortest of the recovered Old Saxon *Genesis* fragments overlaps with a passage near the end of *Genesis B*, and the parallel section confirms the relationship Sievers had inferred: lines 791–817a of the English text closely match lines 1–26a of the Saxon one.[4] For a span of 53 verses of *Genesis B*, then, we can scrutinize the craft of an Old English poet working directly with 51 verses of an Old Saxon poem.[5]

The parallel material reveals that *Genesis B* corresponds far more minutely to its continental vernacular source than does *Genesis A* to its Latin one. We have seen that while most of *Genesis A* stays close to the narrative of the biblical Genesis and regularly includes direct reflections of its wording, the *Genesis A* poet also paraphrased freely within the confines of the biblical sequencing and continually elaborated in directions suggested by vernacular convention, translating not only from one language to another but more comprehensively from one tradition to another. The maker of *Genesis B* took a different path. He or she translated extremely conservatively, favouring word-for-word and verse-for-verse transfer of text between the two cognate dialects and metrical systems to produce a near-exact English counterpart to the Saxon *Genesis*. In this process significant changes of wording were seldom necessary since most Old Saxon words have Old English morphemic and semantic equivalents. Likewise, metrical adaptation in itself presented few challenges to bringing about conformity with acceptable English practice (although *Genesis B* retains a higher incidence of certain permitted verse types than is usual in classical Old English poetry).[6] The translator altered the text mainly by tightening up

3 Bischoff, 'Paläographische Fragen,' 129. I will cite the Old Saxon *Genesis* and *Heliand* from Behaghel (rev. Taeger), *Heliand und Genesis*. On Sievers's hypothesis and Karl Zangemeister's discovery of the Saxon *Genesis*, see ibid., xxxiii–xxxviii; Doane, *Saxon Genesis*, 3–8; and Remley, *Old English Biblical Verse*, 154–7.

4 Lewis ('Metre of *Genesis B*,' 71), following Timmer (*Later Genesis*, 49), would have the overlap begin with l. 790, not l. 791, of *Genesis B*. By this view a single Saxon verse (l. 1a) is rendered by three English verses (ll. 790–1a). However, Vickrey ('*Genesis B*,' 266–8), Doane (*Saxon Genesis*, 57), and Lucas ('Some Aspects of *Genesis B*,' 150 n. 37) offer good reasons to consider only l. 791a of *Genesis B* analogous to line 1a of the Saxon *Genesis*, giving a one-to-one verse correspondence at that point.

5 The translator's addition of two verses will be discussed below.

6 Lucas ('Some Aspects of *Genesis B*') exhaustively documents the relationship of *Genesis B* to classical Old English metrical norms, concluding that it 'conforms to the requirements of OE metre to a remarkable degree' (172): *Genesis B* differs from other English poems in distribution of line types and in the frequency of certain features but very

individual half-lines to better suit the norms of English syntax. Because this close correspondence between the two texts provides an almost laboratory-perfect control of variables, points of divergence have the potential to be enormously informative about Old English poetic craft in the hands of one native practitioner.[7]

This chapter's analysis will focus on denotational differences between *Genesis B* and its Old Saxon source, by which I mean changes to the text's literal, paraphrasable message.[8] By my reading, denotational differences arise at only five points in the textual overlap between *Genesis B* and the Old Saxon *Genesis*.[9] We will see that where the meaning changes, *Genesis B* often amplifies subjectivity through new deployments of traditional diction at the small scale of word and phrase. Observation of this tendency continues to advance my descriptive agenda: as an exceptionally conservative translation into Old English from a closely related poetic tradition,

---

seldom departs from recognized practice in any verse. Lewis too finds *Genesis B* 'metrically similar in most respects to other Old English verse' ('Metre of *Genesis B*,' 109) and concludes that 'the weight of evidence places the work firmly in the Anglo-Saxon tradition' (110). Cf. also Bethel, 'Notes on the Incidence and Type of Anacrusis.'

7 Timmer concluded from lexis that the writer of *Genesis B* was a continental Saxon transliterating (*Later Genesis*, 27–39 and 43–5). Capek supported this view in a short syntactic study ('Nationality of a Translator'), and Schwab also accepts it (*Bruchstücke der altsächsischen Genesis*, 28). However, Vickrey ('*Genesis B*,' 35–9), Lewis ('Metre of *Genesis B*,' 110), Doane (*Saxon Genesis*, 51), and Rauch ('Old English *Genesis B* Poet') persuasively counter the hypothesis of a Saxon translator. In her own reexamination of the linguistic evidence, informed by methodologies designed for investigation of bilingualism and language acquisition, Rauch (ibid.) argues that the *Genesis B* translator was a native Old English speaker with secondary competency in Old Saxon.

8 The translator made different kinds of alterations, most having little effect on meaning. I exclude, for instance, lexical substitutions that preserve essential synonymity. Lewis classifies the types of changes that were made ('Metre of *Genesis B*,' 68–71), and Doane discusses all corresponding verses in comparison (*Saxon Genesis*, 55–64). I do not always agree with either scholar's analysis of the nature of the modifications or the reasons for them, but their commentary helps identify factors that may have been involved in the translator's adjustments.

9 The most plausible case for an additional divergence could be made at Saxon *Genesis*, l. 22a, and *Genesis B*, l. 813a. Doane (*Saxon Genesis*, 63) thinks they say different things at this point, but the Saxon line is badly damaged and the reading conjectural. The Saxon reading as reconstructed by Behaghel and Taeger and usually accepted does not really differ in sense from the English one, although it produces that meaning differently: in forming the compound *scurscead*, the translator seems to have allowed Old English *scur* 'shower' to substitute for Saxon *scûr* 'protection' based on likeness of sound and the equivalence of the resulting statement, despite different denotations of the compound's constituents.

Genesis B can sharpen our understanding of the role of the poetics of mentality within Old English versecraft. But the present chapter develops a literary-critical perspective as well, channelling identification and description into a program of interpretation that acknowledges the poetics of mentality. Where the English translator produces new sense, we need to be as precise as we can about the nature of the change and about what factors – translational, contextual, and traditional – appear to have motivated the adjustment, but that is only half the story. It is equally important to consider how the newly introduced elements in *Genesis B* might function for Anglo-Saxon audiences, asking not just where institutionalized diction referencing mentality is found, but how it interacts with Old English poetic tradition to make meaning.

This chapter has three major sections. The first is chiefly theoretical and methodological, but it will begin by introducing two of the five changed statements in the overlap between the Saxon *Genesis* and *Genesis B*. Brief discussion of these two straightforward cases will provide a concrete starting point for considerations of interpretive method that must precede more intensive analysis of the remaining three cases, those which are directly involved with the poetics of mentality and thus most central to my argument. Following this section's discussion of the hermeneutics of conventional, already-familiar language within a highly traditional poetics, the next will turn to the remaining three instances of denotational difference in the *Genesis B*/Saxon *Genesis* overlap, attending to the influence of English poetic traditionality in each case. The final section of the chapter will reevaluate the precise nature of the translator's activity to learn what his or her work can reveal about the place of the poetics of mentality in Old English poetic tradition more broadly.

Interpreting Traditional Diction

Two Cases of Denotational Difference between the Texts

The material shared between *Genesis B* and the Saxon *Genesis* in their present states consists entirely of a speech Adam makes to Eve after they recognize the gravity of their mistake in eating the forbidden fruit. In the Saxon original, midway through his complaint – part lamentation, part accusation of Eve – Adam asks a desperate question:

> Hû sculun uuit nu libbian, efto hû sculun uuit an thesum liahta uuesan?
> (Saxon *Genesis*, l. 14)

[How are the two of us going to live now, or how are we going to continue in this life?]

In the corresponding line of *Genesis B*, the English poet condenses the b-verse syntactically but also replaces a key word, substituting Old English *land* for Old Saxon *lioht*:[10]

Hu sculon wit nu libban oððe on þys lande wesan? (*Genesis B*, l. 805)

[How are the two of us going to live now, or continue in this land?]

The rhetorical thrust of Adam's question may remain the same: 'How will we carry on?' However, that some change in literal meaning was made consciously with the revision from Old Saxon *lioht* 'light, life, world, existence' to Old English *land* 'land' is confirmed by the *Genesis B* poet's use elsewhere of English *leoht* (cognate to Saxon *lioht*) in a sense more typical of its Old Saxon usage, implying direct retention of the word from the source in those lines and thus its availability to the translator here as well if no semantic adjustment were intended.[11] The use of *land* instead at line 805b suggests in Adam an anxiety over the loss of his and Eve's habitation in Paradise rather than a general concern for their lives or state of life. The new overtones that come with this word choice anticipate Adam and Eve's imminent status as the prototypical earthly exiles and thus tie into a prevalent theme in Old English poetry.

A few lines later, as Adam goes on to describe the hardships that he and Eve are now doomed to suffer, he worries that

kumit haglas skion himile bitengi,
ferid ford an gimang. (Saxon *Genesis*, ll. 17–18a)

[a cloud of hail will come, touching heaven – will advance forward simultaneously (sc. with harsh wind, mentioned previously).]

10 In discussion, I will spell Old Saxon words in the regularized forms they are given in Behaghel and Taeger's glossary.

11 Both Doane (*Saxon Genesis*, 61 and 259) and Schwab (*Einige Beziehungen*, 94), in commenting on the change to *land*, observe the use of Old English *leoht* elsewhere (*Genesis B*, ll. 258a and 310b) with its Saxon meaning.

The world's first weather forecast is a little different in the English version:

cymeð hægles scur   hefone getenge;
færeð forst on gemang.   (*Genesis B*, ll. 808–9a)

[a storm of hail will come, touching heaven; frost will come at the same time.]

There are two changes to this sentence. First, in reference to hail, the Saxon 'cloud' has become an English 'shower' or 'storm,' and in the third verse 'frost' is added. The latter makes the greater difference denotationally, but both offer important clues to the translator's priorities and procedures.

The shift from Old Saxon 'haglas skion' to Old English 'hægles scur' is a case of Saxon poetic language being converted to familiar English poetic language,[12] as comparison with a few other poems quickly reveals. In *The Seafarer* we find a similar tight collocation of *hægl* with *scur* ('hægl scurum fleag' [hail flew in spates], l. 17b), and in both *Andreas* (l. 1257a) and *The Menologium* (l. 35b) a compound *hæglscur* is formed to express the same concept 'shower of hail'; and all three of those occurrences of *hægl* + *scur* share an additional feature, the alliterative collocation of *hægl* with *hrim* 'frost.' In *The Rune Poem*, *scur* again finds a place in a more protracted description of *hægl*:

ᚻ [=hægl] byþ hwitust corna;   hwyrft hit of heofones lyfte,
wealcaþ hit windes scuras,   weorþeþ hit to wætere syððan.   (ll. 25–6)

[Hail is the whitest of grains; it swirls out of the air of heaven, storms of wind toss it, (and) finally it turns into water.]

We may note too that the kenning used for hail in these lines from *The Rune Poem*, 'hwitust corna' [whitest of grains], has one close counterpart in the corpus: it circles us back again to *The Seafarer*, where the second time that poem uses the word *hægl* – collocating it once again with *hrim* – it is defined variationally as 'corna caldast' [coldest of grains] (ll. 32–3a).

12 I can locate no evidence for Doane's claim that in changing OS *skion* to OE *scur* the English poet substitutes 'a prose concept' (*Saxon Genesis*, 62), and his more detailed commentary on the line (ibid., 305) does not clarify. While *hægl* does appear within concatenations of weather terms in prose, outside of verse I find no contextual association of *scur* with it and no other expression of the concept 'shower (or storm) of hail.'

Taken all together this is a modest but well-distributed body of information: the commonalities of *The Seafarer*, *The Rune Poem*, *The Menologium*, *Andreas*, and *Genesis B* attest closely related molecules of diction in five different manuscripts. The simplest explanation is that a traditional poetic concept 'shower of hail' existed, that the co-occurrence of the free morphemes *scur* and *hægl* that forms its lexical core might also reach beyond a direct grammatical interaction while keeping those words linked in a recognizable pattern of usage, and that this lexical association was apt to intersect with a related concept having its own customary phraseology, the description of hail as the '*q*-est of grains.'

Just after the *Genesis B* poet's 'shower of hail' comes the larger change to the meaning of the same statement, the substitution of English *forst* 'frost' for Saxon *forð* 'forth.' As reflected in the translations given above, this time the difference of a single word alters the whole shape of the sentence, introducing a new grammatical subject (frost to go along with the hail) and thus rewriting as an independent clause what had originally been a continuation of the hail-cloud's predicate. This added juxtaposition of frost with hail is hardly surprising given the tendency of weather words to cluster in Old English verse; indeed a parallel to this sentence's threefold linkage of *hægl*, *scur*, and *forst* occurs in the same line of *Andreas* referenced above as containing the compound *hæglscur*: 'Weder coledon / heardum hægelscurum, swylce hrim ond forst' [The weather grew cold with severe hail-showers, likewise rime and frost] (ll. 1256b–7).

Both of these details in lines 808–9a of *Genesis B* – the poet's use of *scur* and *forst*, deviating from the Saxon *Genesis* as we have it – belong to a category of imagery long recognized as a mainstay of traditional concept and language in Old English poetry, that of harsh weather. We see the poet developing that aspect of these verses, or at the very least (if we suppose that *frost* 'frost' was the reading of a lost Saxon exemplar from which the translation was made),[13] ensuring the weather imagery's continued rhetorical impact for the poem's new audience by translating the hailstorm image into an institutionalized form, the *hægl/scur* collocation, that would be recognizable to readers of English verse. Like the simpler case of word substitution in line 805b, where English 'land' replaces Saxon *lioht* and evokes the idea of exile, the modifications here tie into a well-represented

13 Doane (*Saxon Genesis*, 62) speculates that OS *frost* may have been the original reading of the Saxon *Genesis*, reflected in *Genesis B* from an exemplar that differed from the Vatican manuscript of the source poem.

poetic motif in Old English, and I do not believe this similarity between them is incidental. Changes of this kind, if found regularly, bespeak an active attraction on the translator's part to familiar elements and devices of Anglo-Saxon vernacular poetics, and this is exactly what I will suggest can be seen in each of the three additional alterations to be analysed in due course. It is of great significance to my larger argument, then, that those three other denotational differences between the Saxon *Genesis* and *Genesis B* all have to do overtly with the language of mentality: one replaces a description of hellmouth's gaping open with a common formula subjectivizing hell as 'greedy and insatiable'; another enhances and interiorizes a statement of Adam's and Eve's distress; and the third newly characterizes God as 'angry-hearted.' In each case the poet uses particles of demonstratively traditional diction that function in precise, definable ways within the Old English poetic register.

These three remaining instances differ in kind from the two I have discussed thus far, and that difference raises a methodological complication. It is easy to make interpretive claims about the alterations to lines 805b and 808–9a of *Genesis B*, because the first of them ties into a preoccupation of Anglo-Saxon poets (exile) that can be accepted as a purely conceptual likeness, and the second connects to passages from other poems which, while they do involve impressive dictional overlaps, also participate in an often-noted conceptual and rhetorical complex that uses weather imagery to evoke intense human emotion. We already know that references to harsh weather index a traditional subjectivity and stereotyped situations that are understood to correlate to it: this class of imagery powerfully connotes exile (thus complementing the change of *lioht* to *land* a few lines earlier), isolation, privation, and the vulnerability that comes with the lack of a sheltering lord or community – associations whose appropriateness at this moment in *Genesis B* is obvious, both situationally and in terms of the emotions Adam is expressing.[14] Because the concepts involved show sufficient continuity among various texts to justify regarding them as relevant analogues, an argument that those changes by the *Genesis B* poet contribute to an awareness of Adam and Eve's subjective position as soon-to-be exiles need not rest directly on verbal patterning, although when such intertextual patterning exists (as with the weather imagery) it can easily enough be acknowledged as strengthening a primarily conceptual connection.

---

14 Cf. Stévanovitch, *Genèse du manuscrit Junius XI*, 2:734.

However, while such a comparison of discrete units of 'content' across the boundaries of individual works seems intuitive because they are self-evidently meaning-bearing and thus submit readily to our normal apparatus of literary analysis, we often cordon off conventional dictional units, when they do not clearly participate in a larger, stable conceptual package to which they may be subordinated, as a matter of 'form': part of the poetry's shape as distinguished from its meaning. They may thus be rendered invisible to analysis, leading, ironically, to interpretive neglect of some of the tradition's defining features. The constitutive role of traditional diction in the very substance of Old English poetry means that in order to interpret its presence and meaning in a given instance, nothing less is needed than an explicit hermeneutic program, a theory of how to read formulaic and other familiarly patterned phraseology in its own right.

The Old English poetic emphasis on subjectivity differs, in the phenomenology of reading, from more easily recognized and discussed 'themes' like Harsh Weather or Exile. It is pervasive and fluid, emerging from features of diction (which can seem trivial in isolation) and narrative technique (which can seem intangible) as well as concept. Its perception in the three remaining denotational changes in *Genesis B* depends on the interpretation of traditional diction. Whereas the significance of the translator's substitution of *land* for *lioht* can be approached only through concept (because it involves no formulaic or other conventional dictional unit), and the enhancement of the harsh weather motif can be approached either through concept or through patterned, institutionalized language (and so need not rely on the latter for demonstration), the three modifications yet to be discussed operate primarily at the level of the translator's choices of word and phrase. Because they actualize the poetics of mentality through the connotative properties of familiar diction, the relationship of traditional language to meaning in Old English poetry must be considered as a prerequisite to their analysis.

Reading Traditional Diction: Considerations of Theory and Method

Study of the meaning and function of language choices recognized as conventional has come a long way, in different fields of inquiry largely insulated from one another, since the oral-formulaic theory of the Parry–Lord school. Here I will describe and evaluate current theories of conventional diction that have high mutual relevance but have never been brought into substantive contact, arguing that their synthesis produces a coherent framework within which to analyse the presence and operation of traditional language in Old English poems. It is useful to organize thought on traditional dictional units around three questions: *what* they are, *how* they make meaning for audiences also fluent in the tradition, and *why* they are called upon, by individual poets or by a tradition of verse-making.[15] This chapter requires attention mainly to the first two.[16]

The best current understanding of the 'what' and the 'how' in specific reference to Old English poetry was developed by John Miles Foley and fully articulated in the early 1990s, giving us the most well-rounded theory yet of what Anglo-Saxon poets were doing and how they were doing it when they used formulas and other traditional structures.[17] Foley's work can now be recontextualized in a couple of different ways, however, in view of recent approaches to fundamental issues from other directions. I will suggest that ongoing research in linguistics provides unrecognized validation of one of his central theses, on the metonymic referentiality of traditional forms, by strengthening the argumentative basis for his insight on this point; yet some reevaluation of Old English poetry's metonymic dimension as posited by Foley is needed with respect to the concept of discursive register and to the mechanics of traditional processes in human communities. In the final analysis, integrating Foley's pathbreaking work with current developments in both linguistic and cultural theory of received units of meaning clarifies the methodological demands posed by certain phenomena we must deal with in interpreting Old English poetry.

The basis of Foley's theory, as argued in *Traditional Oral Epic*, is the principle of 'tradition-dependence,' which proceeds from the simple fact that languages differ. Because languages differ, so also will those systems of poetic form that are conditioned by such elements of natural language as morphology, syntax, and stress patterning, which determine the sonic contours of utterances and language-users' sense of their constitutent parts. The dissimilar prosodical and metrical systems that result will, in turn, encourage different kinds of traditional structures to emerge in the orally formed poetics of different languages. Foley's argument for this

---

15 This formulation is a composite of precedents in the work of John Miles Foley and John D. Niles. Foley (*Immanent Art*) emphasizes that the crucial question, once traditional forms have been identified and defined, is *how* they mean. Niles (*Homo Narrans*, e.g., 201) speaks of moving from the *what* of traditional oral(-derived) art to the *why*.

16 Chapter 3 will take one of several possible approaches to the question of 'why.'

17 Foley, *Traditional Oral Epic* and *Immanent Art*. Foley had paved the way for this work with a survey of the field of oral-formulaic studies, outlining its development and outstanding issues, in *Theory of Oral Composition*; see pp. 65–74 for Old English.

principle has an implicit but deep kinship with the contemporaneous development by other scholars, working on metre, of the concept of Old English 'metrical grammar' or 'verse grammar.'[18] Foley's rigorous demonstration of tradition-dependence overcame a serious weakness of early 'oral-formulaic' study of Old English poems, namely the imposition of a model of 'the' poetic formula derived from Homeric Greek on the utterly dissimilar prosody and metre of Old English.[19] The ill fit of one language's poetic formula to another language's formulaic poetry had hampered real understanding of Old English verse no less – although perhaps less conspicuously – than had fallacious assumptions about the literary-historical implications of formulaic language's prominence.[20]

Foley's work linking traditional poetic structures to underlying linguistic ones through the mediating system of metre made possible for the first time the analysis of Old English traditional diction on its own terms and in well-defined relation to other elements of the poetic and linguistic systems in which it participates. It revealed, for example, that formulas in Old English poetry naturally vary: rather than maintaining a fixed relationship of wording to both metrical form and fundamental concept (the trifecta Milman Parry had used to define the Homeric formula), the linguistic and

18 Formulaic language had been spoken of as a kind of 'grammar' of oral poetry by earlier theorists, but they meant this as an analogy (to Chomskyan generative/transformational grammar) indicating that formulaic diction acted as a generative system. When a real relationship was posited between the grammar of the language and the 'grammar' of poetry, it was seen as superimposition of the latter discrete system of rules upon the former; that is, the rules of Old English metre were taken as an additional mediating filter, within the larger system of linguistic production, that shaped poetic utterances as such but whose own shape was essentially arbitrary (e.g., Conner, 'Schematization'; for citation of earlier comments along these lines, see Niles, 'Formula and Formulaic System,' 400–1). However, some connections between the rules of Old English metre and those of the language itself, such as constraints on placement and alliterative precedence based on word-type, were defined long ago, and more recent approaches have sought to demonstrate these relationships more holistically: e.g., Donoghue, *Style in Old English Poetry*; Lucas, 'Some Aspects of the Interaction'; Russom, *Old English Meter*; Kendall, *Metrical Grammar of 'Beowulf'*; and Momma, *Composition*.

19 See Foley, 'Oral Theory in Context.'

20 Magoun ('Oral-Formulaic Character') and his school assumed that a high incidence of formulaic language indicated oral composition, but several opponents exposed the faulty reasoning involved, most decisively Benson ('Literary Character'). It is now generally agreed that the presence of formulaic language directly implies nothing about the medium of composition, nor does its presence in poems known to be fully literary undermine the association of such features with oral art earlier in the formation of the tradition.

consequent metrical features of Old English cause its poetic formulas paradigmatically to involve some shaping action in the individual instance, such as the selection of a key word to use within a metrisyntactic template that has enough other fixed components to be recognizable and useful as a traditional unit.[21]

A clear formula might consist, for example, of a shared stressed morpheme and several non-trivial grammatical, metrical, semantic, or other features repeated among instances, but also include a lexical variable (which I have been representing as *q*) to be selected according to the needs of the immediate context, most often providing the point of contact between the formula and the alliterative pattern of the line. To take an example of variability within pattern-sustaining constraints from the poetic descriptions of hail discussed above, *hwitust corna* and *corna caldast* have obvious differences, but they share a number of properties which in aggregate make them immediately recognizable as actualizations of a single underlying formal template, *corna q-st*, where *q-st* is an adjective inflected to the superlative degree. The variable word order is no obstacle here – either way the phrase scans Sx | Sx – so this formula unites a stable metrical profile, a stable lexical core, stable word-morphology, a stable grammatical relationship between elements, and a stable semantic function in figurative reference to hail.

The linguistically constrained formation of Old English poetic diction around the heavily stressed morpheme sustains other structures too, such as traditional collocations of certain words that repeatedly appear within a line together, bound by alliteration but not joining into a formulaic phrase and with no fixed grammatical relationship between them; or, beyond the alliterative reach of the single poetic line, groups of traditionally associated

21 The need for a more flexible concept of the poetic formula than that used for Greek had long been recognized (see Foley, *Theory of Oral Composition*, 69–72); Foley's innovation was to connect this apparent idiosyncrasy to properties of the language itself. Niles ('Formula and Formulaic System') shows that even what appear to be fixed formulas in Old English usually are not, because although they appear in the exact same form more than once, most are still products of formula systems other realizations of which are also attested. Thus – and this point cannot be emphasized strongly enough – one cannot interpret verbatim repetitions as fixed formulas without seeking negative evidence in the form of systemic affiliations. Those relatively few identifiable formulas that cannot be subsumed into attested systems may be true synchronic isolates, or they may be members of synchronic systems whose alternative realizations happen not to occur in the surviving record.

words that recurrently cluster together.[22] We have already seen these dictional patterns in the lexical association of the morphemes *hægl* and *scur*, which twice combine into a compound word, twice group into a phrase together, and once occur in adjacent lines (*Rune Poem*, ll. 25–6a) as if '[hægl] byþ hwitust corna' had created a likelihood that *scur* would crop up too, even if in slightly illogical reference to a different component of the meteorological event (the wind rather than the shower of hail itself).

Similar dictional flexibility also attends larger, concept-driven structural units, which in Old English do not rely upon specific recurrent phrases: complexes of conventional details and linked ideas will trigger corresponding webs of key words and phraseology that may coincide significantly from one instance to the next but may also vary a great deal, with no particular lexical component or combination amounting to a sine qua non.[23] Anyone familiar with the appropriate Old English poems can identify the Beasts of Battle motif, for example, and it is easy to follow Francis Magoun's lead in listing several of its characteristic elements, both conceptual and lexical;[24] yet despite its readily recognizable identity as a traditional poetic package, its actualizations do not have a very high correspondence of working to cue that recognition. Foley's work showed that such phraseological fluctuation in a given motif of this kind is a predictable part of its character as an Old English poetic unit.

In *Immanent Art*, his follow-up to *Traditional Oral Epic*, Foley moves from the 'what' to the 'how,' considering the type of communication traditional poetic structures bring about for audiences whose own experience within the poetic culture enables them to tune in to the transmission. He defines the 'traditional referentiality' of formulas and other conventional dictional structures as metonymic in nature, meaning that the individual traditional form evokes a field of associations generated by its iterations in similar contexts. While formulas and other traditional structures certainly assist oral poets in meeting the demands of composition ex tempore, Foley argues that their traditionality also bestows on these forms a unique aesthetic and semantic power, and that this is what accounts for their persistence in oral-derived written traditions like that of Old English. The

22 Foley, *Traditional Oral Epic*, 201–39.

23 These larger, concept-driven units' lack of dependence on particular recurrent dictional packages became clear very early in the history of their study in Old English: see Foley, *Theory of Oral Composition*, 68–9, and *Traditional Oral Epic*, 329–35. For Foley's illustrations of their dictional flexibility, see ibid., 339–42 and 354–8.

24 Magoun, 'Theme of the Beasts of Battle.'

structures of association they establish are cognitive and cultural categories according to which the poem's meaning is organized through the connection of the given episode, motif, phrase, or poetically marked word to larger bodies of implication, which a reader or hearer who is also proficient in the special idiom perceives quasi-instinctively.[25] Thus skilful traditional poets make meaning not in spite of the received structures and methods – succeeding even while shackled, as it were, by convention – but by means of them.

We have seen an example of this process in the *Genesis B* poet's substitution of a familiar parcel of weather diction (the *hægl* and *scur* collocation) in place of a less familiar one (the Old Saxon word *skion* has a counterpart in English but it does not participate in attested formulas or collocations), which along with the addition of *forst* for good measure could help make available to audiences the stereotyped situation of exile and vulnerability. The specific context is appropriate to this meaning, with Adam and Eve's disobedience of God's command and the substitution just a few lines before of *land* for *lioht* implying Adam's worry that he and Eve will not be allowed to remain in their homeland; but nothing in the weather language itself suggests this meaning except its familiar, institutionalized associations.

Foley's work on traditional referentiality theorizes a phenomenon that had been previously noticed from the standpoint of critical practice, but only in a more piecemeal fashion. Scholars of traditional Old English conceptual units, starting with Magoun and Stanley B. Greenfield, had seen the need to understand the individual instance in light of its participation in recurrent patterns extending beyond the single text.[26] With respect to more purely dictional structures, however, the necessity of this more capacious view, taking in more than the individual text to help in determining meaning, was less widely acknowledged although it had been asserted at times, as by Randolph Quirk in an early analysis of lexical collocations in Old English, and especially by Anita Riedinger in a brilliant essay on what she called 'thematic formulas' which anticipated with a narrower topical focus what Foley would soon posit more generally in *Immanent Art*.[27]

25 Foley, *Immanent Art*, e.g., 51 and 60.

26 Greenfield, 'Formulaic Expression,' esp. 205; Magoun, 'Theme of the Beasts of Battle,' makes one or two comments in passing that indicate the same recognition.

27 Quirk, 'Poetic Language'; Riedinger, 'Old English Formula in Context.' The germ of this way of thinking about the signification of formulaic language was present as early as 1955, again in Greenfield's work ('Formulaic Expression,' 205).

The principles involved do not seem to be controversial,[28] but on the whole, this line of thinking about small units of poetic diction in Old English has not had great impact on literary criticism. To say that traditional forms may project rich connotative fields based on their patterns of prior usage, and that this is intrinsically part of their signifying action in the minds of speakers and hearers who share the same competencies and experience-based frames of reference, is to say that they function much like individual words do in ordinary language: both are structures that connect, through convention and association, to concepts, implications, and functions that lie outside the range of any amount of analysis of their constituent parts. Foley treats the 'wordlike' signifying properties of traditional forms as a strong analogy, and as such it is helpful in illustrating traditional elements' claimed ability to surround themselves with connotational meaning deriving from poets' and readers' awareness of usage patterns extending beyond the single text.[29] But because it remains an analogy,[30] if offered as a basis for a proposed way of reading traditional forms it might well seem like an argumentative leap. Within the methodologies customarily available to the analysis of Old English texts there is no clear way to get beyond an assertion of likeness and present direct evidence that formulas work like lexemes.

In recent years, important developments in linguistics have revealed that the functional similarity of recognized multiword units and individual lexemes is more than an analogy: it is an organizational principle of language use itself, tied to the processing capabilities of the human brain and to the formation and architecture of linguistic competence. Working from a very different disciplinary perspective, and almost totally out of contact with modern work on formulaic poetics,[31] experimental, clinical,

---

28 In a context of approving reference to Foley, Trilling has recently gone so far as to call a metonymic hermeneutics 'the commonly accepted model of interpretation for Anglo-Saxon poetry' (*Aesthetics of Nostalgia*, 39).

29 See Foley, *Traditional Oral Epic*, 44–50; *Immanent Art*, 147–8 and 202; *Singer of Tales in Performance*, 23, 53, and 101; and *How to Read an Oral Poem*, esp. 11–19.

30 Even where Foley sums up this likeness of traditional forms to words with the dictum 'Oral poetry works just like language, only more so,' his explanations and examples stress the putative difference of oral(-derived) poetry from ordinary language (*How to Read an Oral Poem*, 127–8). The signifying operation of phrases such as those he points to as 'bigger words' is treated as specific to oral tradition.

31 Linguists often acknowledge the very early work of Parry and Lord as a precedent in recognizing formulaic language use, and Pawley ('Grammarians' Languages,' 17–19) reports that awareness of the Parry–Lord fieldwork was one stimulus to some of the first

and theoretical research on formulaic constructions in normal language has reached conclusions consistent with the position stated more intuitively by Foley in reference only to traditional poetic units. In the past decade linguists interested in formulaic phenomena have come to agree widely that a variety of structures treated by language-users as conventional units do indeed work like single words: even though they often can be analysed into smaller meaningful segments, they are not so analysed in practice if discursive context allows holistic, quasi-lexical interpretation.[32]

The most inclusive and powerful account of such 'formulaic sequences' thus far is Alison Wray's theory of their relationship to the individual language-user's lexicon.[33] Wray shows strong evidence, assembled from

---

investigations by linguists of formulaic constructions in other contexts. However, real discussion of possible relationships between formulaic poetry and non-poetic formulaic language has been rare (though see Kuiper and Haggo, 'Livestock Auctions'; Kuiper, 'Formulaic Performance'; and Wray, *Formulaic Language: Pushing the Boundaries*, 37–48), and I have found few signs of awareness among linguists that research on formulaic poetry has advanced at all since Parry and Lord. Pawley ('Grammarians' Languages'; cf. Pawley, 'Developments,' 5–14) and Lee ('Formulaic Language in Cultural Perspective,' 471–4) shed light on some of the trends or biases involved.

32 At present, the movement for corpus-based linguistics – which shuns the structuralist grammar/lexicon model and begins with semantics as the foundation of linguistic production, focusing on the patterned behaviour of individual words in the service of message and in the presence of collocates (see, e.g., Sinclair, *Corpus, Concordance, Collocation* and *Trust the Text*; Stubbs, *Words and Phrases*) – presents the main challenge to this school of thought, but the theoretical move granting formulaic sequences wordlike status does not inherently depend on the structuralist model. The semantic ecology that emerges from the study of collocations in large corpora can dovetail with emerging theories of formulaic language if corpus linguists will allow formulaic sequences to be regarded as units within interactions of selection and meaning – as words, essentially – rather than as instances of proximity of their constituent lemmas. Sinclair recognizes the necessity of multiword units 'occasionally' but sees them as problematic (*Trust the Text*, 197 n. 9; cf. *Corpus, Concordance, Collocation*, 110–15); Stubbs discusses 'extended lexical units' that include variability but is also quick to fall back on treating their connotational meaning as a feature of their components' individual semantic profiles conditioned by co-occurrence (*Words and Phrases*, e.g. 58–60, 222–3). The work of Wray (see next note), among others, shows the inadequacy of the corpus linguists' approach to conventional units.

33 Wray, *Formulaic Language and the Lexicon* and *Formulaic Language: Pushing the Boundaries*; see also Wray and Perkins, 'Functions,' and Wray, 'Identifying Formulaic Language.' When I refer to conventional dictional units as a class from the perspective of linguistics, I will use the term 'formulaic sequence' favoured by Wray and since adopted by others. This terminology allows the word 'formula' to retain for my purposes the special, more limited sense – as just one of several kinds of traditional

studies done under a wide range of methodologies, that the brain's lexicon is heteromorphic, storing not just words and combining morphemes but also larger, structured units whose component parts (if recognized by the language-user) are stored independently as well. As fundamental meaning-bearing units, known formulaic sequences have a status in an individual's lexicon no different from that of known words or other irreducible units of meaning or function. Discourse is processed in a large-to-small procedure according to 'needs-only analysis,' such that the reader or hearer first seeks the more economical, holistic interpretation of any recognizable unit and only works down to more processing-intensive analytical interpretation as required by the unsatisfactory resolution of meaning at higher levels of structure. So, for instance, to decode a statement like

> Back in the day, Mary Smith got her share of marriage proposals.

fluent speakers of American and some other dialects of English need not break down the phrase 'back in the day' to comprehend it. Indeed, because it is an idiom (one long-recognized type of formulaic sequence), we would comprehend it *less* well if something caused us to switch off our holistic processing and attempt to handle the phrase analytically, as a learner of English would have to do unless previously alerted to its idiomatic nature. With reference strictly to its constituent parts, even the basic meaning of the phrase is obscure (back in which day?), to say nothing of its implied rhetorical distancing of the present time and situation from some prior one, its connotation of nostalgia, the degree of intimacy or informality it may convey, and any other describable features of non-denotative, pragmatic meaning that come as part of its formulaic package.[34]

Not all formulaic language consists of fixed phrases, and in fact most formulaic sequences in natural language vary in one or more ways, often by including variables to be defined by the language-user's selection of lexical or phrasal elements to fit the situation and communicative needs. In these cases what is properly formulaic is the 'frame,' in Wray's terminology: a

---

forms – that it has acquired in the study of oral(-derived) poetry. Linguists do sometimes refer to all formulaic sequences as 'formulas' or 'formulae,' but sometimes they, too, give the simplex various special senses differing from that used in discussions of traditional poetics; see comments on terminology in Wray, *Formulaic Language and the Lexicon*, 8–10, and Schmitt and Carter, 'Formulaic Sequences in Action,' 3–4.

34 Pragmatics looks beyond strict denotation to include all aspects of meaning actualized between speaker and hearer in acts of communication.

template defined by whatever lexical components and grammatical relationships may be fixed, along with the slots designated for variables. As these formulaic frames are learned – and learned to be conventional – they enter the language-user's lexicon just as words and unvarying phrases do. The sample sentence given a moment ago contains a formulaic structure of this kind too. In the clause 'Mary Smith got her share of marriage proposals,' not only the subject, its corresponding pronoun, and the grammatical attributes of the finite verb must be supplied, but also the object of the preposition 'of' (let us call that object *q*). Unlike 'back in the day,' a plausible meaning for this clause can easily be construed from its components. But for fluent English speakers it normally has a somewhat different meaning that cannot be inferred by tackling the series of words analytically. Within discursive environments that do not rule it out in some way, its understated message, that Mary Smith got not 'the requisite number' of *q*s but actually 'more than enough' of them, is stable and intrinsic to whatever further communicative work this clause does: a sign that it is a formulaic sequence. That Mary Smith got 'more than enough' *q*s is its default denotation as a whole unit based on shared usage patterns within the experience of speaker and hearer.

For it to have this meaning, a language-user need only have this conventional unit in his or her repertoire and find it contextually possible to derive appropriate meaning from holistic processing of the sequence. Apart from reference to a certain person, the example statement I gave offers very little context – only the preceding 'back in the day' formulaic sequence and the embedded selection of *q* – but the informal, idiomatic style of the former and the chosen subject matter of the latter (*q* in this formulaic sequence tends to be culturally marked as something either especially sought after or especially to be avoided) reinforce or confirm the holistic option. A hearer may choose to go beyond this efficient interpretive process to a more analytical one for special reasons, but there is no need to do so in normal communication. Along with the denotation that is basic to the meaning of this formulaic sequence as a unit, it has pragmatic patterning in more fully contextualized usage: seeing formulaic sequences as quasi-lexical units allows them, like individual words, to exhibit what corpus linguists call 'semantic prosody,' 'a consistent aura of meaning with which a form is imbued by its collocates.'[35] In this case what gives the formulaic sequence its semantic

35 Quotation from Louw, 'Irony in the Text,' 157. Semantic prosody (also called 'discourse prosody') is a promising focal point of corpus-based semantic research.

prosody, which may best be summed up as wryness, whether jocular and congratulatory or disapproving, is the conventional constraint on *q* that assigns it to something either very desirable or very undesirable and thus tends to interact ironically with the sequence's institutionalized understatement. An arbitrary distribution of usage – the fact that certain applications seemingly allowable by the sequence's denotation, taken analytically rather than holistically, are almost always selected for and others against – is another sign of its conventionality; and that felt conventionality is all that is needed to further support the expression's holistic denotative value 'more than enough,' with all its pragmatic potential.

As long as no disjunction with satisfactory situational meaning is encountered, our first strategy as fluent hearers or readers will be to understand this clause as a whole, familiar unit carrying familiar connotations. Only if context does not support that strategy by producing acceptable sense within the discourse situation will we resort to slower and neurolinguistically more demanding analytic procedures. In a context of public distribution of food rations, for example, it might be recorded that

> On Monday, 19 October, Mary Smith got her share of turnips but did not receive any cheese.

Now the formulaic possibility will be instantly found irrelevant, if indeed it is entertained at all: contextual elements of the new version – such as the official-sounding specificity of date and time (by contrast to 'back in the day'), the mismatch of 'turnips' with the categories of referents that conventionally attach to the *q* slot, and the continuation of the clause in a manner that enforces its grounding in a very literal communicative context – might altogether preempt recognition of the potential for holistic processing by establishing discourse parameters other than those with which

---

Because it is rooted in measurable patterns of co-occurrence rather than 'fuzzy' speaker intuition, it has helped to legitimize connotation – once regarded as idiosyncratic, subjective, and thus peripheral to serious study of semantics – as an important and investigatable part of how people use linguistic resources to make meaning. See Sinclair, *Corpus, Concordance, Collocation*, esp. chap. 8; Sinclair, *Trust the Text*, esp. 122, 173–5, 131–48, and 196–8; Stubbs, 'Collocations and Semantic Profiles'; and Stubbs, *Words and Phrases*, esp. 65–6, 87–8, 105–8, and 197–218. Schmitt and Carter ('Formulaic Sequences in Action,' 7–9) precede me in applying the concept of semantic prosody to formulaic sequences considered as units. In such cases the relationship between a formulaic frame and an item selected to fill its *q* slot can function as a collocation, just like the patterned co-occurrence of two ordinary words.

its formulaic interpretation is compatible. Either way, meaning must now be constructed, built up from the composed clause's lexical and grammatical features, and the construction will not, cannot, express the semantic prosody that is proprietary to the formulaic usage.

Work in linguistics that addresses formulaic structures as a component of language in general has thus begun to delineate a larger theoretical environment within which the specifically poetic subset of formulas and other traditional structures can be evaluated and understood. This recontextualization allows Foley's analogy between traditional units and words to be upgraded to functional identity, without exceeding the mechanisms and processing strategies present in ordinary language use, and validates key elements of his theory of traditional referentiality as applied to Old English poetry. First, multiword units can and very often do stand as single components of the lexicon whose significance within a discursive context is attached to them holistically rather than generated anew in each instance by their construction from a set of analysable constituents. Second, the holistic identity of such conventional multiword structures exists because they are recognized in processing as conventional; it is their detection by language-users as new instances of familiar patterns that makes economical, holistic interpretation of them possible. Third, their holistic functionality does not depend on fully fixed form, but is compatible with lexical and other variations within formulaic frames that nevertheless retain their recognizability through the convergence of several other, stable attributes that define the conventional unit. Finally, analysis of the use of formulaic sequences in ordinary language shows clearly that the meaning they carry is not only denotational, but may involve complex connotation and implication which attaches to them *as* conventional units. It turns out that the 'value-added,' greater-than-literal signifying power that Foley had argued endows traditional poetic units with communicative nuance and efficiency is not only plausible, but certain, indeed normal.

Old English poetry's special diction can thus be drawn into more evident continuity with the pragmatic resources of language as a whole. Even within Anglo-Saxon studies it has been pointed out that the liberal use of formulaic constructions is not confined, as a compositional practice, either to verse or to the vernacular.[36] Now research in linguistics indicates that in

---

36 See Lapidge, 'Aldhelm's Latin Poetry,' and several works by Orchard: 'Crying Wolf'; *Poetic Art of Aldhelm*, esp. 119–25; 'Oral Tradition'; 'Old Sources, New Resources'; and 'Looking for an Echo.'

fact formulaic sequences are everywhere, much more frequent and essential to normal language use than previously imagined, and importantly, counterindicates any supposition that recognizing the connotational richness of those found in oral-derived poetry requires positing a whole separate way of making meaning unique to one special type of language. That affirmation of their normality, and with it the removal of theoretical barriers to acknowledging their metonymic operation, could come at a price, however, in seeming to deny traditional poetic language its allegedly unique character. So, if traditional forms within Old English poetry are a specialized expression of a phenomenon that typifies not just oral or oral-derived poetry but language itself, and if traditional referentiality is not necessarily dependent on oral tradition, where does that leave Old English poetry's putatively extraordinary charge of metonymic meaning?

It need not be nullified or even weakened, but it does need some redefining, and here, too, linguistic theory proves helpful. The power of traditional units in Old English poetry resides in the special register the poetry embodies, and which those units themselves play a major role in delineating.[37] As already suggested by the 'Mary Smith' example, much of the

37 I adopt 'register' as a technical term from the linguistic subdiscipline of discourse analysis, where it denotes a definable type of discourse produced through the systematic interaction of linguistic choices with situational context, and follow the classic model developed by M.A.K. Halliday beginning in the 1950s: see *The Essential Halliday*, ed. J. Webster, esp. chaps 3 and 20; also Biber, 'Analytical Framework,' and de Beaugrande, '"Register" in Discourse Studies.' Biber and Conrad ('Register Variation,' 175) demonstrate that although registers are normally defined situationally rather than linguistically (through the identification of parameters having to do with the social context and media of their production), they can be studied by examining clusters of grammatical and pragmatic features whose frequencies are register-sensitive.

Foley's *Singer of Tales in Performance* takes up the register of Old English poetry but depends on ideas about what oral-derivation implies that I do not believe are finally tenable. In Hallidayan terms, Foley's definition of the relevant register gives great weight to a 'field of discourse' (the setting or activity within which a language production has a function), namely, in his view, poetic performance, whereas I prefer to foreground a 'mode of discourse' (the channel or type of communication used), namely (written) poetry in the traditional style, because that is what is attested directly in the manuscript record. Foley's approach to register, indebted primarily to anthropological linguistics, works well in the study of living oral traditions, where the field of discourse (performance-of-orally-composed-poetry) and the mode of discourse (poetry-composed-in-oral-performance) coextend, such that neither has meaning outside of their conjunction and to observe one is to observe the other. But unless we are willing to claim that the Old English poetry we have was transcribed during composition-in-performance, then no matter how its mode of discourse originated, its written medium necessarily

work done by formulaic sequences falls within the purview of pragmatics and discourse analysis, which examine language as a behaviour of socially situated humans communicating with each other in order to achieve objectives.[38] The fullest meaning of many formulaic units will have much to do with pragmatic message (every element of the understanding that passes between speaker and hearer, including connotation and implication no less than forthright denotation and reference); and their operation within a social, situational context will be tightly bound to discourse-level goals and functions appropriate to the selected register. The register of polite conversation, for example, is replete with formulas of interaction that serve such purposes as easing social contact among parties who have limited prior acquaintance, meeting the expectations and gaining the approval of others, avoiding conflict with persons who may have competing interests, and so on. They are components in a system which, if successfully navigated by those producing and interpreting utterances, endows them with indispensible effectual 'meaning.' The formulas are inseparable from what the discourse containing them accomplishes, within the situational environment of their recognized register; their functions on the small scale complement the purpose of the whole verbal exchange at a larger scale and contribute directly to it through their messages such as (in this example) goodwill, pleasure in the interaction, and interest in others.

The same is true of more linguistically distinctive, definitively marked registers. Consider the language of a formal legal contract in Modern English, conspicuous for its specialized vocabulary, conventional use of syntactic patterns not often encountered in spoken language, and frequent reliance on dedicated large- and small-scale formulaic sequences. This register is so heavily marked as to be partially self-referential: its distinctive characteristics create a kind of feedback loop in which the text reminds readers continually that it is a legal document, and in so doing asserts the power of the law, with all the resources, linguistic and otherwise, that go with it, in order to impart a shared sense of enforceable obligation. A

---

dissociates mode from any putatively performative field. See Foley, *Singer of Tales in Performance*, chap. 3, esp. pp. 65–6 and 72–6.

38 If pragmatics is the study of how meaning is made and received in a specific context, discourse analysis is the study of how that meaning goes on to function socially within an interpersonal scenario of language use. This maps at least roughly onto the traditionality/traditionalism distinction I posit (see above, introduction, p. 31, and chap. 3 below): traditionality is part of a text's pragmatics; examination of traditionalism takes us into discourse analysis.

contract does its discursive job in part by referencing the tradition in which it participates through highly visible features that are understood to index that register: this is, in fact, a kind of 'traditional referentiality.' As it draws power from the legal tradition to aid in the achievement of its immediate purposes, a formal contract simultaneously falls in line with that tradition to sustain it and to shore up the authority of similar linguistic productions in the future. Here again, as with polite conversation, there is little point in trying to keep the work of the larger discourse segment separate from that of the formulaic phrases, sentences, and content-structuring frameworks that largely constitute it: the pragmatic and discursive 'meaning' of each can be analysed individually, of course, but it exists in cross-scale continuity with the whole. For uninitiated audiences, this register's conventional forms of expression may defeat diligent attempts at full comprehension, but for those with appropriate experience – including the development of not just linguistic but situational (i.e., legal) knowledge – those same structures amount to highly efficient packages of communication, a significant part of which takes place above and around denotative meaning and can work only by assuming a shared frame of reference in legal procedures and principles.[39]

Much like the legal register, the special register of traditional Old English poetry is marked by several objective features in combination, including the constraints of classical metre with its clear alliterative groupings, particular recurrent subject matter,[40] and the presence of dedicated vocabulary, some of it with very pronounced semantic prosody. It is likewise characterized by dictional patterns, including a high density of formulas and other traditional units. Some of its conventional diction is shared with prose, to be sure: Old English poetry is a subset of Old English, and the resources it draws on are linguistic resources, not exclusively poetic ones. But many of its traditional forms are unique to that register. That being the case, the poetic idiom will predictably be 'esoteric' in the linguistic sense, which is to say, characterized by a high intensity of inexplicit, inferred meaning that depends on a grasp of its conventions of

39 On the importance of situational knowledge (which includes subject-matter knowledge) to the production of appropriate formulaic language, see Kuiper, 'Formulaic Performance,' esp. 43–4, 48–9, and 51–2, and Pawley, 'How to Talk Cricket.'

40 For Halliday the subject matter itself is part of the field of discourse: not every imaginable thing can be said within a given register, because the range of eligible subject matter is part of the situation being negotiated by means of the language selections made from the set of all possible choices.

usage. The inexplicit aspects of a given text will be accessible to insider audiences through experience they have gained with that register in the past, on the basis of which they will have added many of its conventional units to their individual lexicons – and hence, pragmatically, to their interpretive repertoires – so that in processing they can grasp, as if intuitively but actually through the recognition of patterns they have internalized, the aura of implication surrounding what is said. Any language production in an esoteric register of this kind is, by its nature, dependent on shared frames of reference and a basis of similar experience; through these the individual utterance helps to cement bonds of shared knowledge and community among speakers and hearers, writers and readers while continually affirming, and making use of, values traditional to that register.

The important point is that because register-specific formulaic language is connected to what discourse in that register needs to achieve, then whatever we believe Old English poetry does, its register-specific features will necessarily help it do: the language choices typical of this mode of discourse cannot be separated from fulfilment of its communicative and social purposes. As with formulaic language in any register, the traditional diction of Old English poetry will thus convey several types of meaning and carry out communicative and interactive functions which (like ordinary words in their real contexts of use) go well beyond semantic denotation or reference. It will be intrinsic to whatever the business is of classical Old English poetry, as a culturally specific linguistic register, not just because it occurs within an Old English poem, but crucially, because it plays an essential role in making one.

As a register-specific phenomenon, then, viewed from the perspective of discourse analysis, traditional Old English poetic diction can be expected to do several things. It will ease processing, both in production and in interpretation, for anyone who has sufficiently internalized its patterns of usage to become sensitive to its pragmatic and discourse-functional properties. It will help to maintain and reinforce the poetic register as the discursive habitat of particular transmitted messages. Its high intensity of register-marking features will produce a kind of reflexive functionality by which a given text asserts itself as traditional poetry, claiming its oneness with that heritage and assuming whatever cultural authority goes along with it: part of what traditional forms reference is tradition itself. Conventional units of language will have social and interactive functions, predicated on that authority and on the poetry's special status as a pleasurable discursive venue for the affirmation and exploration of culturally defined values. And as a constitutive part of a communicative medium, much of an Old English poem's formulaic language will signify metonymically, involving itself with the text's pragmatic conveyance of stories and situations in the fullness of their narrative, ethical, and aesthetic dimensions. If it did not, those communicative purposes could hardly be achieved, given the density of formulaic language in this register.[41] In this and other specialized registers, what unites traditional forms across their many purposes is efficiency: ease of production, for speakers and writers who need to convey complex meanings or fulfil intricate social and linguistic tasks, and the availability to fluent audiences of an immediate, quasi-intuitive grasp of that nuanced message or situational purpose.

The question before us has been whether it is justifiable to attribute specific connotative meaning to a traditional dictional unit, based on that unit's patterns of usage, without relying on a larger-scale conceptual motif, like the imagery of harsh weather in its association with human destitution that we have seen introduced into *Genesis B*. That is to say, can a formula or other unit of diction have a semantically rich functional identity of its own without being subordinated to a particular unit of content that is seen as the primary, definable traditional entity? As it happens, that question is largely answered as soon as we have recognized the diction as markedly traditional, because contemporary linguistics tells us that part of the regular pragmatic and discursive work of patterned, formulaic language is the institutionalization of connotative meaning. When the affiliations of the individual instance with other instances are clear and consistent, what we know about conventional language in general combines with what we know of the register-specific properties of Old English poetry to warrant seeing the unit in question as an economically compressed package of implication that acts upon and within the particular context for readers who have appropriate experience with that tradition. When a small-scale dictional element can be shown to have an active traditional life in Old English poetic expression, indicated by consistent alignments of usage and especially when that usage seems arbitrarily constrained in some way,

41 This does not mean that every instance of traditional diction has to be richly and metonymically significant, at a pragmatic level of meaning-making, any more than it is the case that all vocabulary items in a language must carry intense semantic prosody in their contextual use. One thing the linguistic study of formulaic sequences is very clear on is variety of function. Foley too notes in *Immanent Art* (e.g., 21–2) that there is a natural spectrum of intensity of metonymic meaning for different instances of traditional diction, with some being highly significant denotationally and connotationally while others perform more general functions of marking and maintaining the traditional idiom.

there is no reason to doubt that its *in*vocation *e*vokes whatever cognitive record exists of its previous contexts and instances, within the individual reader's or hearer's experience, to make its field of meaning available through that individual's associative reflex.

Another name for that combination of experience with associative reflex is pattern recognition, which is foundational to all aspects of human culture, including the use of language; and when pattern recognition prompts recurrence of voluntary behaviour in response, we are dealing with tradition as recently defined by Michael Drout. Drout's meme-based cultural theory of tradition, including traditions of style in verbal art whether oral or written, reminds us that systematic strategies for making and interpreting meaning, such as the inference of larger patterns from smaller or only partially expressed ones, are but one class – albeit a fundamentally important one – of traditional behaviour more broadly.[42] Emphasis on recurrent behaviour as an essential component of tradition has the effect of reconceptualizing traditional referentiality as a form of pattern recognition and reproduction that can perpetuate cycles of metonymic meaning: poets familiar with the register shape elements of poems in ways resembling previously experienced analogues strongly enough that initated readers or hearers will respond by understanding them through a complementary act of pattern recognition and reproduction.[43] Provided that a certain complex of associations exists within a given reader's familiarity, if even part of it occurs in a favourable environment the stated element can trigger pattern recognition, cuing him or her to supply other elements cognitively and thus saturate the present instance with connotation. The ability of discourse in a heavily marked register to generate a feedback loop of self-referentiality, whereby the tradition itself is continually renewed and reinforced, sustains the constituent patterns

42 Drout, *How Tradition Works*. Drout's work could fruitfully be linked, too, to that of linguists on formulaic language use, and at a deeper level, to all language use, particularly through a usage-based theory of grammar (that is, a theory positing that grammar is 'the cognitive organization of one's experience with language'), such as that applied to formulaic language by Bybee ('From Usage to Grammar'; quotation from 711). See also Corrigan et al., 'Introduction,' xxiii–xxiv, stressing that language itself is one of many pattern-driven human behaviours and, as such, requires processing that can handle whole-to-part relations.

43 See Drout's accommodation of Foley's concept of traditional referentiality in his larger theory of patterning and response (*How Tradition Works*, esp. 40–2 and 170–7).

powerfully and enhances their likelihood of continuing to be reproduced in some form within future contexts that include appropriate elements.[44]

Nevertheless, even the most traditional poets are socially formed and historically situated agents, making choices of which they have infinitely varying but often high levels of consciousness. While it is at times convenient to speak of 'tradition' as an abstraction, it does not exist independently of its expression through human action: any tradition is constituted by the totality of its enactments, and for any individual, it is constituted by its enactments within his or her own experience, indirect awareness through others of such enactments, and beliefs (accurate or not) about what has been done in the past.[45] Bearing these points in mind can keep our own thought about tradition tethered both to the material and social environment in which it exists and to the essential ingredient of personal experience, which provides and limits the strategies available to individuals and which conditions the preferences that guide their own activity.[46]

While traditional behaviour (including choices made by writers working within a recognized style or register) can feel natural and go unexamined by practitioners, it is also possible for agents of tradition to interact with received patterns in a deliberate fashion, using them to some further purpose while sharing in them or introducing changes in the process of recycling them.[47] Both ways of working within tradition are real and both matter greatly in the study of Old English poetry. Considerations of agency in relation to tradition are one way of addressing the last of the three questions about poetic tradition raised at the start of this discussion: *why*

44 In Drout's analysis of cycles of tradition, this process is part of the drift of the 'Universal Tradition Meme' – which answers the implicit question of why a pattern should be enacted again with a hard-to-gainsay 'Because we have always done so' – toward the 'Unconscious Imperative,' the most preemptive form of justification for traditional behaviour in the sense that the question 'why?' has at that point become totally submerged and the action habitual.

45 See Drout, *How Tradition Works*, esp. 30–8.

46 Drout's materialist orientation to traditional processes usefully avoids implying that the 'whole' tradition is continuously 'out there' somewhere, thus keeping in plain sight the reliance of traditionality on the things that individual humans know and do, singly or in groups, at discrete moments. For Drout, repeated actions – existing in a conceptual system that includes cognizance of those actions as a response to particular conditions as well as their understood justifications – *are* the tradition, connected from one iteration to the next by human memory (often aided by technologies such as writing).

47 On 'strong tradition-bearers,' who shape and reshape traditional verbal art through active engagement with it in the course of transmission, see Niles, *Homo Narrans*.

traditional poetic style may be called upon. To move through the 'how' to the 'why' of tradition is to move from traditionality to traditionalism. That move will for the most part be deferred until chapter 3, but the simple fact of active personal agency within tradition will have a role in the present chapter's analysis of *Genesis B*, and I will return in good time to the nature of its translator's traditional agency.

For now it is important that we avoid any assumption of inherent conflict between formulaic language and structures, on the one hand, and meaningful poetic expression on the other: a modern prejudice which besides being anachronistic proceeds from a false dichotomy.[48] If formulaic sequences are processed cognitively as wordlike entities, then in principle they have the same capacity for nuanced and creative deployment as do lexemes themselves. This may take the form of adept evocation and use of the institutionalized values and relationships they bring into view, or else the manipulation of traditional units in unconventional ways, working in dialogue with anticipated audience expectations; and as always, much aesthetic and rhetorical impact proceeds from a given element's interaction with its immediate context of other conceptual and linguistic choices. It would never occur to us to worry that the entire English language is condemned to artlessness by the fact that the words we use come to us laden with meanings and affinities that we as individual speakers and writers did not invent. On the contrary, we understand those semantic constraints, the complexities of received denotation and connotation to which our linguistic experience gives us access, to be the very substance from which we fashion any verbal art. Likewise, there is no reason to suppose that the presence of formulaic language, even in high density, indicates against the active use of those traditional resources in the service of desired meaning in a present context. The traditionality of the idiom in itself places no

48 There are really two dichotomies at work, 'formulaic' versus 'novel' and 'formulaic' versus 'creative.' Literary critics sometimes still entertain the 'formulaic' versus 'creative' dichotomy – in the plain-English, artistic sense of 'creative' – but the skilful and creative poets of any age are those who most adeptly manage the interface of form, function, and content, and this is no less true when the formal features include a full complement of conventional structures, such as formulas, than at any other time in literary history. Linguists have a more restricted and less value-laden usage of the term 'creative,' which is interchangeable with 'novel' in the discipline-specific sense of 'newly generated' and which they axiomatically oppose to that which is 'formulaic.' But serious objections even to this dichotomy can be raised: with my comments in the remainder of this paragraph, cf. Wray, *Formulaic Language: Pushing the Boundaries*, 21 n. 2 and 33–4.

special burden on the poet: any constraints that inhere in it are only the flip side of resources that skilful hands may manage for chosen effects.

That same traditionality of the idiom does, however, put a special burden on us as readers. Knowledge of the connotations and associations that a particular selection of Modern English words will summon feels natural to highly competent speakers and hearers of this language, and the same was no doubt true for Anglo-Saxons generating and interpreting utterances in their own vernacular; but present-day readers of Old English, reaching across a millennium of linguistic and cultural change, must painstakingly reconstruct connotation, taking account if possible of many attested instances of a word's real usage. Only by that means can we become sensitive to the nuances of its application on a given occasion. Because of the wordlike nature of formulaic sequences, no different is the necessity of paying attention to the real patterns of usage attaching to a formula or other traditional dictional form, as fully as careful use of the record will allow, in order to determine its semantic and functional qualities.[49] The corpus of Old English poetry is neither comprehensive nor uniform and must be analysed with intelligence, but it contains the best evidence we will ever have of usage in that register. If we fail to use the information it provides about the pragmatic behaviour of traditional dictional units, just as we do for individual words, we are only guessing.

Genesis B and the Making of Old English Verse

The foregoing discussion has been a long preamble of a tale, but the issues it covers are methodologically fundamental to the interpretation of dictional features like those that differentiate *Genesis B* from its source. Previous study of the parallel section has been hampered by the English poem's affiliation with the Saxon *Genesis*. Those scholars who have dealt with this material at all have usually regarded *Genesis B* as the nearest thing to an exact cross-dialectal reproduction, even a 'transcription' into English, that the translator was able to achieve.[50] The infelicity of that view lies not in the proposition in itself – a reasonable enough starting point for analysis given the exceptional closeness of rendering that is plainly evident – but in

49 Cf. M. Irvine, 'Medieval Textuality,' 199.

50 The only exception of which I am aware among focused comparisons of *Genesis B* with the Saxon *Genesis* is Jager, 'Word in the "Breost."' Jager's point is confined to the translator's use of the word *breost* and will be addressed in my discussion of the relevant line below.

two corollaries that it has been taken to imply, neither of them necessary and both unhelpful in addressing certain textual facts: first, that whatever differences do exist between the two texts must have been forced in a fully deterministic way (that is, with no compositional agency involved except of the most 'automatic' or 'mechanical' kind); and second, that any attempt to analyse what the Anglo-Saxon writer might actively have been doing at those points of difference, as the maker of an English poem, would therefore not repay the effort.[51]

One practical objection to approaching *Genesis B*'s relationship to its source through these assumptions is that sometimes there is poor agreement among scholars on the nature or even the existence of the problem that is supposed to have prompted a given modification: if the translator's production of the English text was really as mechanical as is often thought, it is curious how elusive the provoking factors have proved to be as we work backward from observed alterations. Thus, for example, in reference to the shift from a cloud of hail to shower of hail that has been discussed above, it is tempting to suggest, as an impetus to the rewording, the unavailability of a cognate to Old Saxon *skion* because the attested Old English cognate (*sceo*) is found only once in the corpus.[52] That singularity of occurrence is tantalizing if the change must be explained in terms of simple causality on the presumption that it would have happened only if the translator could not avoid it, but there is a world of difference between zero attestations of a word and one attestation. If we, now, know the word *sceo*, and know it because we find it in another poem whose vocabulary is not especially strange or arcane, is it not incalculably more likely that the Anglo-Saxon translator knew it too? Differential awareness of uncommon lexemes by producers of texts is very possible, and commentators on *Genesis B* are not the only ones to resort to it as an explanation of textual change, but argumentative reliance on the hypothesis of a native writer's unfamiliarity with a word that is documented in our limited record of the Old English language is surely an undesirable position to find oneself in. In discussing each of the three denotative changes analysed below I will summarize the explanations that have previously been offered for it. My own opinion is that in each instance the translator did encounter some sort of complication or obstacle, a bump in the road, that stimulated a

---

51 The words placed in quotation marks in this paragraph are all among Doane's characterizations (*Saxon Genesis*, passim), but they represent a commonly held view of *Genesis B*.

52 Riddle 3, l. 41b. Doane suggests that OE *sceo* was 'perhaps ... unknown to the transcriber' (*Saxon Genesis*, 305).

temporary shift to freer adaptation. However, in each case the problem was probably superable through more conservative means than those chosen.

Regardless of the reasons for initiating change at a given point, it is not enough then to regard the text at that point as merely unlike the source, as if the bare fact of difference told us all we need to know. Once the translator made the choice to deviate or felt compelled to do so, the text still had to arrive at some positive form; it is that form in which any early audience of the poem as we now have it would have encountered it as well; and the writer's selection of that new form therefore warrants consideration as a compositional act. The fact that the poet added new elements of meaning each time rather than taking another course (such as rearrangement or synonym substitution), and the kinds of preferences that appear to have caused some options to be favoured over others, can reveal much about his or her priorities. I see the traditionality of Old English poetic diction as an inherently attractive force for the translator: this is the explanation that best combines simplicity with plausibility in the cases to be examined now, just as in the two already considered. But having noticed the traditional character of the altered language, we still need to find out what the new wording is likely to have brought to that textual environment for an audience of Old English poetry. Each of the three denotative changes discussed below not only shows gravitation to attested units of Old English traditional diction, but also finds the English poet introducing or developing some dimension of subjectivity, and doing so in ways inseparable from employment of the marked poetic idiom.

Making Genesis B, Lines 792b–3a, from the Saxon Genesis, Lines 2b–3a

The first denotational difference comes near the beginning of the overlap between the poems. In an earlier part of *Genesis B* – and we must assume in the Saxon *Genesis* as well, given the length of the earlier passage and the tight correspondence between the texts where we can compare them – Eve had temporarily enjoyed a vision of heaven after eating the forbidden fruit.[53] Now Adam declares to her an exact reversal of this earlier vision, whether his statement is to be taken literally or metaphorically:[54]

53 *Genesis B*, ll. 599ff. T.D. Hill, 'Pilate's Visionary Wife,' argues that Eve's vision in *Genesis B* derives from an episode in *Heliand*. Hill mentions that *Genesis B* is a translation of an Old Saxon poem (174) but does not take account of what a close rendering it is where comparison is possible. The limited evidence gives no basis for belief that the Anglo-Saxon poet made the large addition of content that Hill suggests.

54 Cf. Doane, *Saxon Genesis*, 300; Stévanovitch, *Genèse du manuscrit Junius XI*, 2:734.

Nu maht thu sehan thia suarton hell
ginon grâdaga. (Saxon *Genesis*, ll. 2b–3a)

[Now you can see dark hell gape, greedy.]

Gesyhst þu nu þa sweartan helle
grædige and gifre. (*Genesis B*, ll. 792b–3a)

[Now you see dark hell, greedy and insatiable.]

In his edition of *Genesis B*, B.J. Timmer takes this clause as a question, presumably on the basis of its altered syntax which deletes the auxiliary and places the now-finite main verb in first position.[55] Verb-initial word order need not signal a question in Old English, however, and the balance of evidence in Mary Blockley's study of clauses like this one, while not justifying certainty, gives no reason to suppose that the English writer meant to effect a change from the source's statement to a question.[56] The syntactic adjustment is part of *Genesis B*'s usual shortening of longer verses in the Saxon text and may function for emphasis in what is in any case a pointedly ironic observation of the transformation of what Eve can 'see,' recalling her prior, diabolically induced vision of heaven.

More important than the rewording of the first verse, which brings about no real denotational change, is the substitution in the next verse of the adjectival doublet 'greedy and insatiable' for the infinitive + adjective 'gape, greedy.' It would not have been difficult for the English writer to retain the wording of the original. Timmer, Lewis, and Doane all note the existence of the Old English verb *ginian*, equivalent to Old Saxon *ginon*, and point out that rather than using it to reproduce the verse found in the source the translator opts for a formula attested elsewhere in Old English.[57] Because both the existence of change and the outcome of change can be informative, there are two separate matters to consider here: the avoidance of an available cognate verb in Old English and the adoption of a familiar formula in its place.

55 *Later Genesis*, 49.

56 *Aspects of Old English Poetic Syntax*, 19–46, 215–16. More generally on verb-initial declarative sentences, see Mitchell, *Old English Syntax*, esp. §§1645 and 3930–3.

57 Timmer, *Later Genesis*, 49; Lewis, 'Metre of *Genesis B*,' 69; Doane, *Saxon Genesis*, 58. The English verb can present either Class I or Class II weak morphology and is cited variously by commentators; I select the Class II form *ginian* to match the source text's *ginon*.

On the first point, all three commentators just cited remark that Old English *ginian* is a prosaic word and seem satisfied that this distributional fact explains the poet's rejection of it.[58] It is a well-known fact of Old English usage that in addition to the large stock of words eligible for indiscriminate use in both verse and prose, certain words are found exclusively, or nearly exclusively, in verse and others are found exclusively, or nearly exclusively, in prose. However, it is also known that neither group's boundaries are impenetrable: hence the need for the qualifier 'nearly' in describing a non-trivial proportion of both the poetic and prosaic sets of lexemes.[59] Certainly we can expect the prosaic nature of Old English *ginian* to have been a factor in the translator's choice, but another factor, also known to have guided the maker of *Genesis B* – his or her amply demonstrated wish to keep the wording as close to that of the Saxon source as possible – pointed in the opposite direction and might very well have counteracted the norms of *ginian*'s usage. After all, there was nothing to prohibit the translator from using the prosaic English cognate, no diction police on the lookout for contaminators of the poetic lexicon. Confirmation that acceptance of *ginian* was available as a serious option is found in this poet's practice elsewhere: while *Genesis B* is not extreme in its permissiveness toward prosaic words, it does include a somewhat higher incidence of them than many other Old English poems (and we will see one example below).[60] So while the prosaic marking of *ginian* may have been a factor, it cannot have been an automatically decisive one. A choice was made and it went against the inertial tendency of very literal translation.

Recognizing this fact of writerly agency sets up a more positive (and accurate) framework of analysis than does viewing the translator's procedures

58 Doane adds that the poet may have been 'concerned ... to avoid a stressed infinitive, which would change the metrical complexion of the line' because 'in OS the infinitive is not stressed' (*Saxon Genesis*, 57). However, adjectives in Old English verse are stressed just like infinitives, so the poet's substitution of *gifre* creates the same prosodical complications as a stressed *ginian*.

59 Stanley, 'Studies in the Prosaic Vocabulary'; Frank, 'Poetic Words in Late Old English Prose.' It is not clear whether, from the standpoint of compositional practice, poetic and mostly-poetic words were perceived as separate categories (and likewise prosaic and mostly-prosaic words), or whether the felt propriety was simpler – poetic versus prosaic – with 'seepage' of prose words into verse and verse words into prose being an occasional phenomenon that we observe for some words and not others due to accidental distribution in a limited record.

60 Approximate incidence is easy to calculate using the lengths of poems and the number of prosaic words in each one as listed in Stanley, 'Studies in the Prosaic Vocabulary.'

as mechanical. Insofar as the English poet's aversion to *ginian* had to do with its prosaic character, the relevant constraint was not – to be precise – the conventional prosaic/poetic tagging of vocabulary, but the desire to observe that tagging: the wish, with respect to diction and at that moment, to write in a traditional way. That desire was strong enough here to overcome the competing desire, also strong and at times sufficient to admit prosaic vocabulary, to transpose the text from one dialect to the other with minimal lexical intervention. By choosing to avoid a prosaic word rather than following the path of least resistance, the translator makes an affirmative statement in favour of traditionality in his or her craft.

The same affirmation inheres in the choice to substitute a familiar parcel of traditional diction, and since prosaic words are used elsewhere in the text, independent attraction to it seems to have made the difference in this case. The resonance of the new language introduced by the translator can be understood by analysing both the traditional co-occurrence of the words *grædig* and *gifre* (which appear together as a reversible formula or in a metrically flexible collocation) and by study of the added word *gifre* itself, which turns out to have a traditional identity of its own as a lexeme whose semantic prosody overlaps with but is independent of its usage in tandem with *grædig*. These two avenues together allow a full appreciation of the change in pragmatic meaning effected by the translator's choice here. I will begin with the traditional conjunction of the words *grædig* and *gifre* and then move to the marked poetic usage of *gifre* by itself, with which the formulaic usage dovetails in this passage.

Grædig and gifre or *gifre and grædig*, a whole-verse formula, is found six times outside of *Genesis B*, always in the a-verse of the line (in keeping with the classical prohibition of double alliteration in the b-verse). In another Junius 11 poem, *Christ and Satan*, it has the same form it takes here. The other five times the adjectives are in the opposite order:[61] once more in the Junius manuscript (*Christ and Satan*, l. 191a), once in the Vercelli Book (*Soul and Body I*, l. 74a), and three times in the Exeter Book (*Soul and Body II*, l. 69a, *The Seafarer*, l. 62a, and inflected to the superlative degree in riddle 84, l. 30a).[62] Besides these instances of the formula strictly

61 Acker (*Revising Oral Theory*, esp. chap. 1) shows 'syndetic' formulas like this one (i.e., consisting of two main words, both the same part of speech, connected by a conjunction or other semantically light element) often to be reversible.

62 The basic metrical contour of this formula, regardless of the order of the adjectives, is Sx | (x)Sx. The inflection of *gifre* never causes it to deviate from the shape Sx. Inflection of *grædig* without syncope would give it the shape Sxx, resulting in the verse form Sxx |

defined as such, two other times in the Exeter Book the words *grædig* and *gifre* appear in an alliterating collocation (*Guthlac A*, l. 738a; *The Phoenix*, l. 507). I will discuss these alongside the formula, because in this case both traditional constructions are found to function the same way.[63]

This formula, together with the supporting collocation, is abundantly enough represented that it is possible to define a field of associations which the pairing of *gifre* with *grædig* can bring with it into new realizations. The two occurrences in *Christ and Satan* apply it to the rebel angels collectively, both times in passages that reference their fall from heaven, and use the phrase to describe the insatiable desire that drove them to strive with God. The appearance of the formula here in *Genesis B* thus aligns topically with both of those other Junius 11 uses, but this time figuring hell itself, not its denizens, as a diabolical entity of limitless appetite: both the Saxon poet and the English translator almost certainly intended for their audiences to visualize hellmouth, the iconographic portrayal of hell as a great demonic monster gulping down the damned.[64] In three of its occurrences outside of that manuscript the formulaic or collocational pairing of *gifre* with *grædig* describes other forces of inexorable, elemental destruction: the apocalyptic fires that will devour all earthly wealth in *The Phoenix*, and death and decomposition, embodied in the *moldwyrmas* 'earthworms' that will consume human flesh, in both *Soul and Body I* and *II*. The elemental connection, with the explicit threat of destructive force, is present too in riddle 84, which by turns describes water's benefits and its extreme (and dangerous) power: the lines evoke an image of a rushing torrent, water at its 'fromast ond swiþost, / gifrost ond grædgost' [strongest and most powerful, most insatiable and most ravenous] (ll. 29b–30a).

The occurrences of this traditional language in *Guthlac A* and *The Seafarer* differ from the others in tone, but in common with the other members of the set, both of these poems still use the phrasing to describe

---

(x)Sx or Sx | (x)Sxx depending on word order, but orthography in two instances (*grædge*, *grædgost*) indicates syncope and retention of the metrical pattern Sx | (x)Sx at least in those cases.

63 See Acker, *Revising Oral Theory*, chap. 1, on the tendency of elements of a syndetic formula also to join as a non-formulaic alliterating collocation. In some cases these less rigid entities appear as extensions outward from received formulas and in other cases have an independent traditional existence with which the stricter formulas interact.

64 Doane believes the image of hellmouth motivated only the Saxon poet and is stripped away by the English one (*Saxon Genesis*, 57–8), but the ready-made associations of *grædige and gifre* with an insatiable drive to consume (discussed below) seem rather to reinforce the reference.

consuming entities beyond the reach of rational governance. Both apply the dictional unit to hungry birds whose nature it is to search endlessly for food, literally in *Guthlac A* and metaphorically in *The Seafarer*. When wild birds leave off their agitated seeking and flock peacefully to St Guthlac, their tameness is miraculous, and the use of the traditional collocation foregrounds the contrast of their 'grædum gifre' [greedily ravenous] nature with their narrated actions. In *The Seafarer*, the formula most interestingly refers to the speaker's quasi-avian *hyge* 'mind, thought,' an *anfloga* 'solitary flier,' after it 'ofer hwæles eþel hweorfeð wide, / eorþan sceatas' [wheels about widely over the whale's country, the regions of the earth] (ll. 60–1a) and returns to him, now impelling him to set out on the sea driven by a strange yearning to try its hardships.[65]

Despite its denotational attachment to subjective states familiar to humans, the *gifre and grædig* formula and collocation are never connected directly to the consciousness of a human being. This bias in usage, totally arbitrary from a semantic standpoint, confirms that the combination has a traditional pragmatic dimension; it is not a bundle of words to drop into any context that would be acceptable with respect to the ordinary meaning of its constituent parts, but a marked unit of poetic language with a particular field of reference. This restricted usage must also have made its application to a semi-autonomous or non-volitional faculty of the mind in *The Seafarer* striking to an early audience and added to the sense of dissociation in that poem between the reflecting, analysing speaker and the acts and urges of his freely roving, zoomorphic *hyge*.[66] The figurative leanings of this word-pairing, too, are part of its semantic prosody as a traditional form. Taken analytically, it could indicate intense insatiable hunger, but in only three of its eight occurrences does the physical sensation of craving food have any connection at all to what the phrase actually describes, and even in two of those three, the associations of horrific,

65 In the seminal discussion of the mind-as-bird passage, Clemoes ('*Mens absentia cogitans*') identifies the *Seafarer* poet's probable source of these lines' concept and imagery in Alcuin's *De animae ratione liber*. The use of the *gifre and grædig* formula, which Clemoes notices in passing (70 and n. 1), suggests a convergence in *The Seafarer* of Alcuin's imagery with a traditional way of describing the insatiability of natural forces and entities.

66 Godden ('Anglo-Saxons on the Mind') first argued that Old English poetry implies a theory of the mind as non-monolithic, with some of its parts or operations not always available to conscious apprehension. Godden discusses this aspect of *The Seafarer* on pp. 293–5, distinguishing its concepts somewhat from those of the probable Alcuinian source.

animate-yet-elemental consuming violence seem primary: the *moldwyrmas* in the two versions of *Soul and Body* are the perpetually devouring mouths of the very earth, irresistible assailants of corporal integrity, as much as they are living creatures. What the *gifre/grædig* unit evokes is more a disposition than a bodily sensation, a drive to seek out and consume experienced by an agent that is more often figuratively than literally ravenous: devils, hell, fire, water, even the desiring mind with its tenuous connection to rational guidance.

In all of its contexts, this parcel of traditional diction implies a pair of contrasting subjective positions, making its work ethical as well as attributive. One, directly described as irrationally *gifre* and *grædig*, belongs to boundlessly craving diabolical, wild, or elemental entities whose nature is to be indifferent at best to any desire to control or avoid them. The other is an observing, evaluating perspective on whatever is disturbingly *gifre* and *grædig*, a human perspective or one with whose interests humans (including those who read the poems) are presumed to identify: God, St Guthlac, the conscious self, or 'us' in general. Intrinsic to this dictional unit's usage is tension between a normative, rational perspective and that which is ungoverned. The opportunistic replacement in *Genesis B* of a prosaic verb with the adjective *gifre*, taking advantage of the word *grædig* brought over from the source, metonymically evokes this adversarial structural relationship between two sets of interests and the corresponding field of associative meaning.

The translator's use of a formula of non-human subjectivity in place of a description centred on a physical action (gaping open) enhances in several related ways the traditional character of the verse within an English context, including gravitation toward mental attribution. The change in the structure of the clause matters here. The Saxon text emphasizes what Eve sees; the English one finishes more quickly with that and puts greater syntactic and lexical stress on the nature of hell, as can be known only through poetic access to that figurative entity's subjective quality of insatiability. Both the Saxon writer and the English one metaphorically animate hell when they imagine it as a devouring mouth, but the English writer's altered presentation also puts its concrete power into static antithetical relation to human interests. The Saxon poem tells us visually what hell does; the English one tells us existentially what hell is, defining it imaginatively through Adam's perception of its subjective orientation as a menace to his and Eve's needs and desires. The traditional diction used here goes beyond describing an observed hell to assimilate it to a known category as an irrational consuming force, its relationship to humankind well and efficiently defined through the familiar joint usage of *grædig* and *gifre*.

Apart from its participation in the *grædig/gifre* combination, the simplex *gifre* has its own poetic traditionality and semantic prosody through its involvement in repeated conceptual and (subordinately) lexical clusters. Seeing their pertinence to *Genesis B* requires a slightly fuller view of the context of its occurrence there:

Hwæt, þu Eue, hæfst yfele gemearcod
uncer sylfra **SIÐ**. Gesyhst þu nu þa **SWEARTAN HELLE**
GRÆDIGE and **GIFRE**; nu þu hie grimman meaht
heonane gehyran. Nis heofonrice
gelic þam **LIGE**. (*Genesis B*, ll. 791–5a)

[Truly, Eve, you have evilly determined our fate. Now you see dark hell, greedy and insatiable; now you can hear it rage from here. The kingdom of heaven is not like that fire.]

Words presented in bold small capitals are those that will recur in passages to be cited in the next pages.[67] The concepts they represent are where the traditional action is, more than those words themselves, but concept clustering will sometimes lead to lexical overlap. Displaying the words shared between *gifre*'s context in *Genesis B* and its contexts elsewhere has no independent argumentative value, then, but emphasizes the affinity of thought among many of these passages.

Gifre occurs twenty-six times in the verse corpus.[68] Setting aside for the moment its pairings with *grædig*, which we have seen have their own identity as a traditional unit, all the remaining poetic instances of *gifre* co-occur with one of two topics in context: either fire or hell (in which category I include its extension into the world in the person of devils). References to fire and hell often coincide, unsurprisingly, and other concepts closely associate as well, especially darkness; but the two do not always appear together, and when one of them is not notionally present in the close vicinity of *gifre* the other always is.

---

67 All but *gifre* are brought over directly from the Old Saxon *Genesis*, ll. 1–5a.

68 Two different words are spelled *gifre* in Old English, one having a long and the other a short root vowel. The word found in *Genesis B* and under discussion here is *gīfre* 'ravenous,' to be distinguished from *gĭfre* 'useful.' The forms *gifre* in riddle 26, l. 28, and *gifrum* in riddle 49, l. 3, represent *gĭfre*, not *gīfre*, as is clear in context, and so are excluded from my count.

The basic association of *gifre* with fire is illustrated in *Beowulf* (bold small capitals show lexis shared with *Genesis B* as highlighted above, and italics indicate shared concept but not wording):

Guðrec astah,
wand to wolcnum; wæl*fyra* mæst
hlynode for hlawe. Hafelan multon,
bengeato burston ðonne blod ætspranc,
laðbite lices; **LIG** ealle forswealg,
gæsta **GIFROST**. (*Beowulf*, ll. 1118b–23a)

[The battle-smoke rose, twisted to the heavens; the greatest of carrion-fires roared before the barrow. Heads melted, wound-gates burst, hateful bites of the body, when the blood sprang out; fire devoured everything, most ravenous of spirits.]

The fire association of *gifre* is also marked dictionally as traditional by another formulaic phrase (underlined above): a kenning for fire as the 'most insatiable' or 'most ravenous of spirits.' There are additional examples of *gifre*'s textual association with earthly fire,[69] and it also describes metaphorical fire in reference to physical affliction or death throes,[70] but a prominent application, pertinent to the salvation-history dimension of its occurrence in *Genesis B*, is to the world-consuming conflagration that will attend Doomsday. It is in this context that Cynewulf deploys the fire kenning just seen in *Beowulf*:

Þonne frætwe sculon
byrnan on *bæle*; blac rasetteð
recen reada **LEG**, reþe scriþeð
geond woruld wide. Wongas hreosað,
burgstede berstað. *Brond* bið on tyhte,
æleð ealdgestreon unmurnlice,
gæsta **GIFRAST**. (*Christ II*, ll. 807b–13a)

69 *Azarias*, ll. 182–8; *Maxims I*, ll. 69–71. The latter is especially interesting as a case of a traditionally encouraged junction: there is no link of thought between the word *gifre* and the proximate reference to fire; the association is purely juxtapositional and concatenates two sections of the poem as divided in the manuscript.

70 *Guthlac A*, ll. 374–9; *Guthlac B*, ll. 978–99.

[Then treasures must burn in fire. Bright will rage the sudden red flame; fierce, it will sweep far and wide throughout the world. Fields will perish, cities break apart. The fire will be on the move, will burn ancient treasure remorselessly, the most ravenous of spirits.]

Another outstanding apocalyptic example from *Christ III* recalls the fire kenning (in the phrase underlined below) and includes the frequently affiliated concept of darkness as well as a more intensive cluster of shared language. Both *sweart* and *lig* come up repeatedly, as simplices and in compounds, along with *gifre* itself:

Đonne eall þreo   on efen nimeð
won fyres wælm   wide tosomne,
se **SWEARTA LIG**, sæs mid hyra fiscum,
eorþan mid hire beorgum,   ond upheofon
torhtne mid his tunglum.   Teon**LEG** somod
þryþum *bærneð*   þreo eal on an.
. . . .
Swa se **GIFRA** *gæst*   grundas geondseceð;
hiþende **LEG**   heahgetimbro
fylleð on foldwong   *fyres* egsan,
widmære *blæst*   woruld mid ealle,
hat, heoro**GIFRE**.
. . . .
Þonne wihta gehwylce,
deora ond fugla,   deað**LEG** nimeð,
fæeð æfter foldan   *fyr***SWEARTA LEG**,
weallende wiga.   (*Christ III*, ll. 966–71, 974–8a, 981b–4a)

[Then far and wide all at once the dark surge of fire, the black flame, will take all three together: the seas with their fish, the earth with its mountains, and the bright sky with its stars. Powerfully the destruction-flame will burn all three together as one ... Thus the insatiable spirit will search throughout lands; the ravaging flame will fell high-built things to the plain in the terror of fire, the widely known blaze (will bring down) the world entirely, hot, battle-ravenous ... Then the death-flame will seize every living creature, (each) animal and bird; fire-dark flame will travel the earth, a surging warrior.]

Further examples of the eschatological subset of *gifre*'s fire-associated usage are found in *Christ III*, lines 1044ff, and *The Phoenix*, lines 499–514.

For *gifre*'s other, overlapping pattern of co-occurrence, its association with references to hell or devils, we can again begin with *Beowulf*. That poem's sole instance of *gifre* outside of the fire kenning comes at the start of Grendel's mother's quest for revenge and contributes to the demonic aura the poet consistently gives the Grendelkin:

... ðy he þone feond ofercwom,
gehnægde HELLE gast. Þa he hean gewat,
dreame bedæled deaþwic seon,
mancynnes feond, and his modor þa gyt
GIFRE ond galgmod gegan wolde
sorhfulne SIÐ, sunu deoð wrecan. (*Beowulf*, ll. 1273b–8)

[... so he (i.e., Beowulf) overcame that demon, put down the spirit of hell. Then wretched, parted from joy, he (i.e., Grendel) went to see the place of death, enemy of the human race; but his mother, unsatisfied and gallows-minded, still wanted to take the sorrowful journey to avenge the death of (her) son.]

Similar in using *gifre* in the context of reference to hell or devils, but not fire, are *Guthlac A*, in which devils attack St Guthlac 'gifrum grapum' [with rapacious clutches] (l. 407a); *Andreas*, where the Mermedonians, directly incited by a devil, likewise attack Andreas 'gifrum grapum' (l. 1335a); and *The Descent into Hell*, where John the Baptist says on behalf of all the imprisoned souls in hell that they have put themselves there 'þurh gifre mod' [through insatiable spirit] (l. 95b).[71]

The hellish associations of *gifre* are compatible with the *grædig and gifre* formula already discussed and sometimes intersect with it: three examples of the formula show the traditional conceptual (and to some degree, lexical) affiliations of *gifre*, in addition to pairing it with *grædig* and activating the associations of that dictional unit. Its context in *Soul and Body II*, for instance, shares with the relevant lines of *Genesis B* prominent reference to hell and the adjective *sweart* when the soul complains that it must

secan þa hamas þe þu me ær scrife,
ond *þa arleasan eardungstowe*,

71 The *gifre* devil in *Solomon and Saturn I*, l. 145b, should perhaps be included in this group, although there has been a reference to fire several lines earlier, in l. 136b.

ond þe sculon moldwyrmas monige ceowan,
seonowum beslitan **SWEARTE** wihte,
GIFRE OND GRÆDGE. (*Soul and Body II*, ll. 65–9a)

[seek out the abodes you previously appointed for me, those honourless dwelling-places; and many earth-worms shall consume you – dark creatures, insatiable and greedy – shred you to the sinews.]

Notice that *Soul and Body II* even positions the word *sweart* in precisely the same way in relation to the formula as *Genesis B*, even though the shared referent of all these adjectives is now different: it is now the worms that are said to be dark, ravenous, and insatiable. *Christ and Satan*'s two instances of *gifre*, both involving it in the formula with *grædig*, variously express the same knot of concepts of hell, fire, and darkness found in *Genesis B*. The first instance is largely descriptive:

Him ðær wirse gelamp,
ða heo in **HELLE** ham staðeledon,
an æfter oðrum, in *þæt atole scref*,
þær heo *brynewelme* bidan sceolden,
saran sorge, *nales swegles leoht*
habban in heofnum heahgetimbrad,
ac gedufan sceolun in ðone deopan *wælm*
niðer under nessas in ðone neowlan grund,
GREDIGE AND GIFRE. (*Christ and Satan*, ll. 24b–32a)

[When one after another they established their home in hell, in that horrible pit, it befell them the worse there, where in the fire-surge they had to endure grievous sorrows and by no means have the high-built light of the sky in heaven, but must plunge into the deep blast, down under the headlands into the deep abyss, those greedy and insatiable ones.]

The second moves from Satan's own lamenting speech into a homiletic exhortation:

'Sceal [ic] nu wreclastas
settan sorhgcearig, **SIÐAS** wide.'
Hwearf þa to **HELLE** þa he gehened wæs,
godes andsaca; dydon his gingran swa,
GIFRE AND GRÆDIGE, þa hig god bedraf

in þæt *hate hof* þam is HEL nama.
. . . .
Læte him to bysne hu þa *blacan* feond
for oferhygdum ealle forwurdon. (*Christ and Satan*, ll. 187b–92, 195–6)

['Now anxious with sorrows (I) must lay exile-tracks, wide wanderings.' Then he returned to hell where he was punished, the enemy of God; so also did his followers, insatiable and greedy, when God drove them into that hot home for which the name is hell ... May it serve as an example (to each person), how the black fiends all perished through overweening.]

Descriptively, then, usage of the simplex *gifre* is subject to an impressively stable set of restrictions: in the entire poetic corpus it is always either connected alliteratively to *grædig* (in a collocational unit having its own traditional identity) or textually proximate to references to either fire or hell. Considering that *gifre* is a fairly frequent word, it is remarkable that not a single one of its twenty-six poetic occurrences fails to meet at least one of those criteria, and most meet more than one. Reference strictly to the citational, lexicographical meaning of the word cannot account for the regularity of these contextual links, and its pairing with *grædig* has associative dimensions not explicable by analytical processing of the component parts. This strong semantic prosody, seemingly arbitrary yet consistently upheld and thus reinforced, is a telltale sign that *gifre* has a widely perceived traditional value. It participates in received packages of phraseology and concept that signify metonymically, by reaching outside the single text to create meaning by reference to a larger received and recognized field of implication, rather than depending solely on what is provided in the immediate textual surroundings.

Gifre's insertion point in *Genesis B* takes advantage of all these traditional attachments, not only pairing it formulaically with *grædig* but also sandwiching it between *helle* 'hell' and *lig* 'fire.' In introducing the word the *Genesis B* poet responds to what he or she found already present in the Saxon *Genesis*: those three words are all inherited from the source text, as are two other concept-words that we have also seen come up repeatedly in similar Old English passages (*sið*, *sweart*) and could have contributed further to a sense of appropriateness. Even though *gifre* is a near-synonym to the already-present *grædig*, its involvement with traditional cognitive and dictional structures brings with its addition much more than the dilation of an original detail. Two different sets of traditional associations converge here to intensify the sense of hell's irresistible agonistic power, enhancing the connotative resonance of the hellmouth scene that was already present in the Saxon version by attributing to hell itself the same bestial insatiability and elemental unconcern with rational human self-interest that other instances of the *grædig/gifre* pair connote. Incapable of satisfaction, hell is eager to consume Adam and Eve and inevitably will do so. Perhaps for some readers *gifre*'s apocalyptic associations also contributed to its semantic prosody. If so, the novel use of that word in direct description of hell itself might secondarily evoke for them the similarly unearthly, all-consuming fires of the apocalypse: Adam and Eve's disobedience results in not just their personal deaths but in universal death, and thus telescopes God's imminent judgment of them into the eventual judgment of all humankind on Doomsday.

Making Genesis B, Lines 802b–4, from the Saxon Genesis, Lines 12b–13

The next denotational change made by the *Genesis B* translator is the most extensive. Here he or she adds a full line to the source:

Nu thuingit mi giu hungar endi thrust,
bitter balouuerek, thero uuâron uuit êr bêđero tuom.
(Saxon *Genesis*, ll. 12b–13)

[Now hunger and thirst oppress me, bitter harm; we used to be free of both of those.]

Nu slit me hunger and þurst
bitre on breostum, þæs wit begra ær
wæron orsorge on ealle tid. (*Genesis B*, ll. 802b–4)

[Now hunger and thirst oppress me, bitter in the breast; we used to be undistressed by that, (by) both, for all time.][72]

72 Lucas ('Some Aspects of *Genesis B*,' 150 n. 38) points out that morphologically, 'bitre' in the Old English could be either an adverb or a nom. pl. adjective agreeing with 'hunger and þurst'; I treat it as the latter. I take 'þæs' as a demonstrative to allow the structure of the clause it opens to be interpreted as similarly to that of the source as the language will support, but this requires reading a slight mix-up of number (reflected in my translation). It is possible that the translator intended a change to a conjunctive use of 'þæs' (the construal Lucas favours: ibid., 150) to indicate that the hunger and thirst oppress harshly *inasmuch as* they are completely unfamiliar sensations, but the alternative seems more natural to me in reading, if a little ragged.

The first verse of the *Genesis B* passage closely translates the corresponding verse in the Saxon *Genesis*, substituting the English verb *slitan* for the synonymous Saxon *thwingan*, which lacks an Old English cognate.[73] The real change begins in the next half-line, where 'bitter balouuerek' [bitter harm], a noun phrase in appositive variation with 'hungar endi thrust' [hunger and thirst], is changed to the adjective + prepositional phrase 'bitre on breostum' [bitter in the breast]. Timmer and Lewis have both sought to explain this verse in isolation. Timmer thought the translator could make no direct transference of Saxon 'bitter balouuerek' because no word corresponding to the Saxon compound is known to have existed in English, where the expected form would be **bealoweorc*.[74] Lewis rightly rejects Timmer's reasoning on the grounds that Anglo-Saxon poets did not hesitate to form nonce compounds and that several compounds in *bealo–* exist as potential models.[75] One might add that compounds in *–weorc* are also abundant.[76] As far as any lexical considerations may take us, then, a direct Saxon-to-English transfer of *baluwerk* to **bealoweorc* was available to the translator, and the productivity of both *bealo–* and *–weorc* as combining morphemes (along with the immediate cue of the Saxon source) make the calque such an obvious possibility that it must have been considered by the English writer.

Lewis identifies a potentially more serious obstacle to such a simple solution, classifying line 803a of *Genesis B* as the one and only verse within the Saxon *Genesis/Genesis B* overlap that he believes was changed for metrical reasons, since a hypothetical verse **biter bealoweorc* would have produced an unattested metrical shape.[77] Even this complication would not have forced the English translator to abandon the Saxon wording, however. Doane notes the possibility of realizing *biter* as *bitter*, a metrical disyllable, just as in Old Saxon.[78] Alternatively, by simply inverting the phrase

73 Timmer, *Later Genesis*, 50; Lewis, 'Metre of *Genesis B*,' 69; Doane, *Saxon Genesis*, 60.

74 *Later Genesis*, 50.

75 'Metre of *Genesis B*,' 71 n. 20.

76 Cf. Schwab, *Einige Beziehungen*, 123.

77 Lewis, 'Metre of *Genesis B*,' 71. Independently, both *biter* in the first foot and *bealo–* in the second would normally resolve. There are no instances of a verse of this stress pattern in which resolution that would normally be triggered in each foot is blocked in one of them, as would be required here to maintain the minimum four metrical positions.

78 *Saxon Genesis*, 60 n. 2. The word is probably a metrical disyllable in *The Phoenix*, l. 404b. There exist additional instances in which OE *bit(t)er* is spelled with a medial double *t*, but all of them occur in verses that could scan as normal types either with or without the assumption of resolution, so their orthography cannot be proved to have metrical significance.

to **bealoweorc biter* the English poet could have produced a well-attested pattern.[79] The metrical situation we find here, then, is somewhat analogous to the lexical decision not to use the prosaic word *ginian* in the first passage analysed above: technical factors having to do with Old English poetic norms may well have figured into the translator's thinking or instincts, but still a choice was made to forgo the solution that would have kept closest to the Saxon exemplar, and that decision in itself has meaning.

The nature of the poet's chosen solution is interesting, but it cannot be seen by examining this half-line out of context. Here, I will suggest, we can observe the poet engaging intensively with both the Saxon *Genesis*, outside of this passage, and Old English poetic tradition. To see how will require bringing into the discussion the next three verses of *Genesis B*, lines 803b–4, which have themselves caused trouble for modern commentators and must be given a moment's attention as a separate group before we return to line 803a.

Timmer claimed that these verses' changes to the original were necessitated by the absence in Old English of a cognate to the Old Saxon word *tôm*,[80] but several scholars have since pointed out that a corresponding form is attested in *Christ III* (l. 1211).[81] Nevertheless Doane returns to the essence of Timmer's suggestion that the verses were shaped by cascading effects of a problem with Old Saxon *tôm*, forced now however to speculate that the Old English word *tom*, having the same meaning, was probably 'not known … to the reviser.'[82] Without going so far, especially seeing that the Saxon version of the word was apparently understood, we may allow the possibility that the uncommonness of the word *tom* gave the poet pause for one reason or another.

Dissatisfied with Timmer's explanation and writing before Doane's revival of it, Lewis treats lines 803b–4a as an 'expansion' of line 13b of the Saxon *Genesis* and concedes its motivation to be 'unclear.'[83] Lewis classifies

---

79 I owe this observation to Thomas A. Bredehoft in personal communication.

80 *Later Genesis*, 49.

81 E.g., Capek, 'Nationality of a Translator,' 94 n. 8; Lewis, 'Metre of *Genesis B*,' 71 n. 18; and Lucas, 'Some Aspects of *Genesis B*,' 150–1. The status of OE *tom* in *Christ III* was once entangled with the question of whether *Christ III* itself might have a Saxon element in its vocabulary (see, e.g., Hofmann, 'Altsächsische Bibelepik,' 177–8). This must be why Timmer discounted it: the existence of *tom* in *Christ III* and its relationship to OS *tôm* had long been under discussion, so it is unlikely that he overlooked it altogether. Binnig's study of the word and its cognates ('Altsächsisch *tōm*') finds no reason to doubt its genuine presence in Old English.

82 *Saxon Genesis*, 60.

83 'Metre of *Genesis B*,' 71.

the change in this way only for descriptive purposes; but thinking of it in the first place as an expansion can lead to a focus on the formal fact of the translator's having added half-lines, and I suggest that in the present case looking through that lens will magnify problems rather than reveal answers, given that in negotiations of form the translator elsewhere prefers to keep step with the source verse-by-verse and often reduces the length of individual verses. Here, in the sole known case of dilation, we might do better to turn away from formal considerations and ask first what the new material *does*, both in context and in view of Old English poetic tradition. Then we may be in a position to see why the translator was attracted enough to this wording to depart from the usual practice of matching or reducing verses and add a line to the source instead.

The adaptation of the Saxon *Genesis*, line 13b, makes the most sense when viewed as an interaction with the rest of the solution the English poet found, which in practice would probably have developed all of a piece. Doane sees the meaning of Saxon *tôm* as having been pushed forward into the next verse in 'a circumlocution that adds two feeble half-lines.'[84] But there has been a change of meaning that this summation does not address. Having put his brief analysis of line 803b in terms that make it sound as though what is wanted is simply a synonym for *tôm*, Doane implicitly treats *orsorg* as if it were just that;[85] however, this is not as straightforward a case as the substitution of *slitan* for Saxon *thwingan* in the previous line. The Old English prefix *or–* 'without' in *orsorg* approximates the meaning of Old Saxon *tôm*, but rather than referring back to hunger and thirst as *tôm* had done, *or–* is part of a composed lexeme the other element of which, *–sorg* 'sorrow, care, anxiety,' has meaning not prompted by this line of the Saxon text. In *Genesis B* Adam does not say merely that he and Eve have previously lacked hunger and thirst, but that they have lacked sorrow or distress as brought on by experiencing those hardships. It may not have been possible to contain the full meaning of line 13b of the Saxon *Genesis* within a single verse of Old English,[86] but even if spillover was inevitable, denotative change was not strictly necessary; other ways of expressing the same concept in Old English were

84 *Saxon Genesis*, 60.

85 Likewise Stévanovitch, 'Translator,' 133.

86 Bredehoft, *Early English Metre*, 27–8, indicates that a normal verse cannot begin with a foot in the shape Sxs. This constraint would disallow the use of *tom* (or a synonymous monosyllable) to give *Genesis B*, l. 803b, a form like *'þæs wit begra ær tom wæron,' *(xx)Sxs | Ssx. On the impossibility of reducing the verse sufficiently to avoid adding a line, cf. Schwab, *Einige Beziehungen*, 124.

certainly available, especially with the freedom granted by the extra line. It is reasonable to assume, then, that the content of *Genesis B*, line 804, in the form that line took as a result of the poet's choices, had its own pragmatic appeal.

I think two factors operated in concert to create that appeal. One is the poetics of mentality as a general impulse, for which I am arguing. The other is the larger dictional context of this passage, much of it lost from the fragmentary Saxon text but reflected in *Genesis B*. This brings us back to the verse 'bitre on breostum' and to how the word choice in the following verses, lines 803b–4a, interacts with it. Here is the changed statement again, now given with the lines preceding it, and with words or morphemes important to my comments below shown in bold small capitals:

Nu wit **HREOWIGE** magon
SORGIAN for þis **SIÐE**, forþon he unc self bebead
þæt wit unc wite warian sceolden,
HEARMA mæstne. Nu slit me hunger and þurst
BITRE on **BREOSTUM**; þæs wit begra ær
wæron or**SORGE** on ealle tid. (*Genesis B*, ll. 799b–804)

[Now (well) can the two of us, mournful, be sorry for this fate, because he himself commanded us that we must guard ourselves from pain, greatest of harms. Now hunger and thirst oppress me, bitter in the breast; we used to be undistressed by that, (by) both, for all time.]

There are three key words involved in the change: *breost*, an addition; *sorg*, a root that occurs in the received context (as a verb a few lines earlier, in l. 800a) but is now replicated in the added *orsorg*; and *biter*, which is found in the source's phrase 'bitter balouuerek' but has now been alliteratively bound to the new word *breost*. The section of overlap between the Saxon and the English text is the first surviving part of the Saxon one, but in *Genesis B*, 556 lines precede it that are certainly based on a now-lost portion of the Saxon original. It has not been noted in previous scholarship that the section of *Genesis B* leading up to the start of the overlap contains a high concentration of the very words most central to this changed statement: *breost*, *sorg*, and *biter*.[87] Taking these three words together, within a

87 Jager alone has noticed any larger dictional pattern, suggesting that it influenced the poet's introduction of *breost* here ('Word in the "Breost"'). His consideration of the occurrences of *breost* throughout *Genesis B* does not involve the more immediate cluster of associated and collocated terms to which I draw attention.

span of seventy-five lines preceding the start of the overlap they occur a total of twelve times.[88] If we add three of the other significant words in the passage under analysis, *hreowig*, *sið*, and *hearm*, the total count within those seventy-five lines increases to twenty;[89] and both *sið* and *hearm* make one more appearance each within the fifteen-line interval at the start of the surviving portion, at lines 792a and 797b respectively, so with their inclusion one could say that the run of densely repeating key words continues unbroken into the overlap.

If the *Genesis B* poet's generally conservative practice in the section of text where we can directly observe it is representative of his or her work throughout, it is not plausible that very much of this diction was added in translation. We must infer that the English poet found in that now-lost portion of the source text a recurrence of both concept and lexis leading up to this passage and strengthened that pattern by resuming it here. It appears, then, that features of the Saxon *Genesis* itself provided part of the impetus for making an insertion. The words from this cluster that do occur at this point in the source apparently nudged the English translator toward adding a reference to the *breost*, in a verse that definitely required no new wording, and a second reference to sorrow, this time negated with *or–* to fit the context and bring in the pragmatic value of *tôm*, as part of a more complex redistribution of content. The resonance already available to these extra references within the target idiom of Old English verse may have been an additional attraction, and in any event, once new dictional elements were added, their full pragmatic character became present for any audience of *Genesis B*.

The phrase 'bitre on breostum' manifests traditional usage of the word *breost* in two different ways, each clearly definable. The first is its participation in the formula *q on breostum*, always whole-verse except once when it appears in a hypermetric environment (*Genesis A*, l. 2867a). In this formula *q* always has the metrical profile S or Sx,[90] thus yielding the basic verse pattern Sx | Sx with or without an extrametrical syllable preceding the second foot.[91] As would be expected, being the first strong stress of its

88 Forms of *sorg* six times (ll. 733b, 755a, 765b, 776b, 785b, and 789a), forms of *breost* four times (ll. 715b, 734a, 751a, and 777a), and forms of *biter* twice (ll. 725a and 763a).

89 A form of *hreowig* one other time (l. 771a), forms of *sið* three times (ll. 718a, 721a, and 733a), and forms of *hearm* four times (ll. 736b, 754b, 759b, and 781a).

90 The only lexical trisyllable attested in this formula, *egesa*, resolves to the metrical shape Sx.

91 If *q* is metrically disyllabic (Sx), the preposition *in/on* would be properly scanned according to its syntax as an extrametrical syllable proclitic to *breostum* to give the verse pattern Sx | (x)Sx. If *q* is a metrical monosyllable (S), *in/on* must be scanned as part of

verse *q* always participates in the alliterative linkage of its half-line with the one opposite to it; and when the formula occurs as a whole a-verse, as here in line 803a, *q* always alliterates also with *breostum*. This is a widely attested formula expressing mental containment, a model of mentality whose prevalence in Old English poetry has been studied elsewhere.[92]

Aside from the *q on breostum* formula, there is a second way the phrase *bitre on breostum* ties into traditional language. No instance of *q on breostum* except this one happens to involve the word *biter* or *bitre* (adjective and adverb, respectively). However, a separate dictional unit strongly associates those words with *breost*: *biter/bitre* and *breost* (or compounds using it) make a traditional collocation providing line-alliteration. The speaker of *The Seafarer* has suffered 'bitre breostceare' [bitter heart-anxiety] (l. 4a) and 'sorge … / bitter in breosthord' [sorrow bitter in the heart-treasury] (ll. 54b–5a); in *Judgment Day II* 'breostgehyda and se bitera wop' [thoughts of the heart and bitter weeping] (l. 173) will run through all the sinful simultaneously; and in *Juliana* the devil confesses to St Juliana how he assails the spiritually unguarded: 'ic ærest him / þurh eargfare in onsende / in breostsefan bitre geþoncas' [first through arrow-shooting I send bitter thoughts into his heart] (ll. 404b–5). In *Beowulf*, after the dragon attacks Beowulf's tribe,

Þæt ðam godan wæs
hreow on hreðre, hygesorga mæst;
wende se wisa þæt he wealdende
ofer ealde riht, ecean dryhtne
bitre gebulge; breost innan weoll
þeostrum geþoncum. (*Beowulf*, ll. 2327b–32a)

[That was grievous in the heart of the good one, the greatest of mind-sorrows; the wise one thought that he had bitterly angered the ruler, the eternal lord, in violation of ancient law; his heart roiled within with dark thoughts.]

---

the first foot despite its syntactic attachment to *breostum*, giving the verse pattern Sx | Sx, in order to satisfy the minimum requirement of four metrical positions per verse (for cases like this, see Bredehoft, *Early English Metre*, e.g., 37–8 and 46–7). Thus the alternation between disyllabic and monosyllabic values for *q* creates no fundamental metrical variation in the formula, only the presence or absence of an extrametrical syllable.

92 Esp. Mize, 'Representation.'

The phrase *bitre on breostum* in *Genesis B* line 803a, then, is not only a case of traditional language, but the unique intersection in surviving Old English verse of two traditional units: one a 'having in the heart' formula and the other a 'troubling of the heart' collocation.

The odd thing about the instance in *Genesis B* is that it starts out as a description of the physical sensation of hunger, inherited from the Saxon *Genesis*. *Breostum* was probably suggested to the poet's ear both by its frequent alliterative link to *biter/bitre* and because of its familiar role in a formula that likewise fit *biter* contextually, having a variable lexical element *q* that 'bitre' could appropriately fill. The semantic ambivalence of *breost*, able to accommodate the literal, corporal sense 'chest, abdomen' as well as the extended, metaphysical sense 'mind,' must also have been a factor given the observation of hunger to which the source text limits itself. But in poetry the mental sense is the more common usage of *breost*, and here in *Genesis B* the half-line constituted by the formula seems to be pulled by the gravitational force of traditional usage away from the source's focus on corporal perception and toward the more mental experience that fits the word's poetic usage. The English poem presents the experience not just of hunger and thirst, but of anguish over hunger and thirst.

So far as meaning goes, the use of *orsorg* in association with a phrase like 'bitre in breostum' makes perfect sense in generating a traditional-sounding mentality proposition of a kind ubiquitous in Old English verse, but the lexeme *orsorg* itself is unexpected in poetic diction.[93] Its acceptability here perhaps can be explained by reference to the fact that the two elements of the word *orsorg* connect with different parts of a sequence that was developing as a unit; each component has its own justification that may have helped to authorize, as it were, the selection of the composed form *orsorg*. *Or–* translates *tôm* and, being a bound morpheme, needs to attach to something. *Sorg*, both as a simplex and as an element in composed forms, is frequent in poetry and already had an ambient presence in this passage, occurring (as we have seen) just a few lines earlier and several times in the preceding section. Here the poet apparently allows the independent practical and contextual attractiveness of *or–* and of *–sorg* to override the poetic unattractiveness of *orsorg*, finding the generated meaning

93 Lucas ('Some Aspects of *Genesis B*,' 151) notes that *orsorg* is a mostly prosaic word, as does Schwab, *Einige Beziehungen*, 125–6 (both citing Stanley, 'Studies in the Prosaic Vocabulary,' in which see pp. 389 and 398).

and the continuation of the lexical cluster more compelling at this moment than vigilance against prosaic words.

Finally we must not neglect line 804b, 'on ealle tid,' a whole added verse that has been largely ignored in commentary because it has been perceived as a content-poor metrical filler needed to patch in the supposedly jerry-rigged 804a.[94] It is understandable that an adverbial indicator of time might not seem promising, but upon examination it turns out that the phrase *on ealle tid* actualizes a formula with a distinct pattern of usage informing its appearance here. Its core is the verse-final foot *q tid*, where *tid* serves as the object of the preposition *in/on* occurring in the first foot. When *q tid* follows an x-foot containing *in/on*, a set of conditions that exists sixty-one times in the corpus by my count, *q* is always metrically disyllabic. This already suggests a traditionally restricted formation – a lexical and metri-syntactic template for the prepositional phrase *in/on q tid* – because there is no metrical reason why *q* in the second foot could not be a mono- or trisyllable in this environment.[95]

Obviously any number of different adjectives and genitive nouns might fulfil *q* with the rhythm Sx to form a familiar-sounding metrisyntactic unit pivoting on the fixed lexeme *tid*. This template alone does not create much basis for more specific traditional meaning, serving more to mark and maintain register. But *in ealle tid* belongs to a subset of its possible realizations that is further restricted lexically, paradigmatically fulfilling *q* with the appropriately inflected form of the word *eall* 'all,' as here in *Genesis B*, but also allowing the sonically similar vowel-initial adjectives *ælc* 'each' and *ece* 'eternal.'[96] Although these three words are not synonyms, the use of the formula is indistinguishable regardless of which one is there: whereas in prose the phrase *in ealle tid* means 'at all times, all the time,' just as

94 Thus Schwab (*Einige Beziehungen*, 124) views the verse as a prosaic makeweight ('eine Zugabe'). Cf. also ibid., 130; Doane, *Saxon Genesis*, 60; and Stévanovitch, 'Translator,' 133.

95 The foot contour is always Sxs, never Ss or Sxxs, both of which are metrically permissible (although an Ss realization would require at least a disyllabic first foot). Several lexical trisyllables are found in the *q* position of this formula, but all of them are subject to resolution and thus metrically disyllabic, and the same ones occur repeatedly (only 4 forms produce the 11 instances: *sumeres* 4×, *dagana/dagena* 2×, *æðelan* 3×, *openan* 2×): strong indications that the disyllabic value of *q* is a traditional constraint on this dictional unit. I have excluded the *Paris Psalter* from all figures I give on this formula, but if included it would merely add five more instances conforming to the patterns I have stated, including one additional resolved trisyllable.

96 Found once each (*Christ I*, l. 406b; *Exodus*, l. 288a).

one would expect given the denotation of *eall*,[97] the poetic usage of *in ealle/ælce/ece tid* always signals not consuetude but constancy, like Latin *in saecula saeculorum*; the distinction between the prosaic and the poetic usage is the distinction between 'all the time' and 'for all time,' between 'continually' and 'perpetually.' The poetic formula produces a temporal frame of reference that conceives of time durationally and in indefinitely long epochs, never with an orientation to points in time (no matter how many of them) or on a scale comprehended by human experience. This is exactly what would be expected when *q* is fulfilled by *ece* 'eternal,' but that word is a minority variant. Only traditionality within the poetic register can account for this formula's stable contextual meaning, a little off-centre for the paradigmatic *eall* and especially so for the other variant, *ælc*.

The contextual indications are consistent. In the Exeter Book the formula is found repeatedly in environments of reference to eternity and divine constancy. *The Panther* describes that otherwise benevolent beast's perpetual animosity toward the dragon:

þam he in ealle tid   ondwrað leofaþ
þurh yfla gehwylc   þe he geæfnan mæg. (ll. 17–18)

[he lives with hostility toward that one for all time, because of every kind of evil he can bring about.]

Later in the poem the panther is allegorized as God, and this exception to its otherwise universal goodwill correspondingly signifies God's unremitting, static wrath toward Satan. In the hortatory conclusion of *The Seafarer*, *in ealle tid* is grouped with terms of honour for God that emphasize his timeless, eternal lordship in contrast to the vicissitudes and turmoil of the mundane life and specifically describes his once-and-for-all justification of humankind through Christ:

Uton we hycgan   hwær we ham agen,
ond þonne geþencan   hu we þider cumen,

97 This is its normal meaning when it occurs in homilies, such as Ælfric's *Lives of Saints*, 19.59. A search for *on ealle tid* in the *Dictionary of Old English Web Corpus* turns up a handful of additional examples, all similar. The phrase also comes up twice in the *Paris Psalter* (105.3, l. 3, and 118.20, l. 3); these two instances are part of that text's significant debt to prosaic usage and derive from the gloss tradition, where the phrase directly represents the Latin *in omni tempori*.

ond we þonne eac tilien, þæt we to moten
in þa ecan eadignesse,
þær is lif gelong in lufan dryhtnes,
hyht in heofonum. Þæs sy þam halgan þonc,
þæt he usic geweorþade, wuldres ealdor,
ece dryhten, in ealle tid. Amen. (ll. 117–24)

[Let us consider where we possess a home and then contemplate how we may arrive there; and let us, then, also strive that we might be allowed to enter eternal blessedness, where there is life proceeding from the love of the Lord, joy in heaven. May there be thanks to the Holy One for this, that he made us worthy, Ruler of Glory, eternal Lord, for all time.]

A very similar environment flavours its appearance in *Christ I*, where it is found in the Sanctus of the seraphim and angels:

Halig eart þu, halig, heahengla brego,
soð sigores frea, simle þu bist halig,
dryhtna dryhten! A þin dom wunað
eorðlic mid ældum in ælce tid
wide geweorþad.
. . . .
Sie þe in heannessum
ece hælo, ond in eorþan lof,
beorht mid beornum. Þu gebletsad leofa,
þe in dryhtnes noman dugeþum cwome
heanum to hroþre. Þe in heahþum sie
a butan ende ece herenis. (ll. 403–7a, 410b–15)

[Holy, holy you are, King of Archangels, true Prince of Victory, ever are you holy, Lord of Lords! Your earthly praise will last forever among men, widely honoured for all time … Everlasting hosanna to you in the heights, and on earth glory, brilliant among men. Live blessed, you who have come to people in the name of the Lord as a comfort to the abject. Eternal praise be to you, forever without end, on high.]

This example, with its selection of the word *ælc* 'each' instead of the more usual *eall* 'all,' is particularly valuable for illustrating the connotations of the formula because holistic traditional meaning overrides what would be a significantly different analytical interpretation of the phrase, which would indicate repetition with discreteness of innumerable instances. Its context here shows that its force is that which the phrase 'for all time' carries in Modern English: the praise of God is to be as eternal, as unceasing, as God himself.

Especially salient to consideration of the formula's addition in *Genesis B* is its occurrence in *The Phoenix*, which coincides with that in *Genesis B* not only in its choice of traditional phrasing but also in its topic. Like Adam in our *Genesis B* passage, the *Phoenix* poet is here describing a paradisiacal garden:[98]

Ne feallað þær on foldan   fealwe blostman,
wudubeama wlite,   ac þær wrætlice
on þam treowum symle   telgan gehladene;
ofett edniwe   <u>in ealle tid</u>
on þam græswonge   grene stondaþ,
gehroden hyhtlice   haliges meahtum,
beorhtast bearwa.   (ll. 74–80a)

[There no fruits, the splendour of forest trees, drop withered onto the ground, but the branches on the trees there (are) always wondrously laden; fruits remain freshly ripe for all time in that grassy place, the brightest of groves pleasantly adorned by the might of the Holy One.]

Readers of the poem are asked to imagine not cycles of ripening wherein some of the fruit is mature at any given time, but timeless perfection: an absence of botanical dynamism (which is associated with the curse of agricultural labour and the expulsion from Eden) corresponding to the absence of any variation in altitude or fluctuation of weather that is described elsewhere in *The Phoenix*. The abundance of constantly ripe fruit complements Adam's recognition in *Genesis B* of the loss of his perfect citizenship in Eden, a recognition brought about in that poem by his new experience of hunger. What *The Phoenix* here presents as the divinely ordained perfection of Paradise is precisely what Adam is beginning to understand he has sundered himself from through sin: the forever-and-always experience of plenty; perpetual satisfaction.

98 See Steen, *Verse and Virtuosity*, 40–55, for comparison of representations of the garden of the Phoenix to Old English and Latin descriptions of both the Garden of Eden and heaven.

This formula is found once in the Junius manuscript outside of *Genesis B*. In *Exodus*, it describes the parting of the Red Sea:

Wegas syndon dryge,
haswe herestræta, holm gerymed,
ealde staðolas, þa ic ær ne gefrægn
ofer middangeard men geferan:
fage feldas, þa forð heonon
in ece tid yðe þeahton,
sælde sægrundas. (ll. 283b–9a)

[The paths are dry, silver highways, the sea (is) opened, ancient foundations which never before throughout the earth have I heard people to travel: gleaming plains which ever since then waves have covered for all time, sealed sea-floors.]

In both of its appearances in the Junius manuscript – this passage in *Exodus* and the point of its introduction into *Genesis B* – the formula comes in the context of an abrupt and singular reversal of created order, throwing into sharp relief the disruption of a static, otherwise everlasting norm. For the Israelites in *Exodus*, the parting of the sea, previously closed and which forevermore 'in ece tid yðe þeahton' [waves have covered for all time], constitutes a spectacular intervention of God in the physical world. In *Genesis B*, Adam and Eve violate a state of original perfection intended by God to have been eternal: as catastrophic a disruption of the universe as the parting of the Red Sea is a triumphant one. When Adam notices his hunger and thirst, a new sensation with which he and Eve have previously been unafflicted, he has lost his integral participation in perfect Creation, designed to have lasted in perpetuity, and he knows it.

As it turns out, the English poet's added verses do a good deal of traditional work. With the substitution of *orsorg* as a subjectivizing and interiorizing alternative to Old Saxon *tôm*; 'bitre in breostum' beginning as a description of the bodily sensation of hunger but realizing a troubling-of-mind formula and then confirmed in that direction by *orsorg*; and finally the injection of *in ealle tid* as a formula with its own semantic prosody enhancing the sense of Adam's devastation at the loss of perfection, the English poem produces a bundle of associations conveying something harmonious with the Saxon source, but not in it, about the Fall and the experiential human perspective on that event.

Making Genesis B, Lines 814b–15a, from the Saxon Genesis, Lines 23b–4a

Both of the adaptations examined so far in this section have introduced or developed mentality content and have done so by means of added language that is demonstrably traditional within Old English verse. One final instance shows the same pattern:

uuit hebbiat unk giduan mahtigna god,
uualdand uurêđan. (Saxon *Genesis*, ll. 23b–4a)

[we have made mighty God, the Ruler, angry toward us.]

ac unc is mihtig god,
waldend, wraðmod. (*Genesis B*, ll. 814b–15a)

[but toward us mighty God, the Ruler, is angry-hearted.]

The main denotative change in this statement from that found in the Saxon original is *Genesis B*'s removal of explicit acknowledgment of human responsibility, from 'we have made God angry at us' to (in effect) 'God is angry at us.' Doane calls attention to the difference and considers it symptomatic of 'a certain insensitivity to the point of the passage.'[99] Other interpretations are possible. The absence of the admission of fault for God's wrath is conspicuous in direct comparison and could, for instance, be seen as a melioration of Adam and Eve's culpability consistent with the famous narratorial apology in *Genesis B* for Eve's capitulation to the tempting devil.

However, without comparative reference to the Saxon text – that is, as an early audience would have encountered *Genesis B* – the statement seems much less bold. I do not think a deflection of human responsibility was the objective of the adjustment, or even that it is truly a feature of these lines at all, although it might appear so without taking into account what I will suggest is the real nature of the revision. The rewrite of the first verse is part of the translator's formal practice, pursued continually in the overlap between the Saxon *Genesis* and the Old English *Genesis B*, of editing the wording of the original to eliminate some unstressed metrical and

99 *Saxon Genesis*, 63.

some extrametrical positions. But as I have been arguing, even changes motivated by formal considerations still have to take some positive shape in the hands of the translator, and we have seen in each of the two cases analysed above that he or she exhibits an attraction to traditional diction and expressive devices. The same is true here, and again we will need to ask not only what the stimulus to change was, but also what the traditionality of the outcome can tell us about the meaning of the new wording for an early English audience.

The shift in the statement's meaning has little to do – superficially, at least – with the compound word *wraðmod* 'angry-minded' that is introduced into *Genesis B*, line 815a, but I need to begin there because it raises several issues that turn out to be pertinent. Doane allows that the change to *wraðmod* in line 815a is 'perhaps a conscious stylistic alteration' but points out, following Timmer, that it is 'one also forced by meter, since the nominative would otherwise yield the three-syllable [half-]line **waldend, wrað*.'[100] Because a simple shift of the adjective to the nominative case (caused by the syntactic contraction of the previous half-line) would reduce the verse by a syllable due to the loss of an inflectional ending, thereby leaving it one metrical position too short to be an acceptable English verse, the motivation behind an adjustment to the source seems more straightforward here than in the other cases we have examined: *wraðmod* solves a clear problem by restoring a fourth metrical syllable.

Discussion of the change has seldom continued beyond that observation, and when it has, it has focused on the question of *wraðmod*'s Englishness. The word is not attested in Old English outside of *Genesis B*, where it occurs twice. John Frederick Vickrey Jr is 'fairly sure' that it is an 'Old Saxonism,' and Lewis points to *wraðmod* as a case of the translator's 'taking over Old Saxon compounds which are otherwise unknown in Old English.'[101] The suggestion that it is adopted from Old Saxon, even though it did not occur at this point in the source, is very plausible: the equivalent Saxon formation *wrêðmôd* is attested in *Heliand*,[102] and it could have been present in the full Saxon *Genesis* as well, in the now-lost Old Saxon verse underlying line 547a of *Genesis B* (the other place in Old English where

100 *Saxon Genesis*, 63; Timmer, *Later Genesis*, 50. Cf. Schwab, *Einige Beziehungen*, 92–3, emphasizing the interaction of the addition in *Genesis B*, l. 815a, with the reduction that took place in l. 814b.

101 Vickrey, '*Genesis B*,' 32; Lewis, 'Metre of *Genesis B*,' 71 and n. 20.

102 Doane is mistaken in stating that it is 'not recorded in OS' (*Saxon Genesis*, 63): *Heliand*, l. 5210a, describes Pilate as 'uulank endi uurêðmôd' [proud and angry-hearted].

wraðmod occurs). But we cannot rule out other possibilities: that it was a known English compound which happens not to exist in any other texts that now survive, or that it was an independent formation by the *Genesis B* poet in accord with well-accepted practices of poetic diction, as already discussed in reference to the hypothetical **bealoweorc* and in chapter 1 regarding *geomorfrod* in *Genesis A*.

Let us suppose, though, that the translator did get the idea of augmenting what would have been the metrically deficient default outcome, *wrað*, to *wraðmod* from this or another Saxon poem. Still, to introduce an acquired Saxon compound into a poem which one is in the process of turning into English, at a place where the Saxon source lacks it, is a compositional act; and even when content is generated by form, that content is then present, a real feature of the poem for anyone who reads it. What is really at issue is not whether or where *wraðmod* is attested in Old English or Old Saxon, or the undoubted metrical motivation for introducing something not in the original at this point. Given the evidence we have seen that the *Genesis B* poet worked in active cognizance of both Old English poetic tradition and the text-internal patterns of the Saxon *Genesis*, the important questions are these: first, whether the choice of word would have seemed in any way out of place in an English poem such as might prevent its being fully transparent and functional in terms of English poetic diction; and if not, then second, what meaning its use here would have for readers of *Genesis B*, as conditioned by both specific context and resonance within Old English tradition.

In addressing the first of these two questions I suggest that not only does the change to *wraðmod* fit very well within the norms of Old English poetic practice, it fits so well as to be perfectly camouflaged there regardless of whether the specific combination of the simplices *wrað* and *mod* was previously familiar. The Old English poetic corpus presents a great many adjectival compounds in *–mod*. This group of words is one important nexus of the poetics of mentality with the formal and dictional qualities of the tradition, much like the ubiquitous *q on mode* formula to which it is related.[103] The *–mod* compounds should be seen, too, as part of a larger family including similarly formed compounds in *–heort* and *–ferhð*, with a smaller number of analogues in *–hygd*: all together, this is one of the most robust and productive complexes of compound words in Old English verse.

103 *Wrað* realizes *q on mode* twice in *Genesis B* (ll. 405 and 745), as well as in *Genesis A* (l. 2262). Its two instances in *Genesis B* will be discussed below.

The majority of the attested *–mod* compounds (28 of 45 separate lemmas by my count) have in their zero-inflected form the same metrical profile as *wraðmod*, Ss.[104] Several of them occur once only,[105] and a few others are found just twice, like *wraðmod*,[106] so the rarity of *wraðmod* in itself is no knock against its use by the translator in converting the Saxon *Genesis* into an English poem. *Þearlmod*, which appears only in *Judith* (ll. 66a and 91a), even provides an analogue among the *–mod* compounds for a poet's possibly introducing a new word but then using it again in the same work.[107] Lexically, then, *wraðmod* presents no difficulties. It actualizes according to well-established patterns a template for compound formation, denoting a mental state or quality, that was enormously productive in Old English poetry, and it has a distribution similar to that of several other such compounds that unquestionably participate in traditional dictional patterns. Nine perfect metrical analogues to *Genesis B*, line 815a, position a *–mod* compound just as it is found here,[108] so formally, too, there is no reason to regard the translator's use of *wraðmod* as a suspect choice with respect to normal English poetic practice. It may have been a manipulation of the poetic lexicon, but if so it was a manipulation of a very familiar or even expected kind amply paralleled elsewhere – that is to say, a kind of manipulation that was itself a normal part of verse composition in Old English – that allowed the *Genesis B* poet to retain the first foot of the half-line as he or she found it in the Saxon *Genesis* while approximating the metrical profile of the second foot in a pattern normal to English metre.

---

104 Self-evidently *anmod, bliðmod, deormod, eaðmod, forhtmod, galmod, gealgmod, glædmod, gleawmod, guðmod, heahmod, heanmod, heardmod, hreohmod, hwætmod, leohtmod, mihtmod, ormod, rummod, sceohmod, stiðmod, styrnmod, swiðmod, torhtmod, tornmod*, and *þearlmod*; and with expected resolution in the disyllabic first component, *micelmod* and *ofermod*.

105 *Bliðmod, forhtmod, galmod, guðmod, heardmod, leohtmod, micelmod, mihtmod, rummod, sceohmod, styrnmod*, and *tornmod*.

106 *Heahmod, hwætmod*, and *þearlmod*.

107 In the parallel *–heort* and *–ferhð* sets, additional analogues to this repeated usage within a single text of a word not found outside of it include *gleawferhð*, limited to *Genesis A* (ll. 1152a and 2448a); *forhtferð*, unique to *Andreas* (ll. 1549a and 1596a); *steorcheort*, only in *Beowulf* (ll. 2288b and 2552a); and *wulfheort*, with three occurrences, all in *Daniel* (ll. 116a, 135a, and 246a).

108 *Genesis A*, ll. 1650b and 1662a (with resolution); *Exodus*, l. 203b; *The Rune Poem*, l. 4a; *Christ and Satan*, l. 246a; *The Dream of the Rood*, l. 40a; *Daniel*, l. 229a; and *Beowulf*, ll. 1785a and 2296a.

Just as important as its compatibility with Old English poetic language and form from a compositional standpoint, however, is the fact that from a reception perspective *wraðmod* would likewise not seem 'marked,' foreign, or unusual. Regardless of where the poet got the idea to use this word, within the frame of reference of Old English poetry it gives the appearance of having been generated in English through a widespread formula of mentality that was present in the idiom and highly productive. A reader who did not happen already to know of a precedent for *wraðmod* in Old Saxon would have had no more reason to suspect it than a speaker of Modern English encountering the term 'world view' for the first time would have to suspect that is a calque from German (*Weltanschauung*). For readers as well as poets the *q-mod* template for compound formation was readily available, a common dictional component of this and other Old English poems, and *wraðmod* looks and feels like a natural activation of it.

So, to come to the second question anticipated above, what does the compound *wraðmod* do in this text? A partial answer is that it brings the statement in which it newly appears into association with others elsewhere in *Genesis B*. Besides occurring in exactly the same form one other time in *Genesis B*, *wraðmod* has an obvious relationship to the phrase *wrað on mode*, found twice in *Genesis B* as well as outside of it,[109] which is one realization of the very productive *q on mode* formula discussed in chapter 1. That a set of connections is being either formed or strengthened with the use of *wraðmod* in line 815a is true regardless of what may have stood behind any of these other *Genesis B* lines in the lost portions of the Saxon *Genesis*, because we know the English writer to have introduced the word here, and that is the compositional choice that concerns us. The three prior passages in *Genesis B* containing either *wrað on mode* or *wraðmod* may provide clues to the usage of the compound at line 815a.

The one earlier appearance of *wraðmod* comes when the devil that has been dispatched from hell to Paradise to ruin humankind, having been rebuffed by Adam, goes to tempt Eve:

Wende hine <u>wraðmod</u> þær he þæt wif geseah
on eorðrice Euan stondan ... (*Genesis B*, ll. 547–8)

[The angry-hearted one made his way to where he saw the woman, Eve, stand in the kingdom of earth.]

109 See n. 103 above.

Here the substantive adjective expresses the nature of the representative Satan has sent from hell like a warrior into battle. It defines this antagonist to human bliss, summing up something essential about him: he simply *is* angry-hearted. When he returns to hell with his report of the successful corruption of humankind, in the middle of it he gives a synopsis of the devils' own fall from heaven that includes the *wrað on mode* formula:

> forþon unc waldend wearð wrað on mode,
> on hyge hearde and us on helle bedraf ... (*Genesis B*, ll. 745–6)

> [For that the ruler grew angry at heart toward us, hard in thought, and drove us into hell.]

This is the second occurrence of the phrase *wrað on mode* in *Genesis B*. The first has come during the earlier council in hell, when the devils resolve to disrupt God's design by bringing about the downfall of his favoured creation. If they can corrupt humankind, they decide,

> þonne weorð he him wrað on mode,
> ahwet hie from his hyldo, þonne sculon hie þas helle secan
> and þas grimman grundas ... (*Genesis B*, ll. 405b–7a)

> [Then he will grow angry at heart toward them, cast them from his favour; then they must seek out hell and these grim depths.]

The statement here, although it refers to an imagined future, describes a scenario like the retrospective account of the fall of the angels that uses the same phrase, but with a different object of God's punitive actions. The parallelism between the situations that these passages construct is meaningful: the devils' plan is to turn God's just wrath, which they have experienced, against humankind now as well, redirecting it as their own weapon against his prized creation.

Both instances of *wrað on mode* are used with the verb *weorðan* 'become.' This is true each time it appears outside of *Genesis B*, too, implying a traditional norm of usage: the phrase *wrað on mode* occurs only in a construction that emphasizes the inception of anger, a transition into a particular mental state.[110] Both occurrences in *Genesis B* describe God's

110 *Genesis A*, ll. 2261–2; and for whatever it may be worth, *Paris Psalter* 84.4, ll. 1–3.

wrath specifically, and clearly this association with God's anger aligns with line 815a. But there is something special about that instance, too, in the type of statement in which it occurs. *Wraðmod*, packaged as a character-defining *-mod* compound, emphasizes a dispositional characteristic, presumed to be static, rather than a dynamic process. Anglo-Saxon poets often seem concerned to differentiate the occupation of a mental state from movement into a state: one type of information about mentality with which they continually present audiences is the distinction between apparent fixity and transparent process. The devil that comes to Paradise to trick Adam and Eve into rebellion against God is deeply and truly vicious, *wraðmod* toward God and humankind alike. When *wraðmod* gets used in line 815a, to say that God 'is angry-hearted,' the statement does not just declare that God happens to be angry – a state of mind responsive to circumstances and therefore perhaps reversible – but conceives of him as an angry God.

From a receptional perspective, this, and not the reconfiguration of the clause's verbal syntax, is the real change from the Saxon text. In *Genesis B* God has a mental space, as it were, consisting of his righteous wrath, formed in relation to the rebellion of the angels. Hell is its cosmological enbodiment, and Adam and Eve have now reserved a place there, on behalf of all posterity, by aligning themselves with the fallen angels against God's rule. According to the diction of the poem God has not so much become angry at humankind as humankind has positioned itself within God's anger: henceforth, in Adam's formulation, that wrath will define the shape of the universe that he and Eve inhabit. From their perspective, God now must be as uncompromisingly hostile toward them as the poet has said the tempting devil to be in seeking their undoing.

Just as when the *grædig and gifre* formula is used for hell, what the poet offers here is more a definitional than a narrative proposition, telling not what God does but what God is. Adam's statement has a rhetorical absoluteness not unlike that of saying that Scyld Scefing was a good king, or that the aurochs is a brave and aggressive creature. The *Genesis B* translator's alterations to the presentation of both God here and hellmouth in the passage previously analysed suggest a kind of truth that is prior to circumstantial considerations and not contingent on the conditions of any moment. This absoluteness suits the context because what is being recounted is, after all, the once-and-for-all-time Fall of Man. Of course, both we and any likely early audience of *Genesis B* know that God's wrath toward humanity will turn out to be less permanent and irrevocable than Adam assumes it will; the eventual reconciliation made possible through Christ will be the ultimate point of this story for the Saxon and Anglo-Saxon poets alike. But within the wide context of Old English poetic discourse and the narrower one of this poem, the statement Adam is given here in *Genesis B* powerfully expresses his sense, from his situated perspective, that his and Eve's favoured status with their divine lord has been exchanged for permanent enmity.

The Likelihood that These Changes Occurred during Translation

The unknown manuscript of the Saxon *Genesis* from which the Anglo-Saxon translator worked may or may not have been substantively identical in every line to the Vatican text we have, and indeed at a few points *Genesis B* has been plausibly conjectured by previous scholars to reflect readings in its Saxon source manuscript different from those in the fragmentary sole witness.[111] It is necessary to ask whether the denotational differences I have identified between the extant Saxon text and *Genesis B* can be reasonably presumed to have attended the translation process, or whether there is a good chance that any of them merely reflect in Old English a variant already present in the lost Old Saxon exemplar behind the translation. As far as I know it has never been doubted that each of the specific points of difference analysed in this section originated in the transfer of the text into English, so I have taken the liberty of deferring this question until those divergences themselves had been presented and discussed, along with possible motivations for what I have interpreted as changes made by the translator. But the evidence should be considered, and now that we have the full information before us it is possible to do so concisely.

In the first of the three cases, the textual difference centres on the word *gifre*. No cognate is known in Old Saxon,[112] whereas it is a fairly common lemma in Old English, so its presence alone would seem to imply the intervention of an English writer and a change of language. Moreover, as we have seen, *gifre* manifests a robust traditionality in Old English poetry which its use at this point in *Genesis B* exploits in two different ways. Its

111 See, e.g., Doane, *Saxon Genesis*, 61 (on 'færeð' in *Genesis B*, l. 807b), 62 and 300 (on 'forst' in l. 809a), and 64 and 301 (on 'to hwon' in l. 816b).

112 Holthausen (*Altenglisches etymologisches Wörterbuch*) does not include *gifre* in his main listings but adds it in his appendix of 'Nachträge und Berichtigungen' (421), showing only an Old Icelandic cognate. Doane (*Saxon Genesis*, 58) notes that it is not attested, and no form cognate to *gifre* appears in Holthausen, *Altsächsisches Wörterbuch*, or Köbler, *Altsächsisches Wörterbuch*.

occurrence in *Genesis B*, that is to say, is not just a fitting but a rather impressive example of its traditional life in Old English verse. To suppose that a Saxon cognate to *gifre* had been present in the *Genesis B* poet's original would require assuming not only the existence of an unattested word in Old Saxon, but also probably a similar complement of traditional associations for it, giving it a formulaic usage and a semantic prosody like that which it manifests in Old English. Nothing about the scenario is impossible, but there is no evidence in support of it.

In the second divergent statement, *orsorg* and *in breostum* appear in a whole line not found in the Vatican manuscript. As discussed previously, these two verses are enmeshed in a somewhat complex alternative arrangement of the sentence's concept elements, possibly a workaround of the Saxon word *tôm* (whose Old English cognate is rare), combined with the introduction of some mentality content not present in the Vatican text. Here again we find a word with no equivalent attested in Old Saxon, *orsorg*, but in this case little weight can be attached to that fact. Cognates to both of its constituent elements, a bound morpheme *or–* and a simplex *sorga*, are represented in Old Saxon, so in principle **orsorga* could be a composed form in that language as well; and given the scantness of the prose remains of Old Saxon,[113] we would have very little chance of finding it, even if it did exist, if it had the same predominantly prose distribution as Old English *orsorg*. Better circumstantial evidence lies in the syntactic entanglement of the line with the previous one, in a way that suggests a spillover of content, and the embedding of the concept of lack (expressed with a simplex in the Saxon text) in a compound word in *Genesis B*. Both seem to imply that the more concise Vatican version represents the state of the text before, not after, a change was made. In principle a revision of this kind could occur at any time, and I know of no linguistic factor that would determine the extra line found in *Genesis B* to have been composed in Old English rather than in an undocumented stage of textual development within Old Saxon, but in the absence of other indications it is reasonable to group this change with others that are more surely associated with the translation process.

The third point of divergence I take to be unambiguous. The disyllable *wraðmod* solved a metrical problem created by a shift in grammatical case that removed a syllabic inflectional ending. That case change was part of

113 For a catalogue of the extant specimens of Old Saxon outside of *Genesis* and *Heliand*, see Gallée, *Altsächsische Grammatik*, 4–8.

the English poet's systematic tightening of syntax in transferring the text from one dialect to the other: here the syntactic compression included replacing a more expansive verb phrase with the copula, in the process turning what had been its accusative object into a predicate nominative.

The first and third denotational alterations, then, those involving *gifre* and *wraðmod*, seem clearly to originate in the English version, and it is the simplest explanation for the second as well, the addition of the line including *orsorg* and *in breostum*. However, that the question of which language formed the environment of these textual divergences even has to be dealt with in this way underscores the similarity of Old English and Old Saxon poetry: the answer would probably be more self-evident if the traditions had fewer linguistic and metrical features in common. The sibling languages themselves had become distinct enough by the ninth century to warrant translation but obviously remained very close; the poetics of both were descended from the same prediasporic West Germanic tradition of oral verse-making; and more immediately, the biblical poetry of each language emerged from a transmarine system of monastic communities that were not only similar but directly connected through the work of Anglo-Saxon missionaries. Any comparison between Old English and Old Saxon texts must take account of the two traditions' special if indefinite relationship, and this is the task of this chapter's final section. Whereas *Genesis B*'s consanguinity with the Saxon *Genesis* has usually been seen as a barrier to learning anything useful about Old English poetry from the translated text, I will argue that it positions *Genesis B* uniquely well to clarify certain aspects of the operation of the poetics of mentality in Old English.

What We Can Learn from *Genesis B*

The fragmentary state of both *Genesis B* and the Saxon *Genesis*,[114] the brevity of the single overlapping section, and the closeness of the translation, such that substantive differences are few and minor, conspire to encourage an atomistic conception of any element one wishes to compare. But while the texts we have are imperfect, the Saxon poem was once much longer, and the original version of *Genesis B* may have had an autonomous

114 It is certain that *Genesis B* as it now exists is not the entirety of the translated matter because it is not the entirety of the interpolation into *Genesis A*: Lucas, 'MS Junius 11,' 16–17, estimates a loss of interpolated matter, prior to the current l. 235, of roughly 70 lines on two leaves.

existence and run to the same length before being excerpted and embedded in *Genesis A*. Verse-by-verse linguistic and technical negotiations played a great part in the ninth-century translator's work at a practical level, but he or she was not just matching a list of Old Saxon words or phrases to a list of Old English ones in the manner of a glossary-maker. In the wider view the project was to turn a Saxon poem into one that could be successfully experienced through the frame of reference of English poetic discourse. As informative as line-by-line comparison can be when focused on the individual textual alteration, then, that analysis needs to be contextualized by a fuller perspective on what the Anglo-Saxon translator, as a reader of poetry, found in the Saxon *Genesis* and how he or she responded to it.

Underneath certain relatively superficial features of the text – artefactual traces of the Saxon language and statistically unusual metrical distributions – *Genesis B* works very much like a 'normal' Old English poem. This generalization applies to its mentality language and content as well as to many of its other characteristics. Furthermore, it is all of *Genesis B*, and not just its intersection with the surviving Saxon *Genesis*, that engages continually with emotion and with states and actions of mind. Yet we cannot suppose the *Genesis B* poet to have created the emphasis on mentality out of a void: in the three passages studied in detail, we find the translator enhancing or elaborating mentality language twice while introducing it only once, and even then doing so in continuation of a pattern present in the pre-overlap section of *Genesis B* that presumably reflects features of the source. So on the one hand we have no reason to believe that the Anglo-Saxon translator peppered *Genesis B* with new mentality references; yet on the other we have observed a clear tendency to develop that dimension of the text.

If we assume that the portion of *Genesis B* corresponding to the first fragment of the Saxon *Genesis* is representative of the translator's method on the whole – and we can hardly assume differently – we must regard a given instance of mentality language and content anywhere in *Genesis B* as potentially derived from its source, whether unchanged or taking an augmented or enhanced form in the English poem. Examination of the other, more extensive surviving portions of the Saxon *Genesis* indeed suggests that within its own vernacular tradition, known already to be closely akin to that of Old English in many ways, something very like the Old English poetics of mentality may also have been at work. Limitations of space do not allow full demonstration here of this likeness of method between Old English and Old Saxon versecraft; the crucial point is its existence, represented obliquely in the above analysis by the fact of the English poet's amplification, rather than total creation, of mentality content. While the impact of the poetics of mentality on the *Genesis B* poet's new compositional choices remains evident, then, the relationship of that poem's mentality language and content to that of the Saxon *Genesis* is no simple matter of presence in the one contrasting with absence in the other, as often was the case with *Genesis A* considered alongside its biblical source.

With regard to that aspect of the text, along with many others, the Anglo-Saxon poet who produced *Genesis B* from the Saxon *Genesis* was working more within a single tradition than between traditions. The recognition that ample reference to mentality was shared between Old English tradition and the Old Saxon *Genesis*, combined with the English translator's peculiar conservatism, suggests that translation may not be the only paradigm of textual propagation that is applicable in this case. The Saxon *Genesis* provided enough of the traditional infrastructure familiar from Old English poetry for the *Genesis B* writer to act in the ways that scribes are known sometimes to have done within textual cycles of vernacular poetic production. Katherine O'Brien O'Keeffe, A.N. Doane, Carol Braun Pasternack, and others have stressed that we cannot talk about texts of Old English poems without alertness to scribes' shaping influence upon them, an influence to be rather analysed than deplored.[115] The blurring of distinctions between poet and scribe that is sometimes touted as an implication of such reevaluations can be overstated, but it is clear that while working within a general framework of textual transmission some Anglo-Saxon scribes engaged in activity that must properly be called compositional;[116] and to my own interchangeable references throughout this chapter to *Genesis B*'s maker as its 'poet,' 'translator,' and 'writer' I now add acknowledgment that his or her behaviour may be characterized also as 'scribal,' at least according to one of the more aggressive and engaged modes of scribal work within the documented range of practice.

If the extent of change, being local and small-scale, may appropriately be considered scribal, the type of change in *Genesis B* is nevertheless

115 O'Brien O'Keeffe, *Visible Song*; Doane, 'Ethnography of Scribal Writing' and 'Oral Texts, Intertexts, and Intratexts'; Pasternack, *Textuality of Old English Poetry*. However, cf. now Bredehoft's reconsideration of the author-function in Old English poetry (*Authors, Audiences, and Old English Verse*, esp. 3–38).

116 Orton reasserts that vernacular scribes often attempted very close fidelity to their exemplars (*Transmission*, 206–7), but he also finds much variation in scribal goals and in the intensity and type of their interaction with exemplars, discussing more freehanded kinds of scribal work in chaps 5–6.

poetic. O'Brien O'Keeffe has argued influentially for independent poetic traditionality on the part of scribes, claiming that Old English poems surviving in two or more manuscripts sometimes show the residue of what she calls 'formulaic reading,' by which individual copyists anticipated certain wording or phrasing on the basis of poetic tradition and made substitutions accordingly.[117] For O'Brien O'Keeffe this is a by-product of vernacular poetry's continuing involvement with the voice and the ear, even in processes of textual transmission.[118] Doane goes a step further to theorize the production of a written text within a highly traditional milieu as itself a full-fledged performance of tradition, complete with some of the same commitments that define other traditional performances: for Doane, the scribe as a 'transmitter of traditional vernacular messages ... differs in his behavior from a scribe preserving authoritative messages in Latin' in being 'responsible to that [vernacular] tradition, not to an unknown "author" or to a dead piece of sheepskin, as he exercises his memory and competence to produce the tradition for a particular audience on a particular occasion.'[119] These characterizations make good sense in theory as one version of scribal activity, and particularly as articulated by O'Brien O'Keeffe they have gained considerable assent. It stands to reason that a scribe who admits substantive alterations into a text might consciously or unconsciously use any filter of perceived appropriateness that his or her experience could activate, and that these filters might include a proficient sense of poetic praxis. In principle, the vernacular work of Anglo-Saxon scribes no less than that of poets might be, under the right circumstances, traditional in nature; some known types of textual transmission would accommodate poetic enhancement according to familiar techniques if the needed personal competencies were in place.

Yet sure signs of scribal poetic traditionality have been elusive.[120] Very often, where comparison of multiple copies of a single text is possible in

117 *Visible Song*.

118 More important to my argument than the aurality implicit in scribes' handling of written Old English poetry is the putative poetic traditionality of that handling, for which see n. 120 below.

119 'Ethnography of Scribal Writing,' 435; cf. Doane, 'Oral Texts, Intertexts, and Intratexts,' 83–7.

120 Doane ('Ethnography of Scribal Writing') focuses on the theoretical role he posits of scribe-as-performer and does not attempt to make a case for the traditionality of individual textual variations. O'Brien O'Keeffe's proposed 'formulaic reading' is plausible as a mode of vernacular textual reception of Old English poetry, but few cases she presents involve straightforwardly poetic features such as documented formulas. For

order to identify divergences, what appears to be missing is not the scribal tendency to modify the exemplar but the specifically poetic sensibility or formal concern to guide those changes in the directions hypothesized by O'Brien O'Keeffe and Doane.[121] I believe we find just that sensibility and that concern in *Genesis B*'s intersection with the first Saxon *Genesis* fragment. In precisely that way in which the translation of the Saxon *Genesis* is most anomalous as a piece of Old English verse translating a known source – that is, in its exceptionally tight adherence to the Saxon text – it can be perfectly well described as exhibiting a 'scribal' level of occasional variance at the level of the word and phrase; and insofar as it is legitimate to fit *Genesis B* to a scribal transmission paradigm on grounds of its general procedure of transdialectal copying, it bears the fingerprints of the sought-after scribe-cum-poet. *Genesis B*'s strangeness as a translation is its normality as a scribal re-production – and one in which we find textual adjustments that are also, manifestly, tiny acts of traditional poetic composition.

If we combine the denotational differences between the Saxon *Genesis* and *Genesis B* into a single reading, the effect of these compositional acts is not radical, but the English poem's vision of the Fall is at once more absolute and more subjectively realized. Viewed in the double context of Old English poetic tradition and *Genesis B*'s inherited specific features, the changes tend to crystallize humankind's new place in the conflict between God and the enemies of the divine order. Adam's narrative in the Saxon poem, in which he and Eve make God angry and hell gapes at them menacingly, becomes in the English version more a static image of the human condition unreconciled to God: activity and process yield ground to a schematized siting of Adam and Eve in a cosmic relational system, caught between two adversarial entities and now irremediably (as it seems from Adam's subjective perspective) threatened by both.

The dispositions of God and hell toward them are imagined concretely through added traditional language; the human position, too, is more emotionally defined, stressing the forlornness of alienation from God's favour and consequent, inevitable doom. Adjustments to the language about the harsh weather that Adam anticipates show the writer's wish to maintain that motif as a poetically active part of the translation, and as

some objections to her evidence, see Orton, *Transmission*, 203–5, and O'Donnell, *Cædmon's Hymn*, 187–90.

121 This observation emerges repeatedly from Orton's analyses (*Transmission*, e.g., 198–9, 206). However, see Doane's interesting comments on the tendencies of *Beowulf*'s Scribe B ('"Beowulf" and Scribal Performance').

such it can be expected to come with associations of emotional destitution and lack of community, especially in the context of another added detail, a few lines previously, reconceptualizing the sudden hardships Adam experiences as primarily an interior problem of worry or care. Similarly, the translator's modification of Adam's rhetorical question, in the situational context of his speech, makes available the paradigm of exile. The *Genesis B* poet's subscription to traditional Old English poetic resources thus enhances in several ways the desolation experienced by Adam and Eve and made by them the inheritance of all humankind: in the presentation of God's wrath as apparently permanent, the irresistable elemental menace presented by the ever-eager jaws of hell, and the interiorized desperation of the fallen condition, the situation Adam laments is both emotional and universal. This kind of associative logic seems very much at home in an Old English poem. Perhaps it would have been equally at home in an Old Saxon poem; but be that as it may, these associations happen not to have been present in this passage of this Saxon poem. Here, they are a product of modifications that reflect the traditional poetics of mentality.

In historical literary analysis we often interpret changes made to a source text as signs of a seamless master plan which the critic discerns across the centuries with aquiline clear-sightedness. Possibly the translator of *Genesis B* deliberately arranged each of the elements analysed here to join together into the interpretation I have offered, thinking along lines similar to those I have laid out, but there is no need to be dogmatic. It also may be that the individual changes, proceeding from the same mind with the same understanding of the Fall and sharing as they do a strong emphasis on subjectivity, each took shape in alignment with norms of English poetic practice to produce a coherent interface between traditional fields of meaning and an immediate context of events and relationships. Some of the added dictional items are centred in connotative semantics: the *grædig/ gifre* unit and the formula *in ealle tid* with aurally similar variants, just like the word *gifre* itself, come with semantic prosody that helped prompt them here due to appropriateness of context. The suggestion of exile and the development of the weather motif complement them by calling upon well-defined poetic concepts. In all of these cases we see the translator working with stable traditional ideas. He or she selects, combines, and fashions, but does not invent, these elements with their connotative meanings. The combinations and selections may be unique and the message therefore in a sense novel, yet these traditional forms, and in turn this passage of *Genesis B*, can do the pragmatic communicative work they do only because of readers' propensity to experience-based pattern recognition.

The *q-mod* and *q in breostum* dictional units are less content-distinctive than the others: they insist on access to subjectivity but leave the particular quality of that subjectivity to be assigned by *q*. Their versatility allows them to splice any number of given narrative situations economically into traditional frames of reference as needed. Yet their status as recognized, constrained, meaning-bearing dictional structures makes them anything but interpretively negligible templates even though their particular content varies: through the cognitive categories activated by traditional forms as such, they are one means by which Anglo-Saxon poets can place different experiential perspectives into relation to one another within an ethical framework. Thus the changes made by the *Genesis B* translator each contribute to a consistent vision of events in part because the substance from which they are formed is ideally suited, within this tradition, to the production of certain structures of both language and thought. It is the business of an Anglo-Saxon poet writing in the classical style to evoke, in reference to textual particulars, the concepts and values indexed within this poetic idiom by its traditional diction. The metonymic construction of significance comes from endowing a new composition with a strong component of recognized patterns that reference networks of topical or situational meaning, in relation to which the individual textual elements will resonate together through their artful juxtaposition.

To analyse an Old English poem's traditionality, then, is not to deny its creator artistic agency, but to reconceptualize that agency. It bears repeating that this chapter has found the *Genesis B* translator to be working with the source text in a thoughtful and fully engaged manner. Such a characterization bears little resemblance to the picture we are usually given of this writer, who has more often been seen as a kind of scriptorial automaton, feeding each successive Old Saxon verse into a dialect-conversion machine that plunked out a slightly bent Old English verse on the other side. The mechanistic view of the *Genesis B* poet's work has always failed to account very well for some of the changes that can be observed in the overlapping section; it has discouraged investigation of whether they might draw upon features of Old English poetic discourse that transcend metrisyntactic stencils to include meaning; and it is incapable of accommodating, or even discerning, the Anglo-Saxon writer's recognition of patterns in the Saxon text extending over many lines and creative response to them through new deployments of his or her traditional craft.

The closeness of the translation is unusual, but we must not be misled by the anomaly into insensitivity to those decisions that were being made. The similarity of Old Saxon and Old English poetic tradition, which allows the translation to be as close as it is in the first place – arguably lying within the purview of scribal activity – can help clarify the *Genesis B* poet's motivations, the nature of his or her work, and finally the role of the poetics of mentality in the making of Old English verse. In contrast to the *Genesis A* poet, the writer who produced *Genesis B* was emphatically not driven by a need to 'English' the poem in any sense except the dialectal and perhaps, to a lesser degree, the metrical. The changes we observe in the overlapping section must not have been introduced for the purpose of making the Saxon poem English-traditional, because it already would have been so once the dialect transformation had been effected. What we do see is that when changes were being made, at points where the translator may have been prompted by some sort of difficulty to take a slightly freer hand with the text, they were made in complete harmony with English poetic tradition, and that in keeping with practices we have observed elsewhere, they exhibit a clear tendency to produce or amplify traditional subjectivities.

With no necessity of completely supplying an emphasis on subjectivity in order to build up conformity with English poetic practice, two possible factors could give rise to these changes: the inherent attractiveness of mentality content to the poet, such that he or she would be moved to develop it frequently, or a high enough degree of seemingly natural involvement of those concepts with the Old English poetic register that any changes, made for whatever reason, would be likely in practice to employ traditional language and associations proper to the poetics of mentality. If we posit the former scenario, the additions and developments were made as more or less deliberate enhancements, because as we have seen, the Saxon *Genesis* already contained an abundance of such features. If we posit the latter one, a certain likelihood of producing mentality language and content anytime new compositional acts are happening for any reason, we find in *Genesis B* an illustration of the way that traditional diction, far from being insignificant filler, generates content which then efficiently combines with other traditional structures of language and meaning to produce a web of metonymic signification. Either way – and although I have stated them here as alternatives, these two scenarios are not exclusive – the propensity to continue manifesting the poetics of mentality even where features suitable to it are already present in the source is testimony to its powerful traditionality and its nature as a generative element of Old English poetic composition.

The uniqueness of *Genesis B* has been an obstacle in the past to finding a meaningful place for it within Anglo-Saxon poetic tradition, and for good reason. One would be ill-advised to depend on it for any claims about Old English lexis or metrical norms, for example. But this chapter's study of its overlap with the Saxon *Genesis* has suggested some ways we can put this text's hybridity to work for us. *Genesis B* offers a vantage point unlike any other on the poetic culture(s) it represents, one that happens to both confirm and elucidate the importance of the poetics of mentality in Old English verse composition. Its translator encountered familiar conditions (features of style and register, conjunctions of concept and lexis) that activated certain expectations or flagged certain attractive potentials, and he or she pursued them, at points where departure from the source presented itself as convenient or desirable, by reshaping the text in ways suggested by his or her personal competence in the techniques of Old English poetry.

Understanding the changes in this way helps to situate the denotational differences between the Saxon *Genesis* and *Genesis B* realistically on a spectrum of intentionality such that we need not either relegate them to the category of the 'automatic' or make assumptions about elaborate plans on the part of the translator. Sometimes people do things because doing them feels normal. Writers make stylistic choices, with varying levels of reflection and deliberation, that seem right or effective to them within the context of the individual project, the genre, and the larger tradition in which they understand themselves to be working. It is not necessary to argue that the *Genesis B* poet was unaware of making the changes we have examined; or that doing so was in any way compulsory, somehow mandated by tradition; or that he or she consciously resolved at the outset to dial up the mentality elements and then set about systematically doing so. Perhaps moment by moment it just made sense, within the frame of reference of classical Old English poetry, to continue engaging with an active category of meaning for which rich traditional resources were readily available. This, too, is part of how tradition works.

3 Traditional Subjectivities in the Political World

Metre 1 of the Old English *Boethius*, a narrative poem offered as a contextualizing historical introduction to the translation of Boethius's *Consolation of Philosophy*, is adapted from a chapter of the earlier, all-prose version of the *Boethius* that has no direct Latin source. As an Old English versification of a prose text that is itself original to Old English, Metre 1 stands in a relation to its vernacular comparandum dissimilar from those of *Genesis A* (a verse translation from Latin prose, with an English prose analogue) and *Genesis B* (a verse-to-verse translation across dialects), making possible another angle of approach to my thesis that the poetics of mentality played a shaping role – and one not sensitively dependent on any particular conditions of composition – in the creation of poems in the traditional style. After a brief section on the two versions of the *Boethius*, the first half of this chapter will define Metre 1's fashioning from the English prose text on which it is based, illustrating the poem's traditionality and, as a part of that traditionality, its consistent subjectivization of the received story. This analysis will complement chapter 2's study of poetic diction by concentrating on larger elements of structure and technique, those more self-evidently involved in the communication of message and values. The second half of the chapter will integrate those observations into a holistic interpretation of Metre 1 as a product of a specific political environment. There, my treatment of the poem will move from its traditionality – the quality of being traditional – to its traditionalism: the deployment and rhetorical impact of traditionality in a real world of writers and readers. I will argue that the *Boethius* poet's production of traditional subjectivities interacts with narrative particulars, within a larger discursive context, to make political meaning inseparable from Metre 1's identity as an Old English poem in the classical style.

The Nature and Relationship of the Two Texts of the *Boethius*

Boethius's sixth-century *Consolation of Philosophy*, a technical masterpiece of the Latin 'mixed form' or *prosimetrum* (the alternation of prose and verse),[1] was adapted into Old English in two versions. The first, entirely in prose, survives only in Oxford, Bodleian Library, MS Bodley 180 (hereafter B), a manuscript of the very late eleventh or very early twelfth century.[2] An additional fragment (N), probably from the all-prose version, survived to modern times but is now lost; it was an Early West Saxon text dating from the early decades of the tenth century or possibly the very late ninth.[3] The second version of the Old English *Boethius*, based directly on the first, is a precocious vernacular example of the mixed form, a formal approximation of the Latin original.[4] It too now exists in a single manuscript, British Library MS Cotton Otho A.vi (C), a mid-tenth-century book that suffered severe damage in the Cotton Library fire of 1731.[5] In this prosimetrical version of the English work, most of the sections from the first translation that corresponded to Boethius's Latin *metra* have been newly versified and re-integrated into the whole, in sequence with the chapters that were carried over unchanged from the all-prose version.[6] Yet by an editorial convention stemming from Franciscus Junius's crucial seventeenth-century transcriptions, until very recently the verse portions of the prosimetrical *Boethius* have always been printed as an uninterrupted series of thirty-one poems separated from the prose sections with which they are carefully intercalated in C.[7]

1 The genre and the use of the term *prosimetrum* are surveyed by Ziolkowski ('Prosimetrum in the Classical Tradition'). See also Eckhardt, 'Medieval *Prosimetrum* Genre.'

2 Godden and Irvine, *Old English Boethius*, 1:9–18.

3 For discussion and an edition of N see Godden and Irvine, *Old English Boethius*, 1:34–41 and 543–4. N likely represents the prose version, based on line counts in relation to the reported dimensions of the leaf; but Kiernan ('Source of the Napier Fragment') emphasizes that this cannot be known for certain, and Godden and Irvine reserve judgment (*Old English Boethius*, 1:35–6 and 48).

4 *Prosimetra* would later be written in several medieval languages. Dronke (*Verse with Prose*) and Eckhardt ('Medieval *Prosimetrum* Genre') discuss a number of vernacular examples.

5 Godden and Irvine, *Old English Boethius*, 1:18–24.

6 Griffith, in his contribution to the Godden and Irvine edition, lists the few Latin *metra* that were represented in the all-prose English version but not redone as verse ('Composition of the Metres,' 81–2 n. 5). Because Griffith's work is a self-contained chapter presenting its own arguments, I will cite it individually by his name.

7 On Junius's transcriptions see Godden and Irvine, *Old English Boethius*, 1:24–34. Kiernan ('Alfred the Great's Burnt Boethius') discusses their influence on editorial history.

Only with the new edition by Malcolm Godden and Susan Irvine, who present both texts of the Old English *Boethius* in full, are the Metres restored to the places they were designed to occupy.[8]

The *Boethius*'s prose preface (present in both B and C before the first leaves of C burned) makes reference to the work's existence in two forms and attributes both unequivocally to King Alfred of Wessex (r. 871–99), explaining that he first rendered the whole into prose and then made verse from the prose:

> Ælfred kuning wæs wealhstod ðisse bec and hie of boclædene on Englisc wende, swa hio nu is gedon. Hwilum he sette word be worde, hwilum andgit of andgite, swa swa he hit þa sweotolost and andgitfullicast gereccan mihte for þam mistlicum and manigfealdum woruldbisgum þe hine oft ægðer ge on mode ge on lichoman bisgodan. Ða bisgu us sint swiþe earfoþrime þe on his dagum on þa ricu becoman þe he underfangen hæfde, and þeah ða he þas boc hæfde geleornode and of Lædene to Engliscum spelle gewende, þa geworhte he hi eft to leoð, swa swa heo nu gedon is. (B, preface, 1–9)
>
> [King Alfred was the translator of this book and turned it from book-Latin into English, as it now stands. Sometimes he put down word for word, sometimes sense from sense, just as he could interpret it most clearly and with best understanding in the face of the various and manifold worldly troubles that troubled him both in mind and in body. The troubles are hard for us to number which in his day came upon the kingdoms he had received; and nevertheless, when he had learned this book and turned (it) from Latin into an English account, he reworked it into song, as it now stands.]

Although this preface is almost certainly a later addition,[9] its assertion of Alfred's authorship of the *Boethius* itself, or at least his personal

---

8 Godden and Irvine, *Old English Boethius*. I will cite both versions of the Old English text from this edition but often silently depart from editorial punctuation.

9 It does little to create an impression of being in Alfred's voice or that of anyone close to him: against the first person of its closing bid for prayer for the king and affirmation of the author's modesty (not quoted here), which are highly conventional, it speaks rather distantly of events 'in Alfred's day' that are less than fully known 'to us,' and the 'troubles' of his reign are presented as an object not of experience but of historical imagination. I think it probable that the prose preface simply repeats the claim of Alfredian authorship found in the other, verse preface and explains the existence of two versions of the *Boethius* by outlining the sequence of the double composition, based on hearsay or inference. For useful recent discussion of the prose preface, see Frantzen, 'Form and

involvement in the translation, has usually been accepted following the pathbreaking work of Dorothy Whitelock and Janet Bately.[10] Recently, however, Malcolm Godden has argued that such evidence as exists does not readily conform to a theory of the king's personal translation of Boethius's Latin, and in view of analogous attributions of royal authorship that we do not take at face value, such as those from the court of Charlemagne, Godden suggests that the preface's claims bring little weight to the other side of the balance.[11] Certain details in the poems and the prose underlying them imply differences in background knowledge or understanding that make the poet of the Metres unlikely in any case also to have been the writer of the all-prose *Boethius*, regardless of whether either person was Alfred.[12] The order of composition stated by the preface, on the other hand, is clearly correct; it has been supported directly or indirectly by every close analysis of the two texts.[13]

What can be determined about the environment(s) in which the Old English *Boethius* was produced, and whether its two realizations represent a single vision or project, are questions that demand continued investigation, but one or both versions may well originate in the West Saxon courtly circle of scholars and advisers gathered by King Alfred, as some other,

---

Function,' 132–3; Godden, 'Did King Alfred Write,' 16–17; Discenza, 'Alfred the Great and the Anonymous Prose Proem'; and Godden and Irvine, *Old English Boethius*, 1:138, 1:141–2, and 2:242–5.

10 Esp. Whitelock, 'Prose of Alfred's Reign,' and Bately, 'Old English Prose.'

11 'Did King Alfred Write.' Not every line of argument Godden pursues is equally compelling: Pratt ('Problems of Authorship and Audience,' 180–4), writing before publication of Godden's 2007 article, critiques some assumptions about the text's reception and interpretation (expressed in Godden's previous writings, but represented also in 'Did King Alfred Write') which Godden believes imply composition away from the royal court. Bately ('Did King Alfred Actually Translate') answers some of Godden's linguistic and stylistic claims. However, her analysis of lexis implies only shared authorship of certain texts, not necessarily Alfredian authorship; and other points raised by Godden, now presented also in his edition with Irvine (*Old English Boethius*, 1:140–5), are sound, making it difficult to justify attributing the translation to Alfred himself.

12 Godden and Irvine, *Old English Boethius*, 1:146–51.

13 Benson, 'Literary Character'; Conlee, 'Note on Verse Composition'; Metcalf, *Poetic Diction*; Monnin, 'Poetic Improvements'; Donoghue, 'Word Order'; Griffiths, *Alfred's Metres*, 11–12; Stévanovitch, 'Envelope Patterns'; Griffith, 'Verses Quite Like *Cwen to Gebeddan*'; and most decisively, Griffith, 'Composition of the Metres.' Kiernan ('Alfred the Great's Burnt Boethius,' 11–13 and 25–6) has challenged the long-standing consensus without developing a full argument.

contemporaneous English translations of Latin books certainly did. Godden and Irvine express doubt on textual grounds that the all-prose and prosimetrical versions were produced near one another in time and place, but the evidence they adduce seems to me to point toward rather than away from relatively early textual co-occurrence and an entwined manuscript history for the prose and verse components of the *Boethius*.[14] In any case, no textual feature of the Metres demands a discontinuity with the first version more profound than a lack of common authorship. On thematic grounds, too, Godden and Irvine are hesitant about the usual assignment of the work to a courtly milieu and argue effectively that an Alfredian environment of production cannot be taken for granted.[15] However, to criticize foolish and prideful kings, as the *Boethius* does within a buffering fiction, is not to impugn all kings and could indeed compliment a presumptively wise and just one;[16] the nature of its commentary on kingship in itself argues neither for nor against courtly production.[17] On date, Godden and Irvine point out that either version of the *Boethius* could theoretically have been created at any time from about 890 to the mid-tenth century but favour c. 930 as a closing terminus.[18] For reasons that will become clear in the later sections of this chapter, I believe that without any improbable interpretation of the evidence – and taking into consideration what is known of the lost fragment N, a West Saxon text of early date – we can lean strongly toward production of both texts in either the last years of Alfred's reign or the early part of his son Edward the

14 This point cannot be elaborated here. Bredehoft's reconstruction of a group of poems that he believes were both available at Alfred's court and drawn on by the *Boethius* poet (*Authors, Audiences, and Old English Verse*, chap. 2), if accepted, would provide another circumstantial reason to suspect a connection between the production of the Metres and that of the all-prose *Boethius*.

15 *Old English Boethius*, 1:143–5. Cf. Godden, 'King and Counselor,' 203–7; Godden, 'Player King,' 140–6; and opposing view in Pratt, 'Problems of Authorship and Audience.'

16 Cf. Wallace-Hadrill, *Early Germanic Kingship*, 124–51.

17 Godden and Irvine give another rationale for doubting courtly authorship of the versified portions when they point to aspects of the text possibly indicative of 'a more ecclesiastical perspective' than in the all-prose version (*Old English Boethius*, 1:151). But even if the features identified do represent a specifically ecclesiastical point of view, this would hardly preclude court attachments on the part of the poet. Cf. Pratt, 'Problems of Authorship and Audience,' esp. 180–4, 190.

18 *Old English Boethius*, 1:145–6.

Elder's. My treatment of the *Boethius* will in no way presuppose Alfredian authorship or controlling influence, but I maintain the working hypothesis that West Saxon court-associated origin, in the very late ninth or very early tenth century, is circumstantially the most likely for both versions.

The dual form of the Old English *Boethius* gives it potentially great value in describing and defining the traditional poetics of mentality, but one aspect of the relationship between the two texts needs to be defined more precisely. Although most scholars regard each version of the *Boethius* as complete and finished, the all-prose one has occasionally been seen as a draft of the prosimetrical one rather than a finished product in its own right.[19] Because this view could call into question the intentional status of the prose version and thus its viability as a comparandum, the draft theory should be addressed briefly.[20] One difficulty with it is the very existence of B, a late copy: drafts not meant for circulation would not ordinarily be reproduced over a span of two centuries unless the final version were unavailable. Yet the existence of both texts in the same sphere of personal knowledge and manuscript availability after the composition of the Metres is virtually certain from the prose preface's association with both versions despite strictly fitting only the prosimetrical one: if the all-prose version represented a stemmatic offshoot of the text in an unfinished state, surviving in isolation from knowledge or availability of the finished prosimetrical version, it is hard to see how a preface written for that later version could have become attached to it. The draft theory derives from the prose preface's comment on the two forms of the *Boethius*, but the preface neither says nor implies that the second text superseded the first. If such had been the belief of the preface-writer, the reference to the all-prose version

19 K. Sisam never asserts that the all-prose version is only a draft but outlines a scenario in which this could be the case ('Authorship of the Verse Translation,' 294–5). Frantzen (*King Alfred*, 44) comments briefly on the prose text as a draft, and since then, Griffiths (*Alfred's Metres*, 12 and 41), Kiernan ('Alfred the Great's Burnt Boethius,' 26), and Szarmach ('*Metre 20*,' 29) have also made this claim, each of them a little carelessly. The comments of Griffiths proceed from a misapprehension about Latin *opera geminata*; see n. 22 below. Kiernan gives the prose preface too much authority and a questionable reading. Szarmach invokes 'scholarly consensus,' citing Greenfield and Calder's *New Critical History*, but the consensus to which Szarmach must intend to refer is on the prose version's priority, not its 'draft' status: Greenfield and Calder never suggest the latter and only mention the consensus that the Metres are a 'poetic paraphrase of the earlier Old English prose translation' (*New Critical History*, 245).

20 In addition to the points I will raise here, cf. arguments in Godden, 'Editing Old English,' 167–8, and Godden and Irvine, *Old English Boethius*, 1:45–6.

would be a needless piece of trivia about the process by which the work was composed. The remark makes sense, rather, as an explanation or announcement of the fact that the *Boethius* exists in two forms, both known to be in circulation.[21]

I suggest that the text's superficially odd doubleness of form, with its alternative presentations of Boethius's original *metra* as prose and verse, may be best understood in the literary-historical context of the *geminus stilus*. This mode of composition, in which both prose and verse versions of the same work were prepared, was well known to the Anglo-Saxons, three of whom, Aldhelm, Bede, and Alcuin, produced major examples of it.[22] In each of the Anglo-Latin *opera geminata* it is clear that the prose and metrical realizations were understood by their authors not in a hierarchical relationship of draft and finished product, but as dual, 'twin' products having a stylistic complementarity that accommodated, perhaps, different audiences and circumstances of use.[23] Statements within the works themselves indicate that both versions were expected to find a readership,[24] and their manuscript histories show that they did so: the alternative versions were copied, disseminated, and received separately more often than together in a single codex, just as the all-prose and the prosimetrical texts of the Old English *Boethius* come down to us independently in manuscripts B and C.[25] In the context of these influential Anglo-Latin writings of previous

21 This is so even if the statement reflects a remark in Lupus of Ferrières' commentary on the metrical forms used in Boethius's *Consolation*, as suggested by Godden, 'King Alfred and the *Boethius* Industry,' 138.

22 Aldhelm's *De virginitate*, Bede's *Vita sancti Cuthberti*, and Alcuin's *Vita sancti Willibrordi*. Essential surveys of the tradition are Wieland, '*Geminus Stilus*,' and Godman, 'Anglo-Latin *Opus Geminatum*.' The only previous association of the Old English *Boethius* with the *geminus stilus* that I have found is made in passing by Griffiths (*Alfred's Metres*, 12), who cites Aldhelm and Bede. However, Griffiths considers the earlier versions of these works 'drafts' of the later versions (a misconception flagged by Godden and Irvine, *Old English Boethius*, 1:45 n. 1).

23 See Wieland, '*Geminus Stilus*,' esp. 114–17 and 124–6; Godman, 'Anglo-Latin *Opus Geminatum*,' 222–6; and Schrader, 'Caedmon and the Monks,' 54–6. Only Alcuin explicitly indicates an expected divergence of readership and use, but such might likewise have been assumed by Aldhelm and Bede as a natural function of the stylistic dissimilarity to which they do call attention (see Wieland, '*Geminus Stilus*,' 122). Brown (*Companion to Bede*, 79–85) succinctly characterizes the different styles and purposes of Bede's two versions of the *Vita sancti Cuthberti*.

24 See authorial comments collected by Wieland, '*Geminus Stilus*,' 115–17.

25 Only four of the ten early manuscripts of Alcuin's *Vita sancti Willibrordi* include both forms of that work; just eight of thirty-eight copies of Bede's prose *Vita sancti*

generations, apart from vernacularity itself there is nothing anomalous about the existence of two formally differentiated renderings of Boethius's *Consolation* into Old English, each having a public textual life.[26]

All three of the substantial Anglo-Latin *opera geminata* call attention to their double form and comment on the relationship between the two versions,[27] and seen from this vantage point, the explanation of the two-part composition process in the *Boethius*'s prose preface may come into clearer focus. The verse preface goes a step further, giving a reason reminiscent of remarks by Alcuin in both versions of his *Vita sancti Willibrordi* that associate his metrical version with the Muses and with suitability for students. The use of poetry is presented as an accommodation for readers who might lose interest without the incentive of literary enjoyment to encourage diligence: Alfred, according to the preface, greatly desired

> ðæt he ðiossum leodum leoð spellode,
> monnum myrgen, mislice cwidas,
> þy læs ælinge ut adrife
> selflicne secg, þonne he swelces lyt
> gymð for his gilpe. (C, verse preface, ll. 4–8a)

> [that he might utter poetry for these people, various sayings, entertainment for men, lest tedium drive away the self-absorbed man when in his pride he cares little for such a thing.]

Perhaps what we have in the double text of the Old English *Boethius*, or in the production of the Metres that created that bifurcation, is an imitation of not just the mixed form of the *Consolation*, but the dual form of the *opera geminata* of past Anglo-Saxon luminaries – the most recent of whom, Alcuin, was part of the circle of scholars around Charlemagne (a

---

Cuthberti also have the corresponding metrical text; and not a single one of the forty-one manuscripts of either version of Aldhelm's *De virginitate* contains both the verse and the prose (Wieland, '*Geminus Stilus*,' 123–4; Godman, 'Anglo-Latin *Opus Geminatum*,' 223).

26 The biform of the *Boethius* is not all-prose and all-verse, but all-prose and *prosimetrum*, and in this of course it differs from the *opera geminata* of Aldhelm, Bede, and Alcuin, but the only partial rather than full versification can be explained as an imitation of the authoritative Latin original.

27 See citations assembled by Wieland ('*Geminus Stilus*,' 115–17). Godman ('Anglo-Latin *Opus Geminatum*') further discusses the reasons given by authors for producing double forms.

precedent for Alfred's own intellectual coterie) and appears to have had a personal role in the Carolingian popularization of Boethius's *Consolation.*[28]

In suggesting that the second version of the Old English *Boethius* is designed to deliver the special pleasures of poetry to an audience expected to demand those pleasures, the writer of this preface highlights its use of verse as its essential defining characteristic from the standpoint of imagined reception. The Metres differ from the prose chapters underlying them, that is to say, specifically in doing the things poems do to bring about the kinds of effects that poems bring about. This Anglo-Saxon perspective on the relationship between the texts, combined with the fact that (unlike the other versified portions of the *Boethius*) Metre 1 adapts an Old English prose narrative that is itself an original composition in English, makes it potentially an excellent source of information about the special character of Old English poetry.

Metre 1's Traditional Poetics of Mentality

The Traditionality of Metre 1's Versification

In carrying out the transformation of the *Boethius*'s historical introduction into verse, the poet proceeds with a continuous sense of connection to the underlying prose, maintaining contact with it as well as can be accomplished while remaking the text in the traditional poetic style. Throughout the Metres the versifier typically makes poetic lines by pairing one verse fashioned from lexical material found in the prose with a new, more independently constructed verse centring on a stressed lexeme marked more or less strongly as poetic, as Allan A. Metcalf first demonstrated.[29] Such a procedure balances a desire to stay close to the prose with a desire to traditionalize the language so that the text will participate recognizably in the

28 Bullough (*Alcuin*) argues that Alcuin's importance at the Carolingian court has been overestimated, but he also documents the burgeoning of Alcuin's posthumous reputation in the ninth century, and it is this reputation that would have relevance in Alfred's day. On Alcuin's role in the surge of interest in the *Consolation*, see Bolton, 'Study of the *Consolation of Philosophy*'; Gibson, 'Boethius in the Carolingian Schools'; Godden, 'Alfred, Asser, and Boethius'; and Godden, 'King Alfred and the *Boethius* Industry.' Charlemagne's court and its achievements are widely seen as a model for Alfred's, a view both fleshed out and refined by recent work: see esp. Story, *Carolingian Connections*, and Pratt, *Political Thought*.

29 *Poetic Diction*; cf. Conlee, 'Note on Verse Composition.'

special Old English poetic register. Mark Griffith has recently reaffirmed this compositional character of the Metres' lexis and finds parallel strategies in the versifier's handling of metre, prosody, and metrical grammar. Griffith's work in particular shows us a *Boethius* poet who is fully familiar with the technical norms of classical Old English poetry and handles them skilfully, with departures usually being attributable to some specific cue in the prose source.[30]

The poet's adherence to the underlying prose by retaining its language when practical implies the possibility of a damping effect on verse-specific strategies of expression. For the purposes of confirming the view of Old English poetic method for which I have been arguing, such a tendency of verbal overlap between the prose and the verse represents a potential hindrance that is actually useful. It means that should there exist any bias at all in the evidence, that bias will be of a kind that would work against demonstration of my thesis. If, on the other hand, the poetics of mentality can be clearly observed in Metre 1 of the *Boethius* despite lexical interference from the prose, this will strongly corroborate the analyses of *Genesis A* and *Genesis B* already presented.

The *Boethius* poet's competence with and investment in classical poetic style is not limited to metrical, metrisyntactic, and lexical practice, but extends as well to his or her informed use of traditional poetic diction in its full pragmatic character. This writer's frequent use of formulaic language has long been known as a quantitative fact. Contributions to the interpretation of that fact were made decades ago in Larry D. Benson's watershed examination of formulas' implications for the orality/literacy debate and in John W. Conlee's profile of the *Boethius* poet's patterns of formula use.[31] But like most studies of formulaic diction before them and many since, those by Benson and Conlee focused on the incidence and distribution of formulas and on conclusions that were thought to follow from those facts in themselves. The question of how formulas actually work in the Metres – not in the construction of verses, but in the making of meaning for writer and readers – has gone unasked. In order to perceive this aspect of Metre 1's traditionality, we need to attend to the

30 Griffith, 'Composition of the Metres.' Cf. the determination of Griffiths (*Alfred's Metres*, 47–51), based on indicators drawn from Amos, *Linguistic Means*, that the Metres have much more in common with classical Old English poetry than with late; and Bredehoft's placement of the Metres, with their 'lack of diagnostic late [half-line] forms,' firmly within the classical tradition ('Ælfric and Late Old English Verse,' 106).

31 Benson, 'Literary Character'; Conlee, 'Note on Verse Composition.'

communicative functionality, in this context, of its traditional forms based on patterns of usage in the existing corpus of classical-style Old English verse: the pragmatic dimension of a text in the poetic register can be discerned only in this way.

The *Boethius* poet's use of traditional diction exhibits his or her command of its semantic prosody and metonymic properties. I will illustrate this general characteristic of the versifier's practice only representatively, in the interest of moving along to a discussion of the poetics of mentality that takes full account of features above the level of diction. Analysis of a short sample of text, just the first five lines of Metre 1, will suffice to introduce the writer's techniques and can serve as a foundation for a more thematically oriented study of mentality throughout the poem.

Metre 1 opens thus:

Hit wæs geara iu   ðætte Gotan eastan
of Sciððia   sceldas læddon,
þreate geþrungon   þeodlond monig,
setton suðweardes   sigeþeoda twa;
Gotene rice   gearmælum weox. (C, Metre 1, ll. 1–5)

[It was long ago that the Goths from the east bore shields from Scythia, thronged with (their) host many a nation, established two conquering nations to the south. The domain of the Goths grew year by year.]

The first verse, 'hit wæs geara iu,' is a formula found five times in the Vercelli and Exeter Books.[32] It is built on the phrase *geara iu* (scanned Sxs) and precedes that phrase with an x-foot, usually amounting to two metrical syllables, the most common form for x-feet, to give the scansion xx | Sxs for the half-line.[33] In practice this formula appears to be limited to the a-verse. Its pragmatic function, as an introductory element establishing a chronologically remote setting, probably creates a lean toward the a-verse in usage, but it is hardly a necessary limitation and may be an arbitrary convention: transitions in thought often occur mid-line in Old English

32 *The Dream of the Rood*, l. 28a; *Vainglory*, l. 57a; *The Wanderer*, l. 22a; *Guthlac A*, l. 40a; and *The Order of the World*, l. 11a.

33 Once, in *The Order of the World*, l. 11a, it has a single-syllable first foot and thus the verse shape x | Sxs.

poetry, and other verses having the same metrical shape are as common in the b-position as in the a-.[34]

The *geara iu* formula aids in a construction of narratorial authority ostensibly based not on books but either on recollected personal experience (as in *The Dream of the Rood* and *The Wanderer*) or on another, more communal kind of memory, wise lore passed down through the generations, which *The Order of the World* invokes explicitly. Similar overtones attend the *geara iu* formula in *Vainglory*, where it introduces the account of the fall of the rebel angels as part of what 'se witga song, / gearowyrdig guma' [the wise one sang, a man ready of words] (ll. 50b–1a), in his warning to contemporaries not to grow similarly prideful. Both *The Order of the World* and *Vainglory* present themselves as a wise man's monologue; but even in *Guthlac A*, where *geara iu* occurs in reference to the making of scriptural prophecy – in Anglo-Saxon reality a decidedly textual and Latinate discourse – taken in context (ll. 35–58) the traditional phrase helps to colour that prophecy as the utterances of sages whose teachings on a favourite Old English sapiential theme, the ongoing decline of human and earthly order, have been handed down and are now being transmitted in turn by the poet. This formula's use at the outset of Metre 1 establishes a setting that is both chronologically distant and indefinite, and it ensures that from the very beginning of the prosimetrical *Boethius* – from Metre 1, line 1, verse a – readers are primed for poetry of the traditional kind, complete with its pretence of person-to-person transmission forming a community of lore. We are a very long way here, in register and mode of thought, from the opening of the prose version ('when the Goths of the Scythian tribe raised war against the kingdom of the Romans'), which by comparison seems packed with journalistic specifics.[35]

'Sceldas læddon' in line 2b is an easily recognizable formula in a rigorous sense of the term despite the fact that this exact combination of words

34 I base this claim on figures compiled by Hutcheson (*Old English Poetic Metre*, 216–17). The metrical configurations represented by real instances of this formula are xxPxS and xPxS in his notation.

35 'On ðære tide ðe Gotan of Sciððiu mægðe wið Romana rice gewin up ahofon' (B, 1.1–2). I am speaking in terms of rhetoric, not historical accuracy. My own understanding of the history of Theodoric's reign for the purposes of this chapter is based primarily on study of Tabacco, *Struggle for Power*, 37–72; Moorhead, *Theoderic in Italy*; and Amory, *People and Identity*. On the events concerning Boethius, I have also consulted Bark, 'Theodoric vs. Boethius'; Chadwick, *Boethius*, 1–68; Matthews, 'Anicius Manlius Severinus Boethius'; Morton, 'Marius of Avenches'; and Marenbon, *Boethius*, esp. 7–16.

occurs nowhere else in the poetic corpus. Whereas many formulas combine a metrisyntactic template with one stable lexical component, this one replaces lexical with semantic constancy and applies the semantic constraint across the whole verse: it always consists of a direct object + verb configuration, scanning Sx | Sx, with the meaning 'carry shields.'[36] *Beran*, *wegan*, and *lædan* 'carry' and *scild*, *rand*, and *lind* 'shield' appear in several different pairings while maintaining the same metrical form, word order, and syntactic relationship. Thus *The Battle of Maldon* – a late poem, but one intent on hitting many traditional notes[37] – can meaningfully be said to use the same formula twice in consecutive b-verses even though the two lines share not a word between them:

Wodon þa wælwulfas (for wætere ne murnon),
wicinga werod, west ofer Pantan,
ofer scir wæter scyldas wegon,
lidmen to lande linde bæron. (*Battle of Maldon*, ll. 96–9)

[The slaughter-wolves advanced – didn't worry about water – west across the Panta, the troop of vikings, carried shields over bright water; the seamen bore linden-shields to land.]

Once in *Beowulf* (l. 1889b) it is not shields but byrnies that are borne, but this is still a defensive article of war-gear, having therefore a reasonably close semantic link to shields, and in this more marginal case the affiliation with an already-familiar formula probably remained apparent.

The formula as a whole indicates the organized movement of an armed troop,[38] and its connotations befit the combination of reference to collective movement with the naming of a primarily defensive piece of weaponry:

36 *Genesis A*, l. 2049b; *Exodus*, l. 332b; *Beowulf*, ll. 2365a, 2653b, and 2850b; and *The Battle of Maldon*, ll. 98b and 99b. The verb in this formula may be either the infinitive form or a disyllabic finite form; for the scansion, see Bredehoft's foot combination rule 3a (*Early English Metre*, 27–8) and 'last word stressed' rule (ibid., 39–40 and 138–9 n. 8).

37 E.g., Bredehoft ('Ælfric and Late Old English Verse') singles out *The Battle of Maldon* as largely lacking in half-lines of types symptomatic of changing metrical norms. *Maldon* exemplifies formal 'conservatism in its most powerful mode' (91) and is 'consciously (or at least conspicuously) archaizing' (107).

38 G. Clark, 'Beowulf's Armor,' 434, references 'the theme of the advancing army' in a passage of *Beowulf* that uses similar language, citing fuller analysis in his doctoral dissertation. There, he does not identify this formula as such but discusses many instances of men being said to carry shields or to be shield-carriers ('Some Traditional Scenes,'

the 'carry shields' formula always indicates not an immediate transition into the act of fighting but a military relocation ('move men and arms in an organized fashion'). In *Beowulf*, where it occurs four times (including the instance substituting byrnies for shields), the formula first describes the young protagonist, now an accomplished monster-fighter, and his band of warriors returning home to resume their service to Hygelac (l. 1889b), and later the Hetware moving to defend their allies during Hygelac's raid on the Frisians (l. 2365a). During Beowulf's fight with the dragon, this particular kind of shield-carrying is what Wiglaf urges his companions against (l. 2653b), exhorting them not to leave at the moment of their lord's greatest need; there the formula calls to mind an organized retreat of a fighting force that would in context be a negative action.

Those earlier instances suggest a sharp irony in *Beowulf*'s fourth and last evocation of the 'carry shields' formula, when the retainers – who did flee from the dragon fight after all – return sheepishly to the site of Beowulf's death:

> Ða ne dorston ær   dareðum lacan
> on hyra mandryhtnes   miclan þearfe,
> ac hy scamiende   scyldas bæran,
> guðgewædu,   þær se gomela læg.   (ll. 2848–51)

> [Those (men) had not dared before to fight with spears in their lord's great need, but growing ashamed, they bore shields, war-gear, to where the old man lay.]

There is no doubt about the ethical status of the deserters. They are said in these lines to be ashamed; the narrating voice has here and previously identified their actions as cowardly; and in a moment they will be excoriated by the faithful Wiglaf. That these warriors whom the poet understatedly calls 'hildlatan' [late to battle] (l. 2846a) should now 'bear shields' to the scene of the fight they earlier abandoned is worse than belated. So much has always been clear to modern readers, but the use of this formula at this moment, with its connotation of organized military movement, enhances the effect: the warriors who previously ran away now move collectively and purposefully, though well aware of their ignominy, to occupy

14–67). The associations of the particular metrisyntactical and semantic unit on which I focus are more specific.

a position that has been made safe by the death of their lord. Their formulaically borne shields will resolve into devastating concreteness in Wiglaf's ensuing speech as the poet seizes on the traditional image and gives it body, making a rhetorical focal point of the material weaponry the men are said to carry. In his condemnation of the cowardly retainers, Wiglaf calls attention explicitly to their arms – both to their failure to use them on this occasion, and to the objects' social-symbolic value as gifts from their lord. The disgraced men stand over the body of Beowulf holding and wearing signs whose original meaning has reversed: their weapons now signify trust misplaced, honour wasted, and obligation shirked.

Outside of *Beowulf*, the 'carry shields' formula is connected every time it appears with purposeful, controlling movement into territory not previously possessed by the group described, but still is never used in immediate description of fighting. In *Genesis A* it occurs at the beginning of Abraham's expedition to recover hostages and possessions that have been taken from the king of Sodom (l. 2049b). In *Exodus* it comes during the crossing of the Red Sea (l. 332b), which is of course – from the perspective of writer and anticipated reader – a glorious movement into territory previously unoccupied by the principals and toward the new, divinely ordained homeland of Canaan. In these two cases the movement is divinely endorsed; the troops moving out are understood to be on the side of right. Metre 1's incursion of a conquering force into territory with whose Christian defenders poet and audience are expected to identify has more in common with the double use of the formula in *The Battle of Maldon* quoted above, where it is the 'wælwulfas' [slaughter-wolves], the 'wicinga werod' [troop of vikings] (ll. 96–7a), who file across the causeway onto what is, in that poet's perspective, home turf guarded righteously but inadequately.

Both verses of Metre 1, line 3, participate in traditional dictional forms. Line 3a, 'þreate geþrungon,' is a marginally attested formula, but probably a genuine one, further supported by a traditional collocation. Its core structure is the combination of a verb with the root *þring*– 'throng, press' with a dative/instrumental (and thus disyllabic) form of the noun *þreat* 'crowd.' The construction seen in Metre 1 is matched twice in the Exeter Book poem *The Phoenix*: 'þreatum biþrungen' (l. 341a) and 'þreatum þringað' (l. 501a). In all three instances the noun *þreat* precedes the verb, and the basic metrical pattern is Sx | Sx (with an extrametrical syllable proclitic to the second foot twice present, in the prefixed forms of the verb, and once absent). As is often the case with formulas having more than one stable lexical element, those constituents can also be found in close contact outside of the formulaic structure strictly defined. *Þreat* and *þringan* are paired in alliterative collocation in *Elene* (l. 329) and *Judith* (l. 164), both times grouped also with the same third alliterating term, *þrym*. These two lines do not coincide closely enough metrically or semantically to call the recurrence they share a formula, but it is apparent that the conjunction of the alliterating terms *þreat* and *þringan*, and of *þrym* with one or both of them (it appears in collocation with *þringan* twice in *Vainglory*, at ll. 24 and 42), had a comfortable ring to the Anglo-Saxon poetic ear.

Line 3b of Metre 1, 'þeodlond monig,' is another formula with stable lexical components: a whole-verse construction *q-lond manig*, the first word of which is always a disyllabic compound, giving the metrical shape Ss | Sx. The exact phrase found in Metre 1 occurs also in *Genesis A* (l. 1766a). Other realizations are 'sidland manig' (*Genesis A*, l. 2207a) and 'eglond monig' (*Maxims I*, l. 15a).[39] What each of these instances has in common with the others, contextually, is reference to a territory whose abundance is emphasized and whose occupants are said to hold it by divine ordination. In Metre 1, this formula combines with that in the preceding half-line, 'þreate geþrungon,' to characterize the Gothic overrunning of vast tribal territories as an act of unjustified aggression. The received semantic prosody is called upon to create a connotation of judgment transcending the human and of wrongness beyond the merely political.

The *Boethius* poet also shows mastery of another kind of traditional metrical-semantic construction, the formation of poetic compound words. An example of the practice in the opening lines of Metre 1 is 'gearmalum' (l. 5b), otherwise attested nowhere in verse or prose but representing the sole intersection of a group of poetic compounds in *gear–* and another group in *–mæl*. Looking a few lines beyond the first five, we find another apparent nonce compound, 'folcgewinnes' (l. 10a); and similarly, while itself unique, it takes its place among numerous attested compounds in either *folc–* or *–gewinn*. Despite being *hapax*, through their relationships to familiar sets of poetic compound words both *gearmæl* and *folcgewinn* succeed in sounding completely traditional, as lexical isolates so often do (paradoxically, to modern sensibilities) in Old English poetic diction. They function exactly like other poetic compounds found nearby that

39 A variant with a genitive plural, 'ealanda mænig,' occurs in *Paris Psalter* 96.1, l. 4a, but as previously noted (chapter 1, n. 5), the *Paris Psalter* cannot be counted on for evidence of traditional style. This is a case in point: the verse 'ealanda mænig' would be best scanned Ssx | Sx, disrupting the metrical shape of the formula that the phrase superficially appears to realize.

happen not to be unique, such as *sigeþeod* (l. 4b), *lindwigend* (l. 13a), and *eðelweard* (l. 24b), which likewise participate in larger networks of composed lexemes to which both their first and second components link them. In forming verses around compounds like these, including nonce compounds, the poet exploits a traditional device of Old English versecraft. In addition to having their individual signifying properties as words occurring in their own contexts, they join the other dictional features we have seen in continually affirming the classical poetic register as the operative communicative medium.

Formulaic and other traditional diction such as we have seen represented in the first five lines abounds throughout Metre 1.[40] In this way too, as well as through the general adherence to classical norms of metre and the introduction of poetically marked vocabulary to balance language retained from the prose source, the *Boethius* poet displays a strong sense of traditionality and competence in acting on it.

Metre 1's Subjectivization of the Received Story

With this awareness of the traditional nature of the poet's versecraft in Metre 1, then, let us look topically at his or her presentations of subjective experience and mentality throughout the poem. The historical introduction of the all-prose version begins,

> On ðære tide ðe Gotan of Sciððiu mægðe wið Romana rice gewin up ahofon and mid heora cyningum, Rædgota and Eallerica wæron hatne, Romane burig abræcon and eall Italia rice þæt is betwux þam muntum and Sicilia þam ealonde in anwald gerehton, þa æfter þam foresprecenan cyningum Þeodric feng to þam ilcan rice. (B, 1.1–6)

> [In the time when the Goths of the Scythian tribe raised war against the kingdom of the Romans and with their kings (they were called Rædgota and Alaric) sacked the city of the Romans and brought into their rule the whole kingdom of Italy, which is between the mountains and the island of Sicily, then – after those aforementioned kings – Theodoric succeeded to that same kingdom.]

40 In the remainder of this chapter, I will not catalogue traditional dictional structures in Metre 1 but will cite them where they bear directly on discussion.

The versifier turns what started out as a single sentence into over thirty lines of verse, expanding the material to about two and a half times its original length by word count:

Hit wæs geara iu   ðætte Gotan eastan
of Sciððia   sceldas læddon,
þreate geþrungon   þeodlond monig,
setton suðweardes   sigeþeoda twa;
Gotene rice   gearmælum weox.
Hæfdan him gecynde   cyningas twegen,
Rædgod and Aleric;   rice geþungon.
Þa wæs ofer Muntgiop   monig atyhted
Gota gylpes full,   guðe gelysted,
folcgewinnes.   Fana hwearfode
scir on sceafte.   Sceotend þohton
Italia   ealla gegongan,
lindwigende.   Hi gelæstan swua
efne from Muntgiop   oð þone mæran wearoð
þær Sicilia   sæstreamum in,
eglond micel,   eðel mærsað.
Ða wæs Romana   rice gewunnen,
abrocen burga cyst;   beadurincum wæs
Rom gerymed.   Rædgot and Aleric
foron on ðæt fæsten;   fleah casere
mid þam æþelingum   ut on Crecas.
Ne meahte þa seo wealaf   wige forstandan
Gotan mid guðe.   Giomonna gestrion
sealdon unwillum   eþelweardas,
halige aðas –   wæs gehwæðeres waa –
þeah wæs magorinca   mod mid Crecum,
gif hi leodfruman   læstan dorsten.
Stod þrage on ðam.   Þeod wæs gewunnen
wintra mænigo,   oðþæt wyrd gescraf
þæt þe Ðeodrice   þegnas and eorlas
heran sceoldan.   (C, Metre 1, ll. 1–31a)

[It was long ago that the Goths from the east bore shields from Scythia, thronged with (their) host many a nation, established two conquering nations to the south. The domain of the Goths grew year by year. They had two lawful kings, Rædgota and Alaric; those powerful ones flourished. Then many a

> Goth full of pride was enticed over the Alps, delighted with war, the strife of peoples. Shining banner waved on shaft. Shooters, shieldbearers, meant to overrun Italy entirely. They advanced so from the Alps all the way to the famous shore where Sicily, the great island in the sea-currents, bounds the homeland.[41] Then the kingdom of the Romans was defeated, the best of cities sacked; Rome was laid open to warriors. Rædgota and Alaric entered that stronghold; the emperor fled with the princes out to the Greeks. The woeful remnant could not resist the Goths with battle, with warfare. The guardians of the homeland unwillingly gave them the treasure of (their) ancestors (and) holy oaths – there was misery over both – yet the mind of the young warriors was with the Greeks, if they might dare to support the leader of the people. So things remained for a while. The nation stayed conquered for many years until fate ordained that thanes and nobles must obey Theodoric.]

This passage epitomizes the kinds of changes made by the poet as he or she transforms the historical introduction of the all-prose *Boethius* into verse. More detail is provided, to be sure, but although the poet adds some new information (such as the idea that the emperor fled when the Goths entered the city,[42] or that the protectors of the nation continued to hope for outside help when forced by circumstances to submit), this is not done in the manner of a writer who believes that an inadequate basis of fact has been offered by the prose: the elaboration has a decidedly poetic rather than historiographic timbre. The versifier is working the matter provided by the prose into the traditional register, and amplifications occur in the process of re-expressing the narrative through poetic diction, syntax, and motifs. Where the supplied material is conformable enough to verse to be accommodated easily, it is retained; where it suggests a familiar poetic motif, it is shaped in that direction; and where new or slightly different content would aid in translating the narrative core into Old English verse, the *Boethius* poet does not hesitate to make such adjustments. Here and throughout Metre 1, just as we have found in other texts, traditional language, traditional content, and traditional narrative techniques are inseparable: the poetics of mentality comes into play partly as it permeates traditional expressive forms, partly as it guides the poet's sense of what is

41 On the translation of *mærsian* 'declare, make known' in l. 16b as 'bound, demarcate,' see Kern, 'Zu altenglisch *mǽrsian*,' and his citation (395–6) of another instance with the same meaning in the all-prose *Boethius* (B, 33.178).

42 In fact, at this time the Western empire was governed from Ravenna, where the emperor remained in 410 and whence Theodoric would rule Italy after killing Odoacer in 493.

worth saying, and partly as it exerts a subjectivizing pull on the representation of recounted events.

Already in these opening lines of Metre 1 we see the poet imaginatively developing subjective dynamics, in the process trading heavily on motifs and experiential moments that are familiar fare at the table of Old English verse: armed conflict, defeat and exile, the desperation of the leaderless. In this passage derived from just the first sentence of the prose, two separate runs of lines seize upon an available locus of subjectivity without precedent in the source text. The first (ll. 8–13a) follows the introduction of the Goths as a tribe overrunning Western Europe and makes the transition to their invasion of Rome. Prior to these lines the movements of the Goths have been recounted objectively, as if observed from the outside. But here, as they reach the region with whose interests readers are meant to identify (subalpine Italy will be called *eðel* 'the homeland' and formulaically demarcated just after this in ll. 14b–16, and in l. 18a Rome will be *burga cyst* 'the best of cities'),[43] they become more subjectively realized: they are 'enticed' by an interior quality, *gylp*, which they are assigned using formulaic diction;[44] they like battle; they have intentions.

As if bringing a distant thing into clearer view, the poet discloses the approaching conquerers' interiority and by that means defines their place in an ethical web, positing a causality that consists of a national character expressing itself in antagonistic action. Yet through the same trick of focalization that we have seen in *The Ruin*, the collective subjectivity is simultaneously granular: it is 'many *a* Goth,' not just 'the Goths,' and the adjectival *gelysted* 'delighted' is morphologically singular to match *Gota.* At this moment the poem calls up an image of a single Gothic warrior, but a stereotyped image said to be iterated many times over: the proud, battle-eager individual, behaving autonomously yet representatively, experiencing his own attitudes, perceptions, and emotions but doing so exactly as his fellows do and thus functioning as our lens on his entire tribe. The Gothic army is a dangerous, predatory invader, its members like-minded yet personally motivated.

---

43 Howe, 'Rome,' explores Anglo-Saxons' identification with Rome. Riedinger, '"Home,"' describes the importance of such designations, especially using traditional diction.

44 Line 9a, 'Gota gylpes full,' actualizes an a-verse formula in which *full* is preceded by two words, each a metrical disyllable scanned Sx, the second of them in the genitive case: see *Exodus*, l. 451a; *Christ I*, l. 88a; *Christ III*, ll. 961a and 1657a; and *Phoenix*, l. 267a. In this construction *full* groups with the preceding genitive to form the second foot, on a metrical paradigm set by trisyllabic compounds, scanned Sxs.

The Gothic *gylp* is problematically ungoverned, in general moral terms – they take active pleasure in 'war, the strife of peoples' – but it acquires more specific meaning here in relation to the interests of the ethically privileged Romans. The next lines recount the Goths' entry into Rome and the flight of the emperor, after which we enter a new patch of focalization as this state of affairs is explored through the perspective of the defeated citizens (ll. 22–7). The choice of the rare compound *wealaf* 'survivors of a woeful event' in line 22a warrants scrutiny. Outside of this instance in Metre 1 it occurs only three other times: twice in verse – both of these in *Beowulf*, separated by just thirteen lines – and once in prose.

Wealaf's two appearances in *Beowulf* both come in the lay of Finnsburh, sung by Hrothgar's scop during the celebration of Grendel's defeat. In the scop's tale, the Danish prince Hnæf and his thanes have gone to visit Hnæf's sister Hildeburh and her husband Finn the Frisian, and while they are there, fighting breaks out between the Danes and their hosts. The two sides reach a terrible stalemate: the Danes, having lost their lord Hnæf and now led by Hengest, have a defensible position but are trapped there; the Frisians have lost a large number of men, including the son of Finn and Hildeburh, and now have insufficient strength to bring the fight to a conclusion. Both times it is used here, *wealaf* refers to the thanes of the slain prince Hnæf who are barricaded inside a hall and have been fighting Finn's troops outside from that position:[45]

Wig ealle fornam
Finnes þegnas nemne feaum anum,
þæt he ne mehte on þæm meðelstede
wig Hengeste wiht gefeohtan,
ne þa <u>wealafe</u> wige forþringan,
þeodnes ðegne; ac hig him geþingo budon,
þæt hie him oðer flet eal gerymdon,
healle ond heahsetl, þæt hie healfre geweald
wið Eotena bearn agan moston,
ond æt feohgyftum Folcwaldan sunu

45 This situation is elucidated somewhat by *The Fight at Finnsburh*, which recounts part of the battle preceding the events that are narrated here in *Beowulf*, and in which Hnæf and his men are clearly fighting from within a hall. This reconstruction of the scenario makes literal sense of the term *meðelstede* 'assembly place' used by the *Beowulf* poet for the location of the battle (l. 1082b) and also accounts for the verb *forþringan* 'drive out' (l. 1084b).

dogra gehwylce   Dene weorþode,
Hengestes heap   hringum wenede
efne swa swiðe   sincgestreonum
fættan goldes   swa he Fresena cyn
on beorsele   byldan wolde.
Ða hie getruwedon   on twa healfa
fæste frioðuwære.   Fin Hengeste
elne unflitme   aðum benemde
þæt he þa wealafe   weotena dome
arum heolde. (*Beowulf*, ll. 1080b–99a)

[War took away all but a few of Finn's thanes such that he could by no means win the battle in that meeting-place against Hengest, the prince's thane – could not with warfare drive out the trauma-remnant.[46] So instead they (Finn and company) proposed terms to them, that they would make entirely open to them the other (i.e., Finn's own) hall-floor, the hall and the high-seat, so that they (the Danes) would have control of half along with the sons of the Jutes;[47] and that each day at gift-giving Folcwalda's son (i.e., Finn) would honour the Danes, present Hengest's band with rings, just as much as it pleased him to cheer the race of the Frisians with treasures of plated gold in the beer-hall. Then on both sides they concluded a firm peace treaty. Nobly, with lack of contention, Finn declared to Hengest with oaths that he would govern the trauma-remnant honourably by the judgment of his councillors.]

The first time the word comes up, the situational misery conveyed by the compound focuses the devastation of battle on the cornered survivors' loss of their prince. The second time the Danes are called a *wealaf* comes just after they have accepted vexing terms of peace, formally agreeing to the proposal of their lord's slayer that they assume a place in his reduced retinue alongside his own thanes. Finn offers them equal footing, full

46 Considering the ability of the *ge–* proclitic to create a teleological lexical connotation (Lindemann, *Old English Preverbal Ge–*), in this context it seems to me that *gefeohtan* must mean 'conclude the business of fighting,' i.e., 'win,' just as *gebidan* can mean 'conclude the business of awaiting,' i.e., 'experience,' and *gesecan* can mean 'conclude the business of seeking,' i.e., 'reach, visit, attack.'

47 These 'Jutes,' whoever they are (the term's meaning here is disputed), are either a discrete subset of Finn's retinue or are mingled in it with his Frisians such that poetic licence permits interchangeable use of the terms. What is important here is that they are Finn's men.

access to *healle ond heahsetl*, where (as those juxtaposed words and the verb *geryman* all suggest) both literal and social-symbolic space will be made for their participation in the rituals of community. They are promised honour and gifts, but when imagined from their perspective, this will translate into disgrace so long as their group identity as Danes remains intact as a frame of reference in which past events continue to have present significance.

Finn's gag order in the subsequent lines (ll. 1100–6) is designed explicitly to cover over and eventually erase those past events – and by implication, Danish identity itself – from memory. By forbidding within the terms of the oath any mention of the fact that Finn has taken the place of the Danes' slain lord and they the place of his own fallen retainers, Finn hopes to render the past silent and powerless. But one of *Beowulf*'s conceptual constants is the past's long reverberation in community memory. Most of the characters in the poem, and certainly Hrothgar's scop in narrating this episode as a hall entertainment, accept the legitimate persistence of former events as signifiers in the present, and the desperate peace at Finnsburh will not last. The absorbed party of Danes will indeed retain its identity, its memory of the hostilities having not been removed but merely removed from view, and after an anguished winter spent enveloped by the Frisian hall and warband they will go on to avenge Hnæf's death by killing Finn before returning home triumphantly with the sonless, brotherless, and finally widowed Hildeburh in tow (ll. 1127b–59a). But all of that lies in the future. Here, at the point critical to our understanding of the term *wealaf*, the word signals not just the grief and privation of those driven to extremity by violent conflict, but also their abjection and perhaps even their miserable complicity in the replacement of a correct social order with a perverse simulacrum.

The likeness of situation between the context of the word's use in Metre 1 and in *Beowulf* is striking, and in form, too, its environment in *Beowulf* is curiously close to that in Metre 1 in ways that exceed the usual half- or whole-line reach of dictional formulas and collocations: in addition to pairing *wealaf* with *wig* to make the alliterative connection between half-lines, both poets follow that construction with an infinitive beginning with the prefix *for–* and dependent on the modal verb *magan*. The incidental similarities are close enough that we may be looking here at a direct reminiscence.[48] It is easy to imagine the versifier of the Metres, if he or she

48 It is worth noting that C. Davis ('Ethnic Dating') argues that *Beowulf* was produced in Alfredian Wessex. Davis builds on Lapidge's suggestion of a 'c. 900' West Saxon *Beowulf*

knew *Beowulf*, seizing upon the apt and memorable compound *wealaf* and then compressing the two ideas associated with it, the unfeasibility of continued warfare and the swearing of humiliating oaths (already close together in *Beowulf*), into the passage from Metre 1 quoted above while supplementing them with a traditionally resonant element, the loss of ancestral treasure.

Arguing from dictional elements like *wealaf* that are shared exclusively between the Metres of the Old English *Boethius* and one other poem, Thomas Bredehoft too suspects direct influence of *Beowulf* (along with several other known texts) on the Metres. To Bredehoft, a textual relation of this kind implies the lack of genuine tradition,[49] but the proximate source of a given dictional item does not matter provided it can be recognized by a reader as having the qualities of traditionality that associate it with the special register of classical Old English poetry. All that is needed is the continued viability of the traditional register for writers and audiences, which in the case of Metre 1 the poet's adept use of traditional dictional forms, techniques, and motifs amply indicates.

Suppose, for example, we could be sure that *wealaf* was borrowed directly from *Beowulf* by the *Boethius* poet and was not familiar to writer or audience from any other occurrences. Nevertheless, as a compound formed according to processes intrinsic to poetic diction, the word sustains the register of classical verse in the way that poetic compounds regularly do, including unique ones. A reader of Metre 1 who had never encountered the word before would receive it as a possible nonce formation, one in perfect tune with traditional versecraft, whose elements evoke traditional preoccupations of classical poetry. If, on the other hand, a reader who also knew *Beowulf* happened to recognize it as a precedented usage, it would still look, sound, and feel right in all the same ways, and again would be perceived as participating in the special register of classical verse: not as an allusion to or citation of *Beowulf*, but as a suitably poetic word

---

exemplar (date as characterized by Davis, ibid., 112; but N.B. that Lapidge posits that exemplar's existence tentatively, as it does not necessarily follow from his palaeographical analysis: Lapidge, 'Archetype,' 36). Following Stanley, 'Paleographical and Textual Deep Waters,' Davis sets aside the part of Lapidge's evidence that would point beyond that exemplar to a still prior manuscript of *Beowulf* from c. 700–c. 750 (Davis, 'Ethnic Dating,' 112; Lapidge, 'Archetype,' 29–34). The status of that evidence is still under discussion: see G. Clark, 'Date of *Beowulf*.'

49 *Authors, Audiences, and Old English Verse*, chap. 2.

whose appropriateness to the context was affirmed by a known prior instance. Just as was argued in chapter 2 in reference to *wraðmod*, the form and textually local function of the word, as those characteristics relate intelligibly to classical poetic praxis, are much more important to its decoding by readers than knowledge of a pedigree revealing its proximate or ultimate origins. However the correspondence came about, the connotations of subjugation and privation of accustomed social order in *Beowulf* agree perfectly with the plight of the conquered Romans in Metre 1, and the poet's use of the rare and arresting word *wealaf* in that environment serves a traditionalizing function.[50] The *Boethius* poet's new detail of the emperor's flight takes on additional appropriateness as part of this complex of ideas, making the Roman citizens, like Hengest and his Danish companions, suddenly leaderless.

The lone occurrence of *wealaf* in a prose environment comes in a homily by Wulfstan as he is waxing poetic – or, at least, adopting a highly embellished style, with conspicuous formal patterning, for elevated rhetorical effect.[51] This time *wealaf* follows a cascade of eschatological disasters and thus accords with Roberta Frank's observation that when predominantly poetic words appear in prose, they 'tend to cluster in rhetorical set-pieces' where some verbal pyrotechnics might be expected.[52] I give the prose passage below in an ad hoc lineated setup that makes apparent to the eye its use of formal devices, particularly rhyme. The context is a warning in the voice of God that those who do not heed his commandments will be given into the hands of their enemies, after which

land hy awestað
⁊ burga forbærnað
⁊ æhta forspillað,
⁊ eard hy amyrrað;

50 Cf. Roberta Frank's comments on the archaizing and traditionalizing function of some of the simplices she discusses ('Sharing Words,' esp. 6–11).

51 On Wulfstan's characteristic style, see Orchard, 'Crying Wolf'; on the Jakobsonian poetic function (which foregrounds patterned language and encourages aesthetic response) in Old English outside of classical verse, see now Beechy, *Poetics of Old English*.

52 'Poetic Words in Late Old English Prose,' 90; description of Judgment Day is one of the contexts Frank mentions. Chapman ('Poetic Compounding') finds that similar patterns of rhetorical heightening typify homilists' use of compound words that otherwise occur only in verse.

and þonne land wyrðeð
for synnum forworden
⁊ þæs folces dugoð
swyþost fordwineþ.
Þonne fehð seo wealaf
sorhful ⁊ sarimod
geomrigendum mode
synna bemænan
⁊ sarlice syfian,
þæt hy ⁊ heora yldran
me swa gegremedan
þurh þæt hy noldan
mine lage healdan
ac me ofersawan
on mænigfealde wisan. (Homily 19, ll. 67–73)[53]

[they (i.e., the enemies) will lay the land waste and burn up cities and ruin possessions, and they will spoil the earth; and the land will be destroyed on account of sins, and the multitude of the people will severely dwindle. Then the trauma-remnant – sorrowful and miserable in mind, with mourning mind – will start to bemoan and miserably lament sins: that they and their predecessors so provoked me, in that they would not observe my law but neglected me in many different ways.]

These statements are organized by a combination of sound patterning and rhetorical structure. The whole sequence is given symmetry by rhyme, mainly in the form of homoeoteleuton, which groups the passage into two eight-verse blocks with a smaller set of three verses between them. All but one of the first eight verses (ll. [1–8]) end in the pronunciation [–ə*θ*], and all of the final eight (ll. [12–19]) end in *–an*. This pattern is regular enough to cause one to wonder whether there might be a textual problem behind *forworden* (l. [6]), the only deviation;[54] but as it stands, line [6] remains linked to line [5] by an alliterating half-rhyme *wyrð–/–word–*. Between these two eight-verse concatenations falls the three-verse formal, syntactic, and rhetorical fulcrum of the passage (ll. [9–11]), in which *wealaf* comes as

53 Cited from Bethurum, *Homilies of Wulfstan*. Bethurum presents the text as prose; the bracketed line numbers are my addition for easy reference. I have repunctuated.

54 Bethurum records no textual variants for this word, which falls in her l. 69.

the subject of a new statement. Internally to that three-verse sequence, the second and third verses (ll. [10–11]) link together through repetition of the morpheme *mod*; and externally, this medial three-verse group links to the preceding lines through alliteration on *f*– and to the two that follow through alliteration on *s*– and *m*–. Wulfstan is bringing out the bells and whistles, marking as rhetorically elevated the vatic context that calls forth the poetic word *wealaf*. And this extract from a later prose homily affirms the associations shared by the two instances of *wealaf* in *Beowulf* and the one in Metre 1 of the *Boethius*, capturing (this time prophetically) the emotional predicament of a group diminished in number by violent conflict and subjected to their enemies.

When the *Boethius* poet produces the word *wealaf*, he or she applies marked language to evoke the emotional devastation of war, the sense of loss and regret among the subjugated survivors. The context of its use in Metre 1 gives further reasons for distress beyond defeat and the loss of comrades. As if having to swear fealty to a foreign lord were not bad enough, in relinquishing the treasure of their ancestors the conquered Romans are, in essence, forced to give up their tangible heritage, a token of their collective identity. Their experiential predicament and their anguish over it, both new introductions into the verse version, make for a scenario of deracination, disruption of community, and alienation from social order of just the type that Anglo-Saxon poets are attracted to, so often manifested in the motif of exile but here tapping into many of the same cultural horrors with reference to a stationary conquered population. Once the situation is put into these terms by the poet it resonates in the *Boethius* – just as the similar repudiation of history that the Danes temporarily accept resonates in the Finnsburh episode of *Beowulf* – because of the traditional importance of these and related themes in Old English verse.

The last part of the Metre 1 passage quoted above continues to grant access to the Romans' subjective position as we are told, without precedent in the prose, that their 'minds are with' the Byzantines in hopes that the latter might 'dare' to support the emperor in reclaiming his throne and the Romans in regaining their ancient rights. The idea of loyalty, brought in with the forced oaths to Theodoric, is thus developed in the form of a thought/action disjunction that is a standard part of the representation of duplicity in Old English poetry:[55] the Romans swear oaths outwardly but secretly maintain loyalty to their fled emperor and hoped-for Byzantine

55 Mize, 'Representation,' 83–5.

allies. We can know this only because the narration of the poetic version takes us into their minds through the technique of focalization. Issues of both loyalty and heritage will hover around the remainder of Metre 1, placing Boethius's political actions and his creation of the *Consolation* within a value scheme shaped by these two perennial poetic concerns.

The next passage of the prose introduction continues in its plainspoken style:

> Se Đeodric wæs Amulinga. He was cristen, þeah he on þam Arrianiscan gedwolan þurhwunode. He gehet Romanum his freondscipe, swa þæt hi mostan heora ealdrihta wyrðe beon, ac he þa gehat swiðe yfele gelæste, and swiðe wraðe geendode mid manegum mane. Þæt wæs, toeacan oðrum unarimedum yflum, þæt he Iohannes þone papan het ofslean. (B, 1.6–11)
>
> [This Theodoric was of the Amulings. He was Christian, although he persisted in the Arian heresy. He promised his friendship to the Romans, such that they could be possessed of their old rights, but he kept those promises very badly and finished very cruelly with many a crime. In particular, in addition to countless other evils, he had John the pope slain.]

The information given is descriptive and biographical, part of a profile briefly establishing Theodoric's character by putting him on the wrong side of a moral dividing line through rhetorical pairings in a 'good news, bad news' structure: he was Christian (good news), but of a heretical odour (bad news); he promised to restore the Romans' old privileges (good news), but failed utterly to do so and in fact became vicious (bad news). These statements are of different kinds, the first pair religious and the second pair political, with each new descriptive datum being followed by a qualification indicating Theodoric's shortcomings, in that category, as ruler of Rome. Next, when we get to the report of a particular outrage – that he went so far as to kill the pope – the act is not linked closely to Theodoric's Arianism but presented as the ultimate instance of the cruelty into which the early promise of his reign declined.

When the poetic version picks up at the corresponding place, it handles this material rather differently:

> Wæs se heretema
> Criste gecnoden; cyning selfa onfeng
> fulluhtþeawum. Fægnodon ealle
> Romwara bearn and him recene to

friðes wilnedon. He him fæste gehet
þæt hy ealdrihta ælces mosten
wyrðe gewunigen on þære welegan byrig,
ðenden God wuolde þæt he Gotena geweald
agan moste. He þæt eall aleag.
Wæs þæm æþelinge Arrianes
gedwola leofre þonne drihtnes æ.
Het Iohannes, godne papan,
heafde beheawon; næs ðæt hærlic dæd!
Eac þam wæs unrim oðres manes
þæt se Gota fremede godra gehwilcum. (C, Metre 1, ll. 31b–45)

[That ruler was committed to Christ: the king himself received baptismal rites. All the sons of Romans rejoiced and quickly desired peace from him. He promised them firmly that they could live in possession of every one of their old rights in that prosperous city for as long as God wished that he might have rule of the Goths. He failed to fulfil all that. The Arian heresy was dearer to that prince than the Lord's law: he commanded that John, the good pope, be beheaded – that was no honourable deed! In addition to that there was an untold number of other crimes that the Goth perpetrated against every one of the good.]

The verse rewrite, like the prose, begins with a characterizing statement about Theodoric, but it immediately returns to the mental perspective of the Romans which it had emphasized a few lines earlier in the distress over oath-taking and the loss of their hereditary treasures. Here, Theodoric is a convert who receives baptism;[56] and then the fact of his Christianity leads straight into not a damning qualification of it, as in the prose, but the Romans' reaction to it as they rejoice and desire the new king's peace. It appears to them that the misery emphasized earlier in the poetic version (and absent from the prose) will now be relieved. This feature of the Romans' response to Theodoric's Christianity plays directly into the characteristic poetic emphasis on emotions and their role in ethical relationships: it will be not just the laws and rights of the Romans, but their joyous Christian fellowship that Theodoric later betrays.

---

56 Also noted as a significant alteration by Godden ('Anglo-Saxons and the Goths,' 65) and Godden and Irvine (*Old English Boethius*, 2:497).

Other increases in emphasis on mentality and subjectivity are present here as well. First, Theodoric's heresy, when it is finally mentioned, is conceived of as an expression of his personal desires; and second, his leadership of his own people (and therefore of subjugated Rome) is attributed to God's will, acknowledged by Theodoric himself, thus giving his accession a providential dimension of which he is aware and which he claims as a basis of his rule. The impact of these two additions is easiest to see in relation to the writer's reorganization of information inherited from the prose.

The poet postpones any reference to Theodoric's heretical bent, connecting the promise of restored rights to both his Christianity and God's endorsement of his kingship. By not immediately retracting the positive remark about Theodoric's religion as the prose version had done, and by instead allowing the Romans' joy in Christian rule to stand as a momentary status quo, the poet merges Theodoric's faith, already given an explicitly political dimension in the verse, to his promise to restore Rome's ancient rights. When he fails to keep the oath attached to his divinely permitted rule of Rome, then, what is made in the poem to look like a departure from the true faith that he had only recently accepted implies that he is not just a heretic, but an apostate. The translator here deviates from the prose and from history: in reality Theodoric had been an Arian all along. Insofar as the joy of religious community emphasized in Metre 1 has any basis in historical fact, the detail reflects Theodoric's tolerance of Catholicism and his permissiveness toward conversion away from Arianism. In reference to the last years of his reign – when Theodoric's Arianism began to cause him trouble with the new Byzantine emperor Justin I, who started enforcing legal sanctions against Arians – the poet makes it seem not as though adherence to Arianism had suffered a change in political status, but as though Theodoric's own religious views had undergone a change within a constant religio-political environment.

The delayed mention of Theodoric's heresy also links it much more tightly to his execution of the pope, in part through another reordering of material, as that outrage is moved forward to attach to it in addition to being put in somewhat more graphic terms. In the prose version, it was bad that Theodoric was a heretic, and it was bad that he committed crimes against Rome; it might be said that these two faults converged in his killing of the pope, but no direct connection was asserted. In the verse revision, the fact that Theodoric is a Christian – not a heretic initially, but simply a Christian – works decisively against him, because it is now his apostasy that leads directly into his murder of the pope. Theodoric's actions in Metre 1 bespeak a clash of wills between a powerful, religiously hostile ruler and the faithful: they have become the constitutive signs of a persecution scenario. The arena of activity and conflict is interiorized so that it involves a disjunction between what Theodoric believes, in his perverse, subjective attraction to the heresy that is 'dearer' to him 'than the Lord's law,' and what the Roman Christians are understood to insist both about Christ's divinity and about the status of Rome and its laws, the people's ancient rights.

When devout resistance to a tyrannical persecutor of the true faith leads to death, as it does for Pope John, it graduates to martyrdom. In the poetic version, the apostate Theodoric's execution of the pope clearly and immediately underscores his own status as an enemy of the faith, and this newly demarcated wickedness is confirmed by his categorical opposition to 'the good': 'Iohannes þone papan' [John the pope] (B, 1.11) becomes 'Iohannes, godne papan' [John the good pope] (l. 42), and Theodoric's cruel deeds are not general as they had been in the prose, but now target 'godra gehwilcum' [every one of the good] (l. 45b). The execution of the pope is further emphasized by the exclamation 'næs ðæt hærlic dæd!' [that was no praiseworthy deed!] (l. 43b), formed on a formulaic template of value affirmation that both presumes and strongly asserts the joint participation of poet and audience in an ethical community.[57] The many other cruel deeds are almost an afterthought now.

In aggregate, small changes infuse the poetic version with an agonistic, adversarial moral structure that is absent from the prose. The original writer had presented Theodoric disapprovingly but matter-of-factly as a heretic and a bad ruler who subscribed to an incorrect doctrine, broke promises, and acted cruelly. The conceptual framework of the verse reformulates these criticisms through a system of binary relationships. Each subjective position that will play a part in them is represented, and these different perspectives are all situated within a prior value system that gives them meaning and defines their ethical status. The method of developing relationships via binaries tends to polarize character when conflict is being represented, but there is nevertheless a sincere probing of philosophical and experiential difficulty, for instance in the portrayal of duplicity and

57 Cf. 'that was a good king!' (*Beowulf*, ll. 11b, 863b, and 2390b) and other similarly constructed evaluations: e.g., *Beowulf*, ll. 1075b and 1812b; *Daniel*, ll. 7 and 24; and *Deor*, l. 23b. *Widsith*, l. 67b, parallels Metre 1, l. 43b, in taking a negative form. Niles describes this kind of 'summary judgment' as a traditional feature that 'sets a totalizing stamp of approval on what [the narrator] admires' (*Homo Narrans*, 75). Here, of course, it is a totalizing stamp of disapproval.

the feelings attached to it. From the start it is apparent that such explorations will be carried out on the terms of traditional poetic art, by plotting subjective positions on an ethical grid that will have signifying power for audiences. Complexity arises not through subtleties of 'character' in a more modern sense, but situationally, and takes on meaning with respect to recognized points of reference.

The adjustments we have seen the poet make thus far in Metre 1 have the cumulative effect of collapsing together the religious and the political goings-on in Theodoric's Rome such that the presumption of shared Christian faith, and specifically a model of that faith that places it conceptually within a received tradition of persecution and martyrdom, provides important components of that value framework. But we can also see connections between the earlier passage and this one through Theodoric's oath to protect the Romans' *ealdriht*, their customary senatorial prerogatives and privileges as citizens. In the prose, this is the first time the political relationship between conqueror and conquered has been referenced. In Metre 1, however, that idea has already been contextualized by the giving of oaths and loss of hereditary treasure in the passage analysed prior to this one. The earlier attention to the subjective state of the conquered Romans in the verse casts Theodoric's accessional or baptismal oath as a welcome turnabout in a situation that the poet has already been monitoring. It likewise renders Theodoric's default on that oath a more intensely concentrated betrayal than it was in the prose, complementing the paradigm of apostasy and further contributing to the convergence of religious and political meaning.

Boethius makes his entrance in the next passage of the prose version:

> Þa wæs sum consul, þæt we heretoha hatað, Boetius wæs gehaten; se wæs in boccræftum and on woruldþeawum se rihtwisesta. (B, 1.11–13)

> [Then there was a certain consul – we call it a *heretoga*[58] – named Boethius; both in book-knowledge and in the customs of the world he was the 'right-wisest.']

The word *rihtwis* is used in an unusual way here. In the immediate context of its two limiting phrases, 'in boccræftum' and 'on woruldþeawum,' it

58 See Griffith, 'Composition of the Metres,' 1:118–19, on the use of *heretoga* as a vernacular technical word for consul.

cannot be translated with its Modern English reflex to give good sense: while 'righteous' could fit well enough with the second of these to indicate steadfast virtue in worldly affairs, the co-occurrence of *boccræft* 'scholarship, book-learning' makes the statement hard to interpret. The Bosworth–Toller *Anglo-Saxon Dictionary* cites this sentence from the prose *Boethius* three times as an illustrative quotation, in the entries for *rihtwís*, *weoroldþeáwas*, and *bóccræft*, and exhibits a telling confusion over it. Under both the lemmas *rihtwís* and *weoroldþeáwas*, the phrase 'in boccræftum' is silently omitted from the quotation. No suggested translation of the sentence is given at *rihtwís*, but 'rihtwisesta' within the quotation is not indicated to need modification from the general definition 'righteous, just' at the head of the entry. The entry for *weoroldþeáwas* does offer a translation: 'in the conduct of his life he was most righteous.' The same sentence's handling s.v. *bóccræft*, where of course that lexeme must appear, confirms that the omission of the 'boccræftum' phrase from the other citations was due to the ambiguity caused by its use with *rihtwis*. This time, the other qualifying phrase, 'in woruldþeawum,' is omitted, and the entry gives the translation 'Boethius, in book-learning, was the most wise.' In other words, the Bosworth–Toller dictionary defines a single occurrence of *rihtwis* two different ways to match each of the two phrasal qualifiers associated with it, suppressing the difficulty in all three citations with an unsignalled ellipsis.[59]

Consideration of this statement in its context suggests that the compound is being used analytically or etymologically by the writer such that its constituent elements, *riht* and *wis*, are not totally subsumed into a concept 'righteous' but point to the quality of being 'wise' concerning 'right, rectitude' – or even, arguably, concerning 'rights,' because the usage here, in unbroken sequence with what precedes and follows, connects it semantically as well as lexically with the concept of *ealdriht*, the 'ancient rights' of which Theodoric has deprived the Romans. It is the *ealdriht* that Boethius, here introduced as having wisdom concerning such things according to both traditional practice (worldly custom) and law or history (formal learning), will try to find a way to restore.

59 In their addenda and corrigenda to Bosworth–Toller, neither Toller nor Campbell resolves the jerry-rigged set of definitions, and the *Dictionary of Old English* (s.v. *bōccræft*, the only one of these three lemmas covered to date) does not suggest a meaning for the whole statement.

The verse rendering follows the prose closely in retaining both of these aspects of Boethius's wisdom, one with respect to books and the other with respect to the ways of the world, but distributes them differently:

Ða wæs ricra sum on Romebyrig
ahefen heretoga, hlaforde leof
þenden cynestole Creacas wioldon.
Þæt wæs rihtwis rinc: næs mid Romwarum
sincgeofa sella siððan longe.
He wæs for weorulde wis, weorðmynða georn,
beorn boca gleaw. Boitius
se hæle hatte se þone hlisan geþah. (C, Metre 1, ll. 46–53)

[Then a certain one among the powerful in the city of Rome, dear to his lord while the Greeks controlled the throne, was made consul. That was a just man: there was not a better treasure-giver among the Romans for a long time afterward. He was wise concerning the world, zealous for honour, a nobleman clear-minded about books. The hero who gained that reputation was called Boethius.]

This version leans in a different direction from the prose, being more nuanced in one respect and less so in another. Where the prose statement has a certain precision about the ancient rights and Boethius's suitability to defend them, encapsulated in what must in context be a special use of the word *rihtwis*, the verse shows more interest in evoking schemes of relationships. The poet reverts to the usual sense of *rihtwis* by letting it stand alone, removing book-learning and worldly experience from association with it so that each of them, too, becomes its own independent attribute. In doing so he or she severs any tie between that term and the lost Roman *ealdriht*.

But at the same time, these lines plug Boethius into two different relational systems, one in which he serves a lord and another in which he administers the populace. The poet locates both lord and people in the ethical landscape by granting us access to their perspectives on the medial figure, Boethius, who is an object of perception and opinion from both above and below in the social hierarchy. To his king, Theodoric, Boethius is dear (according to a formula of lordly or familial favour)[60] during the time when

60 In the form *q leof*, where *q* is always a metrical trisyllable in the dative case, for the whole-verse scansion Ssx | S: cf. *Genesis A*, ll. 1183b, 1285b, and 2598b; *Exodus*, l. 355b; and *Menologium*, l. 215b.

Theodoric remains at peace with his own overlord, the emperor in Constantinople;[61] and by the citizenry over whom he holds a position of governance, Boethius is respected, as line 53 affirms his achievement of the reputation that we have been told just previously it is his nature to seek and maintain. The poet has also specified that Boethius is the best 'treasure-giver' Rome would have for a long time, a manner of designating his role that emphasizes his relationship with the citizens, implicitly according to their collective opinion, on a traditional poetic model of benefaction and reciprocal obligation. In complementarity to those aspects of his representation, Boethius's own mental qualities – somewhat developed toward a less precise yet more robust, holistic notion of wisdom and worthiness – define his character in such a way as to trace the ethical contours of the relational networks in which he participates. The descriptions of Boethius as just, wise, learned, and mindful of honour serve as a moral measuring stick by which we may judge both Theodoric, who values Boethius's service prior to his hostilities with the emperor, and the Romans at large, who likewise properly value his leadership.

Nothing done in the verse is really at odds with the prose, but in terms of what is privileged as most important to establish and communicate, the poet proceeds according to an entirely different set of priorities that involve Metre 1 intimately with the methods and preoccupations of traditional Old English poetic discourse, giving mentality and ethical status meaning with respect to each other and within a social framework. The whole presentation of the Romans' situation, the problem with Theodoric, and the attempted solution will continue, in the verse version, to have to do less with realistic statecraft than with the interpersonal relationships and loyalties that characterize the idealized warrior-aristocracy of traditional poetry: the literary construct to which the language of Boethius as a

61 Godden ('Anglo-Saxons and the Goths,' 65–6) and Godden and Irvine (*Old English Boethius*, 2:498) take ll. 47b–8 to refer to service by Boethius to the rightful Roman emperor prior to the Gothic usurpation and thus see the poet as having collapsed widely separated events into Boethius's lifetime. It is true that the poet (like the writer of the all-prose version) understands there to have been only one Gothic invasion of Rome and thinks of Theodoric as a lineal successor to the earlier Gothic kings. However, it is hard to see why the regime of the Roman emperor Honorius, who (according to Metre 1) had fled, would then be characterized as the rule of the 'Greeks,' and the poem seems to indicate that Boethius was made consul during Theodoric's reign. Theodoric – who thus in the poem, as in historical fact, elevated Boethius to the office he held at the time of his arrest – is surely the lord to whom Boethius is dear in these lines, which accurately capture Boethius's service to him as an office-holder prior to Theodoric's falling-out with Emperor Justin I.

'treasure-giver' and a 'hero' of 'reputation' belongs, and proper to the register in which the poet declares of him that 'þæt wæs rihtwis rinc' (l. 49a) in contrast to the formally similar statement 'næs ðæt hærlic dæd' just a few lines before (l. 43b). Because these relationships are traditionally explored in verse through freely circulating access to the perspectives of their participants, as threads in the conceptual fabric they cannot be disentangled from the more easily defined, textually localized manifestations of the poetics of mentality.

The next passage in both versions recounts Boethius's consideration of the problem and his secret dispatch of messages to Constantinople. This section of text already has an interiorizing bent in the prose, which narrates Boethius's thought process before coming to his appeal to the Byzantine emperor for help:

> Se þa ongeat þa manigfealdan yfel þe se cyning Đeodric wið þam cristenan dome[62] and wið þam Romaniscum witum dyde. He þa gemunde þara eðnessa and þara ealdrihta þe hi under þam caserum hæfdon heora ealdhlafordum. Þa ongan he smeagan and leornigan on him selfum hu he þæt rice þam unrihtwisan cyninge aferran mihte, and on ryhtgeleaffulra and on rihtwisra anwealde gebringan. Sende þa digellice ærendgewritu to þam kasere to Constentinopolim, þær is Creca heahburg and heora cynestol, forþam se kasere wæs heora ealdhlafordcynnes. Bædon hine þæt he him to heora cristendome and to heora ealdrihtum gefultumede. (B, 1.13–23)

> [He perceived then the manifold evils that the king, Theodoric, perpetrated against Christian authority and against the Roman senate. Then he was mindful of the comforts and the ancient rights they had had under their ancient lords the emperors. Then he began to contemplate and consider within himself how he might take the kingdom away from that unrighteous king and bring it into the rule of the orthodox and the just. He then secretly sent letters for the emperor to Constantinople, where the capital of the Greeks is and their royal seat, because the emperor was of their ancient royal kin. They (i.e., the letters) asked that he help them back to their Christianity and their ancient rights.]

62 My word-division here differs from Godden and Irvine's. They construe *cristenandome* as a compound word, but the *-an* at the end of what would be its first element (contrast *cristendome*, also dative, later in the same passage) would make it a unique form within the Old English corpus. I take the construction as a phrase, with *-an* being a weak inflection on the adjective *cristen* to agree with the dative form of the simplex *dom*.

Here we have a portrait of a thoughtful, reasoning statesman who first dissects and defines a problem in private contemplation; and only then, once that analytical foundation is secure, acts to effect a solution, responding exactly to the shape of the problem as he has surveyed it. This representation of responsible action *pro patria* as a deliberative procedure with two discrete stages, whereby thought creates a kind of order from which appropriate action can be fashioned, is intellectually of a piece with what we find more protractedly in the Old English *Pastoral Care*'s prose preface, the entirety of which is an extended step-by-step exposition, cast in a reflective Alfredian first-person voice, of precisely this kind of focused, purposeful deliberation.[63] In making a point of narrating the process by which a decision is reached in answer to a seemingly intractable problem, as opposed to (for example) simply stating the resolved-upon solution or presenting its rationale in the form of a list of reasons, both of these prose texts go to some lengths to dramatize the figure of the wise leader thinking carefully about how best to meet the needs of his people, against all odds and amid severe adversity.[64]

In thinking through Rome's plight, the prose writer's Boethius identifies two public interests damaged by Theodoric's rule: the normative status of the Roman form of Christianity and the integrity of the Roman polity. These two species of harm to Roman society continue to be treated in careful parallel in the prose, just as they have been in the previous section. First, the *yfel* 'evils' of Theodoric are said to be committed against both *cristen dom* 'Christian authority' and the *Romanisce witan* 'Roman senate.' Then, after Boethius calls to mind – to his mind for the first time in the prose, and to readers' minds again – the *ealdriht* 'ancient rights' enjoyed by the Romans prior to Gothic rule, he considers how to bring Rome back into the governance of those who are *ryhtgeleaffulle* 'orthodox' and *rihtwise* 'just' ('wise concerning right' or perhaps, in the prose, 'rights'). Finally, his plea to the emperor at the end of the quoted passage likewise invokes the two complementary but distinct value

63 Edited from two manuscripts in Sweet, *King Alfred's West-Saxon Version*.

64 Cf. S. Irvine, 'Wrestling with Hercules,' 174–6, on a similar passage elsewhere in the *Boethius*. K. Davis ('Performance of Translation Theory') analyses in depth the presentation of Alfred the translator in the preface to the *Pastoral Care* as a figure of simultaneous political and sapiential authority; cf. Harbus, 'Metaphors of Authority,' 721–2. If Discenza ('"Wise Wealhstodas"') is right that the prologue to Ecclesiasticus stands behind the *Pastoral Care*'s preface, the disproportionality of the narrative of Alfred's thought process by comparison with that source underscores the rhetorical emphasis I suggest.

systems of the Romans' Christianity (*cristendom*) and their traditional political liberties (*ealdriht*).

As in the previous segment of Metre 1, the poet again changes tack from the prose, most conspicuously by eliminating the earlier writer's consistent twofold articulation of Boethius's religious and political reasons for finding Theodoric's rule unacceptable:

> Wæs him on gemynde mæla gehwilce
> yfel and edwit þæt him elðeodge
> kyningas cyðdon; wæs on Creacas hold,
> gemunde þara ara and ealdrihta,
> þe his eldran mid him ahton longe,
> lufan and lissa. Angan þa listum ymbe
> ðencean þearflice, hu he ðider meahte
> Crecas oncerran, þæt se casere eft
> anwald ofer hi agan moste.
> Sende ærendgewrit ealdhlafordum
> degelice, and hi for drihtne bæd
> ealdum treowum ðæt hi æft to him
> comen on þa ceastre, lete Creca witan
> rædan Romwarum, rihtes wyrðe
> lete þone leodscipe. (C, Metre 1, ll. 54–68a)

> [At every moment the evil and abuse that the foreign kings showed them was on his mind; he was loyal to the Greeks, mindful of the honours and ancient rights that his elders had long held with them, love and joys. He cleverly began to consider secretly, then, how he could turn the Greeks in that direction so that the emperor could again have rule over them. He sent a letter secretly to the lords of old and enjoined them, for the Lord's sake, that they come back to them in that city on account of old loyalties; (Boethius) would let that nation – the senate of the Greeks, possessed of justice – govern the Roman citizens.]

The last several lines of this passage give increased detail about Boethius's plan and his intentions, continuing the augmentation of subjective information to which we are by now accustomed. More important, the amplification is accompanied by a shift of emphasis throughout that continues the trend seen in the previous sections. As before, the goals have changed. The poet simply is not concerned to enunciate a model of leadership based on deliberative judgment, the model shared by the prose version and the preface to the *Pastoral Care*, nor to keep the problems of Theodoric's reign neatly classified according to the religious interests of Rome on the one hand and the political ones on the other.

Instead, there is a subtle change in what precisely Boethius is 'mindful' of. Both the concern for traditional privileges and that for the normative faith are still present in the verse, but the latter is mentioned clearly only once. This is not because religion has ceased to be important in the poet's intellectual construction, but because it has already coalesced with the other field of concern so that Metre 1 presents them as a single problem embodied in the person of Theodoric, assailant of one unified and integrated religio-political scheme of values. Because of what has gone before, for Boethius now to ponder the Roman state is for him to ponder orthodox Christianity, and to address one term of the problem is simultaneously to address the other. It is both revealing and appropriate that the *treow* 'allegiance, good trust' (l. 65a) – the word does not denote religious faith – which Boethius invokes in his communication to the Byzantines is ambiguous in reference, covering bonds of fidelity between the emperor and the Romans, or else their shared fidelity to the Lord God, or both at once. There is little interpretive difference in favouring one or the other construal at this point, because the 'old loyalties' are understood in any case to bind together the religiously orthodox and politically just against a heretical tyrant in a shared history of 'honours and ancient rights ... love and joys.'

The chosen language in this part of Metre 1 is very predominantly political, that field of reference having subsumed the religious to gather under a single rubric all of the trouble caused by a dictatorial apostate. But it is not quite the same concept of the political as was found in the prose, which evoked an institutional power struggle between an autocrat and the senatorial body. The verse treatment is as much about individual relationships of loyalty and trust as it is about law and government, and once again, for the *Boethius* poet those relationships remain configured according to the social paradigm of lordship idealized in traditional verse. Boethius is presented as having genuine prior loyalties that must remain covert while he is elevated to high office by a lord who has turned bad. In the all-prose *Boethius* the entire dimension of Roman allegiance to Byzantine lords that we find in the poetic version of this material is absent. There, Boethius's communication to Constantinople reads like a plea made to a third party whose goodwill can be presumed due to dynastic and political kinship but whose interests are indirect; it asserts no special claim on the emperor's obligation. In Metre 1, Boethius's sense of loyalty to the Byzantines, of their prerogative as part of the Roman imperial heritage, and indeed of their lordly duty to protect steadfast Rome is explicitly defined against the Gothic usurper's royal line, which the poet makes a point (as the prose writer does not) of denigrating as *elðeodig* 'foreign,' and as we have already seen, Boethius is able to appeal to the mutual bond of 'ealdum treowum,' a formulation of political good faith.

According to the poet, Theodoric is guilty of a breach of loyalty not just to the Roman citizenry whose rights he has promised to uphold, but to a higher lord, the emperor in Constantinople. This idea had been introduced previously, in the allusion to the former time 'while the Greeks controlled the throne' during which Boethius had been 'dear to his lord' Theodoric; it is developed here with the statement that Boethius 'remains loyal' to the 'Greeks' when Theodoric breaks his faith. The whole notion that Boethius's turn against Theodoric is a response to Theodoric's rejection of the emperor's rule is an invention of the poet: the prose version had focused on local abuses in Rome and Boethius's desire to defend the Roman people against them. Nowhere else, whether in early medieval historical writing about these events or in the prose of the *Boethius*, do we find the situation encountered in Metre 1, where Theodoric becomes disloyal to the emperor and Boethius then becomes disloyal to Theodoric in order to maintain faith with the emperor. The poet's handling of Theodoric's loyalties goes hand in hand with the treatment of his religion as already analysed above. In historical reality, a change of regime in Constantinople brought about a change of policy toward Arians. But the poet gives no hint of change in either the imperial or the religious situation, making Theodoric appear unstable: a religious apostate and a political one, too.

The sense of socially defined identity developed in the poem marks Boethius's political deception here in Metre 1, like Hengest's oathbreaking in the Finnsburh episode of *Beowulf*, as ethically acceptable or even virtuous; both are understood by the tellers of the respective tales (the narrating voice of the *Boethius* and Hrothgar's scop) as calculated reassertions of a wrongly subverted order. The loyalty added in Metre 1 is mapped onto not just ethical but also psychological points of reference, as the memory of ancient rights is augmented by Boethius's mindfulness of honours, love, and kindness bestowed by the lords of old. This idea is grounded firmly in tradition by the phrase 'lufan and lissa' (l. 59a), a formula whose words' denotations would seem to allow any number of possible applications, but which always in context describes the benefits enjoyed by a favoured retainer in the lord-thane relational paradigm and always connotes the lord's role as protector as well as provider and leader. It is a further sign of

Metre 1's blending of political with religious virtue that the favouring and protecting lord who is referred to in every single instance of this formula outside of this text is God.[65]

The next passage, which concludes the introduction and leads into the opening *metrum* from the Latin *Consolation*, recounts Theodoric's discovery of Boethius's plot, his imprisonment of him, and Boethius's reaction to this turn of events:

> Þa þæt ongeat se wælhreowa cyning Đeodric, þa het he hine gebringan on carcerne and þærinne belucan. Þa hit ða gelomp þæt se arwyrða wer on swa micelre nearanesse becom, þa wæs he swa micle swiðor on his mode gedrefed swa his mod ær swiðor to þa woruldsælþum gewunod wæs, and he þa nanre frofre beinnan þam carcerne ne gemunde; ac he gefeoll niwol ofdune on þa flor and hine astrehte swiðe unrot and ormod hine selfne ongan wepan[.] (B, 1.23–30)

> [When the cruel king Theodoric became aware of that, he ordered him (Boethius) brought to a prison and locked up inside. When it happened that that estimable man came into such great confinement, he was as much more severely agitated in his mind as his mind previously had been the more greatly accustomed to worldly joys, and he did not think on any comfort within that prison then; rather, he fell down prostrate on the floor and stretched himself out, terribly dejected, and began, miserable, to weep for himself.]

This segment of the prose, like the previous one, already includes a great deal of Boethius's interiority. The versification amplifies it a little, but more important is the manner in which this is done:

> Đa þa lare ongeat
> Đeodric Amuling and þone þegn oferfeng,
> heht fæstlice folcgesiðas
> healdon þone hererinc. Wæs him hreoh sefa,
> ege from ðam eorle. He hine inne heht
> on carcernes cluster belucan.
> Þa wæs modsefa miclum gedrefed
> Boetius. Breac longe ær

65 *Genesis A*, ll. 1949a, 2334a, and 2738a; *Guthlac B*, l. 1076a; *Daniel*, l. 339a; and *Azarias*, l. 55a.

wlencea under wolcnum;   he þy wyrs meahte
þolian þa þrage   þa hio swa þearl becom.
Wæs þa ormod eorl,   are ne wende,
ne on þam fæstene   frofre gemunde,
ac he neowol astreaht   niðer ofdune
feol on þa flore,   fela worda spræc,
forþoht ðearle,   ne wende þonan æfre
cuman of ðæm clammum.   (C, Metre 1, ll. 68b–83a)

[Then Theodoric the Amuling became aware of that counsel and seized that retainer, commanded officers of the people to hold that warrior securely. To him belonged a vexed mind, fear of that nobleman. He ordered him locked away in a cell of a prison. Then Boethius's mind was greatly agitated. He had enjoyed prosperity under the heavens for a long time previously; the worse could he endure that hardship, so severe, when it came. The nobleman was miserable then, did not expect mercy, did not think on comfort in that confinement; but he stretched out prostrate, fell down flat on the floor, spoke many words, despaired terribly, did not hope ever to come out from there, out of those fetters.]

The poet adeptly works some of the key words from the prose into traditional dictional forms to describe Boethius's emotional state. In line 74 the participial adjective *gedrefed* 'agitated' fills the *q* position in a stable full-line formula, built on the exclusively poetic compound *modsefa* 'mind,' that is found in *Beowulf* and two Vercelli Book poems.[66] A few lines later not only are the words *frofor* and *gemunan* from the prose brought together into a well-attested formula (*frofre q*), but that formula is combined, in a relationship of poetic variation, with another one (*are q*) having identical metrisyntactic composition and scansion.[67]

66 *Beowulf*, l. 349 ('wæs his modsefa manegum gecyðed' [*manegum* resolves]); *Andreas*, l. 892 ('þa wæs modsefa myclum geblissod'); and *Elene*, l. 875 ('on modsefan miclum geblissod'). The scansion of this formulaic two-verse combination is [x-foot] | Ssx || Sx | (x)Sx, with *modsefa(n)* always supplying the second foot of the a-verse, a metrical disyllable (alliterating of course on *m–*) always giving the first foot of the b-verse, and a past participle with the proclitic syllable *ge–* always occupying the second foot of the b-verse. The first foot of the a-verse scans x or xx. The *Boethius* poet uses the same formula again at Metre 5, l. 39.

67 *Frofre q*: *Beowulf*, ll. 185b and 973b; *Andreas*, l. 1705b; *Soul and Body I*, l. 128b; *Christ II*, l. 722b, *Guthlac A*, l. 508b; *Guthlac B*, l. 1236a; Exeter Book riddle 5, l. 4b; and *Exhortation to Christian Living*, l. 27b. *Are q*: *Beowulf*, l. 1272b; *Genesis A*, l. 1580b;

This mirroring pair of formulas doubly renders the prose writer's statement that Boethius expects no comfort, creating a close similarity of both diction and signification with analogues in *Beowulf* and two Exeter Book poems.[68]

On the larger scale, the poet makes an important change by adding Theodoric's mental perspective (ll. 71b–2a). In the narrative context, either figure could plausibly be said to fear the other, and these lines have been read both ways, but one of several indications that they describe Theodoric's state of mind and not Boethius's is the retention of the word *hreoh* from the prose, where it is the head of a compound (*wælhreow*) used in reference to Theodoric.[69] The way *hreoh* is redeployed in a different construction captures perfectly the shifted focus of the verse version. The poet could easily have kept the compound *wælhreow* and written line 69a as *'Đeodric se wælhreow,' which would not have required the b-verse to be other than it is. But in substituting 'Amuling' as an epithet for Theodoric, the poet chooses again to mark him ethnically as an unwelcome outsider; and instead of making him 'slaughter-*hreoh*,' the verse shifts that term's denotation from his nature to his condition so that now Theodoric is circumstantially *hreoh* in mind – and specifically about Boethius – in a new statement not precedented in the prose source. The result is a neat contrast between Theodoric's trust in Boethius previously (l. 47b) and his agitated fear of him now. Just like the earlier statement that Boethius was 'dear to his lord,' the change in relationship from Theodoric's perspective is conveyed through traditional diction: 'him wæs hreoh sefa' uses a metrisyntactic formula of mental state to denote a ferociously unsettled mind, and

---

Christ I, l. 70b; *Wanderer*, l. 1b; *Deor*, l. 33b; and *Judgment Day II*, l. 156b. In both formulas, *q* is a verb form with an unstressed proclitic (*ge*– or *ne*) giving the verse shape Sx | (x)Sx. (The *are q* formula also has a variant without the extrametrical proclitic on the verb form of the second foot: see *Genesis A*, ll. 1023b and 1842b; *Andreas*, l. 1129b; and *Guthlac A*, l. 480b.)

68 *Beowulf*, l. 185b; *Guthlac A*, l. 508b; riddle 5, l. 4b.

69 The second element of *wælhreow* is etymologically *hreoh* 'fierce' rather than *hreow* 'sorrowful' (see Bosworth-Toller, s.v. *hreow*). Other reasons to see Theodoric as the *him* in these lines: the term *eorl* better fits the king's officer than the king himself (cf. l. 78a); the statement is sandwiched by two others that recount the arrest of Boethius, seeming to explain the king's motivation for an action that began just before this sentence and will conclude immediately after it; and the next lines will describe Boethius's state of mind in turn, an alternation conforming to the usual procedure in Old English verse of serially displaying multiple parties' interior conditions to define the ethical dimension of their interaction.

ege and *eorl* form a traditional alliterating collocation.[70] Neither element of this before-and-after pairing had been present in the prose; both, and the structure they create together, manifest the poetics of mentality and help spin the webs of relationship and obligation that are so important in traditional verse.

By the time we reach the end of Metre 1, the beginning of the *Consolation* proper has been entirely reframed in the prosimetrical version by recognizable lineaments of heroic and elegaic poetry expressed through thoroughly traditional language, motifs, and narrative techniques. As in classical Old English verse in general, in this literary introduction to a very literary work, the literal – not just the 'letter' of reported history, but the whole mode of signification that supposes meaning to be contained entirely within and bounded by the individual text – takes a back seat to the traditional and metonymic. The relationships and ethical valences evoked through Metre 1's subjective dimension require, for appreciation of what they mean beyond the bare facts of one man's circumstances, awareness that beneath this visible, analysable text lies a submerged iceberg-mass of written, read, declaimed, and heard performances, a subset of which is accessible to us, that define the discursive register in which this poem took body as a communicative construction.

This section's look at the poetics of mentality in Metre 1 confirms again how deeply rooted in the soil of Old English poetry is the attentiveness to different loci of subjective experience, and thus to mental states, qualities, and actions, that is encountered at every turn. We are now in a position to see the poetics of mentality take part in the generation of social meaning when a traditionalizing poetic production meets the world. With a firm foothold in the 'what' and the 'how' of the poetics of mentality, through continued consideration of Metre 1 as a case study we can now approach one aspect of the 'why,' redirecting our attention from Metre 1's traditionality, the presence of many traditionalizing elements, to its traditionalism, the larger discursive utility of its shaping and articulation of content in the classical style.

---

70 *Him wæs q sefa*: *Andreas*, l. 1251b; *Elene*, ll. 173b and 627b; *Christ I*, l. 499b; *Beowulf*, ll. 49b and 2419b; and several other close variants. *Ege* (including derived forms) with *eorl*: *Genesis A*, l. 2669; *Elene*, l. 321; *Beowulf*, ll. 6 [emended], 1649, and 1757; *Judith*, l. 257; *Daniel*, l. 718; and *Judgment Day I*, l. 52.

Traditionalism and Interpretation

Both the traditionalizing impulse of the *Boethius* poet and the poetics of mentality as a prominent element of his or her traditionality are continually in evidence throughout Metre 1. They are expressed in small-scale dictional and stylistic features, in technical choices involving shifts of perspective and access to various angles of experience accommodated by the story, and in content that proceeds from or is shaped by that access. We have found the poet of the prosimetrical *Boethius* recreating the original introduction in accordance with typical Old English poetic practice, and in no small measure through the evocation and management of traditional subjectivities: virtually every traditional element of Metre 1 is developed partly through successive narrative entry into multiple subjective positions made imaginatively available by the contours of the story, generating an ethical frame of reference within which events are to be understood.

But we have not yet inquired directly into the desirability or impact of doing so. Traditionality is a historically situated phenomenon in itself, and the *Boethius* poet's attraction to the methods and priorities of classical Old English verse bespeaks perceived value in them, called upon by compositional choices made within a total social and intellectual environment. Each new engagement with tradition is, in fact, new, whatever lengths it may go to to appear timeless.[71] From this fact two observations follow. First, because tradition never stands outside of culture, no new iteration, however conservative in form or intent, can simply draw ever-uniform substance or meaning from it like water from a well. Every realization of any tradition has its own conditioned immediacy; it cannot come into being uninflected by its circumstances of production. And in its particularity, each enactment of tradition must in turn act on that tradition, whether radically or almost imperceptibly, influencing its continuing history and therefore its configuration and significance for subsequent participants. Tradition is endlessly formed and reformed by the quiet redaction, intentional or unwitting, of what has gone before, and its experienced meaning at any time emerges from an indefinite number of just such singular operations.[72]

71 On the stylistically created impression of timelessness in traditional Old English poetry, cf. Tyler, *Old English Poetics*, 3 and 157–60, and Trilling, *Aesthetics of Nostalgia*.

72 Drout (*How Tradition Works*) theorizes the mechanics of these processes in depth.

Second, and as a partial consequence of the principle just stated, we cannot view a writer's adherence to tradition as a strictly passive or 'default' course, no matter how unreflecting it might have been in a given case. Alternatives were available to the *Boethius* poet – beginning with not writing at all – and his or her agency in selecting among them, with or without recognition of their full range, shaped the text. This is true not only in matters of foregrounded, thematic content, but also in small-scale compositional choices made to produce metrisyntactic units, and as we have seen, even very local technical decisions such as those do participate in the production of meaning. Still more fundamentally, we should not overlook the significance of the choice to versify the historical introduction of the *Boethius* in the first place. Because the prose material underlying Metre 1 was original to the English translation and was added outside the bounds of the *Consolation* proper, in principle there is no reason why the project of imitating Boethius's Latin *prosimetrum* with an English one had to lead to the creation of this poem. The reviser could have accepted the prose introduction as a supplied paratext, begun versifying with the opening *metrum* of the Latin work, now represented by Metre 2, and avoided the unique succession of one Metre directly upon another.[73] The existence of Metre 1 testifies that the material in the prose introduction looked to someone as though it both could and ought to be put into verse. The ways in which this transformation was carried out do more than demonstrate that the writer valued tradition. They also underscore the poet's sense of that tradition's salient potential to make meaning within his or her own world, regardless of whether the possibilities were exploited calculatingly or, as can be the case in the production of traditional discourse, seemed simply to represent a convenient or appealing route to follow during the composition process.

It may be useful at this point to recapitulate what the poetic version brings to the fore that was not present or prominent in the prose, because whatever work this text might have done specifically as a piece of traditionalizing verse in the environments of its writing and early reception can be expected to involve those elements. (1) First, we have found in Metre 1 the idealized lord/retainer relationship, based on mutual loyalty derived from culturally scripted roles, that is a mainstay of classical Old English poetry. This conceptual paradigm of lordship, altogether absent from the

73 Godden and Irvine point out the unparalleled juxtaposition of two Metres (*Old English Boethius*, 2:498).

prose version, appears in the poem in a multi-tiered form whereby Boethius is a lord to the Roman citizenry and a retainer to Theodoric; and whereby Theodoric, in turn, is simultaneously king to Boethius and the other Roman nobles and client to the emperor in Constantinople.[74] (2) We have seen the religious element of Theodoric's misrule handled significantly differently in the verse. Theodoric's religion is redefined away from a static model of heresy that was present in the prose and toward a dynamic model of conversion followed by apostasy; and more broadly, his failure to keep the orthodox Christian faith is blended inextricably with his failure to keep political faith with lord and subjects such that it becomes, in effect, one feature of his participation in the schemes of loyalty just described. (3) The Gothic surge across the Alps and into Rome, too, is put into vivid traditional terms, made to strike chords familiar from classical Old English verse on troop movement and warfare. Metre 1 emphasizes the aggression of this act, noting repeatedly the alienness of the Gothic kings while enhancing the contrast with the Romans' own ancient imperial rule and their time-honoured political rights and customs. (4) Finally, freely shifting access to the mentality of all parties reveals the Goths' gusto for violence, the Romans' distress, Boethius's disaffection, and Theodoric's fear of his formerly trusted minister: and indeed that access to multiple subjectivities through both definitional description and narrative focalization, in keeping with the traditional Old English poetics of mentality, is a key means by which each element of Metre 1 that I have listed is realized. This is the material before us for interpretation.

Metre 1, Historical Context, and Political Ideology

Any attempt to understand the workings of poetic tradition in a posited environment of reception obviously must begin by identifying that environment. Two recent articles, one by Richard Scott Nokes and Paige K. Swaim and the other by Susan Irvine, have suggested that the original introductory narrative of the Old English *Boethius* is driven by topical reference to the Scandinavian invasions that disrupted native rule in all Anglo-Saxon kingdoms other than Wessex during the 860s and 870s.[75]

74 This feature of Metre 1 conforms to a pattern, noted by Godden and Irvine but without reference to Metre 1, of the *Boethius* poet's interest in 'hierarchies of authority' (*Old English Boethius*, 1:150).

75 Nokes and Swaim, 'Kingship'; S. Irvine, '*Anglo-Saxon Chronicle*,' esp. 69–73.

In the view of Nokes and Swaim, Metre 1's aggressive Goths stand for conquering Danes by whom the book's audience has been subjugated, such that Boethius's *Consolation* is transformed into 'a text about political resistance,' albeit 'resistance' of a non-confrontational, privately comforting kind.[76] However, although Alfred's kingdom was successfully occupied by Danes under the leadership of Guthrum for some months in 878, it was not under Danish control at any time the *Boethius* might have been written. Irvine's version of the proposed Goths–Danes analogy, which treats the opening section of only the all-prose *Boethius*, is made more plausible by its compatibility with the work's production in 890s Wessex. Irvine compares the *Boethius*'s representation of the Gothic invasion with the *Anglo-Saxon Chronicle*'s retrospective accounts of the events of 878 and other years, which were written in 892.[77] For Irvine, it is the remembered past, not the present, that the translator maps onto more ancient history, and reading the introduction to the *Boethius* alongside *Chronicle* annals reveals that the latter text has 'all the elements that Alfred incorporates into the opening of his *Boethius*: violent occupation of a country by barbarians, submission of the people, swearing of oaths by the enemy, breaking of those oaths, and the stand of one man (Alfred in one, Boethius in the other) against the enemy.'[78]

Irvine's list of shared elements does show an overlap of concerns between the original compiler of the *Chronicle* and the translator of the

76 Nokes and Swaim, 'Kingship,' quotation from 77; 'Alfred produces a myth of spiritual and mental resistance to unjust pagan rulers, thus absolving Anglo-Saxons, who were under Danish rule, by allowing them to claim that while the Danes had conquered them externally, they remained unconquered Christians internally' (ibid., 61).

77 The original compilation of the *Anglo-Saxon Chronicle* extends through the annal for 892, with textual instability in its last couple of annals indicating its writing to have been still in process at the time it began to be copied (see Bately, 'Compilation'), and was used through its record of 887 by Asser in his 893 *Life of Alfred*. (The authenticity of Asser's *Life* as a document of the 890s has been questioned several times but has stood the test: the most recent major challenge, Smyth's contention in his book *King Alfred the Great* that the work is a late tenth-century forgery, is refuted comprehensively by Keynes, 'On the Authenticity,' and Lapidge, 'Asser's Reading,' 44–7.) For a closely reasoned argument that I accept as the current state of knowledge of the *Chronicle*'s first compilation and continuations, see Dumville, 'Anglo-Saxon Chronicle.' For all of my comments about the *Anglo-Saxon Chronicle*, I have consulted texts A through E (Bately, *MS A*; Taylor, *MS B*; O'Brien O'Keeffe, *MS C*; Cubbin, *MS D*; and S. Irvine, *MS E*). Unless otherwise indicated, citations will refer to the text of manuscript A as edited by Bately. In each case I use the annal numbers as given in the edition cited.

78 '*Anglo-Saxon Chronicle*,' 69.

Boethius, suggestive of a perceived correspondence of general political circumstances between Ostrogothic Rome and 870s Wessex as depicted by two roughly contemporary writers near the turn of the tenth century. This commonality marks a desired cultural identification of Wessex with Rome against the 'barbarian' invaders,[79] the larger thesis of Irvine's essay which she substantiates by reference to other passages in the *Boethius* and elsewhere in the cluster of contemporaneous English translations. I agree that along with the presumptive sympathy of the Roman and Boethian perspective, these factors make the Danish presence as overrunners of neighbouring kingdoms, and formerly (in 878) of Wessex itself, a possible association for early readers; and bringing Metre 1 into the field of view allows one to add to Irvine's claims the observation that the poem, in contrast to the prose version of the introduction, emphasizes the intrusive foreignness of Gothic rule in Rome.

But the question remains, I think, of how these implicit likenesses might have operated. The similarity is not of a very historically specific kind, such as might support a straightforwardly parallel reading. For example, the oaths sworn by the enemy and then broken, as cited by Irvine, occur in a different annal of the *Chronicle* (876) and as part of a totally different series of events from those of 878. The two entries both belong to the original compilation of the *Chronicle* and show no sign of divergence in authorship, so there is no objection to seeing them as part of a single literary instalment, but the situation described s.a. 876, where the cornered Danes swear peace with Alfred in order to get out of a tight spot and then promptly attack Exeter, has little in common with that in the *Boethius* introduction, where the oath consists of a promise by the unchallenged king that he will rule the populace justly. Likewise, the comparison between Alfred and Boethius is not self-evidently valid beyond the opposition of both to an invader; and even on that point, in Boethius's case it is eventual opposition only, and Theodoric is not himself an invader but successor to an established line of rulers whom Boethius does not object to serving as long as Theodoric maintains good faith religiously and politically. Moreover, like most treatments of the *Boethius*, Irvine's suggestion is mounted within the frame of Alfredian personal authorship: a frame from which Malcolm Godden (whose writings until recent years shared it as well) and, in collaboration with Godden, Irvine herself have lately and with good reason urged us to break free. At the very least we must now

79 Cf. also Howe, 'Rome.'

recognize that to rely on Alfred's personal, detailed involvement with the text is to make a great assumption.[80]

It might seem that relinquishing confidence in Alfred's own creative control over the *Boethius* can only harm critical inquiry, stripping bare one of the few plots of ground we have thought ourselves able to cultivate for historical interpretation. But perhaps clearing that ground can also make room for new growth. A disadvantage of positing Alfredian authorship has been the concomitant tendency to restrict historicizing study of this work to directly or indirectly biographical forms of interest and often, in order to make the desired connections, to a hermeneutics of political allegory. The character Boethius is too easily reduced to a doppelgänger of Alfred,[81] Theodoric to an exemplum or specimen of bad kingship, and the English text's allowance that Boethius really was working covertly to remove his king from power rather than being falsely accused – an astonishing concession in contradiction to the Latin *Consolation*[82] – to interpretive inconsequentiality. The *Boethius* does reflect intense interest in right rule and principled political action, and as a cultural production I think it makes the most sense when seen as originating in meaningful contact with the West Saxon court during or hard on the heels of Alfred's reign, as I stated at the outset of this chapter. But as long as we read the *Boethius* predominantly with reference to King Alfred, we may miss more subtle and further-reaching ways it locates itself within a social moment.

By reading outward from what Metre 1 explicitly provides, it is possible to gain access to larger discourses that enabled its production and gave it meaning. This chapter's comparison of the poem to the corresponding prose has described ways it differentiates itself, in its specific identity as a poem in the heavily marked classical style, from its source. Now, by focusing on those elements that define it as a discrete text, and considering its discursive affinities with other texts addressing the history of Alfred's

80 See discussion and references on pp. 157–60 above.

81 For some difficulties with such an analogy, see Godden, 'Player King,' esp. 140–6. The importance to the conceptual construction of Metre 1 of Boethius's positioning below higher authorities has also emerged from my analysis in the previous section of this chapter and will continue to inform my interpretation below.

82 Cf. Nelson, 'Political Ideas,' 52–4; Godden, *Translations of Alfred and His Circle*, 12. The representation of Boethius as plotting against Theodoric is precedented in one of the Latin *vitae* of Boethius that sometimes accompany the *Consolation* in manuscript (these are surveyed by Godden, 'King and Counselor,' 194–8). See Godden and Irvine, *Old English Boethius*, 2:255–6.

reign, we can learn more fully what political language Metre 1 speaks: not only what it says and advocates at a level one could associate with authorially planned messages, but what its very articulation of those messages may reveal about a wider system of thinkable thoughts and speakable claims from which this poem emerged and to which it therefore offers us a point of entry.[83] In the remainder of this chapter I propose to deal with Metre 1 as a particle of discourse moved, necessarily, by currents of political language and belief within which it is suspended, and thus able to tell us something about their flow. Because it takes the shape of traditional poetry – poetry whose form, technique, and content continually assert its traditionality – consideration of how this text interacts with the tradition that it calls upon will enable us also to give one kind of answer to the question 'why' asked earlier about traditional verse.

I will argue that the story told by Metre 1, produced through the interaction of the received prose narrative with poetic tradition in the sensibilities of an unknown writer, does stand in a relation to the history of Wessex that is discernible to us, even though it is not, in my opinion, a political allegory or allusion that disguises some scenario from Anglo-Saxon affairs as a contextualization of Boethius's situation. As a traditionalization of the prior prose version's subject matter, Metre 1 projects a vision of political actions and relationships that is endemic to the poet's ideological universe, contributing to cycles of linguistic performance that reinforce a privileged set of beliefs, attitudes, and behaviours. The poem can afford us a glimpse of the discursive field that it inhabits, and upon which its rhetoric relies, through its orientational signals: what points it seems to need to make; what, on the other hand, it is able to take for granted; and who stands to benefit from, or would be positioned to identify with, the principles it affirms. Without having to posit reference to any particular historical event, we can understand Metre 1 to exemplify and reproduce a way of conceptualizing certain political relationships and situations that is itself an artefact of historical particularity.

I will not exaggerate my reading's value as evidence for the dating of the text, but I will contend, in partial support of my working hypothesis of the origins of the Old English *Boethius* as a whole, that Metre 1 finds its best political fit either in the closing years of Alfred's reign or the first few

83 My analysis is indebted to some of the principles explored in Foucault, *Archaeology of Knowledge*. M. Irvine, 'Medieval Textuality,' usefully extends and shapes Foucault's ideas toward the study of Old English texts.

years of his son Edward the Elder's, when certain ideas and perspectives that the poem articulates were demonstrably both present and serviceable in the West Saxon courtly sphere. The *Boethius* poet's traditionalizing conversion from prose to classical-style verse sets forth with seemingly unimpeachable cultural authority certain novel concepts that can also be documented within political rhetoric supportive of these kings. Considering Metre 1's implied ideological background allows the discernment of historical meaning in the text without any need to assume a fully deliberate manipulation of tradition by the poet, whose interpretation and re-expression of received motifs to reflect Alfredian and subsequent political doctrine may have felt only natural.

Current opinion on the group of near-contemporary translations from Latin that includes the Old English *Boethius* considers these works to be designed for not just the education, but the dynastically useful political formation, of the higher-born among Alfred's subjects.[84] This view is of course vulnerable to recent doubts concerning authorship and environment of production, as described at the beginning of this chapter with reference more narrowly to the *Boethius*, and we need to remain open to questions about whether the writing of these books represents a 'program' and the extent to which the individual efforts behind them may have been united under royal sponsorship or direction.[85] But several of these texts do align with one another, and with Asser's *Life of Alfred*, in their interest in matters of moral and effective governance and in sharing a perspective on good rule

84 E.g., Lerer, *Literacy and Power*, 77–88; Abels, *Alfred the Great*, esp. 219–57; K. Davis, 'Performance of Translation Theory'; Nelson, 'Power and Authority'; Discenza, 'Wealth and Wisdom,' esp. 451–66; Discenza, 'Alfred's Verse Preface'; Stanton, *Culture of Translation*, chap. 2; Discenza, *King's English*; Pratt, *Political Thought*, 115–350; and Pratt, 'Problems of Authorship and Audience.'

85 Asser's *Life* does not mention a translation program per se but is compatible with it: see Whitelock, 'Prose of Alfred's Reign,' 74–5; Pratt, *Political Thought*, esp. 120–3; and Wormald, 'Living with King Alfred,' 14 n. 47. Asser does reference Alfred's patronage of Werferth's translation of Gregory's *Dialogues* (*Life of Alfred*, chap. 77) and builds his theme of Alfred's commitment to wisdom and learning to a climax in Alfred's insistence that his officials learn to read or else relinquish their positions (chap. 106); the note on which the *Life* ends is consistent not only with the emergence of a coordinated translation program, but also with the calculated royal image and forms of political thought that scholars perceive in the translations themselves when associating them interpretively with Alfred or his circle (cf. Lerer, *Literacy and Power*, 61–77, and Sheppard, *Families of the King*, 63–70). I cite Asser's *Life of Alfred* from Stevenson's edition and, where I quote, give translations from Keynes and Lapidge, *Alfred the Great*, 65–110.

that equates it with wisdom,[86] and D.A. Bullough and Paul Anthony Booth have assembled evidence that at least for a time the Alfredian plan to extend education to laity of the ruling and administrative classes (spelled out in the preface to the Old English *Pastoral Care*) had an impact in some quarters.[87] As with the narrower question of the unity of purpose and the compositional milieu(x) of the two versions of the *Boethius*, then, so also with the broader proposition of a late Alfredian and early post-Alfredian curriculum of aristocratic reading that served to impart implicit and sometimes explicit political education: the evidence is circumstantial, but to suppose a degree of coordination among the translated texts, originating in some connection with the West Saxon court, is reasonable and, it seems to me, simpler than alternative explanations of the facts. In any event, it can hardly be disputed that this group of books constitutes a coherent body of vernacular instruction and wisdom, at times directly addressing political philosophy and always in communication with it through channels of historiography, moral counsel, and guidance on effective ecclesiastical administration. Whether or not they collectively represent the direct, efficient fulfilment of a royal plan, the texts' existence attests to a discursive formation present in late Alfredian and early Edwardian Wessex.

Within that discursive formation, and as a component of it, the Old English *Boethius* (in either version) presupposes the basic sympathy of its readers and seeks to develop or shape that sympathy in particular directions. Metre 1 offers itself as an uncontentious historical narrative, envisaging no possibility of controversy and assuming that its audience's assent to the values it asserts lies within easy reach. It takes up this rhetorical position through strategies indebted to poetic tradition, instantiating and reinforcing political models already familiar from classical English poetry of the kind that we know was read and learned by at least three generations of West Saxon royalty.[88] The values transmitted by such poetry can

86 See, e.g., Wormald, 'Uses of Literacy,' 105–7; Nelson, 'Wealth and Wisdom'; Pratt, *Political Thought*, 115–350; Abels, *Alfred the Great*, esp. 219–57; Scharer, 'Writing of History'; Kempshall, 'No Bishop, No King'; Discenza, 'Wealth and Wisdom,' esp. 457–66; Discenza, *King's English*; and S. Irvine, 'Wrestling with Hercules.'

87 Bullough, 'Educational Tradition'; Booth, 'King Alfred versus Beowulf,' 44–50. Wormald ('Uses of Literacy,' 107ff.) reaches more negative conclusions. Dumville ('King Alfred') sees Alfred's initiative as underlying the eventual monastic reform.

88 According to Asser (*Life of Alfred*, chaps 22–3 and 75–6), vernacular verse was enjoyed by Alfred's mother and others around his father Æthelwulf's court when he was a child, loved and learned by Alfred himself both in youth and in maturity, studied in turn by at least one of his sons and one daughter, and taught to others at his royal school. Lerer

be presumed to have had some appeal for court-associated individuals like the magnates, officials, and their sons for whom the *Boethius* appears to be intended. We may infer that Metre 1's early readers are unlikely to have come to it lacking prior acquaintance with Old English poetic tradition or very resistant to the constructions of lordship, moral authority, and wisdom embodied by this poem as it took its place in the growing library of learned vernacular texts.[89]

Metre 1 addresses theoretical challenges of rule and subjecthood, and as part of the Old English *Boethius* it does so within a system of political rhetoric that Nicole Guenther Discenza has argued flatters both the king and his supporters as upholders of justice and wisdom while reinforcing their participation in a scheme that enhances royal authority.[90] In its key position opening the prosimetrical *Boethius*, Metre 1 certainly accords with that broader-based encouragement of a particular kind of political subjectivity among readers, and in ways that are directly tied to its traditionalizing features. The poem's formulaic language of treasure-giving, ancient customs, oaths, and private longing for a departed lord brings into play a shared social ideal which, being deeply traditional in the literary culture, can be efficiently evoked rather than fully described or explicitly propounded. The lord-and-retainer model of political obligation that we see ubiquitously in classical Old English poetry, being based on personal, role-driven loyalty, obviously serves the interests of all who are positioned to claim lordship over someone else, that is to say, much of the *Boethius*'s potential audience, if the educational plan outlined in the preface to the *Pastoral Care* is indeed relevant to this text's anticipated or real dissemination. As a political construct, this model can have a socially stabilizing function: it encourages any individual situated within multiple hierarchical relationships, having authority in one sphere and being subject to authority in another (again, a description of most Anglo-Saxon

(*Literacy and Power*, 69) observes that Asser places vernacular poetry within the sphere of book-learning; cf. also Bredehoft, *Authors, Audiences, and Old English Verse*.

89 Cf. remarks by Nelson ('Wealth and Wisdom,' 36–7 and 44–5, and 'Political Ideas,' 135–7) on the use of vernacular poetry to inculcate values similar to those encouraged by the Alfredian-era prose works.

90 See Discenza, *King's English*, on this scheme in the *Boethius* as a whole. Discenza is careful to emphasize (10) that the Metres lie outside the brief of her project. However, a great deal of the prose text that she analyses is present in the prosimetrical version as well and so has contextualizing relevance to the Metres.

men in positions of political consequence), to function as a virtuous subject to his lord in order to enjoy the privileges of his own lordship over others in turn; and to be a good, wise, and just lord in order to enjoy the benefits of protection and favour that come with service to a similarly virtuous higher one.[91]

But while Metre 1 calls upon this familiar relationship of mutual expectation and presupposes its acceptance in principle, the lord-retainer model receives serious complications in the poem, and to pass over them is to ignore much of this text's substance. Its web of loyalties and hierarchical relationships mutates in accordance with shifting ethical judgments as to worthiness and includes counterfeit as well as real allegiances. Theodoric is Boethius's lord; but above Theodoric is the Eastern emperor, to whose geographically distant authority Theodoric and Boethius respond differently. Below Boethius is the citizenry at large, whose collective disappointments, hopes, and desires are emphasized along with their secret loyalty, at the earlier time of their conquest, to their departed Roman emperor (notwithstanding their outward oath-taking before their new Gothic overlords) and to 'the Greeks' in Constantinople to whom he fled. This complexity of perspectival information and interpersonal action is essential to Metre 1's construction, far exceeding the descriptive capacity of any binary scheme of oppressor and oppressed, and it is brought about largely through techniques I have associated with the poetics of mentality.

The headed subsections below will examine three different aspects of Metre 1's presentation of the lord-retainer relationship: transferred allegiance, morally void oaths, and desire for an absent lord. Each proceeds from modifications to the prose source through development of traditional subjectivities, and each has a definable place within the political discourse of Wessex during and shortly following Alfred's reign.

Transferred Allegiance

Metre 1's protagonist, roundly declared honourable and wise, turns against his lord, Theodoric. Such a scenario might seem to present a risk that readers could find in it a ready-to-wear justification for disloyalty to a rightful

91 J.M. Hill (*Anglo-Saxon Warrior Ethic*) explores the literary operation of this model to the political benefit of the house of Wessex.

monarch or lord.[92] I will argue that the opposite is more likely: that Metre 1 reinforces the traditional imperative of allegiance, and does so in a way consonant with policies and practices of the West Saxon kings that appear to begin with Alfred.

First, the very fact that the poem draws on the diction and concepts that embody the received model of lordship based on personal loyalty will imply for readers some endorsement of it, because it is a highly traditional package the expectation of which is readily activated. For the same reason, it will be difficult for the narrative particulars to disrupt that model's presumptive rightness accidentally, although they do stand in tension with it and thus require resolution. The traditionality of language and style implies a complex of received ideas even as the story's details deviate from its more typical realization. In such a situation, readers tuned in to those cues will tend to rationalize or circumscribe ambiguities in a manner that protects the anticipated and approved scheme of values if possible. Metre 1 invites a hermeneutic logic of exceptionalism: Boethius is emphatically described as virtuous, and he is said to be a good lord to the Romans and a trusted subordinate to Theodoric; virtuous men who understand and participate in the institution of lordship do not act treacherously in defiance of it; therefore Boethius's betrayal of his lord must somehow be just, and must be accommodated within the idealized lord-retainer model. Theodoric, by contrast, is a tyrannical heretic. This polarization of character, which as we have already seen is effected in part by a mapping of ethical terrain through access to various interacting subjectivities, requires a reader to choose sides, and without flouting the text's direct propositions it is not possible to make a choice contrary to the several affirmations of Boethius's goodness and wisdom. In this sense the manner of representation, through traditional poetic forms and concepts, is likely to have a more determining role in interpretation than the bare fact of the story's oppositional structure, inherited by the poet from history and the original English prose.

Yet the fact remains that Metre 1 features the protagonist's abandonment of loyalty to a ruler, and it must be central to any reasonable interpretation of the poem. The reconciliation of Boethius's actions against Theodoric with the a priori claim of a lord upon the fidelity of subordinates takes the form here of an assumed rather than stated, yet very clear, limitation placed on loyalty: it is owed only to those who fulfil the obligations of their

92 Cf. Godden, 'King and Counselor,' 203–7.

station and keep their promises.[93] First we are told that when Boethius became *heretoga* the 'Greeks' controlled the Roman throne, during which time Boethius was dear to his lord, Theodoric; then, when there was a change, with Theodoric breaking his promises and committing the atrocities that were previously narrated, Boethius himself remained *hold* 'loyal' to the Byzantines and tried to devise a way for the emperor to regain power over Rome. Boethius is justified in opposing Theodoric once the Gothic king proves himself disloyal both to his own lord the Byzantine emperor and to his Roman subjects by betraying Christianity and the hereditary rights of the citizenry. Although Theodoric's rule began well, he is the scion of unwelcome foreign rulers; in this respect his religious conversion in Metre 1 is as much a correlative to his unexpected early political goodness as it is a datum about his own faith. When he reneges, he slips back into the adversarial niche occupied by his forebears not only as heathens but as oppressors of protagonistic Rome.

When Metre 1 collapses the religious into the political, so that Theodoric's political breach of faith and his religious breach of faith form two sides of a single coin, it simplifies matters in a way that suits royal interests.[94] There was always the potential for conflict in the interacting prerogatives of churchmen on the one hand and king and secular nobles on the other, and the kings of Wessex did at times take over, or force the exchange of, ecclesiastical and monastic lands for strategic purposes.[95] The situation was complicated by the intersection of two orders of governance, the religiously and the politically authorized, such that many individuals had dual roles and potentially disjunctive combinations of interests.[96] Kings of Wessex directed the appointment of some bishops, created some abbots (by granting land to noblemen for the establishment of new monasteries), and influenced the election of others.[97] Powerful ecclesiastics had

93 Cf. Nelson, 'Political Ideas,' 152–4.

94 Discenza ('Alfred's Verse Preface') makes a parallel suggestion with regard to the verse preface to the Old English *Pastoral Care*.

95 See Yorke, 'Bishops of Winchester,' esp. 64–5; Fleming, 'Monastic Lands'; Dumville, 'Ecclesiastical Lands'; Smyth, *King Alfred the Great*, 41–6; Abels, *Alfred the Great*, 243–6; Blair, *Church in Anglo-Saxon Society*, 323–41; Wormald, '*On þa Wæpnedhealfe*,' 274–5; Thacker, 'Dynastic Monasteries,' 251–4; and Rumble, 'Edward the Elder.' Broader treatments of royal-episcopal relations that provide background to Alfredian policy include J. Campbell, 'Placing King Alfred,' 6–11, and Brooks, *Early History*, esp. 197–206.

96 Cf. Kempshall, 'No Bishop, No King.'

97 See, e.g., Pratt, *Political Thought*, esp. 45–8 and 56.

a continual presence at gatherings of the West Saxon court, and Alfred in particular pursued a thorough integration of his inner circle of advisors with church governance by installing several of his intimates in episcopal sees and abbatial office, including non-West Saxons who had been brought to the kingdom specifically in the king's service (Asser, Werferth, Plegmund, John the Old Saxon, Grimbald).[98] Bishops and rulers of monastic houses were themselves magnates, generally of noble birth and kinship, who held substantial estates ex officio and often personally as well, and could command their own retinues of thanes.[99] As regional administrators of land and its inhabitants, they delivered not just wisdom but also war in service to the king, sometimes in person.[100]

We should notice that the religious element of Metre 1, even in its use of the apostasy model created through changes to the prose account, focuses not on the divergent theological content of Theodoric's faith – in sharp contrast to portrayals of the Danes in the original compilation of the *Anglo-Saxon Chronicle* and in Asser's contemporaneous *Life of Alfred*, both of which repeatedly remind their readers of the invaders' heathenry – but rather on the act of breaking faith; and strikingly, in Metre 1 this act is defined more as a turn against the static position of a political authority (the imperial court in Constantinople) than as a betrayal of God. The poem's conceptualization of both the political and religious domains in terms of virtuous earthly lordship makes for a very convenient preemption in favour of the king: supporting Christianity means supporting rightful political authority, and undermining the one amounts to attacking the other. In this regard, Metre 1 appears to presuppose a confident royal ideology that might easily use the role of bishops and abbots as loyal advisors and territorial administrators – a role valued by all parties – as leverage against them in pursuing royal prerogatives. The poet need not have set out to make a point of this; the adjustments to the prose, with all their implications, may have

98 Dumville ('Between Alfred the Great and Edgar,' 166) stresses the continuity between Alfred's reign and his son Edward's that these appointments provided; cf. Pratt, *Political Thought*, 52–8.

99 Abels (*Lordship and Military Obligation*, 151–9) discusses several examples. Blair (*Church in Anglo-Saxon Society*, 91–9) uses the career of Wilfrid to illustrate the range of bishops' power and activities.

100 Bishops Ealhstan and Heahmund led troops in battle according to the *Anglo-Saxon Chronicle*, s.aa. 823, 845, and 871. In annal 896 two other bishops, Swithwulf and Ealhheard, are named in a context implying their direct involvement in war against Danish invaders. Abbot Cenwulf is reported killed in battle s.a. 903. See also Brooks, 'Development'; Nelson, 'Church's Military Service'; and Pratt, *Political Thought*, 54.

proceeded from an investment in royal interests that seemed, to him or her, to require no justification.

This reading addresses Metre 1's redirection of attention to the sphere of secular lordship, but it still cannot do justice to the complexities stemming from the poem's more fully developed political hierarchy by comparison to the prose. Whereas in religion faith must always be directed to God, whose ministers are intermediaries and facilitators, in earthly affairs loyalty is presumed to be owed primarily to one's personal, immediate lord. But in Metre 1 Boethius circumvents his own lord, transferring his allegiance from Theodoric to the 'Greek' emperor; by contrast to the prose source, the ethical Boethius's disloyalty to Theodoric turns out actually to constitute a truer and vindicating loyalty. Within a political context, what matters about this sequence of events is that it not only shows the transfer of loyalty from one lord to another one, but represents a theoretical claim that an implicit bond of allegiance to a higher position on the ladder of lordship always exists. The language in which the transition is described seems concerned to assert this: when Theodoric steps out of line, Boethius's break with his lord is portrayed not as a move or shift of any kind, but as an indicator of political stability because his sympathies relative to the 'Greeks' do not change. Rather than putting it in terms of legitimate disloyalty to or abandonment of Theodoric, the poet represents his actions as a static inaction, remaining *hold* 'loyal' to another lord, in terminology that is 'part of the reciprocal vocabulary of the warband.'[101] Metre 1's portrayal of these manoeuvrings, in promoting the claim of an overlord on the allegiance of a lesser lord's retainers rather than assuming the primary bond of loyalty to be automatically proximate, implies a strong pro-royal viewpoint.

Richard Abels has called attention to the practice inaugurated by Alfred of collecting loyalty oaths not just from those who ordinarily answered directly to the king – the magnates of the realm, who were properly part of his court and council, plus free men of any rank in the king's own service through their attachment to royal estates or membership in his personal retinue – but from all subjects of political consequence, including those whose land occupancy or other ties would traditionally have put them only in the direct service of non-royal magnates and lesser lords. This practice is first recorded in the *Anglo-Saxon Chronicle*'s account of Alfred's occupation of London in 886, and it was continued by Alfred's

---

101 So J.M. Hill (*Anglo-Saxon Warrior Ethic*, 50) characterizes the pragmatics of the word *hold*.

successors, taking on the status of policy among West Saxon kings.[102] This radical extension of the loyalty oath intervened in the traditional structure of lordship, encouraging a background sense of obligation that reached straight to the king, without actively disrupting the customary, quotidian claims of lower lords on their men. Kings of Wessex from the late ninth century onward were able to preserve the effectiveness of the more complex hierarchy of lordship for practical administrative and military purposes while establishing the potential that the king might, if necessary, trump subordinates by calling directly upon the formally sworn loyalty of those who served them.

Ideally, for a man immediately subject to the personal lordship of (for example) an ealdorman or bishop, the two lines of this potentially ramified allegiance would remain united. Such would be the case as long as his lord remained in the king's peace, aligned with the royal policies and wishes. But should the lower lord enter into conflict with the king, the subject would find himself forced to make a choice. From a top-downward perspective, the correct course would be to choose the higher lord, the king, a choice that would now be seen from that vantage point as an act of political steadfastness despite violating the traditional precedence of proximate lordship.[103] Because the very notion that a constitutional relationship demanding personal loyalty might extend directly to the king appears to be an innovation of the late ninth century, coinciding with the expanded use of loyalty oaths by the house of Wessex, the appearance in Metre 1 of the idea that one might justly go over the head of a lord who violates his own obligations can be inferred to reflect pro-royal political discourse of the Alfredian and post-Alfredian West Saxon regime. That Boethius does what he does on principle, even in the emperor's absence, is (from this ideological standpoint) impressive – one might even say heroic, given its difficulty and danger – and powerfully compatible with West Saxon royal interests.

The risk that Metre 1 will seem to undermine the accepted principle of loyalty to a lord is negligible, then, although it does refocus it, privileging the highest lord's loftiness of social place over a lesser lord's directness of claim on his man's allegiance. This political principle inheres in the shape the received story is given by the poet. In evaluating this detail of the poem in the political environment from which it proceeds, we should not be

102 Abels, *Lordship and Military Obligation*, chaps 3–4.
103 As described in ibid., chap. 1.

distracted by the fact that Theodoric is a king. His title, inherited from the prose and from history, matters less than the fact that he is not the apex of authority in his political system, being subject himself to the Byzantine emperor. An orthodox Christian king with no overlord, representing an established dynasty and exercising stable leadership, could hardly resemble the poet's Theodoric for readers of Metre 1, and any shift of an individual's loyalty from a lower lord to a constitutionally higher one such as the poem dramatizes would favour a king of Wessex, whose position would be more analogous to that of the emperor. Negative portrayals like the one Theodoric receives, when embedded within a normative ideological framework, are understood by their makers and sympathetic audiences to be about 'them,' not any of 'us': they serve to fortify solidarity of writers and readers against a real or imagined third party. That third party, in the political vision projected by Metre 1, is any one of the powerful who breaks faith with the highest secular lord.

False Oaths

It might seem that a simple, binary relational paradigm of oppressor versus oppressed would be apposite to the period following the temporarily successful Danish invasion of Wessex in 878 and thus might define Metre 1's relationship to the West Saxon past along allegorical lines. But in truth, great political complexity attended even the situation Alfred faced during Guthrum's occupation of his kingdom. Although in the end enough nobles and men of local authority who remained in Wessex rallied and mobilized to defeat the Danes at the Battle of Edington, during the four-month interim when the king's whereabouts and doings were probably unknown to most we must realistically assume a full spectrum of individual responses to the threat to person and property that the Danes presented.[104] Early sources indicate that some West Saxons fled the land entirely, a few (Alfred and Ealdorman Æthelnoth with their retinues) regrouped and worked toward a future counterstrike, and many submitted

104 From January through late March Alfred kept a low profile, raiding as he was able. Only at Easter (23 March) did Alfred and Ealdorman Æthelnoth establish a fortification at Athelney from which Alfred might conduct some type of more systematic warfare (*Anglo-Saxon Chronicle*, s.a. 878; Asser, *Life of Alfred*, chaps 52–5; Æthelweard, *Chronicon*, pp. 42–3). I cite Æthelweard's *Chronicon* (in Latin and English translation) from A. Campbell's edition.

quickly to the invaders.[105] At least some in that last category, the noble and landed men who submitted, must have accepted Guthrum's lordship decisively enough to be regarded later as having irreparably broken faith with their king and thus as deserving of disgrace and dispossession;[106] certainly during the crisis Alfred regarded some West Saxons as united with the enemy and conducted raids on them himself.[107] But subsequent events make clear that also among those who acquiesced for a time to Danish control of the region was a significant number of Alfred's subjects who, although initially choosing self-preservation over abstract loyalty to an absent king, yet proved willing to move under Alfred's direct leadership when called upon.[108]

These circumstances cannot fail to have presented a political quandary once Alfred regained control of Wessex. He would find no advantage in attempting to break all the noble and landed West Saxons who had cooperated sufficiently with the Danes to remain in place during the occupation, some of whom had after all eventually played a part in his victory over Guthrum. Yet any of them who had personally submitted to Guthrum or other leaders of the invading force obviously had not demonstrated unstinting loyalty to their rightful king, however practically necessary their actions may have been and however unlikely it must have seemed that Alfred would ever reclaim power. The lack of opposition to the Danish force entering Wessex by *fyrd*-commanding nobles could easily be construed as cowardly if not criminal, and we know that an interpretation of these events as a moment of ignominy did in fact crop up in some quarters: this is the distinct flavour of Æthelweard's account, produced shortly before 980 but based on earlier materials.[109]

---

105 *Anglo-Saxon Chronicle*, s.a. 878; Asser, *Life of Alfred*, chaps 52–3; Æthelweard, *Chronicon*, 42.

106 Abels (*Alfred the Great*, 152–3 and 177–8) discusses this likelihood with reference to a notable discontinuity between witnesses to charters prior to and subsequent to 878 and draws attention to one probable case, that of the former ealdorman Wulfhere, mentioned in a 901 charter of Edward the Elder. Circumstances possibly surrounding Wulfhere's defection are hypothesized by Nelson ('"King across the Sea,"' 53–5 and 67). Yorke ('Edward as Ætheling,' 35–6) interprets the charter's reference to Wulfhere differently, and Pratt (*Political Thought*, 239) raises doubts about the timing of the event.

107 Asser, *Life of Alfred*, chap. 53.

108 Abels's account of developments in the concept and practice of lordship (*Lordship and Military Obligation*) is invaluable for understanding the events of 878; see esp. 58–62.

109 *Chronicon*, 42. Whitbread ('Æthelweard') gives internal evidence that Æthelweard wrote before 980. Meaney ('St. Neots,' 209) and Bately (*Anglo-Saxon Chronicle: Texts*

Metre 1 of the *Boethius* testifies to the availability of an alternative model by which Wessex's own harrowing period of invasion and apparent conquest might be remembered. In the poem, the character of Boethius, by attempting to orchestrate a strike by the emperor against Theodoric, exemplifies the rejection of an illegitimate authority in favour of a rightful one, covertly and at great personal risk, while pretending continued cooperation with the villainous offender. That pretence is the key. The very intelligibility of a portrayal of virtuous deception implies that such a concept existed within West Saxon political discourse; and if it did, then it could also accommodate a valourizing assessment of Alfred's subjects who had submitted to the Danes for a time in 878 before responding to a summons to act suddenly against them. With the template for political action to which Metre 1 attests at the disposal of post-Edington West Saxons, such subjects could be figured as heroic in the final analysis, like the wise Boethius, a distinctly cautious, deliberating type of *hæle* 'hero' (l. 53a) and *hererinc* 'warrior' (l. 71a) who did not act immediately but thought through the matter *listum* 'cleverly' (l. 59b) and made a plan. Pretended allegiance is in fact a recurrent feature of Metre 1. Particularly interesting when viewed in mind of the events of 878 is the unprecedented detail in the poem that the conquered Romans swore loyalty oaths to the Gothic invaders while hiding in their hearts true fidelity to their own emperor and hoping that the 'Greeks' would act to restore him. The poem thus strongly implies a principle that under threat, even such a binding, weighty act as the swearing of a loyalty oath can be reanalysed as a cunning means of remaining in a position to act on one's real, honourable allegiance should the opportunity arise.

We have already seen a scenario partly parallel to this in another poem: the predicament of Hengest's men in a passage of *Beowulf* having close enough verbal similarities with Metre 1 to raise a real possibility that it was known to the *Boethius* poet. As closely analogous as the episodes are, one difference between them is very informative. Hengest's men, recall, are forced by circumstances to accept unsavoury terms of peace. However, the poet never suggests that they do not mean to abide by those terms. The

---

and Textual Relationships, 59–62) both consider Æthelweard a witness to the earliest reconstructable form of the *Chronicle*, but Bately, like most other scholars, sees the information that is unique to Æthelweard as brought in from elsewhere at some point during transmission (ibid., esp. 41–53 and 60). Whatever source provided the additional details nevertheless would seem to reflect an account of events relatively close to the time of the *Chronicle*'s original compilation (cf. Stenton, 'South-Western Element,' 19–22).

agreement they make with Finn is treated as a straightforwardly binding oath ('Ða hie getruwedon on twa healfa / fæste frioðuwære' [then on both sides they concluded a firm peace-treaty], ll. 1095–6a) which nevertheless is eventually overpowered by the memory of fallen kinsmen and the group identity that sustains the revenge ethos:

> Hengest ða gyt
> wælfagne winter wunode mid Finne;
> he unhlitme eard gemunde,
> þeah þe ne meahte on mere drifan
> hringedstefnan – holm storme weol,
> won wið winde, winter yþe beleac
> isgebinde – oþ ðæt oþer com
> gear in geardas ...
> ....
> Fundode wrecca,
> gist of geardum; he to gyrnwræce
> swiðor þohte þonne to sælade,
> gif he torngemot þurhteon mihte,
> þæt he Eotena bearn inne gemunde –
> swa he ne forwyrnde woroldrædenne –
> þonne him Hunlafing hildeleoman,
> billa selest on bearm dyde,
> þæs wæron mid Eotenum ecge cuðe.
> Swylce ferhðfrecan Fin eft begeat
> sweordbealo sliðen æt his selfes ham,
> siþðan grimne gripe Guðlaf ond Oslaf
> æfter sæsiðe sorge mændon,
> ætwiton weana dæl; ne meahte wæfre mod
> forhabban in hreþre. (*Beowulf*, ll. 1127b–34a, 1137b–51a)

[Hengest yet remained with Finn the slaughter-stained winter; he fervently thought of home, although he could not drive the ring-prowed ship on the sea – the ocean surged in storm, fought the wind, winter locked waves in ice-binding – until the next year arrived in the settlements ... The out-of-place one, the visitor, was eager to leave that habitation, (but) he thought more of vengeance than a sea-voyage: whether he could bring about a confrontation such that he might inwardly recall the sons of Jutes – thus he did not refuse the custom of the world – when he should place on his lap Hunlafing the battle-light, best of swords, whose edges were well known among the Jutes.

(So) once again in the same manner cruel sword-destruction befell the bold-spirited Finn at his own home, after Guðlaf and Oslaf complained of grief, of the grim attack after the sea-journey, blamed (Finn) for a share of woes. The restless mind could not restrain itself in the breast.][110]

The resolve that takes shape within Hengest in these lines is where emphasis falls in the episode's dramatic development, and to imagine the oath as insincere from the beginning would weaken the point of passage. The *Beowulf* poet's interest here lies in the threshold moment of the choice to take revenge before leaving Finn's hall, *despite* having sworn peace and *despite* having successfully endured on noisome terms first the funeral of slain kinsmen and then the long winter, during which homeward seafaring had been impossible.[111]

The emphasis on this moment of decision is produced by the account's unhurried movement through Hengest's ponderings: first his musing that through revenge he might carry away with him a gratifying rather than shameful memory of 'the sons of Jutes' – his thoughts at this stage form a private, prospective narrative of his own leadership as it may become honourably reconciled again to the ceremonies of hall and warband – and then, more publicly, the firming-up again of Danish history with present identity through his own men's rehearsal of the past, all inciting him at last to action. Hrothgar's singer, telling the tale at a feast of celebration, seems

110 This passage has well-known uncertainties of interpretation. I construe *dyde* in l. 1144b as past subjunctive, in parallel with *gemunde*, as *þonne* at the beginning of its clause implies it should be (see Fulk, Bjork, and Niles, *Klaeber's Beowulf*, 189–90), and accordingly I understand Hengest's reasoning to refer to an imagined moment that is future and hypothetical for him, but past to the teller and hearers of the tale: if he takes revenge now, the blade that he will wear or place upon his *bearm* will be able to cue unshameful memories of the visit to Finnsburh. The *wæfre mod* in l. 1150b is almost certainly Hengest's, as the entire quoted passage has been an account of his mental processes: in continuous reading, ll. 1150b–1a most naturally finish a single extended thought by the poet, with a resumptive reference to Hengest (whose brooding has been left unconcluded up to this point), and explain why violence breaks out a second time (as it will do in the lines immediately following these).

111 I agree with Gwara (*Heroic Identity*, 135–80) and others that all parties are sincere in the swearing of the oath, and I concur with his recognition of the poem's emphasis on the decision gradually reached by Hengest to avenge Hnæf. There is nothing inevitable about the revenge taken on Finn in the wake of a truce-oath, and no indication that Hengest responds to a feuding obligation rather than situational pressures and his and his men's desires: cf. J.M. Hill, *Anglo-Saxon Warrior Ethic*, esp. 11 and 60–8, and Jurasinski, *Ancient Privileges*, 79–111.

to think that Hengest finally came to his senses and recounts the revenge and return home with Hildeburh as a suspensefully delayed Danish triumph. However, while the oath at Finnsburh may have been, in the eyes of the scop, a travesty of honour from the start, there is no hint that it was in its conception a mere ruse designed to allow Hengest's Danes to bide their time until a more favourable moment.

Yet that is exactly what the Romans' oaths are said to be in Metre 1. That the concept of heroic temporary inaction, or of secret loyalty to an absent lord in contradiction to an outward, insincere oath to a present one, was born of political expediency in the aftermath of the near-collapse of Wessex – and what posterity might otherwise see as the embarrassingly easy submission of high-ranking subjects whose support Alfred ultimately regained – is a conjecture, but I take it as practically certain that some kind of political accommodation would have been necessary following the crisis of 878. In view of this need, the concepts underlying Metre 1 are the optimal face-saving solution: they support a retrospective vision with the power not only to excuse but to lionize those who, regardless of what they might have done for some months beforehand, proved their loyalty at Edington when it mattered most and helped win back the kingdom. An interpretation of oaths sworn under duress as not only non-disloyal, but in their later falseness actively loyal, could clear a necessary path to redemption for some of Alfred's subjects once he had regained control of his kingdom, and I submit that for at least a generation after the Battle of Edington some ideological construction along these lines would have been an essential means of making peace with history. Metre 1 proves that this attitude was seriously conceivable.

As a matter of fact, we can be sure that a concept very close to this existed at Alfred's court, because it is found in his laws. Following the prologue to Alfred's *Domboc*, and placed prominently at the head of the law code proper, comes Alfred's charge on oath-taking and -keeping:

> Æt ærestan we lærað, þæt mæst ðearf is, þæt æghwelc mon his að ⁊ his wed wærlice healde. (Alfred 1)[112]

112 I cite the law code or *Domboc* of Alfred (incorporating the laws of Ine) from Liebermann, *Gesetze der Angelsachsen*. The law to be discussed here is identified in all manuscripts as item II. However, while the numbering may be archetypal to all extant manuscripts (see Wormald, *Making of English Law*, 266–9), it can hardly be original given the phrase 'Æt ærestan' [first] that identifies this law, internal to its text, as the first to be presented. I cite according to the numbering that Liebermann supplied for the same reason. Cf. Stanley, 'On the Laws,' 213–14.

[First we enjoin that which is most needful, that each man scrupulously observe his oath and his pledge.]

The stress laid on loyalty oaths by the West Saxon kings, already noted above, is sometimes discussed only with reference to the formal oaths of allegiance Alfred and his successors received as they expanded their power into new territories, but an important complement to and possible institutionalization of that practice is here in the laws.[113] Most salient, however, and made all the more remarkable by the house of Wessex's emphasis on oaths, is the qualification to the law just stated that comes in the very next clause:

Gif hwa to hwæðrum þissa genied sie on woh, oððe to hlafordsearwe oððe to ængum unryhtum fultume, þæt is þonne ryhtre to aleoganne þonne to gelæstanne. (Alfred 1.1)

[If anyone should be wrongfully forced into either of these things, either betrayal of his lord or assistance in any injustice, it is more just, then, to deceive than to follow through.]

Contemplation of the possibility that oath-taking might occur under duress, or that such circumstances could give an oath exceptional legal status, is without known precedent in the traditions on which Alfred's law code draws.[114]

In view of the political necessity of finding some satisfactory reconstruction of the events of 878 that could reconcile Alfred with subjects

113 Cf. Keynes and Lapidge, *Alfred the Great*, 306 n. 6, and Wormald, '*Lex Scripta*,' 12. This appears to be the direction Wormald was going with this clause of Alfred's code in *The Making of English Law*: 'Chapter 9 [in the projected vol. 2, not published] will argue that Alfred's law on oaths turned any criminal behaviour into a breach of fealty' (148), and his comments in ibid., pp. 283–4, likewise classify this law as representing a policy innovation; cf. Pratt, *Political Thought*, 232–41.

114 Alfred 1 as a whole may be indebted to chap. 18 of the legatine capitulary of 786 (in Dümmler, *Epistolae Karolini aevi [II]*, 19–29), a document whose influence on Alfred's laws has been suggested by Wormald ('In Search,' 214–17). I am grateful to Bryan Carella for pointing me to it. Keynes and Lapidge (*Alfred the Great*, 306) note in relation to Alfred 1.1 that Bede articulates a principle whereby breaking an oath that entails wrongdoing is preferable to keeping it and cite Gerald Bonner's brief discussion of Bede's homily on the decollation of John the Baptist (Bonner, 'Bede and Medieval Civilization,' 75; Bede's commentary on Herod's oath to Herodias's daughter is 2.23, ll. 108–32, in his *Homeliarum evangelii libri II*). However, none of these possible sources identifies duress as a factor affecting the status of an oath.

who had eventually, but not immediately, proved their loyalty to the West Saxon king, it does not seem coincidental that his very first law takes the form it does. The existence of this innovative distinction in the *Domboc* indicates that oath-taking under duress was a topic discussed at some point in Alfred's court as a problem requiring treatment; my contention is that it could hardly have been otherwise after he regained rule of his kingdom at the Battle of Edington. It would seem that we can document the emergence into West Saxon political discourse of a way of thinking and talking about loyalty oaths, conditions of duress, and the relationship of such oaths to true allegiance to one's lord – allowing that allegiance may be maintained by 'deceiving' an oppressor, in violation of a forced oath – that meshes perfectly with the actions of the Romans in Metre 1 of the *Boethius* and elucidates the particular intimation about their state of mind that the poetics of mentality prompted.

Deliverance by an Absent Authority

We have seen that a defining factor in the *Boethius* poet's modification of the prose account was the construction of a hierarchy in which Theodoric occupied a medial position that could be justly circumvented by allegiance to a higher power. Let us now consider the desperate desire of the oppressed in Metre 1 that that absent imperial authority might triumphantly appear on the scene. This is an iterated and emphatic feature of the poem but not the underlying prose: first, an addition made by the poet portrays the Romans as hoping for help from the East at the time of their conquest; and later, in the core narrative element inherited from the prose version but reshaped and subjectivized in ways already discussed, Boethius seeks that help actively when Theodoric turns tyrannical. The desideratum of the arrival of righteous deliverance in Metre 1 mirrors a recurrent motif in historical accounts of royal actions that first appears in the early 890s and remains available into the reign of Edward the Elder. More than once, if we accept the rhetoric of these narratives, the type of political salvation that the poet tells us Boethius finally ceased hoping for in sixth-century Rome arrived in ninth-century Wessex.

We first find the motif of the desired appearance of a rightful authority in accounts of the events of 878, in sources associated with Alfred's court or at least reflecting royal interests.[115] The *Chronicle*'s annal for that year,

115 Stenton's theory of a non-courtly origin of the *Anglo-Saxon Chronicle* ('South-Western Element') has had an influence out of proportion to its soundness; Smyth's

written about 892, concentrates on the suddenness of Alfred's reunion with his people before Edington and their reaction upon seeing him:

> Þa on þære seofoðan wiecan ofer Eastron he gerad to Ecgbryhtes stane be eastan Sealwyda, ⁊ him to coman þær ongen Sumorsæte alle ⁊ Wilsætan ⁊ Hamtunscir se dęl se hiere behinon sę was ⁊ his gefægene wærun. (s.a. 878)
>
> [Then in the seventh week after Easter (i.e., 4–10 May, 878) he rode to Ecgbert's Stone, east of Selwood, and all of Somerset came to him there, and Wiltshire, and Hampshire – the portion that was on this side of the sea – and they were joyful of him.]

The last words quoted are significant. The terse original portion of the *Anglo-Saxon Chronicle* does not pause to elaborate literarily on what are taken to be the noteworthy events of Alfred's reign or to mention attitudes about those events. Its compiler cleaves closely to what are seen as 'just the facts' of what occurred, and even for those facts provides little – often, for us, confusingly little – orientation, context, or explanation.[116] So even though all we have here is a single statement that Alfred's assembling subjects experienced joy at the reappearance of their king, that any mention of their reaction appears at all suggests that it matters to the writer at the level of historical record: it is in some sense one of the facts, a piece of information that the chronicler thinks ought to be transmitted because it captures, for him or her, an essential aspect of the event.

Given the chronicler's usual choices, the few details of this kind are best seen not as naive outbursts, or as slips in method that contaminate the

---

negative assessment of Stenton's view (*King Alfred the Great*, 471–7) is for the most part just. Dumville notes of the Stenton theory and the opposing courtly, dynastic chronicle theory that there may not be 'as much practical difference' beween them 'as has sometimes been suggested' ('Anglo-Saxon Chronicle,' 71); cf. Meaney, 'St. Neots,' 209. The *Chronicle* of the early 890s was regarded by manuscript compilers and copyists as properly associated with Alfred and Alfredian texts (Bredehoft, *Textual Histories*, esp. 6). Whether or not it was compiled by an individual close to Alfred, it was made within reach of court information and very much within the ambit of West Saxon political interests and was available to Asser almost immediately (see Bately, *Anglo-Saxon Chronicle: Texts and Textual Relationships*, 53–5 and 59–62). I will consider the *Chronicle* a 'court-associated' document.

116 C. Clark's discussion of this 'annalistic' style ('Narrative Mode,' 215–21) rightly rejects the notion that its simplicity equals crudeness and finds it instead to 'constitute in [its] own way a highly artificial manner, especially in [its] avoidance of descriptive elements of all kinds' (218).

account with opinion about the reported incidents,[117] but as interpretable signals of those incidents' received meaning circa 892. A clue to that meaning lies in these comments' quasi-formulaic character. The statement in annal 878 about the joyous return of Alfred is a repetition of one s.a. 855 to describe the people's joy upon the return of his father King Æthelwulf, whose second son Æthelbald refused to relinquish the throne he had held while Æthelwulf was in Rome. The *Chronicle* makes no mention of this conflict within the royal family, saying only that Æthelwulf 'to his leodum cuom, ⁊ hie þæs gefægene wærun' [came to his people, and they were joyful of that] (s.a. 855). It is significant, I believe, that each of these nearly identical announcements of popular rejoicing comes within a whitewashed description of a moment of great tension in the kingdom, when the nobility's loyalties were divided.[118] Asser tells us of the year 855 what the *Chronicle* does not, that Æthelbald had usurped his father's throne with the support of some of the most powerful men of Wessex,[119] and we have already seen the vacillation of Alfred's nobles in 878, which in some cases may have represented something even more alarming to the king than helpless capitulation to the Danes.[120]

Regardless of whether the active threat to Alfred in 878 was strictly external or had an internal element, both 855 and 878 saw serious challenges for the rule of Wessex, challenges of a kind that will naturally create problems for a retrospective, teleologically organized dynastic narrative.[121] The

117 *Pace* C. Clark, ibid., 220.

118 That the whole chain of events, and caution about their presentation, were in the chronicler's mind at the time the 855 account was devised is shown by its leap two years ahead to what it presents as Æthelbald's 857 succession to the West Saxon throne upon his father's death, thereby completing the elision of conflict within the royal family: '⁊ ymb .ii. gear þæs ðe he o[f] Francum com he gefor ... On þa fengon Ęþelwulfes suna twegen to rice, Ęþelbald to Wesseaxna rice ... ⁊ þa ricsode Ęþelbald .v. gear' [and about two years after he came back from Francia he died ... At that time Æthelwulf's two sons succeeded to the kingdom, Æthelbald to the kingdom of the West Saxons ... and then Æthelbald reigned for five years] (s.a. 855). No mention is made of the fact that Æthelbald continued to occupy the throne of Wessex after Æthelwulf's return.

119 *Life of Alfred*, chaps 12–13.

120 Nelson, '"King across the Sea,"' 53–5, and Nelson, 'Power and Authority,' 324–6.

121 Wallace-Hadrill's thesis that the *Chronicle* is a document of some political urgency supportive of the interests of the house of Wessex ('Franks and the English,' 212–14) has been developed by many subsequent historians, often in a more forceful form: e.g., R.H.C. Davis, 'Alfred the Great'; Smyth, *King Alfred the Great*, e.g., 482–6; J. Campbell, 'Placing King Alfred,' 4–5; J. Campbell, 'Asser's *Life of Alfred*,' 124; Scharer, 'Writing of History,' esp. 178–85; and Abels, 'Alfred the Great, the *Micel Hæðen Here*, and the Viking Threat,' esp. 269. Whitelock took sharp exception to this view ('Importance of

rhetoric of these annals might well be expected to show signs of stress. By planting within each of these accounts a united, collective subjectivity with which readers are invited to align themselves, the chronicler provides an ethical grounding for the assimilation of events that had in their own time been controversial into a partisan narrative. The crucial message, formed in hindsight – and it is a message, not an incidental, undisciplined irruption of personal opinion – is that the two returning kings, father and son, were overwhelmingly preferred by the people. In the *Chronicle*, Æthelwulf's reign continues unmarred by any consequences, or indeed any notice, of Æthelbald's overreaching. Likewise, Alfred raises and fulfils the hopes of his loyal subjects by leading them in a triumphant expulsion of the invaders; cognizance of prior West Saxon complicity, which came very close to enabling a real and final Danish conquest of Wessex, simply evaporates.

What happens to the scene of Alfred's arrival at Ecgbert's Stone in Asser's retelling of it, elaborated from an early version of the *Anglo-Saxon Chronicle* at almost the same time as the *Chronicle* itself first began to circulate,[122] speaks volumes as to how the West Saxons' overjoyed reaction in 878 fits into a larger narrative of the recovery of Wessex that was current in the early 890s in Alfred's own circle of associates:

> Iterumque in septima hebdomada post Pascha ad Petram Ægbryhta, quae est in orientali parte saltus, qui dicitur Seluudu ... ibique obviaverunt illi omnes accolae Summurtunensis pagae et Wiltunensis, omnes accolae Hamtunensis pagae, qui non ultra mare pro metu paganorum navigaverant; visoque rege, sicut dignum erat, quasi redivivum post tantas tribulationes recipientes, immenso repleti sunt gaudio. (55.5–14)

> [Presently, in the seventh week after Easter, he rode to Ecgbert's Stone, which is in the eastern part of Selwood Forest ... and there all the inhabitants of Somerset and Wiltshire and all the inhabitants of Hampshire – those who had not sailed overseas for fear of the heathens – joined up with him. When they saw the king, receiving him (not surprisingly) as if one restored to life after suffering such great tribulations, they were filled with immense joy.] (84)[123]

---

the Battle of Edington'), but the writer is clearly a staunch supporter of Alfred, and there is good evidence in the *Chronicle* of 'spin' (though not properly 'propaganda'). See the balanced discussion of Shippey, 'Missing Army.'

122 See Bately, *Anglo-Saxon Chronicle: Texts and Textual Relationships*, 59–62.

123 Here and below, I make one alteration to Keynes and Lapidge's translations, replacing their 'Vikings' with 'heathens' where Asser has *pagani*. The translation 'Vikings'

Asser picks up the *Chronicle*'s calculation of the battle's date from Easter and amplifies the scene by adding a resurrection simile to enhance the expression of Alfred's subjects' elation at his return; and the seventh week after Easter is the feast of Pentecost, celebrating the arrival on earth of the foretold 'Comforter,' the Holy Spirit. It would stretch credulity to suppose that Alfred actually chose this particular week to reassemble his army and to make his dramatic, public return to leadership of his people for the symbolic value of the season: the liturgical celebration of the end of a period of uncertainty between Christ's departure from earth and the arrival of the Paraclete to restore the direct, guiding presence of God to the community of faith, launching the apostolic mission and infusing it with divine power. But quite apart from Alfred's own intentions in 878, fifteen years later and writing as an intimate of the king, Bishop Asser seizes upon the Easter and Pentecost associations and makes Alfred appear as a saviour restored to his people at the moment of their darkest distress. The messianic overtone Asser creates, like the Romans' yearning for rescue from the East in Metre 1 of the *Boethius*, suggests an active conceptual model, among writers associated with Alfred in the 890s, of dramatic political salvation from ruinous oppression through the arrival on the scene of a mighty and righteous royal power.

This narrative template remained available in the service of the West Saxon king for at least a short time after Alfred's death. An extremely interesting account, this time applying the deliverance model to his son Edward, comes to us in Æthelweard's *Chronicon*, which draws in this section on a lost source that in all likelihood originates early in Edward's reign.[124] In relating the events of 893, when a dangerous entrenchment by two Danish armies newly arrived from the continent was more or less successfully contained, Æthelweard gives no information at all about King

---

obscures Asser's emphasis on the non-Christian status of the invaders; cf. ten Harkel, 'Vikings and the Natives,' 181.

124 A. Campbell (*Chronicon Æthelweardi*, xviii) hypothesizes a source from Edward's reign. The inference that the ultimate origins of this account are in the early part of that reign is my own, based on its nature and apparent purpose; the absence of any similar presentations of Edward in *Anglo-Saxon Chronicle* annals of the second continuation (912) or later; and the fact that the first few years of Edward's reign saw a specific source of pressure on his royal story – his cousin Æthelwold's attempt first to seize the throne of Wessex from within the kingdom and then, failing that, to conquer it from outside – that could be expected to generate, during the period up to about 905, a retrospective aggrandizement of Edward's career as an ætheling.

Alfred's military reaction and instead spotlights the ætheling Edward, who was by this time leading some West Saxon forces:

> Pascalique post anni illius eleuatur exercitus, qui de Gallias uenerat partes, subsequendo latebras cuiusdam immanis syluæ quæ uulgo Andredesuuda nuncupatur, protensique sunt Occidentales Anglos usque, ast pedetentim adsitas prouincias uastant, id est Hamtunscire et Bearrucscire. Prænotataque sunt hæc clitoni tum Eaduuerdi, Elfredi filii regis: iam fuerat exercitando per notheas partes Anglorum. Sed post inducuntur et Occidentales Anglos. Fit in occursu minacibus stridens agmine denso Fearnhamme loco. Nec mora, contra insiliunt facta iuuentus, armis irrepti sultant liberati rite clitonis aduentu, ueluti suetam aduectæ post prædam pastoris suffultu pascua bidentes. (49)
>
> [Afterwards at Easter of that year the army which had come from Gaul, following the thickets of a huge wood called Andred by the common people, spread as far as Wessex, and gradually wasted the adjacent provinces, that is Northamptonshire and Berkshire. These matters then came to the notice of Prince Edward, the son of King Alfred. He was at that time moving forces through the southern part of England [? or through Sussex]. Later, however, they [the Danes] penetrated Wessex. He [the prince] came clashing in dense array into collision with the foemen at Farnham. There was no delay, the young men leaped against the prepared defences, and having slipped on their armour they duly exulted, being set free ... by the prince's arrival, like sheep brought to the pastures by the help of the shepherd after the customary ravaging.] (p. 49, bracketed insertions Campbell's)[125]

The focus on Edward even to the complete exclusion of Alfred is striking, because the *Anglo-Saxon Chronicle*'s version of the same events does not so much as mention the prince by name while going out of its way to stress Alfred's tactical effectiveness in hindering the new invaders. Annal 893 in the vernacular *Chronicle*, part of the first continuation written near the end of Alfred's reign, explains in some detail how the king established a position between the two Danish encampments to restrict their activities, surveilled and confronted their smaller raiding parties, and prevented the enemy armies from moving en masse except (as the chronicler puts it) on two occasions: their arrival in Wessex and their departure. Æthelweard's

---

125 I normalize the spelling of personal names in Campbell's translation. The ellipsis omits '[from care],' an insertion by Campbell that eliminates Æthelweard's metaphor.

unknown source is equally determined to make sure Edward gets credit, indeed creating the impression that the ætheling responded independently to the foreign threat. While the two accounts never directly conflict, virtually the only point of positive agreement between them is the fact that the major battle between the West Saxon and Danish forces occurred at Farnham.[126]

Æthelweard's version has the earmarks of a court narrative celebrating a sitting king's precociously regal heroics during his youth and helping to establish his image.[127] It emphasizes Edward's leadership and detaches his status and worthiness from his powerful father by writing Alfred out of the story. But even so, and most significantly for our purposes, we see applied to Edward's actions motifs of captivity and deliverance closely akin to those Asser had invoked in recounting Alfred's assembly of his army for the Battle of Edington. The West Saxon men are exuberant upon seeing Edward come to save the day, and they are 'set free' by their prince as he, like a shepherd, leads them to safety. The importance of this likeness is twofold. First, because this portrayal comes from a source distinct from the *Anglo-Saxon Chronicle* as we have it (unlike Asser's account of 878 and earlier parts of Æthelweard's *Chronicon* itself),[128] it provides independent confirmation of the currency within West Saxon court circles of this paradigm of royal rescue from a foreign predator. Second, because the material drawn from that source is redolent of Edwardian interests, it attests to the continued viability of the 'royal saviour' model into Edward's reign, at least close to his court.

The foregoing examples establish the chronological range of this model's documentation and its usefulness in telling the story of Wessex's internal political integrity against the Danes. But it also had political pertinence to the project of extending West Saxon power into neighbouring regions. Although the series of Danish assaults that overthrew all the other

126 Cf. Shippey, 'Missing Army.'

127 Cf. the analogous emphasis on the military presence of Edmund in *The Battle of Brunanburh*: as Scragg points out ('Reading of *Brunanburh*,' 116–17), Edmund was sixteen years old at the time of the battle, but writing him prominently into the account would make sense as a validating strategy after he had succeeded his brother on the throne.

128 Æthelweard's material from the original compilation of the *Anglo-Saxon Chronicle* stems from an early version from which MS A also derives (Bately, *Anglo-Saxon Chronicle: Texts and Textual Relationships*, 41–53 and 59–62), but for the last years of Alfred's reign and all of Edward's and Æthelstan's, Æthelweard's work is independent of the *Anglo-Saxon Chronicle* continuations.

Anglo-Saxon kingdoms likewise targeted and for a time seriously endangered Wessex, its disruption of Anglo-Saxon geopolitics also contributed to the expansion of West Saxon territorial control, and in the early stages of this process the narrative of political rescue from a foreign invader could be redirected to that purpose. Beginning immediately after the basic stability of Wessex was recovered at the end of the 870s, first Alfred and then his successors positioned themselves as potential beneficiaries of the political turbulence resulting from the ninth-century Danish invasions.

The desire of Boethius in Metre 1 to engineer a transfer of direct rule to the Byzantine emperor seems meaningful in this connection. Whereas in the prose he had sought alliance against Theodoric from the East, the verse states explicitly that he wants an outside government to come in and take over, headed by those imagined to be of distant kinship to the dispossessed and departed Western imperial dynasty and to share legal and religious customs with the Romans. Metre 1's construction of the will of a conquered people happens to be exactly that which would justify the intervention of a West Saxon king in neighbouring regions after the Danish invasions, and we know that Alfred's own political philosophy included an unapologetically expansionist notion of royal success. This is evident in the preface to the Old English *Pastoral Care*,[129] one of the books most securely associated with his patronage if not authorship, and it is equally apparent in Alfred's consistent styling in charters and coinage, from the mid-880s onward, as 'king of the Anglo-Saxons' or 'king of the Angles and the Saxons': an assertion of rule in English Mercia, and a break with the historical West Saxon royal designation 'king of the Saxons,' that is reflected as well in Asser's *Life of Alfred*.[130]

By the time we reach the possible period of Metre 1's composition, the process of establishing West Saxon rule over territories conquered by the Danes, which would continue over several decades, had taken a firm first step in Mercia. We may see the poem as reflecting light from a concept of Wessex's extension of its power as the liberation of subjugated, English-speaking peoples from violent foreigners heedless of ancient native customs and rights: a gratifying version, current within Alfred's ideological community, of the incipient story of West Saxon expansion. It is in this

129 Sweet, *King Alfred's West-Saxon Version*, 3/5–9.

130 See Keynes and Lapidge, *Alfred the Great*, 227–8 n. 1; Keynes, 'Edward'; Keynes, 'King Alfred'; Abels, *Alfred the Great*, 146 and 169–83; Blackburn, 'London Mint'; Blackburn, 'Alfred's Coinage Reforms'; and Asser, *Life of Alfred*, dedication, 1.2, 64.1, 67.1, and 83.1.

context that we can best understand the attempt by writers in Alfred's growing domain to cultivate a germinal 'national' identity that could be trained toward political unity under an ever farther-reaching West Saxon monarchy.[131] In annal 886 of the *Chronicle*, describing Alfred's activities at London, we catch a clear glimpse of the process in action:

> gesette Ęlfred cyning Lundenburg, ⁊ him all Angelcyn to cirde þæt buton deniscra monna hæftniede was; ⁊ he[132] þa befæste þa burg Ęþerede aldormen to haldonne. (s.a. 886)
>
> [King Alfred occupied London, and all the English race which was free of (lit. outside of) the captivity of the Danish men turned to him; and then he entrusted the stronghold to Ealdorman Æthelred to defend.]

It is no accident that we find here the term *Angelcynn* that has been much discussed as an Alfredian instrument of a new political identity encompassing both Angles and Saxons. Asser, recounting the same event, calls Alfred 'Angulsaxonum rex' [king of the Anglo-Saxons] (83.1; Keynes and Lapidge, 97) and says that 'ad quem regum omnes Angli et Saxones, qui prius ubique dispersi fuerant aut cum paganis sub captivitate erant, voluntarie converterunt, et suo dominio se subdiderunt' [all the Angles and Saxons – those who had formerly been scattered everywhere and were not in captivity with the heathens – turned willingly to King Alfred and submitted themselves to his lordship] (83.5–8; Keynes and Lapidge, 98). Both the regal style applied to Alfred by Asser and the language that he and the *Anglo-Saxon Chronicle* use to describe the general submission in London imply a doctrine that once Danish rule is peeled back from a given area, what will be found beneath it is a population of 'the English' or 'the

---

131 The literature on social identity in medieval Britain began to benefit from current models of ethnicity with Reynolds, 'What Do We Mean?' and has grown explosively since the mid-1990s. Studies commenting substantively on ninth-century developments in what would become England are J. Campbell, 'United Kingdom' (but see critiques by Foot, 'Historiography'); Foot, 'Making of *Angelcynn*'; K. Davis, 'National Writing in the Ninth Century'; Reuter, 'Making of England'; Smyth, 'Emergence of English Identity'; Foot, 'Remembering, Forgetting, and Inventing'; Kleinschmidt, 'What Does the *Anglo-Saxon Chronicle* Tell Us?'; Neville, 'History, Poetry, and "National" Identity'; S.J. Harris, *Race and Ethnicity*, chap. 3; Nelson, 'England and the Continent: II,' esp. 22–7; Sheppard, *Families of the King*, esp. chap. 2; and Stodnick, 'Interests of Compounding.'

132 Correcting from MS *hie*, which Bately identifies as a scribal error.

Anglo-Saxons' of whom Alfred is presumptively the rightful king, and who need only be liberated to accept him as such. The language of 'captivity' in both the *Chronicle* and Asser's adaptation of it is pointed; these writers encourage a conceptualization of West Saxon military advances into the Danelaw not as conquest, or even (as some historians have misleadingly called it) reconquest, but rescue.

We have little specific knowledge of Alfred's 886 activity at London, a former Mercian trade centre situated near the convergence of several kingdoms' historical frontiers. The episode used to be seen as a violent conquest of a Danish military position, but it was more likely an unresisted takeover of a point theoretically or sporadically within the bounds of Danish rule or else a display of royal authority at a site already considered by that time to fall under Alfred's control following the end of the unsucceeded Ceolwulf II's reign in Mercia.[133] It may or may not have coincided with an intensification of recognized Alfredian dominion over western Mercia as a whole;[134] and the exact nature of its relationship to the *Treaty*

---

133 Versions of the *Chronicle* other than MS A testify that on one occasion Alfred besieged London (s.a. 884 in MSS B and C; s.a. 883 in MSS D and E). Some have assumed that the annal recording the event is misplaced and belongs to 886, which would make the account given there describe a conquest immediately prior to Alfred's doings in London reported s.a. 886. But against this interpretation should be considered the rather different description by Asser (*Life of Alfred*, 83.1–3; Keynes and Lapidge, *Alfred the Great*, 98–9), which sounds like the peaceful rebuilding and resettlement of a city that had been ravaged by war at an earlier date. For argument that the entry s.a. 883 or 884 in non-A MSS is not mistakenly placed, see Dumville, 'Treaty,' 6–7 and n. 35. Two additional factors are the numismatic evidence, which indicates at least intermittent recognition of Alfred's authority in London from as early as the 870s (Blackburn, 'London Mint'; Keynes, 'King Alfred,' 12–18; Blackburn, 'Alfred's Coinage Reforms,' 212–14), and the fact that the town had mostly moved outside of the Roman wall. Alfred appears to have brought about resettlement of the Roman town at this time (Cowie, 'Mercian London'; Keene, 'Alfred and London'), and I return to Asser's contemporary language, which sounds decidedly civic, gives the impression of a past, but not a present, of war for those receiving Alfred in 886, and in this agrees with the archaeological, numismatic, and documentary evidence.

134 The events following the death or departure of Ceolwulf, whose reign ended no later than 880, are obscure. The direct ruler of western Mercia thereafter is Ealdorman Æthelred, soon to be Alfred's son-in-law, but authoritative contemporary sources carefully avoid assigning him the title 'king' (see, for instance, the summary of relevant charters by Keynes, 'King Alfred,' 27–9). It is not certain whether Alfred's appointment of Æthelred to administer London followed from some formal submission of Æthelred at that time, or whether Æthelred's position with respect to Alfred was already stable and he was simply given responsibility for London in 886.

of Alfred and Guthrum, like that document's relationship to Alfred's influence in Mercian territory more broadly, is ambiguous.[135] What is clear is that 'a major political event' occurred in London in 886,[136] and that Alfred's ensconcement there was a strategic assertion of regional power against the neighbouring, and suddenly once again warlike, East Anglian Danes.[137] The goings-on of that year appear to have marked – both for participants and for the writers close to the occasion who recorded it without, unfortunately, telling us much about it – a new phase in Alfred's reign, in which he could claim persistent overlordship over all of English-speaking Britain that lay outside the limits of Danish domination as they existed at that moment. Simon Keynes has presented good reasons to see in the general submission in London the beginning of a formal union of Wessex and western Mercia as 'the kingdom of the Anglo-Saxons,'[138] although the administrative reorganization of this political entity may never have been completely realized before dynastic attention was redirected toward expansion to the north and east by Alfred's son Edward and daughter Æthelflæd, Lady of the Mercians.[139]

Alfred's 886 occupation of London involved his attainment and retention of notional support, among the politically consequential inhabitants of the region, as a preferable kingly alternative to Danish rule. Just as was the case in accounts of the crisis of 878, from a West Saxon perspective of the 890s Alfred's position in the aftermath of Ceolwulf's reign was analogous not to that of Boethius himself in Metre 1, but to that of the imperial authority whose intervention Boethius and the Romans crave. Again I emphasize,

---

135 An older view, represented for instance by Keynes and Lapidge, *Alfred the Great*, 171, and R.H.C. Davis, 'Alfred and Guthrum's Frontier,' holds that the treaty cannot predate 886. However, other scholars have been unwilling to limit the treaty's date by reference to 886 for various reasons relating to the uncertain nature of that year's events, and many now see the arrangement as proceeding closely from the baptism of Guthrum in 878, the withdrawal of the Danes from Wessex, and (by this view) the assumption of lordship over western Mercia by King Alfred at the end of Ceolwulf's reign: e.g., Abels, *Alfred the Great*, 163–4; Abels, 'Alfred the Great, the *Micel Hæðen Here*, and the Viking Threat,' 277–8; Blackburn, 'London Mint,' 122–3; and Charles-Edwards, 'Alliances, Godfathers, Treaties, and Boundaries,' 55–6.

136 Quotation from Keynes and Lapidge, *Alfred the Great*, 266 n. 200; cf. Keynes, 'King Alfred,' 24–5; Nelson, 'Political Ideas,' 154–7; and Foot, 'Making of *Angelcynn*,' 26–7.

137 The previous *Chronicle* annal (885) has the Danes of East Anglia breaking the peace that had lasted since Guthrum's baptism.

138 Keynes, 'King Alfred' and 'Edward.'

139 On administrative arrangements, see Keynes, 'Edward,' 45–8. Davidson ('(Non)submission,' 204–5) points to the main reasons for reserving judgment as to the total achievement of the new polity Keynes describes.

however, that there is no need to posit a focused political allegory in the minds of the *Boethius* poet or the text's early readers to find in Metre 1 traces of the political discourse of the period: the important dates for understanding the perspective of this poem are not 878 and 886, but 892 to roughly 905, when other texts in close ideological harmony with it were being produced. The prominence in Metre 1 of a paradigm of longed-for rescue from a foreign oppressor, coupled with the presence in contemporaneous historical sources of a model of deliverance and other rhetoric designed to naturalize West Saxon rule of 'the English' in other regions, points less to specific allusion than to a political fantasy of Wessex's relationship to the Anglian kingdoms that had succumbed to Danish invasion.

Metre 1, that is to say, is a poem about a conquered people that appeals to the interests of the unconquered: those within established West Saxon authority, and particularly those wielding it. This text's presuppositions about how subjugated groups might respond to their situation, emotionally, ethically, and politically, originate in an interested perspective outside of the immediate relationship of conquerer and conquered or oppressor and oppressed: the perspective of a third party eager to intervene. Boethius's pretence of remaining loyal to Theodoric while calling on a greater power to come in and remove him places at the centre of Metre 1 a noble protagonist whose virtue consists in having the wisdom to choose an appropriate ruler on whom to fix his loyalty, not limiting his options to those present, and to seek outside help. When we fill in from history the role that is desired but never actualized in Metre 1 – when we insert into the scenario a third party that really does act as Boethius only hopes the Byzantine emperor will do – what the poem represents as covertly resistant behaviour by the conquered becomes in fact acquiescence to the assumption of power by a new ruler who will oppose a foreign usurper on the behalf of the oppressed, and whose re-establishment of righteous lordship will free them to reclaim their formerly accustomed privileges. Metre 1's vision of a vanquished people longing for liberation by the righteous is one more attestation of the rhetorical template of deliverance through the sudden arrival of an absent royal authority that is manifested in contemporaneous historical writing friendly to both the dynastic narrative of the salvation of Wessex and the Alfredian phase of West Saxon expansion.

* * *

Traditional, verse-specific features of Metre 1 are the entrée into that poem for political concepts, current during Alfred's reign and the first part of Edward's, that readily support royal interests of that period in at least three specific ways. First, Metre 1's ideal nobleman – wise, mindful of custom and duty, and loyal both to those in his lordship and to his own worthy lord, Theodoric – opposes Theodoric rather than participating in injustice when Theodoric turns against the emperor and starts to tyrannize Rome. Boethius transfers his loyalty to the highest available political authority through the letters he sends the emperor pleading with the 'Greeks' to step into direct rule of Rome, and in doing so replicates the structure of multiple allegiance, including a direct tie to the top of the hierarchy, established by the loyalty oaths instituted by Alfred and carried on by his dynastic successors. Second, he pursues a solution only secretly. The disjunction between Boethius's private intentions and his actions, which for a time preserves his position while he seeks an opportunity to change the situation, resembles the deliberately false oath-swearing under duress by the Romans that has occurred previously in Metre 1, and both strategies mirror the principle first articulated in Alfred's laws that it is more just to deceive than to carry out an oath that would entail betraying a rightful lord or otherwise constitute a wrong. Finally, both the Romans when newly conquered and later Boethius himself, languishing under the rule of their pagan or heretical oppressors, hope for help from afar from the righteous, politically worthy emperor. Here their desires reproduce a paradigm of political deliverance that appears repeatedly in near-contemporary historical accounts glorifying Alfred's and Edward's military achievements and have the look of a West Saxon political fantasy of liberating grateful neighbours from their tyrannical Danish lords.

Boethius's general situation in the poem of course comes from the Latin original and his plan is inherited from the immediate prose source. Things do not end well for him. But the purpose of Metre 1 is not to advance a focused, topical, political agenda based on any simple identification with the fictional scenario. The protagonist's states and qualities of mind – his wisdom, his discernment, his loyalty to the emperor, his hope, and finally his anguish in prison – are far more central to the poem, in the larger context of the prosimetrical *Boethius*, than any political message, as also were the Romans' misery, longing, and faithful secret commitment to the old regime earlier in Metre 1. The poet's development of Boethius's subjectivity and invention of the Romans', both along highly traditional lines and drawing upon expectations and complexes of meaning supplied by the poetic register, nevertheless take on particular contours which, like the edges of a puzzle piece, reveal something also about the poem's discursive environment, fitting it to identifiable elements of West Saxon political writing.

The political discourse it implies can be dated to the latter part of Alfred's reign and the early years of Edward's, when other texts manifesting all of the same discursive elements exist and when those discursive elements most readily make sense vis-à-vis the historical context. The features of the poem that connect up in this way are precisely those which both emerge from its adaptation into classical verse and manifest the poetics of mentality, affirming once again how entwined the latter is with poetic method. The versifier's development of political relationships in Metre 1 is a complex and subtle demonstration of ways that larger-scale content and message are governed by poetic interest in perspective. It is the consideration of those elements, in their interface with the tradition that they both draw from and subtly act upon, that gives us our best chance of locating the text's specific, meaningful discursive identity.

The power of tradition lies in its ability to seem timeless and natural: a repetition of patterns stretching back to the perspectival vanishing point and, through continued iterations, an extension of those patterns into the indefinite future. Its appeal often rests in its apparent detachment from situational contingencies that are unique to the moment: its apparent superiority to those contingencies so that it may bring them under absolute, ordering control while remaining unaffected by them. That appearance is illusory, but because of the comforting impression tradition can offer of transcendent freedom from the jarring particularities of history, a speaker or writer who succeeds in communicating novel or timely ideas in a markedly traditional way has taken a great stride toward making them feel irresistibly true. We cannot know whether the *Boethius* poet deliberately innovated, or innovated unconsciously by importing presumptions from political discourse into a new traditional production because to him or her they felt natural in poetic discourse as well; but in any case Metre 1's own version of traditionalism trades on political concepts and rhetoric that mattered in Wessex at a certain moment in time. The political images offered by Metre 1 are projected out of concrete historical circumstances, yet are endowed by the poem's method with the aura of abstract, timeless rightness that is characteristic of ideologically freighted representations, and of traditional ones.

Conclusions

Using an array of texts selected to account for variables in compositional scenarios, I have argued that a poetics of mentality inhabits the register of classical-style verse in Old English and makes an integral part of that discourse's traditionality. In order to establish this thesis as rigorously as possible and show that the poetics of mentality operates independently of particular textual relations or circumstances of production, the preceding chapters have examined an English poem alongside an English prose analogue, both based on the same Latin source; an English poem that only slightly adapts its continental Saxon verse source; and an English poem alongside its English prose source. Whether in highly stylized but systematic translation from Latin, in the uncommonly faithful line-by-line modulation of a poem from one to another closely related vernacular, or in the conversion of an English prose text into a fully functional poem in the traditional style, we observe the same thing: the continual amplification of any subjectivity derived from the source and the liberal addition of it where it was absent. My choice of texts has been governed by a comparative methodology because this approach provided the most information-rich opportunities for analysis, but the tendencies described pervade the corpus of classical-style verse.

In narrative works, we have seen the poetics of mentality consistently expressed in at least three descriptively discrete but interlocking ways: (1) at the small scale of word and phrase, through its presence in the formulaic and other traditional diction by means of which verses and lines are constructed; (2) in content-driven features, exhibiting an inclination among poets to comment often on states and processes of mind at scales ranging from the individual statement to the entire episode; and (3) in the technical delivery of narrative information, using focalization to give readers knowledge of various experiential positions within the unfolding story. The relationships among these three manifestations of the Old English poetics of mentality are asymmetrical. The second and third as I have listed them, mentality content and subjectivizing narrative technique, can appear without direct and specific dependency on the first, traditional diction, which proves that they are not strictly a function of the stock of formulas available to poets. However, the first and third, traditional diction and focalization, cannot exist without being involved in some sense with the second, content. Patterned diction brings form to desired content, of course, but it also brings content to desired form, especially in view of the fact that Old English formulas paradigmatically include variable elements. Formulas use real and meaningful language – none the less so for being deployed in highly institutionalized ways – and can endow it with special semantic qualities within the pragmatics of a distinctive, heavily marked register. Likewise, narrative focalization is intrinsically involved with content because it selects among available perspectives and accordingly shapes a reader's knowledge of the story matter. It is well known in literary studies that the form/content dichotomy we find analytically convenient is never absolute, but the participation of traditional forms in the communicative pragmatics of an 'esoteric' register (in the terminology of discourse analysis), like that of Old English poetry, is extreme. The fact that no part of the system exists independently of the register's signifying and other discursive properties implies that no interpretation of a text in that register can afford to neglect traditionality of expression, and I have argued that this traditionality includes the frequency and nature of poetic attention to subjective positions, states, and events.

What, then, are the consequences of these findings for our understanding of Old English poems? Recognition of the poetics of mentality suggests, first, that we cannot build interpretation of individual texts upon the fact that the poet provides information about one or another experiential position. That fact alone tells us nothing in a given case, because it is to be expected within this tradition. To answer in the simplest possible terms a question posed at the beginning of this book, about the Franks Casket's front panel inscription, the emotional state of a stranded whale mattered to the poet because he or she was writing a classical Old English poem. The glimpse of the whale's misery, together with and no less than the verse form and metrical grammar in which it is recounted, contributes to the inscription's identity as a poem in the traditional register.

The situation remains essentially the same as we move from one of the shortest narratives in Old English verse to the longest. Readers of *Beowulf* often comment on the information delivered about the subjectivity or perspectives of some character or group of characters. Scholarship of the academic generation spanning the past thirty years or so has drawn attention to the focalization through Grendel and has commented frequently, if more in passing, on other, similar details, such as the stress laid on Hildeburh's sadness in the Finnsburh episode. There is no doubt that the subjectivized elements of *Beowulf* are handled with great artistry; but I think there is a tendency in the criticism to overinterpret the mere occurrence of this phenomenon as thematically significant and to overestimate the degree to which it differs in kind from what is widely encountered elsewhere in the corpus. Other longer poems, too, have attracted readings that call attention to the putatively remarkable subjective representations of their characters, especially female protagonists.

The poetic acknowledgment of experiential positions that other discourses tend to subordinate ethically (like those of monsters, devils, and animals) or socially (like those of women or fleeing slaves) seems striking to modern readers because we expect it to be anomalous in a pre-modern literature, but it is not unusual in the Old English poetry that we have. It may be exceptional for a poem in the heroic style to have a female protagonist, but once she is there, access to the mind of a Judith is not surprising. If there existed other Old English narrative poems featuring *þyrsas*, we might find that they think and feel very much like Grendel.[1] Arguably the traditionality of Grendel's subjectivity is implied by the maxim sentencing (so to speak) the *þyrs* to solitude in the fen (*Maxims II*, ll. 42b–3a): a state of existence, defined within a symbolic geography, that seems almost to demand development into a narrative of inveterate hostility to human community and to the hall as the centre of an ordered social landscape.[2] I would not wish to oversimplify the range of critical readings that proceed from observing poetic attentiveness to situated perceptions and to qualities and states of mind; they move in various directions and often propose additional lines of reasoning in support of their claims. I only point out

1 As his mother and the dragon more or less do, although their monstrous subjectivities are less often noted. The rare word *þyrs*, usually translated simply as 'monster,' is one of the few simplices the poet uses to denote what Grendel is.

2 Cf. Clemoes, *Interactions of Thought and Language*. Clemoes's theory of poetic semantics leads him to an understanding of maxims as reflecting implicitly narrative thinking about their topics. The gnome about the solitary, fen-dwelling *þyrs* is a prime candidate for such a link between traditional concept and narrative actualization given the poetic associations of both fen and isolation.

that other kinds of evidence must indeed be adduced before arguing for the specific, interpretable meaning of this traditional phenomenon in a given case. To whatever extent a reading rests on an assumption that some pattern of subjective access in itself sets one poem apart from others, or creates within the text a special emphasis of some kind, that reading should be reevaluated.

It must not be supposed, however, that alertness to the poetics of mentality only narrows interpretive possibilities. The attention to subjectivity is real, and it can and should be analysed, both as a cultural phenomenon and as a constituent of poetic meaning in the individual instance. The question is how to do so while taking account of its nature as a facet of Old English poetic traditionality more broadly. It is not necessary, for instance, to dismiss the forlorn whale of the Franks Casket from critical relevance upon recognizing that the detail is motivated by conventional priorities and interests. A sad cetacean is poetically attractive not merely in being a whale (although the stranding of a whale would be a spectacle, and a stroke of luck, that might well inspire epigrammatic memorialization)[3] and not merely in being sad (although Anglo-Saxon poets do seem to savour distress). The poetic centre of gravity is the subjective position the animal occupies, or can imaginatively be made to occupy, within an agonistic system in which its might has been defeated by an even more powerful force of nature:[4] situationally the beached whale is a weather-beaten exile of sorts, out of its proper element, driven from its kind, and accordingly doomed. This reading both honours the traditionality of the poem's construction of the whale's subjectivity and contributes to the solution of a long-standing interpretive challenge by bringing the inscription into intelligible association with the context formed by several of the images on the casket[5] – but only, I would emphasize, through the poem's metonymic

3 See Gardiner, 'Exploitation,' and Szabo, *Monstrous Fishes*. In her vignette of the attempts in 2006 to rescue a whale that had swum up the Thames, Szabo observes that whereas onlookers at that time hoped for the whale's return to the sea, witnesses of a medieval stranding would likely have celebrated the event (282–3).

4 See Neville, *Representations*, 175–7, on the sea as a semi-personified combatant in some Old English poems.

5 See Osborn, 'Picture-Poem' and 'Lid as Conclusion.' My understanding of the whale differs from Osborn's, but I agree with her perception that the concept of displacement unifies various design elements of the casket, including the front panel inscription. More recently, Webster ('Iconographic Programme'), Lang ('Imagery'), and Neuman de Vegvar ('Reading') have all proposed exile as a theme uniting the panels, but without addressing the front panel text in this connection.

pragmatics activated by the conjunction within classical verse form of the whale's misery and its helpless separation, in the sand, from its own 'homeland.'[6]

Readings that take full account of the poetics of mentality are easiest to achieve within critical approaches that focus on traditionality itself or on the traditionalism that makes extratextual use of that traditionality. Katherine O'Brien O'Keeffe's excellent analysis of two very late poems in the *Anglo-Saxon Chronicle*, *The Death of Alfred* (s.a. 1036, MSS C and D) and *The Death of Edward* (s.a. 1065, MSS C and D), can illustrate the point. O'Brien O'Keeffe demonstrates the pronounced traditionality of *The Death of Edward* by contrast to the slightly earlier *Death of Alfred*, a non-traditional poem far removed from classical verse in metrical and dictional technique, and argues that the *Edward* poet's highly conspicuous traditionalism seeks to inculcate a desired political perspective.[7] Bringing the poetics of mentality into the account adds another dimension to her observations: *The Death of Edward* shows the traditional attraction to situational subjectivity and to diction that defines character by mental states and qualities, while *The Death of Alfred* lacks signs of such an attraction. The *Edward* poet memorializes Edward the Confessor not only by his holiness, but also prominently by his mental qualities (he is said to have been 'cræftig ræda' [skilled in counsel] and 'froda' [wise], ll. 5b and 29a); and in a report of his recovery of his proper place reminiscent of the *Beowulf* poet's statement that Scyld Scefing found consolation after starting as a destitute foundling, Edward is said to have been 'a bliðemod, bealuleas kyng' [ever happy-minded, the king lacking in malice] (l. 15) despite his former hardships as a very traditional-sounding exile whose 'deore rice' [beloved kingdom] (l. 19b) had been held by the Danes while he, 'lande bereafod, / wunode wræclastum wide geond eorðan' [bereft of (his) land, inhabited exile-paths far and wide throughout the earth] (ll. 16b–17).[8] To his subjects (whom the poet's encomiastic perspective is

---

6 A traditional concept: several poetic terms for the sea define it as the homeland or habitation of whales. Cf. Clemoes, *Interactions of Thought and Language*, 111–12, on the elemental relationship between the whale and the sea, and Riedinger, '"Home,"' on the traditional resonance of scenarios of removal from home.

7 O'Brien O'Keeffe, 'Deaths and Transformations'; cf. Trilling, *Aesthetics of Nostalgia*, 208–11. Amodio, *Writing the Oral Tradition*, 53–9, also emphasizes the poem's traditionality but does not take up political implications. On the classical-style regularity of this and four other *Chronicle* poems, see Townsend, 'Metre of the *Chronicle*-Verse.'

8 I cite *The Death of Edward* from O'Brien O'Keeffe's edition of *Chronicle* MS C, s.a. 1065, and supply line numbers.

to represent) Edward was *deor* 'beloved' (l. 26b), and he has been served *holdlice* 'loyally,' first by *eall* 'everyone' and then, more specifically, by his successor Harold Godwinson (ll. 13–14, 30b–2). Because the poetics of mentality helps shape *The Death of Edward*'s ethical mapping and its constructions of lordship and allegiance, it has a role in the poem's political work. Awareness of this component of traditional versecraft can similarly inform analysis of other late yet traditionalizing poetry both within and outside of the *Anglo-Saxon Chronicle*, complementing recent discussion of the political value of traditional form in the tenth and eleventh centuries by Martin Irvine, Janet Thormann, Donald Scragg, Elizabeth Tyler, and Renée Trilling.[9]

The work of these scholars reminds us that Old English verse existed as a communicative medium in a social world. Because it was made by and for historically implicated human beings, we need to be alert to all of the purposes (aesthetic, rhetorical, political) served by the choice of stylistic traditionality and, I would add, by the poetics of mentality as a part of it. Classical verse form and style, including dictional and conceptual emphasis on subjective states and qualities of mind, presumably became ever more assertive a statement as options diversified late in the Anglo-Saxon period; it must, by the time of *The Death of Edward*, have become very marked, perceived by readers in explicit contradistinction to newer kinds of verse.[10] Yet even at earlier times, when the choice to make a poem in the traditional style was perhaps less noteworthy and might less complexly gratify aesthetic sensibilities that could be taken for granted, those sensibilities themselves were situated within a cultural moment and had meaning there.

The mostly anonymous and imprecisely datable canon of classical Old English verse presents problems for historicizing readings, but the finer points of a poem's traditionalism may sometimes offer leads. We saw in chapter 3 that the opening Metre of the Old English *Boethius* presupposes a ruling authority's claim on the direct allegiance of one whose immediate lord breaks faith; provides for the validation of loyalties finally proved, even if not at all times expressed, by figuring political equivocation in hard circumstances as strategic; and portrays a desired system of power

9 M. Irvine, *Making of Textual Culture*, 451–60; Thormann, '*Anglo-Saxon Chronicle* Poems'; Scragg, 'Reading of *Brunanburh*'; Tyler, *Old English Poetics*, chap. 5; and Trilling, *Aesthetics of Nostalgia*, chaps 4–5.

10 See Bredehoft, *Early English Metre*, esp. 91–3; O'Brien O'Keeffe, 'Deaths and Transformations'; Tyler, *Old English Poetics*, 157–60; and Trilling, *Aesthetics of Nostalgia*, chaps 4–5.

relationships, stretching across geographic and political boundaries, that might in the short term justify the actions of the West Saxon kings with respect to neighbouring lands under the rule of Danish invaders. Each of these aspects of the poem naturalizes political ideas that had specific utility in Alfredian and early Edwardian Wessex to familiar, authorizing aesthetic structures and conceptual frames of reference. Traditionalism creates a rhetorical field in which innovation can be almost imperceptibly legitimated, and Metre 1 projects images of personal loyalty, wisdom, and ideal subjecthood perfectly suited to West Saxon policy of the period as we currently understand it. Yet it is a historical poem, concerned primarily to tell the poetically elaborated story of Boethius inherited from the prose source, not a political one in the sense of advertising a specific agenda in relation to contemporary circumstances. Metre 1's involvement in political discourse proceeds from the relational and ethical logic of the text, which in turn emerges in large part from the way the poet handles access to loci of subjectivity and shifts in perspective. The meanings that are made cannot be totally divorced from the materials with which they are made, and it is through the poetics of mentality that Metre 1 weaves new colours into the cloth of Old English poetic tradition.

Elsewhere, more conventional manifestations of the poetics of mentality may serve to anchor experimental and ostentatious realizations of the classical poetic form, tethering them to the 'aesthetics of the familiar' (in Tyler's apt phrase). We see this in *The Riming Poem* and *Aldhelm*, each of which has a complicated relationship to classical poetic form yet maintains quite ordinary ties with traditional subjectivity. *The Riming Poem*, with its outrageous melange of sonic effects, presents motifs of mental containment (and its failure) in an elegiac scenario of loss and forlornness that is easily recognizable, despite being very obscure in its particulars due partly to the extreme formal constraints adopted by the poet.[11] The encomiastic *Aldhelm*, a preface to one copy of the prose version of Aldhelm's *De virginitate*, likewise covers the classical poetic metre with a thick display coat of experimentation, mixing Old English and Latin in approximately equal

11 On this poem's formal features and difficulty, see esp. Earl ('Hisperic Style'), who would connect it to Anglo-Latin poetry of the kind studied by Lapidge ('Hermeneutic Style'). Most recently Abram ('Errors') suggests an especially close connection to the alliterating and rhyming octosyllables of Æthilwald. O'Brien O'Keeffe ('Deaths and Transformations,' 154–6) considers *The Riming Poem*'s relationship to traditional verse-craft and the impact of its form on intelligibility. I comment on its use of the motif of mental containment in 'Representation,' 84–5.

proportion and dropping in dabs of Greek.[12] The scholar and poet Aldhelm as portrayed there is formulaically wise, and the text briefly invokes the ad hoc subjectivity of a reader of the work who must apply his mind to study. Most interestingly, the book – which is itself the first-person speaker[13] – seems, when it memorializes Aldhelm 'geonges geanoðe geomres' [with a sad youth's complaint],[14] to mourn him as a disciple laments the departure of the master.[15] In both of these poems what we have is not a rejection of tradition, but rather an exuberant decoration of its essential forms. The poetics of mentality maintains solid contact with poetic traditionality while other aspects of the writers' versecraft challenge expectations. Critical recognition of its constancy amid such explosive experimentation contributes to a picture of these poets' traditionality in some dimensions of their art despite their unconventionality in others.

While inquiries that focus on traditionality and traditionalism can easily incorporate an awareness of the poetics of mentality and be further advanced by that awareness, my findings are potentially more disruptive to the study of psychological representations in individual poems, where the fact of traditionality very directly affects interpretation of the evidence and requires a more considered methodology than has usually been brought to bear. While a great many readings of Old English poems comment on the subjective dynamics within them, they tend to presuppose whatever is observed within a single text to be particular to and circumscribed by that text, taking all its meaning from that immediate environment. Mine is certainly no argument against close reading: because texts are communicative acts, formed in certain moments by certain persons with certain objectives, each has particularity. Yet in a heavily marked register, isolationist readings remain in one real sense non-readings. Without attention to the traditionality of representations of subjective experience, interpretation of a given text comes unmoored from the dictional and other systems that defined its pragmatic properties for early audiences. In classical Old English verse, poetic entry into minds is conventional. What

12 See Lapidge, 'Hermeneutic Style,' 121, and Orchard, *Poetic Art of Aldhelm*, 282–3.

13 On this conceit, see Earl, 'King Alfred's Talking Poems' (noting the example of *Aldhelm* on p. 58); Discenza, 'Alfred's Verse Preface,' 628; and O'Brien O'Keeffe, 'Listening to the Scenes of Reading.'

14 I follow the translation of this phrase given by Orchard, *Poetic Art of Aldhelm*, 282 n. 105.

15 I take the 'youth' in *Aldhelm* to be a student or disciple (it is of course the book representing itself as having learned from Aldhelm). Cf. *Guthlac B*, ll. 1327–79; *Christ II*, ll. 533–40a; and allegorically, *The Phoenix*, ll. 350–4a.

matters in the individual instance is what we find there – what poets think belongs there – and crucially, how it relates to tradition. Every new use of traditional elements will draw meaning simultaneously and dynamically from its accumulated identity as a recognizable expression, from its particularity as it is inflected by the local, immediate, textual context, and from the occasions of its making and reception.

I have tried to illustrate in some detail the interaction of these factors in the case study of Metre 1 of the *Boethius*. The subjectivized elements of that poem are there for all to see, and an understanding of the poetics of mentality was not strictly necessary in order to notice many of the features I have highlighted. Noticing them was probably made more likely by a sensitivity to it, but where such sensitivity really matters is in their interpretation. An isolationist reading of Metre 1 might easily lead to the conclusion that the poet set out to present a psychologized Boethius for sympathetic identification, for example, a view which in turn would encourage seeing the text as an allegorical or straightforwardly exemplary piece. Recognizing that Metre 1's subjective elements are part of its traditionalism, emergent in the conversion of prose to verse, helps us discern something about the discourse around the poem, the environment in which such elements could arise as a matter of course. An Old English poem's strong subjectivizing tendencies can mean both less and more, in a sense, than reading them without reference to the tradition might lead one to believe: less, because they are not necessarily strong assertions of unique conferred meaning in the individual instance; yet also more, because they tell us not just about one writer's goals in a single text, but about how that text fits into a larger discursive environment from which it draws pragmatic meaning.

The chapters above have concentrated on narrative poetry, due to the availability of informative comparanda and also because it is in third-person narration that focalization provides a structural means of selectively granting access to minds. However, shorter classical-style poetry participates in the same register, and there too the principle stands that evaluation of mental content should take traditionality into account. The lyrical, mainly elegiac texts that centre on a state of mind and the progress of contemplation are free-standing, whole-poem productions of fictive subjectivities and can fruitfully be seen as expressions of the same impulse that leads to heavily subjectivized episodes within longer, primarily external narratives. Consider, for instance, that in each case the speaker or focal character is presented as concretely situated within a larger, implied and partially revealed narrative: the death of the Wanderer's lord and companions (compare *Beowulf*'s Last Survivor); the Seafarer's seemingly compulsive self-exile; the Wife's alienation, in *The Wife's Lament*, from her husband and his kindred apparently due to feud (compare the mourning Hildeburh in *Beowulf*); Deor's loss of status with his lord; and so on. All are traditionally charged figures poetically embodied through their quasi-narrative embroilment in traditionally charged situations. The Wanderer, the Seafarer, and the Wife are all constructed according to the exile motif; the Wanderer's philosophical progress is aided by his contemplation of a traditionally resonant ruin that inscribes on the landscape the transience of earthly glory; the Wife seems to be a casualty of over-optimistic exogamy like Hildeburh, or like Freawaru in Beowulf's forecast of her prospects. These are traditional subjectivities in specific, culturally scripted circumstances of hardship, and their particularity in individual texts will be built upon and interactive with their traditionality, whatever else may also be true. We cannot neglect the social embeddedness of the loci of subjectivity to which the poetic discourse is so attracted; in my view it is crucial to, even constitutive of, the phenomenon I have described.[16]

In a register as heavily marked as that of traditional Old English verse, the medium is no small part of the message. To read poetry of this kind without taking account of its poetic properties as such, thus acknowledging the special discursive identity that it constantly declares for itself, is to risk treating it like a linguistic analogue to the postulated but undetectable ether of nineteenth-century cosmologists: an invisible substance that somehow transmits information, like bodies through space, with zero interaction, and which therefore can be omitted from equations. The problem becomes acute when the topic of investigation (as in 'psychological' readings of individual poems) is itself a traditional component of the medium through which we perceive it, as I have argued to be the case for the continual recurrence to subjective positions in Old English poetry. The verbal material of the poems' embodiment, the discourse in which they take on reality as acts of communication and textual performance, is a socially generated code system with its own rules of signification. Because that register itself proceeds from the activities of real men and women making poems for their own purposes, let us return briefly to two topics that have arisen recurrently in this book: the

16 In this respect McGeachy, *Lonesome Words*, is satisfying in its treatment of the elegiac material. I would see many of the features McGeachy studies as part of larger systems of poetic subjectivity.

concreteness of the classical poetic tradition in which the poetics of mentality inheres, and its relationship to creative agency.

To understand how the poetics of mentality functioned within attested Old English poetic culture as part of its broader traditionality, we need to learn more about what likenesses of detail among poems meant for Anglo-Saxon writers and readers. Elizabeth Tyler has rightly stressed that the persistence of classical poetic form for over four centuries is itself a notable fact of literary history that requires analysis, and I have suggested above that alertness to the poetics of mentality can play a part in reading some late poems' resolute traditionalism. But by what means, exactly, such poetry might carry on a viable and active traditionality, as opposed to mimicking a moribund one, is an open question. We still suffer critical fallout from the old idea that formulaic diction and other structures that probably arose in an oral poetic culture must be signs of continuing orality, that is, symptoms of oral composition of the texts in which they appear. Even though that assumption was long ago falsified, we have been reluctant in its absence to fully re-theorize the nature of the tradition that produced extant texts and their shared traits, too often sidestepping the issue by treating it as an amorphous, ambient phenomenon. There are serious problems with this usually unstated perspective, the most fundamental being that even truly oral traditions are constitutionally no more amorphous or immaterial than purely textual ones.[17] Language, ideas, and other components of tradition are always transmitted from person to person through material media, whether the human voice, the written word, or embodied practice. When we explain that something was 'in the air' we only mean that we cannot locate specific paths of connection among instances because too many of the trails have proved ephemeral or because our observational apparatus is unequal to the task. Those connections assuredly existed, however. Tradition keeps both feet firmly on the ground.

This being true even of undoubtedly oral lines of transmission, the tendency to comment on written Old English texts as if they were suspended in a vague jelly of tradition is doubly problematic. The rather transcendental way the operation of tradition has sometimes been described (or not described) would make it easy to imagine that the discernment of solid

17 As J. Harris has recently put it in a different connection, 'oral tradition need not be a disembodied ("superorganic," in the idiom of folkloristics) force moving in mysterious waves; one conceptualizes it so vaguely only when no actual tradition-bearers are available as its vectors' ('Rök Stone,' 44).

textual connections, which of course would argue against true orality in those cases, must also argue against viable, active traditionality. But such an extension of supposed implications would rest ultimately on a fallacious insistence on synchronic concomitance between traditional diction, which is at issue here, and oral poetic culture, which is not. I have been content to treat all extant Old English poetry as arising in a textual compositional matrix, this being the position that requires the fewest assumptions, and I have maintained that this stance has no bearing whatsoever on the question of traditionality.

The record exhaustively and sensitively enough analysed may indeed reveal cells of poetic practice within the larger corpus. The type of work that both Andy Orchard and Thomas A. Bredehoft have recently done toward locating micro-communities or transmissional streams through recoverable textual connections raises exciting possibilities.[18] The successful identification of such communities or lines of influence would open up new vistas of work to be done on Old English poetic culture. However, the imitative nature of the activity so revealed would not in itself imply the non-traditionality of the craft the writers of such poems practised, which, as I have been suggesting, is a separate question requiring other kinds of inquiry. We can reason even a priori that Anglo-Saxon poets learned their craft from other poets and poems, however they encountered them, and that they did so through processes of internalization, imitation, and adaptation within the limits imposed by the recognition and comprehension of audiences. This cycle of interactive behaviour is how children learn language itself, and through continuing iterations of the same process on a higher discursive order it is how adolescents and young adults specialize their developing situational, topical, and pragmatic linguistic competencies into the subsystems of spoken and written performance that we call registers. One of these, in Anglo-Saxon England, was dedicated to poetry in the classical style. The great significance of Orchard's and Bredehoft's findings, if they do show what they are said to show,[19] lies not in the *existence* of textual relations or linear influence, but

18 Orchard, 'Both Style and Substance,' 'Computing Cynewulf,' and 'Intoxication, Fornication, and Multiplication'; Bredehoft, *Authors, Audiences, and Old English Verse.*

19 I do not doubt that the exposed patterns are meaningful, yet in my opinion the nature of their significance is uncertain. Complex methodological questions remain: in brief, more study needs to be given (1) to the rationale for what precisely should be counted, and how, in the collection of data; and – since many of the claims made are underlyingly statistical – (2) to the strength of the correspondences observed in tabulations as

in the discovery of their occasional *visibility* in our surely discontinuous record. The question of register-based traditional pragmatics versus superficial mimicry of marked features still must be answered case by case through the careful evaluation of hypotheses on grounds of their coherence, economy, and explanatory power.[20]

Throughout this book, I have worked from a perspective on Old English poetic discourse that tries to come to grips simultaneously with its undeniable textuality and with what is in my view the equally undeniable traditionality of much of it. This has entailed an awareness of tradition itself not as an immaterial, metaphysical 'force' or 'field,' but as an accumulation of human behaviours, thus always and necessarily material, embodied, and particular in its realization: tradition as practice, each instance concretely connected to prior instances through persons and their technologies of memory. Yet 'tradition' is an ambiguous, literally ambi-valent word: it can refer either to a praxis, considered in itself, or else to a notional entity, invoked within and produced by a larger cultural sign system that refers to such praxis for authority. That is to say, when we call a text 'traditional' we may mean only that it produces familiar constructions and deploys them in a recognizably patterned way, or we may mean that it calls upon that type of patterned production and deployment in its work at a higher, more comprehensive level: that of its rhetorical efficacy within communities of writers and readers, speakers and hearers. This formulation corresponds to the distinction I have used between 'traditionality,' descriptively identifying part of a text's pragmatic character, and 'traditionalism,' identifying a goal-oriented discursive character built upon the pragmatic one. These are two sides of a coin: a writer cannot exploit traditionalism without providing a convincing pragmatics of traditionality, and a text's traditionality must have a role in its greater discursive ambitions. But the distinction is analytically meaningful, and at either level, writerly agency – always present in the fashioning of a text – can take a variety of more and less conscious forms.

---

measured against controls that create systematic opportunities for negative evidence to surface.

20 For example, Bredehoft had previously pointed out that many formulas in *The Death of Edward* are shared with earlier *Chronicle* poetry and suspected that the later poet mainly drew directly from those precedents (*Textual Histories*, 112–13), but based on O'Brien O'Keeffe's analysis ('Deaths and Transformations') he now indicates belief that the *Edward* poet had fuller access to the classical poetic tradition (Bredehoft, *Authors, Audiences, and Old English Verse*, 195 and 197).

Even when what we find is completely conventional, this does not warrant its dismissal as 'just' traditional. To identify a text or feature as traditional is to make a positive statement about how it signifies and what kinds of claims, or demands, it makes on both the competencies and the sensibilities of readers. For a poet to choose to write in that way is to choose to make those claims and demands, and even the most automatic traditionality may generate an analysable traditionalism, often one communicative of great discursive authority. Here Carol Braun Pasternack's concept of 'implied tradition,' as an alternative to the 'implied author' of more modern literatures, is valuable: in her view of Old English poetic culture, a sense of controlling authority emerges from a particular discursive relation between text and audience that renders absent any kind of function we would recognize as 'authorial.'[21] I find helpful Pasternack's argument that a controlling, individual writerly agency is not strongly encoded within classical Old English poetic expression and thus does not have a prominent place in the modes of textuality an early reader would confront. Still, this does not imply that agency did not exist behind the code that obscures it. Living, breathing humans, working from historically situated positions of desire and intentionality, shaped and circulated the poems that we have, even when they fashioned them in the most conventional way from the most conventional materials, and they did so for whatever they understood to be their own reasons. I want to keep within the circumference of our awareness the men and women whose selections, choices, desires, and commitments both produced and responded to the traditionality of this poetry, even when they did not realize they were doing so. Arguably, when agency is submerged or concealed, attempting to locate it is all the more important, and the attempt need not inevitably reinstate the anachronistic projection of the authorial role (as an implied textual function) against which Pasternack makes a strong case.

The poetics of mentality that typifies Old English verse composition in the classical style emerges, then, neither from an amorphous traditionality nor from an impersonal textuality. Rather, it emerges from a concrete, embodied traditionality, actualized in a concrete, embodied textuality, by means of which real people tried to do things with words. Redactive or progressive approaches to tradition by those situated within it are possible, of course. I have argued for them in a few cases myself,

21 *Textuality of Old English Poetry*; cf. the similar perspective of Huisman, 'Subjectivity/Orality,' esp. 320.

elsewhere,[22] and in this book I have asserted that every evocation of tradition is necessarily bound up in a historical particularity that subsequently becomes a part of that tradition's own secret history. But bona fide poetic agency can also accept traditionality as an uncontested good and attempt to comply fully with its received methods and resources. Tradition is a powerful attractor, and we should not be too quick to perceive among makers of Old English verse a restless resistance to its straightforward adoption. Most 'tradition-bearers' are not 'strong' ones (to borrow John D. Niles's application of a useful concept from folklore studies), who take charge of it in a forceful way and give it their distinctive imprint.[23] Strong tradition-bearers are interesting, but so are the others, too: they just tell us different versions of the story.

The story of traditional subjectivities, in all its versions, takes place in a borderland between the particular and the categorical. Classical Old English poetry's play between the two, effected in part through continual access to minds, often makes the modes of subjectivity expressed in this literature perplexing to modern readers, who are prone to interpret as highly specifying and 'psychological' those traditional devices that integrate representations of personal interiority with social or even communal forms of identity, as in *The Ruin* and the description of the Goths in Metre 1 of the *Boethius*. Similar is the easy oscillation one finds between particularizing narrative and generalizing, sententious statements, like those at the end of *The Wife's Lament* (whatever exactly they mean) or those interspersed throughout *The Wanderer*,[24] and the ubiquitous interaction between disposition, which may be defined absolutely, and emotion and thought, which are inextricable from situation.

The traditional subjectivities of Old English poetry are located at the nexus of self and circumstance, with circumstance at times even giving rise to the fictive self. In the Franks Casket inscription, what turns a marine mammal into a poetic subjectivity, a literary consciousness, is not the whale's inward character but its outward predicament. In a sense the experiencer is created by the experience, the subject by the poetically attractive opportunity to produce a traditional subjectivity. This priority of subjectivity to the subject, which in my introduction I discussed in reference to

22 'Manipulations.'

23 *Homo Narrans*, esp. chap. 7.

24 On *The Wanderer*, cf. certain elements of Head's analysis (*Representation and Design*, 27–40).

The Ruin and the Last Survivor in *Beowulf*, is likewise evident in *Aldhelm*, whose writer conjures up the figure of the lamenting disciple in order to eulogize an intellectual giant of a bygone day; and I am not sure the inscrutable implied scenario of *The Riming Poem* ever did more than provide a framework for a familiar kind of subjectivity, strongly evoking poetic tradition, around which to construct a bold formal experiment.

In narrative, these subjective positions generally enter into relational networks in which various represented perspectives interact. Even within the narrow confines of the 'Whalebone' micronarrative, a pair of alliterating words may produce a germinal relational schema, a double-exposure of the scene through two interested positions. The obscure compound *gasric*, a name given to the whale which in the same half-line alliteratively grows *grorn*, appears to be an emotionalizing one, its elements credibly hypothesized to yield the sense 'terror-king.'[25] If this construal is correct, the word compactly evokes an outside, human perspective, that subject position from which an early medieval whale is properly defined as a diabolical, or at least very dangerous, monster from the deep.[26] In every narrative example I have analysed we have seen serial access to the perspectives of protagonists and antagonists, aggressors and their victims, the prudent and the errant. This poetic insistence on the production of subjectively realized relational systems in narration suggests that the lyrics, too, are best seen within larger ethical frameworks from which they derive part of their meaning, not just as free-standing psychological studies of unique characters. Their own dictional and conceptual traditionality, involving partially narrated situations and social structures that define their speakers' subjective identities, implies as much.

The traditional subjectivities found throughout the canon of classical Old English verse are creatures of the poetic discourse itself, their natural habitat a poetic register that knows no firm boundaries between the lyrical, the narrative, and the sapiential.[27] They spring from points of engagement between private and public reality: places where interior mind, character, and disposition confront exterior event, community, and world. This confrontation is called experience, and Old English poetry surrounds experience with an ethical ecology which each interaction of subjectivity with tradition refreshes. The continual stress on subjective

25 A meaning favoured (tentatively) by Page (*Introduction*, 175).

26 Cf. Szabo, *Monstrous Fishes*, 55–6.

27 Cf. Foley, 'How Genres Leak,' esp. 91–101.

experience in fact asserts that the main point of interest for writers and audiences lies at the interface between personal situatedness and the wider world of nature and society; and it is this interface, I will close by suggesting, that the poets are really examining when they look through the lens of subjectivity. Anglo-Saxon writers are everywhere concerned with the individual's relationships to community, the natural and material environment, and moral and soteriological superstructures. Unexpectedly, perhaps, the constant revelation of minds in Old English poetry – seemingly an uncompromising turn inward – serves to locate individuals within a world greater than themselves.

Bibliography

Abels, Richard. 'Alfred the Great, the *Micel Hæðen Here*, and the Viking Threat.' In *Alfred the Great: Papers from the Eleventh-Centenary Conferences*. Ed. Timothy Reuter, 265–79.

– *Alfred the Great: War, Kingship, and Culture in Anglo-Saxon England*. London: Longman, 1998.

– *Lordship and Military Obligation in Anglo-Saxon England*. Berkeley: University of California Press, 1988.

Abram, Christopher. 'The Errors in *The Rhyming Poem*.' *Review of English Studies* ns 58 (2007): 1–9.

Acker, Paul. *Revising Oral Theory: Formulaic Composition in Old English and Old Icelandic Verse*. New York: Garland, 1998.

Æthelweard. *Chronicon Æthelweardi: The Chronicle of Æthelweard*. Ed. A. Campbell. London: Thomas Nelson and Sons, 1962.

Aldhelm. *Aenigmata*. Ed. Fr. Glorie, with trans. by James Hall Pitman. In *Tatuini opera omnia: Variae collectiones aenigmatum Merovingicae aetatis; Anonymus De dubiis nominibus*. Ed. Maria de Marco and Fr. Glorie, 1:359–540. 2 vols. Corpus Christianorum Series Latina 133–133A. Turnhout: Brepols, 1968.

– *Aldhelm: The Poetic Works*. Trans. Michael Lapidge and James L. Rosier. Cambridge: D.S. Brewer, 1985.

Allen, Michael J.B., and Daniel G. Calder, trans. *Sources and Analogues of Old English Poetry: The Major Latin Texts in Translation*. Cambridge: D.S. Brewer, 1976.

Amodio, Mark. *Writing the Oral Tradition*. Notre Dame, IN: University of Notre Dame Press, 2004.

Amory, Patrick. *People and Identity in Ostrogothic Italy, 489–554*. Cambridge Studies in Medieval Life and Thought, 4th ser. Cambridge: Cambridge University Press, 1997.

Amos, Ashley Crandell. *Linguistic Means of Determining the Dates of Old English Literary Texts*. Medieval Academy Books 90. Cambridge, MA: Medieval Academy of America, 1980.

Anlezark, Daniel. 'An Ideal Marriage: Abraham and Sarah in Old English Literature.' *Medium Ævum* 69 (2000): 187–210.

– *Water and Fire: The Myth of the Flood in Anglo-Saxon England*. Manchester: Manchester University Press, 2006.

Arator. *Aratoris Subdiaconi Historia Apostolica*. Ed. A.P. Orbán. 2 vols. Corpus Christianorum Series Latina 130–130A. Turnhout: Brepols, 2006.

Asser. *Asser's Life of King Alfred, Together with the Annals of Saint Neots Erroneously Ascribed to Asser*. Ed. William Henry Stevenson. Oxford: Clarendon Press, 1904.

Avitus, Alcimus Ecdicius. *De spiritalis historiae gestis*. In *Alcimi Ecdicii Aviti Viennensis episcopi opera quae supersunt*. Ed. Rudolf Peiper, 203–74. Monumenta Germaniae Historica [Scriptores: Auctores Antiquissimi] 6.2. 1883; reprint, Munich: Monumenta Germaniae Historica, 1985.

Bal, Mieke. *Narratology: Introduction to the Theory of Narrative*. Trans. Christine van Boheemen. Toronto: University of Toronto Press, 1985.

Bark, William. 'Theodoric vs. Boethius: Vindication and Apology' (1943–4). Reprinted in *Boethius*. Ed. Manfred Fuhrmann and Joachim Gruber, 11–32. Wege der Forschung 483. Darmstadt: Wissenschaftliche Buchgesellschaft, 1984.

Barnhouse, Rebecca. 'Shaping the Hexateuch Text for an Anglo-Saxon Audience.' In *The Old English Hexateuch: Aspects and Approaches*. Ed. Rebecca Barnhouse and Benjamin C. Withers, 91–108. Publications of the Richard Rawlinson Center. Kalamazoo, MI: Medieval Institute Publications, 2000.

Bately, Janet. *The Anglo-Saxon Chronicle: Texts and Textual Relationships*. Reading: University of Reading, 1991.

– 'The Compilation of the *Anglo-Saxon Chronicle* Once More.' *Leeds Studies in English* ns 16 (1985): 7–26.

– 'Did King Alfred Actually Translate Anything? The Integrity of the Alfredian Canon Revisited.' *Medium Ævum* 78 (2009): 189–215.

– ed. *MS A*. Vol. 3 (1986) of *The Anglo-Saxon Chronicle: A Collaborative Edition*. Gen. ed. David N. Dumville and Simon Keynes. 9 vols to date. Cambridge: D.S. Brewer, 1983–.

– 'Old English Prose before and during the Reign of Alfred.' *Anglo-Saxon England* 17 (1988): 93–138.

Battles, Paul. '*Genesis A* and the Anglo-Saxon "Migration Myth."' *Anglo-Saxon England* 29 (2000): 43–66.

Bede. *Homeliarum evangelii libri II*. Ed. David Hurst. In *Opera homiletica; opera rhythmica*. Ed. David Hurst and J. Fraipont, xxiii–403. *Bedae Venerabilis opera*, parts 3–4. Corpus Christianorum Series Latina 122. Turnhout: Brepols, 1955.

Beechy, Tiffany. *The Poetics of Old English*. Farnham, Surrey: Ashgate, 2010.

Behaghel, Otto, ed. *Heliand und Genesis*. 10th ed. Rev. Burkhard Taeger. Altdeutsche Textbibliothek 4. Tübingen: Max Niemeyer Verlag, 1996.

Benson, Larry D. 'The Literary Character of Anglo-Saxon Formulaic Poetry.' *PMLA* 81 (1966): 334–41.

Bessinger, J.B., Jr, and Philip H. Smith, Jr, eds, with Michael W. Twomey. *A Concordance to* The Anglo-Saxon Poetic Records. Ithaca: Cornell University Press, 1978.

Bethel, Patricia. 'Notes on the Incidence and Type of Anacrusis in *Genesis B*: Some Similarities to and Differences from Anacrusis Elsewhere in Old English and in Old Saxon.' *Parergon* ns 2 (1984): 1–24.

Bethurum, Dorothy, ed. *The Homilies of Wulfstan*. Oxford: Clarendon Press, 1957; reprint, 1998.

Biber, Douglas. 'An Analytical Framework for Register Studies.' In *Sociolinguistic Perspectives on Register*. Ed. Douglas Biber and Edward Finegan, 31–56. New York: Oxford University Press, 1994.

Biber, Douglas, and Susan Conrad. 'Register Variation: A Corpus Approach.' In *The Handbook of Discourse Analysis*. Ed. Deborah Schiffrin, Deborah Tannen, and Heidi E. Hamilton, 175–96. Malden, MA: Blackwell Publishers, 2001.

Biblia sacra iuxta Vulgatam versionem. Ed. Robert Weber et al. 5th corr. ed., rev. Roger Gryson. Stuttgart: Deutsche Bibelgesellschaft, 2007.

Biggs, Frederick M. 'Biblical Glosses in Ælfric's Translation of Genesis.' *Notes and Queries* 236 (1991): 286–92.

– 'Deor's Threatened "Blame" Poem.' *Studies in Philology* 94 (1997): 297–320.

Binnig, Wolfgang. 'Altsächsisch *tōm*, angelsächsisch *tōm*, und althochdeutsch *zuomi(g)*.' Appendix to *Einige Beziehungen swischen altsächsischer und angelsächsischer Dichtung*, by Ute Schwab, 223–57. Centro italiano di studi sull'alto medioevo 8. Spoleto: Centro italiano di studi sull'alto medioevo, 1988.

Bischoff, Bernhard. 'Paläographische Fragen deutscher Denkmäler der Karolingerzeit.' *Frühmittelalterliche Studien* 5 (1971): 101–34.

Bitterli, Dieter. 'Exeter Book Riddle 15: Some Points for the Porcupine.' *Anglia* 120 (2002): 461–87.

– *Say What I Am Called: The Old English Riddles of the Exeter Book and the Anglo-Latin Riddle Tradition*. Toronto Anglo-Saxon Series 2. Toronto: University of Toronto Press, 2009.

Blackburn, Mark. 'Alfred's Coinage Reforms in Context.' In *Alfred the Great: Papers from the Eleventh-Centenary Conferences*. Ed. Timothy Reuter, 199–217.

– 'The London Mint in the Reign of Alfred.' In *Kings, Currency, and Alliances: History and Coinage of Southern England in the Ninth Century*. Ed. Mark

A.S. Blackburn and David N. Dumville, 105–23. Studies in Anglo-Saxon History 9. Woodbridge, Suffolk: Boydell Press, 1998.

Blair, John. *The Church in Anglo-Saxon Society*. Oxford: Oxford University Press, 2005.

Blake, N.F. 'Rhythmical Alliteration.' *Modern Philology* 67 (1969): 118–24.

Blanton, Virginia, and Helene Scheck, eds. *Intertexts: Studies in Anglo-Saxon Culture Presented to Paul E. Szarmach*. Arizona Studies in the Middle Ages and the Renaissance 24; Medieval and Renaissance Texts and Studies 334. Tempe: Arizona Center for Medieval and Renaissance Studies in collaboration with Brepols, 2008.

Blockley, Mary. *Aspects of Old English Poetic Syntax: Where Clauses Begin*. Illinois Medieval Studies. Urbana: University of Illinois Press, 2001.

Boenig, Robert, trans. *The Acts of Andrew in the Country of the Cannibals: Translations from the Greek, Latin, and Old English*. New York: Garland, 1991.

– *Saint and Hero:* Andreas *and Medieval Doctrine*. Lewisburg, PA: Bucknell University Press, 1991.

Bolton, Diane K. 'The Study of the *Consolation of Philosophy* in Anglo-Saxon England.' *Archives d'histoire doctrinale et littéraire du Moyen Âge* 44 (1977): 33–78.

Bonjour, Adrien. '*Beowulf* and the Beasts of Battle.' *PMLA* 72 (1957): 563–73.

Bonner, Gerald. 'Bede and Medieval Civilization.' *Anglo-Saxon England* 2 (1973): 71–90.

Booth, Paul Anthony. 'King Alfred versus Beowulf: The Re-Education of the Anglo-Saxon Aristocracy.' *Bulletin of the John Rylands Library* 79 (1997): 41–66.

Bosworth, Joseph, and T. Northcote Toller. *An Anglo-Saxon Dictionary Based on the Manuscript Collections of the Late Joseph Bosworth*. Oxford: Oxford University Press, 1898. Reprint, Oxford: Clarendon Press, 1972, with additional volume containing *Supplement* by T. Northcote Toller (1921) and *Enlarged Addenda and Corrigenda to the Supplement by T. Northcote Toller* by Alistair Campbell (1972).

Boyd, Nina. 'Doctrine and Criticism: A Revaluation of *Genesis A*.' *Neuphilologische Mitteilungen* 83 (1982): 230–8.

Bredehoft, Thomas A. 'Ælfric and Late Old English Verse.' *Anglo-Saxon England* 33 (2004): 77–107.

– *Authors, Audiences, and Old English Verse*. Toronto Anglo-Saxon Series 5. Toronto: University of Toronto Press, 2009.

– 'The Boundaries between Verse and Prose in Old English Literature.' In *Old English Literature in Its Manuscript Context*. Ed. Joyce Lionarons, 139–72. Medieval European Studies 5. Morgantown: West Virginia University Press, 2004.

– *Early English Metre*. Toronto Old English Series. Toronto: University of Toronto Press, 2005.

– *Textual Histories: Readings in the Anglo-Saxon Chronicle*. Toronto: University of Toronto Press, 2001.

Brooks, Nicholas. 'The Development of Military Obligations in Eighth- and Ninth-Century England.' In *England before the Conquest: Studies in Primary Sources Presented to Dorothy Whitelock*. Ed. Peter Clemoes and Kathleen Hughes, 69–84. Cambridge: Cambridge University Press, 1971.

– *The Early History of the Church of Canterbury: Christ Church from 597–1066*. Leicester: Leicester University Press, 1984.

Brown, George Hardin. *A Companion to Bede*. Anglo-Saxon Studies 12. Woodbridge, Suffolk: Boydell Press, 2009.

Buchelt, Lisabeth C. 'All about Eve: Memory and Re-Collection in Junius 11's Epic Poems *Genesis* and *Christ and Satan*.' In *Women and the Medieval Epic*. Ed. Sara S. Poor and Jana K. Schulman, 137–58. The New Middle Ages. New York: Palgrave Macmillan, 2007.

Bueno Alonso, Jorge Luis. '"Less Epic Than It Seems": *Deor*'s Historical Approach as a Narrative Device for Psychological Expression.' *Revista Canaria de Estudios Ingleses* 46 (2003): 161–72.

Bullough, Donald A. *Alcuin: Achievement and Reputation; Being Part of the Ford Lectures Delivered in Oxford in Hilary Term, 1980*. Education and Society in the Middle Ages and Renaissance 16. Leiden: Brill, 2004.

– 'The Educational Tradition in England from Alfred to Ælfric: Teaching *Utriusque Linguae*.' In *La scuola nell'Occidente latino dell'alto medioevo*. [No ed. credited], 2:453–94. 2 vols. Settimane di studio del Centro italiano di studi sull'alto medioevo 19. Spoleto: Presso la sede del Centro, 1972.

Bybee, Joan. 'From Usage to Grammar: The Mind's Response to Repetition.' *Language* 82 (2006): 711–33.

Cable, Thomas. *The English Alliterative Tradition*. Middle Ages Series. Philadelphia: University of Pennsylvania Press, 1991.

Campbell, James. 'Asser's *Life of Alfred*.' In *The Inheritance of Historiography, 350–900*. Ed. Christopher Holdsworth and T.P. Wiseman, 115–35. Exeter Studies in History 12. Exeter: University of Exeter, 1986.

– 'Placing King Alfred.' In *Alfred the Great: Papers from the Eleventh-Centenary Conferences*. Ed. Timothy Reuter, 3–23.

– 'The United Kingdom of England: The Anglo-Saxon Achievement.' In *Uniting the Kingdom? The Making of British History*. Ed. Alexander Grant and Keith J. Stringer, 31–47. London: Routledge, 1995.

Capek, Michael J. 'The Nationality of a Translator: Some Notes on the Syntax of *Genesis B*.' *Neophilologus* 55 (1971): 89–96.

Carmody, Francis J., ed. *Physiologus Latinus*. Paris: Librairie E. Droz, 1939.

Chadwick, Henry. *Boethius: The Consolations of Music, Logic, Theology, and Philosophy*. Oxford: Clarendon Press, 1981.

Chapman, Don. 'Composing and Joining: How the Anglo-Saxons Talked about Compounding.' In *Verbal Encounters: Anglo-Saxon and Old Norse Studies for Roberta Frank*. Ed. Antonina Harbus and Russell Poole, 39–54. Toronto: University of Toronto Press, 2005.

– 'Poetic Compounding in the Vercelli, Blickling, and Wulfstan Homilies.' *Neuphilologische Mitteilungen* 103 (2002): 409–21.

Charles-Edwards, Thomas. 'Alliances, Godfathers, Treaties, and Boundaries.' In *Kings, Currency, and Alliances: History and Coinage of Southern England in the Ninth Century*. Ed. Mark A.S. Blackburn and David N. Dumville, 47–62. Studies in Anglo-Saxon History 9. Woodbridge, Suffolk: Boydell Press, 1998.

Clark, Cecily. 'The Narrative Mode of *The Anglo-Saxon Chronicle* before the Conquest.' In *England before the Conquest: Studies in Primary Sources Presented to Dorothy Whitelock*. Ed. Peter Clemoes and Kathleen Hughes, 215–35. Cambridge: Cambridge University Press, 1971.

Clark, George. 'Beowulf's Armor.' *English Literary History* 32 (1965): 409–41.

– 'The Date of *Beowulf* and the Arundel Psalter Gloss.' *Modern Philology* 106 (2009): 677–85.

– 'Some Traditional Scenes and Situations in Anglo-Saxon Poetry.' Unpublished Ph.D. dissertation, Harvard University, 1961.

– 'The Traveler Recognizes His Goal: A Theme in Anglo-Saxon Poetry.' *JEGP* 64 (1965): 645–59.

Clemoes, Peter. *Interactions of Thought and Language in Old English Poetry*. Cambridge Studies in Anglo-Saxon England 12. Cambridge: Cambridge University Press, 1995.

– 'King and Creation at the Crucifixion: The Contribution of Native Tradition to *The Dream of the Rood* 50–6a.' In *Heroes and Heroines in Medieval English Literature: A Festschrift Presented to André Crépin on the Occasion of His Sixty-Fifth Birthday*. Ed. Leo Carruthers, 31–43. Cambridge: D.S. Brewer, 1994.

– '*Mens absentia cogitans* in *The Seafarer* and *The Wanderer*.' In *Medieval Literature and Civilization: Studies in Memory of G.N. Garmonsway*. Ed. D.A. Pearsall and R.A. Waldron, 62–77. London: Athlone Press, 1969.

Conlee, John W. 'A Note on Verse Composition in the *Meters of Boethius*.' *Neuphilologische Mitteilungen* 71 (1970): 576–85.

Conner, Patrick W. 'Schematization of Oral-Formulaic Processes in Old English Poetry.' *Language and Style* 5 (1972): 204–20.

Corrigan, Roberta, Edith Moravcsik, Hamid Ouali, and Kathleen Wheatley. 'Introduction: Approaches to the Study of Formulae.' In *Formulaic Language*.

Ed. Roberta Corrigan, Edith A. Moravcsik, Hamid Ouali, and Kathleen M. Wheatley, 1:xi–xxiv. 2 vols. Typological Studies in Language 82–3. Amsterdam: John Benjamins, 2009.

Cowie, Robert. 'Mercian London.' In *Mercia: An Anglo-Saxon Kingdom in Europe*. Ed. Michelle P. Brown and Carol A. Farr, 194–209. Studies in the Early History of Europe. London: Leicester University Press, 2001.

Cubbin, G.P., ed. *MS D*. Vol. 6 (1996) of *The Anglo-Saxon Chronicle: A Collaborative Edition*. Gen. ed. David N. Dumville and Simon Keynes. 9 vols to date. Cambridge: D.S. Brewer, 1983–.

Cyprianus Gallus. *Cypriani Galli Poetae Heptateuchos*. Ed. Rudolf Peiper. Corpus Scriptorum Ecclesiasticorum Latinorum 23. Vienna: F. Tempsky, 18[9]1.

Dailey, Patricia. 'Questions of Dwelling in Anglo-Saxon Poetry and Medieval Mysticism: Inhabiting Landscape, Body, and Mind.' *New Medieval Literatures* 8 (2006): 175–214.

Davidson, Michael R. 'The (Non)submission of the Northern Kings in 920.' In *Edward the Elder: 899–924*. Ed. N.J. Higham and D.H. Hill, 200–11. London: Routledge, 2001.

Davis, Craig. 'An Ethnic Dating of *Beowulf*.' *Anglo-Saxon England* 35 (2006): 111–29.

Davis, Kathleen. 'National Writing in the Ninth Century: A Reminder for Postcolonial Thinking about the Nation.' *Journal of Medieval and Early Modern Studies* 28 (1998): 611–37.

– 'The Performance of Translation Theory in King Alfred's National Literary Program.' In *Manuscript, Narrative, Lexicon: Essays on Literary and Cultural Transmission in Honor of Whitney F. Bolton*. Ed. Robert Boenig and Kathleen Davis, 149–70. Lewisburg, PA: Bucknell University Press, 2000.

Davis, R.H.C. 'Alfred and Guthrum's Frontier' (1982). Updated reprint in *From Alfred the Great to Stephen*, 47–54. London: Hambledon Press, 1991.

– 'Alfred the Great: Propaganda and Truth' (1971). Updated reprint in *From Alfred the Great to Stephen*, 33–46. London: Hambledon Press, 1991.

De Beaugrande, Robert. '"Register" in Discourse Studies: A Concept in Search of a Theory.' In *Register Analysis: Theory and Practice*. Ed. Mohsen Ghadessy, 7–25. Open Linguistics Series. London: Pinter Publishers, 1993.

Dictionary of Old English: A to G Online. Ed. Antonette diPaolo Healey et al. Toronto: Dictionary of Old English Project, 2007 release. http://tapor.library.utoronto.ca/doe.

Dictionary of Old English Web Corpus. Ed. Antonette diPaolo Healey with John Price Wilkin and Xin Xiang. Toronto: Dictionary of Old English Project, 2009 release. http://tapor.library.utoronto.ca/doecorpus.

Discenza, Nicole Guenther. 'Alfred the Great and the Anonymous Prose Proem to the *Boethius*.' *JEGP* 107 (2008): 57–76.

– 'Alfred's Verse Preface to the *Pastoral Care* and the Chain of Authority.' *Neophilologus* 85 (2001): 625–33.

– *The King's English: Strategies of Translation in the Old English Boethius*. Albany: State University of New York Press, 2005.

– 'Wealth and Wisdom: Symbolic Capital and the Ruler in the Translational Program of Alfred the Great.' *Exemplaria* 13 (2001): 433–67.

– '"Wise Wealhstodas": The Prologue to Sirach as a Model for Alfred's Preface to the *Pastoral Care*.' *JEGP* 97 (1998): 488–99.

Doane, A.N. '"Beowulf" and Scribal Performance.' In *Unlocking the Wordhord: Anglo-Saxon Studies in Memory of Edward B. Irving, Jr.* Ed. Mark C. Amodio and Katherine O'Brien O'Keeffe, 62–75. Toronto: University of Toronto Press, 2003.

– 'The Ethnography of Scribal Writing and Anglo-Saxon Poetry: Scribe as Performer.' *Oral Tradition* 9 (1994): 420–39.

– ed. *Genesis A: A New Edition*. Madison: University of Wisconsin Press, 1978.

– 'Oral Texts, Intertexts, and Intratexts: Editing Old English.' In *Influence and Intertextuality in Literary History*. Ed. Jay Clayton and Eric Rothstein, 75–113. Madison: University of Wisconsin Press, 1991.

– ed. *The Saxon Genesis: An Edition of The West Saxon Genesis B and the Old Saxon Vatican Genesis*. Madison: University of Wisconsin Press, 1991.

Dodwell, C.R., and Peter Clemoes, eds. *The Old English Illustrated Hexateuch: British Museum Cotton Claudius B.iv*. Early English Manuscripts in Facsimile 18. Copenhagen: Rosenkilde and Bagger, 1974.

Donoghue, Daniel. *Style in Old English Poetry: The Test of the Auxiliary*. New Haven: Yale University Press, 1987.

– 'Word Order and Poetic Style: Auxiliary and Verbal in *The Metres of Boethius*.' *Anglo-Saxon England* 15 (1986): 167–96.

Dronke, Peter. *Verse with Prose from Petronius to Dante: The Art and Scope of the Mixed Form*. Cambridge, MA: Harvard University Press, 1994.

Drout, Michael D.C. *How Tradition Works: A Meme-Based Cultural Poetics of the Anglo-Saxon Tenth Century*. Medieval and Renaissance Texts and Studies 306. Tempe: Arizona Center for Medieval and Renaissance Studies, 2006.

Dümmler, Ernst, ed. *Epistolae Karolini aevi (II)*. Monumenta Germaniae Historica [Epistolae] 4. Berlin: Weidmann, 1895.

Dumville, David N. 'The Anglo-Saxon Chronicle and the Origins of English Square Minuscule Script.' In *Wessex and England from Alfred to Edgar*, 55–139.

– 'Between Alfred the Great and Edgar the Peacemaker: Æthelstan, First King of England.' In *Wessex and England from Alfred to Edgar*, 141–71.

– 'Ecclesiastical Lands and the Defence of Wessex in the First Viking Age.' In *Wessex and England from Alfred to Edgar*, 29–54.

– 'King Alfred and the Tenth-Century Reform of the English Church.' In *Wessex and England from Alfred to Edgar*, 185–205.

– 'The Treaty of Alfred and Guthrum.' In *Wessex and England from Alfred to Edgar*, 1–27.

– *Wessex and England from Alfred to Edgar: Six Essays on Political, Cultural, and Ecclesiastical Revival*. Studies in Anglo-Saxon History 3. Woodbridge, Suffolk: Boydell Press, 1992.

Earl, James W. 'Hisperic Style and the Old English *Rhyming Poem*.' *PMLA* 102 (1987): 187–96.

– 'King Alfred's Talking Poems.' *Pacific Coast Philology* 24 (1989): 49–61.

Early Manuscripts at Oxford University. http://image.ox.ac.uk. Accessed 2 July 2009.

Eckhardt, Caroline D. 'The Medieval *Prosimetrum* Genre (from Boethius to *Boece*).' *Genre* 16 (1983): 21–38.

Eliason, Norman. '*Deor* – A Begging Poem?' In *Medieval Literature and Civilization: Studies in Memory of G.N. Garmonsway*. Ed. D.A. Pearsall and R.A. Waldron, 55–61. London: Athlone Press, 1969.

Ericksen, Janet Schrunk. 'Lands of Unlikeness in *Genesis B*.' *Studies in Philology* 93 (1996): 1–20.

Fleming, Robin. 'Monastic Lands and England's Defence in the Viking Age.' *English Historical Review* 100 (1985): 247–65.

Foley, John Miles. 'How Genres Leak in Traditional Verse.' In *Unlocking the Wordhord: Anglo-Saxon Studies in Memory of Edward B. Irving, Jr.* Ed. Mark C. Amodio and Katherine O'Brien O'Keeffe, 76–108. Toronto: University of Toronto Press, 2003.

– *How to Read an Oral Poem*. Urbana: University of Illinois Press, 2002.

– *Immanent Art: From Structure to Meaning in Traditional Oral Epic*. Bloomington: Indiana University Press, 1991.

– 'The Oral Theory in Context.' In *Oral Traditional Literature: A Festschrift for Albert Bates Lord*. Ed. John Miles Foley, 27–122. Columbus, OH: Slavica Publishers, 1981.

– *The Singer of Tales in Performance*. Bloomington: Indiana University Press, 1995.

– *The Theory of Oral Composition: History and Methodology*. Bloomington: Indiana University Press, 1988.

– *Traditional Oral Epic:* The Odyssey, Beowulf, *and the Serbo-Croatian Return Song*. Berkeley: University of California Press, 1990.

Foot, Sarah. 'The Historiography of the Anglo-Saxon "Nation-State."' In *Power and the Nation in European History*. Ed. Len Scales and Oliver Zimmer, 125–42. Cambridge: Cambridge University Press, 2005.

– 'The Making of *Angelcynn*: English Identity before the Norman Conquest.' *Transactions of the Royal Historical Society*, 6th ser., 6 (1996): 25–49.

– 'Remembering, Forgetting, and Inventing: Attitudes to the Past in England at the End of the First Viking Age.' *Transactions of the Royal Historical Society*, 6th ser., 9 (1999): 185–200.

Foucault, Michel. *The Archaeology of Knowledge*. Trans. A.M. Sheridan Smith. New York: Harper and Row, 1972.

Frank, Roberta. 'Poetic Words in Late Old English Prose.' In *From Anglo-Saxon to Early Middle English: Studies Presented to E.G. Stanley*. Ed. Malcolm Godden, Douglas Gray, and Terry Hoad, 87–107. Oxford: Clarendon Press, 1994.

– 'Sharing Words with *Beowulf*.' In *Intertexts: Studies in Anglo-Saxon Culture Presented to Paul E. Szarmach*. Ed. Virginia Blanton and Helene Scheck, 3–15.

– 'Some Uses of Paronomasia in Old English Scriptural Verse' (1972). Reprinted in *The Poems of MS Junius 11: Basic Readings*. Ed. R.M. Liuzza, 69–98. Basic Readings in Anglo-Saxon England 8. New York: Routledge, 2002.

– 'The Unbearable Lightness of Being a Philologist.' *JEGP* 96 (1997): 486–513.

Frank, Roberta, and Angus Cameron. *A Plan for the Dictionary of Old English*. Toronto: University of Toronto Press, 1973.

Frantzen, Allen J. 'The Form and Function of the Preface in the Poetry and Prose of Alfred's Reign.' In *Alfred the Great: Papers from the Eleventh-Centenary Conferences*. Ed. Timothy Reuter, 121–36.

– *King Alfred*. Boston: Twayne Publishers, 1986.

Frey, Leonard H. 'Exile and Elegy in Anglo-Saxon Epic Poetry.' *JEGP* 62 (1963): 293–302.

Fry, Donald K. 'Old English Formulaic Themes and Type-Scenes.' *Neophilologus* 52 (1968): 48–54.

– 'Old English Formulas and Systems.' *English Studies* 48 (1967): 193–204.

Fulk, R.D. *A History of Old English Meter*. Philadelphia: University of Pennsylvania Press, 1992.

Fulk, R.D., Robert E. Bjork, and John D. Niles, eds. *Klaeber's* Beowulf *and* The Fight at Finnsburg. 4th ed. Toronto: University of Toronto Press, 2008.

Gallée, Johan Hendrik. *Altsächsische Grammatik*. 3rd Auflage. Sammlung kurzer Grammatiken germanischer Dialekte, Hauptreihe 6. Tübingen: Max Niemeyer Verlag, 1993.

Garde, Judith N., and Bernard J. Muir. 'Patristic Influence and the Poetic Intention in Old English Religious Verse.' *Literature and Theology* 2 (1988): 49–68.

Gardiner, Mark. 'The Exploitation of Sea-Mammals in Medieval England: Bones and Their Social Context.' *Archaeological Journal* 154 (1997): 173–95.

Gatch, Milton McC. 'Noah's Raven in *Genesis A* and the Illustrated Old English Hexateuch.' *Gesta* 14.2 (1975): 3–15.

Gelling, Margaret. 'The Landscape of *Beowulf*.' *Anglo-Saxon England* 31 (2002): 7–11.

Genette, Gérard. *Narrative Discourse: An Essay in Method*. Trans. Jane E. Lewin. Ithaca: Cornell University Press, 1980.

– *Narrative Discourse Revisited*. Trans. Jane E. Lewin. Ithaca: Cornell University Press, 1988.

– *Paratexts: Thresholds of Interpretation*. Trans. Jane E. Lewin. Cambridge: Cambridge University Press, 1997.

Gibson, Margaret T. 'Boethius in the Carolingian Schools.' *Transactions of the Royal Historical Society*, 5th ser., 32 (1982): 43–56.

Godden, Malcolm R. 'Alfred, Asser, and Boethius.' In *Latin Learning and English Lore: Studies in Anglo-Saxon Literature for Michael Lapidge*. Ed. Katherine O'Brien O'Keeffe and Andy Orchard, 1:326–48. 2 vols. Toronto: University of Toronto Press, 2005.

– 'The Anglo-Saxons and the Goths: Rewriting the Sack of Rome.' *Anglo-Saxon England* 31 (2002): 47–68.

– 'Anglo-Saxons on the Mind.' In *Learning and Literature in Anglo-Saxon England: Studies Presented to Peter Clemoes on the Occasion of His Sixty-Fifth Birthday*. Ed. Michael Lapidge and Helmut Gneuss, 271–98. Cambridge: Cambridge University Press, 1985.

– 'Did King Alfred Write Anything?' *Medium Ævum* 76 (2007): 1–23.

– 'Editing Old English and the Problem of Alfred's *Boethius*.' In *The Editing of Old English: Papers from the 1990 Manchester Conference*. Ed. D.G. Scragg and Paul E. Szarmach, 163–76. Cambridge: D.S. Brewer, 1994.

– 'King Alfred and the *Boethius* Industry.' In *Making Sense: Constructing Meaning in Early English*. Ed. Antonette diPaolo Healey and Kevin Kiernan, 116–38. Publications of the *Dictionary of Old English* 7. Toronto: Pontifical Institute of Mediaeval Studies, 2007.

– 'King and Counselor in the Alfredian Boethius.' In *Intertexts: Studies in Anglo-Saxon Culture Presented to Paul E. Szarmach*. Ed. Virginia Blanton and Helene Scheck, 191–207.

– 'The Player King: Identification and Self-Representation in King Alfred's Writings.' In *Alfred the Great: Papers from the Eleventh-Centenary Conferences*. Ed. Timothy Reuter, 137–50.

– *The Translations of Alfred and His Circle, and the Misappropriation of the Past*. H.M. Chadwick Memorial Lectures 14. Cambridge: Department of Anglo-Saxon, Norse, and Celtic, University of Cambridge, 2004.

Godden, Malcolm R., and Susan Irvine, eds, with Mark Griffith and Rohini Jayatilaka. *The Old English Boethius: An Edition of the Old English Versions of Boethius's De Consolatione Philosophiae*. 2 vols. Oxford: Oxford University Press, 2009.

Godman, Peter. 'The Anglo-Latin *Opus Geminatum*: From Aldhelm to Alcuin.' *Medium Ævum* 50 (1981): 215–29.

– ed. and trans. *The Bishops, Kings, and Saints of York*. Oxford: Clarendon Press, 1982.

Green, Roger P.H. 'Approaching Christian Epic: The Preface of Juvencus.' In *Latin Epic and Didactic Poetry: Genre, Tradition, and Individuality*. Ed. Monica Gale, 203–22. Swansea: Classical Press of Wales, 2004.

– 'Birth and Transfiguration: Some Gospel Episodes in Juvencus and Sedulius.' In *Texts and Culture in Late Antiquity: Inheritance, Authority, and Change*. Ed. J.H.D. Scourfield, 135–71. Swansea: Classical Press of Wales, 2007.

– 'The *Evangeliorum Libri* of Juvencus: Exegesis by Stealth?' In *Poetry and Exegesis in Premodern Latin Christianity: The Encounter between Classical and Christian Strategies of Interpretation*. Ed. Willemien Otten and Karla Pollmann, 65–80. Supplements to *Vigiliae Christianae*: Texts and Studies of Early Christian Life and Language 87. Leiden: Brill, 2007.

– *Latin Epics of the New Testament: Juvencus, Sedulius, Arator*. Oxford: Clarendon Press, 2006.

Greenfield, Stanley B. 'The Formulaic Expression of the Theme of "Exile" in Anglo-Saxon Poetry.' *Speculum* 30 (1955): 200–6.

– *The Interpretation of Old English Poems*. London: Routledge and Kegan Paul, 1972.

Greenfield, Stanley B., and Daniel G. Calder with Michael Lapidge. *A New Critical History of Old English Literature*. New York: New York University Press, 1986.

Griffith, Mark. 'The Composition of the Metres.' In *The Old English Boethius: An Edition of the Old English Versions of Boethius's De Consolatione Philosophiae*. Ed. Malcolm Godden and Susan Irvine with Mark Griffith and Rohini Jayatilaka, 1:80–134. 2 vols. Oxford: Oxford University Press, 2009.

– 'Convention and Originality in the Old English "Beasts of Battle" Typescene.' *Anglo-Saxon England* 22 (1993): 179–99.

– 'Poetic Language and the Paris Psalter: The Decay of the Old English Tradition.' *Anglo-Saxon England* 20 (1991): 167–86.

– 'Verses Quite Like *Cwen to Gebeddan* in the *Metres of Boethius*.' *Anglo-Saxon England* 34 (2005): 145–67.

– 'Whole-Verse Compound Placement in Old English Poetry.' *Notes and Queries* 251 (2006): 253–62.

Griffiths, Bill, ed. *Alfred's Metres of Boethius*. Rev. ed. Pinner, Middlesex: Anglo-Saxon Books, 1994.

Gwara, Scott. *Heroic Identity in the World of Beowulf*. Medieval and Renaissance Authors and Texts 2. Leiden: Brill, 2008.

Hall, J.R. 'Perspective and Wordplay in the Old English *Rune Poem*.' *Neophilologus* 61 (1977): 453–60.

Halliday, M.A.K. *The Essential Halliday*. Ed. Jonathan J. Webster. London: Continuum, 2009.

Halsall, Maureen, ed. *The Old English Rune Poem: A Critical Edition*. Toronto: University of Toronto Press, 1981.

Harbus, Antonina. 'Anglo-Saxon Mentalities and Old English Literary Studies.' *Revista Canaria de Estudios Ingleses* 55 (2007): 13–21.

– 'Cognitive Studies of Anglo-Saxon Mentalities.' *Parergon* 27 (2010): 13–26.

– *The Life of the Mind in Old English Poetry*. Costerus ns 143. Amsterdam: Rodopi, 2002.

– 'The Medieval Concept of the Self in Anglo-Saxon England.' *Self and Identity* 1 (2002): 77–97.

– 'Metaphors of Authority in Alfred's Prefaces.' *Neophilologus* 91 (2007): 717–27.

Harris, Joseph. 'Beasts of Battle, South and North.' In *Source of Wisdom: Old English and Early Medieval Latin Studies in Honour of Thomas D. Hill*. Ed. Charles D. Wright, Frederick M. Biggs, and Thomas N. Hall, 3–25. Toronto Old English Series. Toronto: University of Toronto Press, 2007.

– 'The Rök Stone through Anglo-Saxon Eyes.' In *Anglo-Saxons and the North: Essays Reflecting the Theme of the 10th Meeting of the International Society of Anglo-Saxonists in Helsinki, August 2001*. Ed. Matti Kilpiö, Leena Kahlas-Tarkka, Jane Roberts, and Olga Timofeeva, 11–45. Medieval and Renaissance Texts and Studies 364; Essays in Anglo-Saxon Studies 1. Tempe: Arizona Center for Medieval and Renaissance Studies, 2009.

Harris, Stephen J. *Race and Ethnicity in Anglo-Saxon Literature*. Studies in Medieval History and Culture 24. New York: Routledge, 2003.

Head, Pauline E. *Representation and Design: Tracing a Hermeneutics of Old English Poetry*. SUNY Series in Medieval Studies. Albany: State University of New York Press, 1997.

Higley, Sarah Lynn. *Between Languages: The Uncooperative Text in Early Welsh and Old English Nature Poetry*. University Park: Pennsylvania State University Press, 1993.

Hill, John M. *The Anglo-Saxon Warrior Ethic: Reconstructing Lordship in Early English Literature*. Gainesville: University Press of Florida, 2000.

Hill, Thomas D. 'Pilate's Visionary Wife and the Innocence of Eve: An Old Saxon Source for the Old English *Genesis B*.' *JEGP* 101 (2002): 170–84.

– 'The "Variegated Obit" as an Historiographic Motif in Old English Poetry and Anglo-Latin Historical Literature.' *Traditio* 44 (1988): 101–24.

Hofmann, Dietrich. 'Die altsächsische Bibelepik ein Ableger der angelsächsischen geistlichen Epik?' *Zeitschrift für deutsches Altertum* 89 (1959): 173–90.

Holthausen, Ferdinand. *Altenglisches etymologisches Wörterbuch*. 2nd ed. Heidelberg: Carl Winter, Universitätsverlag, 1963.

– *Altsächsisches Wörterbuch*. 2nd unveränderte Auflage. Niederdeutsche Studien 1. Cologne: Böhlau Verlag, 1967.

Howe, Nicholas. *Migration and Mythmaking in Anglo-Saxon England*. New Haven: Yale University Press, 1989.

– 'Rome: Capital of Anglo-Saxon England.' *Journal of Medieval and Early Modern Studies* 34 (2004): 147–72.

Huisman, Rosemary. 'Subjectivity/Orality: How Relevant are Modern Literary Theories to the Study of Old English Poetry? What Light Can the Study of Old English Poetry Cast on Modern Literary Theory?' In *The Preservation and Transmission of Anglo-Saxon Culture: Selected Papers from the 1991 Meeting of the International Society of Anglo-Saxonists*. Ed. Paul E. Szarmach and Joel T. Rosenthal, 313–31. Studies in Medieval Culture 40. Kalamazoo, MI: Medieval Institute Publications, 1997.

Huppé, Bernard. *Doctrine and Poetry: Augustine's Influence on Old English Poetry*. New York: State University of New York, 1959.

Hutcheson, B.R. *Old English Poetic Metre*. Cambridge: D.S. Brewer, 1995.

Irvine, Martin. *The Making of Textual Culture: 'Grammatica' and Literary Theory, 350–1100*. Cambridge Studies in Medieval Literature 19. Cambridge: Cambridge University Press, 1994.

– 'Medieval Textuality and the Archaeology of Textual Culture.' In *Speaking Two Languages: Traditional Disciplines and Contemporary Theory in Medieval Studies*. Ed. Allen J. Frantzen, 181–210 and 276–84. Albany: State University of New York Press, 1991.

Irvine, Susan. 'The *Anglo-Saxon Chronicle* and the Idea of Rome in Alfredian Literature.' In *Alfred the Great: Papers from the Eleventh-Centenary Conferences*. Ed. Timothy Reuter, 63–77.

– ed. *MS E*. Vol. 7 (2004) of *The Anglo-Saxon Chronicle: A Collaborative Edition*. Gen. ed. David N. Dumville and Simon Keynes. 9 vols to date. Cambridge: D.S. Brewer, 1983–.

– 'Wrestling with Hercules: King Alfred and the Classical Past.' In *Court Culture in the Early Middle Ages: The Proceedings of the First Alcuin Conference*. Ed. Catherine Cubitt, 171–88. Studies in the Early Middle Ages 3. Turnhout: Brepols, 2003.

Jager, Eric. 'The Word in the "Breost": Interiority and the Fall in *Genesis B*.' *Neophilologus* 75 (1991): 279–90.

Jurasinski, Stefan. *Ancient Privileges:* Beowulf, *Law, and the Making of Germanic Antiquity*. Morgantown: West Virginia University Press, 2006.

Karkov, Catherine. *Text and Picture in Anglo-Saxon England: Narrative Strategies in the Junius 11 Manuscript*. Cambridge Studies in Anglo-Saxon England 31. Cambridge: Cambridge University Press, 2001.

Kartschoke, Dieter. *Bibeldichtung: Studien zur Geschichte der epischen Bibelparaphrase von Juvencus bis Otfrid von Weißenburg*. Munich: Wilhelm Fink Verlag, 1975.

Kaske, R.E. '*Sapientia et Fortitudo* in the Old English *Judith*.' In *The Wisdom of Poetry: Essays in Early English Literature in Honor of Morton W. Bloomfield*. Ed. Larry D. Benson and Siegfried Wenzel, 13–29 and 264–8. Kalamazoo, MI: Medieval Institute Publications, 1982.

Keefer, Sarah Larratt. *The Old English Metrical Psalter: An Annotated Set of Collation Lists with the Psalter Glosses*. New York: Garland, 1979.

Keene, Derek. 'Alfred and London.' In *Alfred the Great: Papers from the Eleventh-Centenary Conferences*. Ed. Timothy Reuter, 235–49.

Kempshall, Matthew. 'No Bishop, No King: The Ministerial Ideology of Kingship and Asser's *Res Gestae Aelfredi*.' In *Belief and Culture in the Middle Ages: Studies Presented to Henry Mayr-Harting*. Ed. Richard Gameson and Henrietta Leyser, 106–27. Oxford: Oxford University Press, 2001.

Kendall, Calvin B. *The Metrical Grammar of* Beowulf. Cambridge Studies in Anglo-Saxon England 5. Cambridge: Cambridge University Press, 1991.

Kern, J.H. 'Zu altenglisch *mǽrsian*.' *Anglia* 28 (1905): 394–6.

Keynes, Simon. 'Edward, King of the Anglo-Saxons.' In *Edward the Elder, 899–924*. Ed. N.J. Higham and D.H. Hill, 40–66. London: Routledge, 2001.

– 'King Alfred and the Mercians.' In *Kings, Currency, and Alliances: History and Coinage of Southern England in the Ninth Century*. Ed. Mark A.S. Blackburn and David N. Dumville, 1–45. Studies in Anglo-Saxon History 9. Woodbridge, Suffolk: Boydell Press, 1998.

– 'On the Authenticity of Asser's Life of King Alfred.' *Journal of Ecclesiastical History* 47 (1996): 529–51.

– 'The Power of the Written Word: Alfredian England, 871–899.' In *Alfred the Great: Papers from the Eleventh-Centenary Conferences*. Ed. Timothy Reuter, 176–97.

Keynes, Simon, and Michael Lapidge, trans. *Alfred the Great: Asser's Life of King Alfred and Other Contemporary Sources*. London: Penguin Books, 1983.

Kiernan, Kevin S. 'Alfred the Great's Burnt Boethius.' In *The Iconic Page in Manuscript, Print, and Digital Culture*. Ed. George Bornstein and Theresa Tinkle, 7–32. Ann Arbor: University of Michigan Press, 1998.

– 'Reading Cædmon's "Hymn" with Someone Else's Glosses.' *Representations* 32 (1990): 157–74.

– 'The Source of the Napier Fragment of Alfred's *Boethius*.' *Digital Medievalist* 1.1 (2005). http://www.digitalmedievalist.org/journal/1.1/kiernan. Accessed 17 Dec. 2009.

Kiricsi, Ágnes. 'From *Mod* to *Minde*: Report from a Semantic Battlefield.' In *What Does It Mean?* Ed. Kathleen E. Dubs, 217–39. Pázmány Papers in English and American Studies 3. Piliscaba: Pázmány Péter Catholic University, 2004.

Kleinschmidt, Harald. 'What Does the *Anglo-Saxon Chronicle* Tell Us about "Ethnic" Origins?' *Studi Medievali*, 3rd ser., 42 (2001): 1–40.

Köbler, Gerhard. *Altsächsisches Wörterbuch*. 3rd ed. (2000). http://www.koeblergerhard.de/aswbhinw.html.

Krapp, George Philip, and Elliott Van Kirk Dobbie, eds. *The Anglo-Saxon Poetic Records: A Collective Edition*. 6 vols. New York: Columbia University Press, 1931–53.

Kuhn, Sherman M. 'Was Ælfric a Poet?' *Philological Quarterly* 52 (1973): 643–62.

Kuiper, Koenraad. 'Formulaic Performance in Conventionalised Varieties of Speech.' In *Formulaic Sequences: Acquisition, Processing, and Use*. Ed. Norbert Schmitt, 37–54. Language Learning and Language Teaching 9. Amsterdam: John Benjamins, 2004.

Kuiper, Koenraad, and Douglas Haggo. 'Livestock Auctions, Oral Poetry, and Ordinary Language.' *Language in Society* 13 (1984): 205–34.

Lang, James. 'The Imagery of the Franks Casket: Another Approach.' In *Northumbria's Golden Age*. Ed. Jane Hawkes and Susan Mills, 247–55. Stroud, Gloucestershire: Sutton, 1999.

Lapidge, Michael. 'Aldhelm's Latin Poetry and Old English Verse' (1979). Updated reprint in *Anglo-Latin Literature, 600–899*, 247–69 and 505–6. London: Hambledon Press, 1996.

– *The Anglo-Saxon Library*. Oxford: Oxford University Press, 2006.

– 'The Archetype of *Beowulf*.' *Anglo-Saxon England* 29 (2000): 5–41.

– 'Asser's Reading.' In *Alfred the Great: Papers from the Eleventh-Centenary Conferences*. Ed. Timothy Reuter, 27–47.

– 'The Hermeneutic Style in Tenth-Century Anglo-Latin Literature' (1975). Updated reprint in *Anglo-Latin Literature, 900–1066*, 105–49 and 474–79. London: Hambledon Press, 1993.

– 'Latin Learning in Ninth-Century England.' In *Anglo-Latin Literature, 600–899*, 409–54. London: Hambledon Press, 1996.

– 'Old English Poetic Compounds: A Latin Perspective.' In *Intertexts: Studies in Anglo-Saxon Culture Presented to Paul E. Szarmach*. Ed. Virginia Blanton and Helene Scheck, 17–32.

– 'The Study of Latin Texts in Late Anglo-Saxon England' (1982). Updated reprint in *Anglo-Latin Literature, 600–899*, 455–98 and 516. London: Hambledon Press, 1996.

– 'Versifying the Bible in the Middle Ages.' In *The Text in the Community: Essays on Medieval Works, Manuscripts, Authors, and Readers*. Ed. Jill Mann and Maura Nolan, 11–40. Notre Dame, IN: University of Notre Dame Press, 2006.

Lee, Penny. 'Formulaic Language in Cultural Perspective.' In *Phraseology and Culture in English*. Ed. P. Skandera, 471–96. Berlin: Mouton de Gruyter, 2007.

Lerer, Seth. *Literacy and Power in Anglo-Saxon Literature*. Regents Studies in Medieval Culture. Lincoln: University of Nebraska Press, 1991.

Lewis, David J.G. 'The Metre of *Genesis B*.' *Anglo-Saxon England* 16 (1987): 67–125.

Liebermann, F., ed. *Die Gesetze der Angelsachsen*. 3 vols. Halle: Niemeyer, 1903–16; reprint, Tübingen: Scientia Aalen, 1960.

Lindemann, J.W. Richard. *Old English Preverbal Ge–: Its Meaning*. Charlottesville: University Press of Virginia, 1970.

Lockett, Leslie. *Anglo-Saxon Psychologies in the Vernacular and Latin Traditions*. Toronto Anglo-Saxon Series 8. Toronto: University of Toronto Press, 2011.

– 'An Integrated Re-Examination of the Dating of Oxford, Bodleian Library, Junius 11.' *Anglo-Saxon England* 31 (2002): 141–73 and plates Ia–IVc.

Louw, Bill. 'Irony in the Text or Insincerity in the Writer? The Diagnostic Potential of Semantic Prosodies.' In *Text and Technology in Honour of John Sinclair*. Ed. Mona Baker, Gill Francis, and Elena Tognini-Bonelli, 157–76. Amsterdam: John Benjamins, 1993.

Low, Soon-Ai. 'Approaches to the Old English Vocabulary for "Mind."' *Studia Neophilologica* 73 (2001): 11–22.

– 'Pride, Courage, and Anger: The Polysemousness of Old English *Mōd*.' In *Verbal Encounters: Anglo-Saxon and Old Norse Studies for Roberta Frank*. Ed. Antonina Harbus and Russell Poole, 77–88. Toronto Old English Series. Toronto: University of Toronto Press, 2005.

Lucas, Peter J. 'Loyalty and Obedience in the Old English *Genesis* and the Interpolation of *Genesis B* into *Genesis A*.' *Neophilologus* 76 (1992): 121–35.

– 'MS Junius 11 and Malmesbury (II).' *Scriptorium* 35 (1981): 3–22.

– 'Some Aspects of *Genesis B* as Old English Verse.' *Proceedings of the Royal Irish Academy*, ser. C, 88 (1988): 143–78.

– 'Some Aspects of the Interaction between Verse Grammar and Metre in Old English Poetry.' *Studia Neophilologica* 59 (1987): 145–75.

Magennis, Hugh. *Images of Community in Old English Poetry*. Cambridge Studies in Anglo-Saxon England 18. Cambridge: Cambridge University Press, 1996.

– 'Treatments of Treachery and Betrayal in Anglo-Saxon Texts.' *English Studies* 76 (1995): 1–19.

Magoun, Francis P., Jr. 'The Oral-Formulaic Character of Anglo-Saxon Narrative Poetry.' *Speculum* 28 (1953): 446–67.

– 'The Theme of the Beasts of Battle in Anglo-Saxon Poetry.' *Neuphilologische Mitteilungen* 56 (1955): 81–90.

Marenbon, John. *Boethius*. Oxford: Oxford University Press, 2003.

Marsden, Richard. 'Ælfric as Translator: The Old English Prose *Genesis*.' *Anglia* 109 (1991): 319–58.

– ed. *The* Old English Heptateuch *and Ælfric's* Libellus de Veteri Testamento et Novo. 1 vol. to date. EETS os 330–. Oxford: Oxford University Press, 2008–.

– 'Old Latin Intervention in the Old English *Heptateuch*.' *Anglo-Saxon England* 23 (1994): 229–64.

– *The Text of the Old Testament in Anglo-Saxon England*. Cambridge Studies in Anglo-Saxon England 15. Cambridge: Cambridge University Press, 1995.

– 'Translation by Committee? The "Anonymous" Text of the Old English Hexateuch.' In *The Old English Hexateuch: Aspects and Approaches*. Ed. Rebecca Barnhouse and Benjamin C. Withers, 41–89. Publications of the Richard Rawlinson Center. Kalamazoo, MI: Medieval Institute Publications, 2000.

Matthews, John. 'Anicius Manlius Severinus Boethius.' In *Boethius: His Life, Thought, and Influence*. Ed. Margaret Gibson, 15–43. Oxford: Basil Blackwell, 1981.

Matto, Michael. 'True Confessions: *The Seafarer* and Technologies of the *Sylf*.' *JEGP* 103 (2004): 156–79.

– 'A War of Containment: The Heroic Image in *The Battle of Maldon*.' *Studia Neophilologica* 74 (2002): 60–75.

McGeachy, M.G. *Lonesome Words: The Vocal Poetics of the Old English Lament and the African-American Blues Song*. The New Middle Ages. New York: Palgrave Macmillan, 2006.

McIlwain, James T. 'Brain and Mind in Anglo-Saxon Medicine.' *Viator* 37 (2006): 103–12.

McIntosh, Angus. 'Wulfstan's Prose.' *Proceedings of the British Academy* 35 (1949): 109–42.

Meaney, Audrey L. 'St. Neots, Æthelweard, and the Compilation of the *Anglo-Saxon Chronicle*: A Survey.' In *Studies in Earlier Old English Prose: Sixteen*

Original Contributions. Ed. Paul E. Szarmach, 193–243. Binghamton: State University of New York Press, 1986.

Metcalf, Allan A. *Poetic Diction in the Old English Meters of Boethius*. De Proprietatibus Litterarum, series practica, 50. The Hague: Mouton, 1973.

Mirsky, Aaron. 'On the Sources of the Anglo-Saxon *Genesis* and *Exodus*.' *English Studies* 48 (1967): 385–97.

Mitchell, Bruce. *Old English Syntax*. 2 vols. Oxford: Clarendon Press, 1985.

– 'The Relation between Old English Alliterative Verse and Ælfric's Alliterative Prose.' In *Latin Learning and English Lore: Studies in Anglo-Saxon Literature for Michael Lapidge*. Ed. Katherine O'Brien O'Keeffe and Andy Orchard, 2:349–62. 2 vols. Toronto: University of Toronto Press, 2005.

Mize, Britt. 'Manipulations of the Mind-as-Container Motif in *Beowulf*, *Homiletic Fragment II*, and Alfred's *Metrical Epilogue to the Pastoral Care*.' *JEGP* 107 (2008): 25–56.

– 'The Meaning of "Fisc Flodu Ahof" on the Franks Casket.' *Notes and Queries* 256 (2011): 373–8.

– 'The Representation of the Mind as an Enclosure in Old English Poetry.' *Anglo-Saxon England* 35 (2006): 57–90.

Molinari, Maria Vittoria. 'Overcoming Pagan Suffering in *Deor*.' Trans. Richard Davies. *Linguistica e Filologia* 8 (1998): 7–28.

Momma, H. *The Composition of Old English Poetry*. Cambridge Studies in Anglo-Saxon England 20. Cambridge: Cambridge University Press, 1997.

Monnin, Pierre-Eric. 'Poetic Improvements in the Old English *Meters of Boethius*.' *English Studies* 60 (1979): 346–60.

Moorhead, John. *Theoderic in Italy*. Oxford: Clarendon Press, 1992.

Morris, Richard, ed. *The Blickling Homilies of the Tenth Century*. 3 vols. EETS os 58, 63, and 73. London, 1874–80.

Morton, Catherine. 'Marius of Avenches, the "Excerpta Valesiana," and the Death of Boethius.' *Traditio* 38 (1982): 107–36.

Nelson, Janet L. 'The Church's Military Service: A Contemporary Comparative View?' *Studies in Church History* 20 (1983): 15–30.

– 'England and the Continent in the Ninth Century: II, Vikings and Others.' *Transactions of the Royal Historical Society*, 6th ser., 13 (2003): 1–28.

– '"A King across the Sea": Alfred in Continental Perspective.' *Transactions of the Royal Historical Society*, 5th ser., 36 (1986): 45–68.

– 'The Political Ideas of Alfred of Wessex.' In *Kings and Kingship in Medieval Europe*. Ed. Anne J. Duggan, 125–58. King's College London Medieval Studies. London: King's College London Centre for Late Antique and Medieval Studies, 1993.

– 'Power and Authority at the Court of Alfred.' In *Essays on Anglo-Saxon and Related Themes in Memory of Lynne Grundy*. Ed. Jane Roberts and Janet Nelson, 311–37. King's College London Medieval Studies 17. London: King's College London Centre for Late Antique and Medieval Studies, 2000.
– 'Wealth and Wisdom: The Politics of Alfred the Great.' *Acta* 11 (1986): 31–52.
Neuman de Vegvar, Carol. 'Reading the Franks Casket: Contexts and Audiences.' In *Intertexts: Studies in Anglo-Saxon Culture Presented to Paul E. Szarmach*. Ed. Virginia Blanton and Helene Scheck, 141–59.
Neville, Jennifer. 'History, Poetry, and "National" Identity in Anglo-Saxon England and the Carolingian Empire.' In *Germanic Texts and Latin Models: Medieval Reconstructions*. Ed. K.E. Olsen, A. Harbus, and T. Hofstra, 107–26. Mediaevalia Groningana 2. Leuven: Peeters, 2001.
– *Representations of the Natural World in Old English Poetry*. Cambridge Studies in Anglo-Saxon England 27. Cambridge: Cambridge University Press, 1999.
Niles, John D. 'Formula and Formulaic System in *Beowulf*.' In *Oral Traditional Literature: A Festschrift for Albert Bates Lord*. Ed. John Miles Foley, 394–415. Columbus, OH: Slavica Publishers, 1981.
– *Homo Narrans: The Poetics and Anthropology of Oral Literature*. Philadelphia: University of Pennsylvania Press, 1999.
– *Old English Enigmatic Poems and the Play of the Texts*. Studies in the Early Middle Ages 13. Turnhout: Brepols, 2006.
– 'Toward an Anglo-Saxon Oral Poetics.' In *De Gustibus: Essays for Alain Renoir*. Ed. John Miles Foley, 359–77. Albert Bates Lord Studies in Oral Tradition 11. New York: Garland, 1992.
Nodes, Daniel J. *Doctrine and Exegesis in Biblical Latin Poetry*. ARCA Classical and Medieval Texts, Papers, and Monographs 31. Leeds: Francis Cairns, 1993.
Nokes, Richard Scott, and Paige K. Swaim. 'Kingship in Alfred's *Meters of Boethius*.' *Carmina Philosophiae* 13 (2004): 61–74.
North, Richard. *Pagan Words and Christian Meanings*. Costerus ns 81. Amsterdam: Rodopi, 1991.
O'Brien O'Keeffe, Katherine. 'Deaths and Transformations: Thinking Through the "End" of Old English Verse.' In *New Directions in Oral Theory*. Ed. Mark C. Amodio, 149–78. Medieval and Renaissance Texts and Studies 287. Tempe: Arizona Center for Medieval and Renaissance Studies, 2005.
– 'Listening to the Scenes of Reading: King Alfred's Talking Prefaces.' In *Orality and Literacy in the Middle Ages: Essays on a Conjunction and Its Consequences in Honour of D.H. Green*. Ed. Mark Chinca and Christopher Young, 17–36. Utrecht Studies in Medieval Literacy 12. Turnhout: Brepols, 2005.

– ed. *MS C*. Vol. 5 (2001) of *The Anglo-Saxon Chronicle: A Collaborative Edition*. Gen. ed. David N. Dumville and Simon Keynes. 9 vols to date. Cambridge: D.S. Brewer, 1983–.

– *Visible Song: Transitional Literacy in Old English Verse*. Cambridge Studies in Anglo-Saxon England 4. Cambridge: Cambridge University Press, 1990.

O'Donnell, Daniel Paul. 'Bede's Strategy in Paraphrasing *Cædmon's Hymn*.' *JEGP* 103 (2004): 417–32.

– ed. Cædmon's Hymn*: A Multimedia Study, Archive, and Edition*. Society for Early English and Norse Electronic Texts (SEENET), ser. A, 7. Cambridge: D.S. Brewer in association with SEENET and the Medieval Academy, 2005.

Olsen, Alexandra Hennessey. 'Old English Women, Old English Men: A Reconsideration of "Minor" Characters.' In *Old English Shorter Poems: Basic Readings*. Ed. Katherine O'Brien O'Keeffe, 65–83. Basic Readings in Anglo-Saxon England 3. New York: Garland, 1994.

Orchard, Andy. 'Both Style and Substance: The Case for Cynewulf.' In *Anglo-Saxon Styles*. Ed. Catherine E. Karkov and George Hardin Brown, 271–305. Albany: State University of New York Press, 2003.

– 'Conspicuous Heroism: Abraham, Prudentius, and the Old English Verse *Genesis*' (1994). Reprinted in *The Poems of MS Junius 11: Basic Readings*. Ed. R.M. Liuzza, 119–36. Basic Readings in Anglo-Saxon England 8. New York: Routledge, 2002.

– 'Computing Cynewulf: The *Judith*-Connection.' In *The Text in the Community: Essays on Medieval Works, Manuscripts, Authors, and Readers*. Ed. Jill Mann and Maura Nolan, 75–106. Notre Dame, IN: University of Notre Dame Press, 2006.

– *A Critical Companion to* Beowulf. Cambridge: D.S. Brewer, 2003.

– 'Crying Wolf: Oral Style and the *Sermones Lupi*.' *Anglo-Saxon England* 21 (1992): 239–64.

– 'Enigma Variations: The Anglo-Saxon Riddle-Tradition.' In *Latin Learning and English Lore: Studies in Anglo-Saxon Literature for Michael Lapidge*. Ed. Katherine O'Brien O'Keeffe and Andy Orchard, 1:284–304. 2 vols. Toronto: University of Toronto Press, 2005.

– 'Intoxication, Fornication, and Multiplication: The Burgeoning Text of *Genesis A*.' In *Text, Image, Interpretation: Studies in Anglo-Saxon Literature and Its Insular Context in Honour of Éamonn Ó Carragáin*. Ed. Alastair Minnis and Jane Roberts, 333–54. Studies in the Early Middle Ages 18. Turnhout: Brepols, 2007.

– 'Looking for an Echo: The Oral Tradition in Anglo-Saxon Literature.' *Oral Tradition* 18 (2003): 225–7.

– 'Old Sources, New Resources: Finding the Right Formula for Boniface.' *Anglo-Saxon England* 30 (2001): 15–38.
– 'Oral Tradition.' In *Reading Old English Texts*. Ed. Katherine O'Brien O'Keeffe, 101–23. Cambridge: Cambridge University Press, 1997.
– *The Poetic Art of Aldhelm*. Cambridge Studies in Anglo-Saxon England 8. Cambridge: Cambridge University Press, 1994.
– 'Reconstructing *The Ruin*.' In *Intertexts: Studies in Anglo-Saxon Culture Presented to Paul E. Szarmach*. Ed. Virginia Blanton and Helene Scheck, 45–68.
Orton, Peter. *The Transmission of Old English Poetry*. Westfield Publications in Medieval and Renaissance Studies 12. Turnhout: Brepols, 2000.
Osborn, Marijane. 'The Lid as Conclusion of the Syncretic Theme of the Franks Casket.' In *Old English Runes and Their Continental Background*. Ed. Alfred Bammesberger, 249–68. Anglistische Forschungen 217. Heidelberg: Carl Winter, Universitätsverlag, 1991.
– 'The Picture-Poem on the Front of the Franks Casket.' *Neuphilologische Mitteilungen* 75 (1974): 50–65.
Page, R.I. *An Introduction to English Runes*. 2nd ed. Woodbridge, Suffolk: Boydell Press, 1999.
Pasternack, Carol Braun. *The Textuality of Old English Poetry*. Cambridge Studies in Anglo-Saxon England 13. Cambridge: Cambridge University Press, 1995.
Pawley, Andrew. 'Developments in the Study of Formulaic Language since 1970: A Personal View.' In *Phraseology and Culture in English*. Ed. Paul Skandera, 3–45. Topics in English Linguistics 54. Berlin: Mouton de Gruyter, 2007.
– 'Grammarians' Languages versus Humanists' Languages and the Place of Speech Act Formulas in Models of Linguistic Competence.' In *Formulaic Language*. Ed. Roberta Corrigan, Edith A. Moravcsik, Hamid Ouali, and Kathleen M. Wheatley, 1:3–26. 2 vols. Typological Studies in Language 82–3. Amsterdam: John Benjamins, 2009.
– 'How to Talk Cricket: On Linguistic Competence in a Subject Matter.' In *Currents in Pacific Linguistics: Papers on Austronesian Languages and Ethnolinguistics in Honour of George W. Grace*. Ed. Robert Blust, 339–68. Pacific Linguistics, ser. C, 117. Canberra: Department of Linguistics, Research School of Pacific Studies, Australian National University, 1991.
Peeters, L. 'The Franks Casket: A Judaeo-Christian Interpretation.' *Amsterdamer Beiträge zur älteren Germanistic* 46 (1996): 17–52.
Pratt, David. *The Political Thought of King Alfred the Great*. Cambridge Studies in Medieval Life and Thought, 4th ser. Cambridge: Cambridge University Press, 2007.

– 'Problems of Authorship and Audience in the Writings of King Alfred the Great.' In *Lay Intellectuals in the Carolingian World*. Ed. Patrick Wormald and Janet L. Nelson, 162–91. Cambridge: Cambridge University Press, 2007.

Quinn, Karen J., and Kenneth P. Quinn. *A Manual of Old English Prose*. New York: Garland, 1990.

Quirk, Randolph. 'Poetic Language and Old English Metre.' In *Early English and Norse Studies Presented to Hugh Smith in Honour of His Sixtieth Birthday*. Ed. Arthur Brown and Peter Foote, 150–71. London: Methuen, 1963.

Rauch, Irmengard. 'The Old English *Genesis B* Poet: Bilingual or Interlingual?' *American Journal of Germanic Linguistics and Literatures* 5 (1993): 163–84.

Raw, Barbara. 'The Construction of Oxford, Bodleian Library, Junius 11.' *Anglo-Saxon England* 13 (1984): 187–205.

– 'The Probable Derivation of Most of the Illustrations in Junius 11 from an Illustrated Old Saxon *Genesis*.' *Anglo-Saxon England* 5 (1976): 133–48.

Remley, Paul G. 'The Latin Textual Basis of *Genesis A*.' *Anglo-Saxon England* 17 (1988): 163–89.

– *Old English Biblical Verse: Studies in* Genesis, Exodus, *and* Daniel. Cambridge Studies in Anglo-Saxon England 16. Cambridge: Cambridge University Press, 1996.

Renoir, Alain. '*Judith* and the Limits of Poetry.' *English Studies* 43 (1962): 145–55.

– 'Point of View and Design for Terror in *Beowulf*.' *Neuphilologische Mitteilungen* 63 (1962): 154–67.

Reuter, Timothy, ed. *Alfred the Great: Papers from the Eleventh-Centenary Conferences*. Studies in Early Medieval Britain. Aldershot, Hampshire: Ashgate, 2003.

– 'The Making of England and Germany, 850–1050: Points of Comparison and Difference.' In *Medieval Europeans: Studies in Ethnic Identity and National Perspectives in Medieval Europe*. Ed. Alfred P. Smyth, 53–70. London: Macmillan, 1998.

Reynolds, Susan. 'What Do We Mean by "Anglo-Saxon" and "Anglo-Saxons"?' *Journal of British Studies* 24 (1985): 395–414.

Richards, Mary P. 'Prosaic Poetry: Late Old English Poetic Composition.' In *Old English and New: Studies in Language and Linguistics in Honor of Frederic G. Cassidy*. Ed. Joan H. Hall, Nick Doane, and Dick Ringler, 63–75. New York: Garland, 1992.

Richardson, Peter. 'Point of View and Identification in *Beowulf*.' *Neophilologus* 81 (1997): 289–98.

Riedinger, Anita R. 'The Formulaic Relationship between *Beowulf* and *Andreas*.' In *Heroic Poetry in the Anglo-Saxon Period: Studies in Honor of Jess B. Bessinger Jr.* Ed. Helen Damico and John Leyerle, 283–312. Studies in Medieval Culture 23. Kalamazoo, MI: Medieval Institute Publications, 1993.

– '"Home" in Old English Poetry.' *Neuphilologische Mitteilungen* 96 (1995): 51–9.

– 'The Old English Formula in Context.' *Speculum* 60 (1985): 294–317.

Roberts, Jane. 'The Old English Prose Translation of Felix's *Vita Sancti Guthlaci*.' In *Studies in Earlier Old English Prose*. Ed. Paul E. Szarmach, 363–79. New York: State University of New York Press, 1986.

Roberts, Michael. *Biblical Epic and Rhetorical Paraphrase in Late Antiquity*. ARCA Classical and Medieval Texts, Papers, and Monographs 16. Liverpool: Francis Cairns, 1985.

– 'Vergil and the Gospels: The *Evangeliorum libri IV* of Juvencus.' In *Romane Memento: Vergil in the Fourth Century*. Ed. Roger Rees, 47–61. London: Duckworth, 2004.

Rumble, Alexander R. 'Edward the Elder and the Churches of Winchester and Wessex.' In *Edward the Elder, 899–924*. Ed. N.J. Higham and D.H. Hill, 230–47. London: Routledge, 2001.

Russom, Geoffrey. 'Dating Criteria for Old English Poems.' In *Studies in the History of the English Language: A Millennial Perspective*. Ed. Donka Minkova and Robert Stockwell, 245–65. Topics in English Linguistics 39. Berlin: Mouton de Gruyter, 2002.

– *Old English Meter and Linguistic Theory*. Cambridge: Cambridge University Press, 1987.

Scharer, Anton. 'The Writing of History at King Alfred's Court.' *Early Medieval Europe* 5 (1996): 177–206.

Schmitt, Norbert, and Ronald Carter. 'Formulaic Sequences in Action: An Introduction.' In *Formulaic Sequences: Acquisition, Processing, and Use*. Ed. Norbert Schmitt, 1–22. Language Learning and Language Teaching 9. Amsterdam: John Benjamins, 2004.

Schrader, Richard J. 'Caedmon and the Monks, the *Beowulf*-Poet, and Literary Continuity in the Early Middle Ages.' *American Benedictine Review* 31 (1980): 39–69.

Schürr, Diether. '*Hron* und *Fisc* auf Franks Casket.' *Amsterdamer Beiträge zur älteren Germanistic* 60 (2005): 27–37.

Schwab, Ute, ed. *Die Bruchstücke der altsächsischen Genesis und ihrer altenglischen Übertragung: Einführung, Textwiedergaben und Übersetzungen, Abbildung der gesamten Überlieferung*. Göppinger Beiträge zur Textgeschichte 29. Göppingen: Kümmerle Verlag, 1991.

– *Einige Beziehungen swischen altsächsischer und angelsächsischer Dichtung*. Centro italiano di studi sull'alto medioevo 8. Spoleto: Centro italiano di studi sull'alto medioevo, 1988.

Scragg, D.G. 'A Reading of *Brunanburh*.' In *Unlocking the Wordhord: Anglo-Saxon Studies in Memory of Edward B. Irving, Jr.* Ed. Mark C. Amodio and Katherine O'Brien O'Keeffe, 109–22. Toronto: University of Toronto Press, 2003.

Sedulius, Caelius. *Carmen paschale*. In *Sedulii opera omnia*. Ed. Johannes Huemer. Rev. ed. Rev. Victoria Panagl. Corpus Scriptorum Ecclesiasticorum Latinorum 10. Vienna: Verlag der Österreichischen Akademie der Wissenschaften, 2007.

Sheppard, Alice. *Families of the King: Writing Identity in the Anglo-Saxon Chronicle*. Toronto Old English Series 12. Toronto: University of Toronto Press, 2004.

Shippey, Thomas A. 'A Missing Army: Some Doubts about the Alfredian *Chronicle*.' *Geardagum* 4 (1982): 41–55.

Šileikytė, Rūta. 'In Search of the Inner Mind: Old English *Gescead* and Other Lexemes for Human Cognition in King Alfred's *Boethius*.' *Kalbotyra* 54.3 (2004): 94–102.

Sinclair, John. *Corpus, Concordance, Collocation*. Describing English Language. Oxford: Oxford University Press, 1991.

– *Trust the Text: Lexis, Corpus, and Discourse*. Ed. with Ronald Carter. London: Routledge, 2004.

Sisam, Kenneth. 'The Authorship of the Verse Translation of Boethius's Metra.' In *Studies in the History of Old English Literature*, 293–7. Oxford: Clarendon Press, 1953.

Sisam, Kenneth, and Celia Sisam. 'The Psalm Texts.' In *The Paris Psalter: MS. Bibliotheque Nationale Fonds Latin 8824*. Ed. Bertram Colgrave, 15–17. Early English Manuscripts in Facsimile 8. Copenhagen: Rosenkilde and Bagger, 1958.

Smyth, Alfred P. 'The Emergence of English Identity, 700–1000.' In *Medieval Europeans: Studies in Ethnic Identity and National Perspectives in Medieval Europe*. Ed. Alfred P. Smyth, 24–52. London: Macmillan, 1998.

– *King Alfred the Great*. Oxford: Oxford University Press, 1995.

Sorrell, Paul. 'Like a Duck to Water: Representations of Aquatic Animals in Early Anglo-Saxon Literature and Art.' *Leeds Studies in English* ns 25 (1994): 29–68.

Springer, Carl P.E. *The Gospel as Epic in Late Antiquity: The Paschale Carmen of Sedulius*. Supplements to *Vigiliae Christianae*: Texts and Studies of Early Christian Life and Language 2. Leiden: E.J. Brill, 1988.

Stanley, E.G. 'Alliterative Ornament and Alliterative Rhythmical Discourse in Old High German and Old Frisian Compared with Similar Manifestations in

Old English.' *Beiträge zur Geschichte der deutschen Sprache und Literatur* 106 (1984): 184–217.

– '*The Judgement of the Damned* (from Cambridge, Corpus Christi College 201 and Other Manuscripts), and the Definition of Old English Verse.' In *Learning and Literature in Anglo-Saxon England: Studies Presented to Peter Clemoes on the Occasion of His Sixty-Fifth Birthday*. Ed. Michael Lapidge and Helmut Gneuss, 363–91. Cambridge: Cambridge University Press, 1985.

– 'Old English Poetic Diction and the Interpretation of *The Wanderer*, *The Seafarer*, and *The Penitent's Prayer*.' *Anglia* 73 (1956): 413–66.

– 'On the Laws of King Alfred: The End of the Preface and the Beginning of the Laws.' In *Alfred the Wise: Studies in Honour of Janet Bately on the Occasion of Her Sixty-Fifth Birthday*. Ed. Jane Roberts and Janet L. Nelson with Malcolm Godden, 211–21. Cambridge: D.S. Brewer, 1997.

– 'Paleographical and Textual Deep Waters: <a> for <u> and <u> for <a>, <d> for <ð> and <ð> for <d> in Old English.' *American Notes and Queries* 15.2 (2002): 64–72.

– 'Studies in the Prosaic Vocabulary of Old English Verse.' *Neuphilologische Mitteilungen* 72 (1971): 385–418.

Stanton, Robert. *The Culture of Translation in Anglo-Saxon England*. Cambridge: D.S. Brewer, 2002.

Steen, Janie. *Verse and Virtuosity: The Adaptation of Latin Rhetoric in Old English Poetry*. Toronto Old English Series. Toronto: University of Toronto Press, 2008.

Stenton, F.M. 'The South-Western Element in the Old English Chronicle.' In *Essays in Medieval History Presented to Thomas Frederick Tout*. Ed. A.G. Little and F.M. Powicke, 15–24. 1925; reprint, Freeport, NY: Books for Libraries Press, 1967.

Stévanovitch, Colette. 'Envelope Patterns in Translation: The Old English *Metres of Boethius*.' In *The Medieval Translator. Vol. 6, Proceedings of the International Conference of Göttingen (22–25 July 1996)*. Ed. Roger Ellis, René Tixier, and Bernd Weitemeier, 101–13. Turnhout: Brepols, 1998.

– ed. and trans. *La Genèse du manuscrit Junius XI de la Bodléienne: edition, traduction, et commentaire*. 2 vols. Publications de l'Association des Médiévistes Anglicistes de l'Enseignement Supérieur, hors série, 1. Paris: Université de Paris IV Sorbonne, 1992.

– 'The Translator and the Text of the Old English *Genesis B*.' In *The Medieval Translator / Traduire au Moyen Age*. Vol. 5. Ed. Roger Ellis and René Tixier, 130–45. Turnhout: Brepols, 1996.

Stodnick, Jacqueline A. 'The Interests of Compounding: *Angelcynn* to *Engla Land* in the *Anglo-Saxon Chronicle*.' In *The Power of Words: Anglo-Saxon*

Studies Presented to Donald G. Scragg on His Seventieth Birthday. Ed. Hugh Magennis and Jonathan Wilcox, 337–67. Medieval European Studies 8. Morgantown: West Virginia University Press, 2006.

Story, Joanna. *Carolingian Connections: Anglo-Saxon England and Carolingian Francia, c. 750–870*. Studies in Early Medieval Britain. Aldershot, Hampshire: Ashgate, 2003.

Strauss, Jürgen W. 'Compounding in Old English Poetry.' *Folia Linguistica Historica* 1 (1980): 305–16.

Stubbs, Michael. 'Collocations and Semantic Profiles: On the Cause of the Trouble with Quantitative Studies.' *Functions of Language* 2 (1995): 23–55.

– *Words and Phrases: Corpus Studies of Lexical Semantics*. Oxford: Blackwell, 2001.

Sweet, Henry, ed. *King Alfred's West-Saxon Version of Gregory's Pastoral Care*. Corr. reprint. 2 vols. EETS os 45 and 50. London: Oxford University Press, 1958; reprint, Millwood, NY: Kraus, 1978.

Symphosius. *Aenigmata*. Ed. Fr. Glorie, with trans. by Raymond Theodore Ohl. In *Tatuini opera omnia; Variae collectiones aenigmatum Merovingicae aetatis; Anonymus De dubiis nominibus*. Ed. Maria De Marco and Fr. Glorie, 2:611–721. 2 vols. Corpus Christianorum Series Latina 133–133A. Turnhout: Brepols, 1968.

Szabo, Vicki Ellen. *Monstrous Fishes and the Mead-Dark Sea: Whaling in the Medieval North Atlantic*. Leiden: Brill, 2008.

Szarmach, Paul E. '*Meter 20*: Context Bereft.' *American Notes and Queries* 15.2 (2002): 28–34.

Tabacco, Giovanni. *The Struggle for Power in Medieval Italy: Structures of Political Rule*. Trans. Rosalind Brown Jensen. Cambridge: Cambridge University Press, 1989.

Taylor, Simon, ed. *MS B*. Vol. 4 (1983) of *The Anglo-Saxon Chronicle: A Collaborative Edition*. Gen. ed. David N. Dumville and Simon Keynes. 9 vols to date. Cambridge: D.S. Brewer, 1983–.

ten Harkel, Letty. 'The Vikings and the Natives: Ethnic Identity in England and Normandy, c. 1000 AD.' In *The Medieval Chronicle IV*. Ed. Erik Kooper, 177–90. Amsterdam: Rodopi, 2006.

Terasawa, Jun. *Nominal Compounds in Old English: A Metrical Approach*. Anglistica 27. Copenhagen: Rosenkilde and Bagger, 1994.

Thacker, Alan. 'Dynastic Monasteries and Family Cults: Edward the Elder's Sainted Kindred.' In *Edward the Elder, 899–924*. Ed. N.J. Higham and D.H. Hill, 248–63. London: Routledge, 2001.

Thormann, Janet. 'The *Anglo-Saxon Chronicle* Poems and the Making of the English Nation.' In *Anglo-Saxonism and the Construction of Social Identity*. Ed. Allen J. Frantzen and John D. Niles, 60–85. Gainesville: University of Florida Press, 1997.

Timmer, B.J., ed. *The Later Genesis*. Oxford: Scrivener Press, 1948.

Toswell, M.J. '"Awended on Engliscum Gereorde": Translation and the Old English Metrical Psalter.' *Translation and Literature* 5 (1996): 167–82.

– 'The Translation Techniques of the Old English Metrical Psalter, with Special Reference to Psalm 136.' *English Studies* 75 (1994): 393–407.

Townsend, Julie. 'The Metre of the *Chronicle*-Verse.' *Studia Neophilologica* 68 (1996): 143–76.

Trahern, Joseph B., Jr. 'Working the Boundary or Walking the Line? Late Old English Rhythmical Alliteration.' In *Intertexts: Studies in Anglo-Saxon Culture Presented to Paul E. Szarmach*. Ed. Virginia Blanton and Helene Scheck, 33–44.

Trilling, Renée R. *The Aesthetics of Nostalgia: Historical Representation in Old English Verse*. Toronto Anglo-Saxon Series 3. Toronto: University of Toronto Press, 2009.

Tyler, Elizabeth M. *Old English Poetics: The Aesthetics of the Familiar in Anglo-Saxon England*. York: York Medieval Press, 2006.

Vandersall, Amy L. 'The Date and Provenance of the Franks Casket.' *Gesta* 11.2 (1972): 9–26.

Vickrey, John Frederick, Jr. '*Genesis B*: A New Analysis and Edition.' Unpublished Ph.D. dissertation, Indiana University, 1960.

Victorius, Claudius Marius. *Alethia*. Ed. P.F. Hovingh. In *Commodiani Carmina; Claudii Marii Victorii Alethia*. Ed. Josef Martin and P.F. Hovingh, 115–93 and 269–97. Corpus Christianorum Series Latina 128. Turnhout: Brepols, 1960.

Wadstein, Elis. *The Clermont Runic Casket*. Skrifter utgifna af Kongl. Humanistiska Vetenskaps-Samfundet i Upsala 6.7. Uppsala: Almqvist & Wiksells Boktryckeri-A.-B., 1900.

Wallace-Hadrill, J.M. *Early Germanic Kingship in England and on the Continent: The Ford Lectures Delivered in the University of Oxford in Hilary Term, 1970*. Oxford: Clarendon Press, 1971.

– 'The Franks and the English in the Ninth Century: Some Common Historical Interests.' *History* 35 (1950): 202–18.

Webster, Leslie. 'Encrypted Visions: Style and Sense in the Anglo-Saxon Minor Arts, a.d. 400–900.' In *Anglo-Saxon Styles*. Ed. Catherine E. Karkov and George Hardin Brown, 11–30. SUNY Series in Medieval Studies. Albany: State University of New York Press, 2003.

– 'The Iconographic Programme of the Frank's Casket.' In *Northumbria's Golden Age*. Ed. Jane Hawkes and Susan Mills, 227–46. Stroud, Gloucestershire: Sutton, 1999.

– 'Stylistic Aspects of the Franks Casket.' In *The Vikings*. Ed. R.T. Farrell, 20–32. London: Phillimore, 1982.

Whitbread, L. 'Æthelweard and the *Anglo-Saxon Chronicle*.' *English Historical Review* 74 (1959): 577–89.

– 'Notes on the Old English *Exhortation to Christian Living*.' *Studia Neophilologica* 23 (1951): 96–102.

– 'Two Notes on Minor Old English Poems.' *Studia Neophilologica* 20 (1948): 192–8.

– '"Wulfstan" Homilies XXIX, XXX, and Some Related Texts.' *Anglia* 81 (1963): 347–64.

Whitelock, Dorothy. 'The Importance of the Battle of Edington' (1977). Reprinted in *From Bede to Alfred: Studies in Early Anglo-Saxon Literature and History*, chap. 13. London: Variorum Reprints, 1980.

– 'The Prose of Alfred's Reign.' In *Continuations and Beginnings: Studies in Old English Literature*. Ed. Eric Gerald Stanley, 67–103. London: Nelson, 1966.

Wieland, Gernot. '*Geminus Stilus*: Studies in Anglo-Latin Hagiography.' In *Insular Latin Studies: Papers on Latin Texts and Manuscripts of the British Isles, 550–1066*. Ed. Michael W. Herren, 113–33. Papers in Mediaeval Studies 1. Toronto: Pontifical Institute of Mediaeval Studies, 1981.

Wood, Ian N. 'Ripon, Francia, and the Franks Casket in the Early Middle Ages.' *Northern History* 26 (1990): 1–19.

Wormald, Patrick. 'In Search of King Offa's "Law Code"' (1991). Updated reprint in *Legal Culture in the Early Medieval West: Law as Text, Image, and Experience*, 201–23. London: Hambledon Press, 1999.

– '*Lex Scripta* and *Verbum Regis*: Legislation and Germanic Kingship from Euric to Cnut' (1977). Updated reprint in *Legal Culture in the Early Medieval West: Law as Text, Image, and Experience*, 1–43. London: Hambledon Press, 1999.

– 'Living with King Alfred.' *Haskins Society Journal* 15 (2006): 1–39.

– *The Making of English Law: From Alfred to the Twelfth Century*. Vol. 1, *Legislation and Its Limits*. Oxford: Blackwell, 1999.

– '*On þa Wæpnedhealfe*: Kingship and Royal Property from Æthelwulf to Edward the Elder.' In *Edward the Elder: 899–924*. Ed. N.J. Higham and D.H. Hill, 264–79. London: Routledge, 2001.

– 'The Uses of Literacy in Anglo-Saxon England and Its Neighbours.' *Transactions of the Royal Historical Society*, 5th ser., 27 (1977): 95–114.

Wray, Alison. *Formulaic Language and the Lexicon*. Cambridge: Cambridge University Press, 2002.

– *Formulaic Language: Pushing the Boundaries*. Oxford: Oxford University Press, 2008.

– 'Identifying Formulaic Language: Persistent Challenges and New Opportunities.' In *Formulaic Language*. Ed. Roberta Corrigan, Edith A. Moravcsik, Hamid

Ouali, and Kathleen M. Wheatley, 1:27–51. 2 vols. Typological Studies in Language 82–3. Amsterdam: John Benjamins, 2009.

Wray, Alison, and Michael R. Perkins. 'The Functions of Formulaic Language: An Integrated Model.' *Language and Communication* 20 (2000): 1–28.

Wright, Charles D. 'More Old English Poetry in Vercelli Homily XXI.' In *Early Medieval English Texts and Interpretations: Studies Presented to Donald G. Scragg*. Ed. Elaine Treharne and Susan Rosser, 245–62. Medieval and Renaissance Texts and Studies 252. Tempe: Arizona Center for Medieval and Renaissance Studies, 2002.

Yorke, Barbara. 'The Bishops of Winchester, the Kings of Wessex, and the Development of Winchester in the Ninth and Early Tenth Centuries.' *Proceedings of the Hampshire Field Club and Archaeological Society* 40 (1984): 61–70.

– 'Edward as Ætheling.' In *Edward the Elder, 899–924*. Ed. N.J. Higham and D.H. Hill, 25–39. London: Routledge, 2001.

Ziolkowski, Jan. 'The Prosimetrum in the Classical Tradition.' In *Prosimetrum: Crosscultural Perspectives on Narrative in Prose and Verse*. Ed. Joseph Harris and Karl Reichl, 45–65. Cambridge: D.S. Brewer, 1997.

Index

Footnotes are referenced only where the listed name or concept does not also occur in the main text of the same page. The index omits instances of personal names found in quotations but having no presence in surrounding discussion. Other than the Vulgate Bible, the Ælfrician prose *Genesis* and *Judith*, and the poems attributed to Cynewulf, references to works by known authors are absorbed into the author's entry.

Toronto Anglo-Saxon Series

1 *Preaching the Converted: The Style and Rhetoric of the Vercelli Book Homilies,* Samantha Zacher

2 *Say What I Am Called: The Old English Riddles of the Exeter Book and the Anglo-Latin Riddle Tradition*, Dieter Bitterli

3 *The Aesthetics of Nostalgia: Historical Representation in Anglo-Saxon Verse*, Renée Trilling

4 *New Readings in the Vercelli Book*, edited by Samantha Zacher and Andy Orchard

5 *Authors, Audiences, and Old English Verse*, Thomas A. Bredehoft

6 *On Aesthetics in* Beowulf *and Other Old English Poems*, edited by John M. Hill

7 *Old English Metre: An Introduction*, Jun Terasawa

8 *Anglo-Saxon Psychologies in the Vernacular and Latin Traditions*, Leslie Lockett

9 *The Body Legal in Barbarian Law*, Lisi Oliver

10 *Old English Literature and the Old Testament*, edited by Michael Fox and Manish Sharma

11 *Stealing Obedience: Narrative of Agency and Identity in Later Anglo-Saxon England*, Katherine O'Brien O'Keeffe

12 *Traditional Subjectivities: The Old English Poetics of Mentality,* Britt Mize

www.ingramcontent.com/pod-product-compliance
Lightning Source LLC
LaVergne TN
LVHW090152080826
844660LV00013B/780/J